No Moral Conscience

The Hospital for
Sick Children
and the death
of Lisa Shore

Sharon Shore

© Copyright 2004 Sharon Shore.
All rights reserved. No part of this publication may be reproduced, stored in a retrieval system, or transmitted, in any form or by any means, electronic, mechanical, photocopying, recording, or otherwise, without the written prior permission of the author.

Note for Librarians: a cataloguing record for this book that includes Dewey Decimal Classification and US Library of Congress numbers is available from the Library and Archives of Canada. The complete cataloguing record can be obtained from their online database at: www.collectionscanada.ca/amicus/index-e.html
ISBN 1-4120-4346-8

Interior book design by Fiona Raven
Book cover design by Art Department Design and Eric Gertzbein
Printed in Victoria, BC, Canada

TRAFFORD

Offices in Canada, USA, Ireland, UK and Spain
This book was published *on-demand* in cooperation with Trafford Publishing. On-demand publishing is a unique process and service of making a book available for retail sale to the public taking advantage of on-demand manufacturing and Internet marketing. On-demand publishing includes promotions, retail sales, manufacturing, order fulfilment, accounting and collecting royalties on behalf of the author.

Book sales for North America and international:
Trafford Publishing, 6E–2333 Government St.,
Victoria, BC v8t 4p4 CANADA
phone 250 383 6864 (toll-free 1 888 232 4444)
fax 250 383 6804; email to orders@trafford.com

Book sales in Europe:
Trafford Publishing (uk) Ltd., Enterprise House, Wistaston Road Business Centre,
Wistaston Road, Crewe, Cheshire cw2 7rp UNITED KINGDOM
phone 01270 251 396 (local rate 0845 230 9701)
facsimile 01270 254 983; orders.uk@trafford.com

Order online at:
www.trafford.com/robots/04-2154.html

10 9 8 7 6 5 4 3 2

*To the memory of
my daughter, Lisa Shore
November 20, 1987 – October 22, 1998
and
my father, Philip Grief
March 6, 1933 – November 21, 1998*

TABLE OF CONTENTS

List of people   vi
Acknowledgments   viii
Preface   ix
INTRODUCTION   xiii

PART ONE: February 1998 – October 1999   1
  1. The beginning of the end   3
  2. Ambush   19
  3. Searching for help   31
  4. Boston   39
  5. Lisa gets her life back   46
  6. October 21, 1998   57
  7. October 22, 1998   66
  8. Mourning and evening and mourning again   78
  9. Records and questions   82
  10. The coroner's office   91
  11. The anonymous letter   98
  12. The coroner's investigation   104
  13. Waiting for the inquest   111
  14. Mediations and meetings   116

PART TWO: November 1999 – February 2000   131
  15. Preparations   133
  16. The inquest begins   140
  17. The small stuff   147

18. A surprise theory   149
19. *If* there was a monitor   155
20. The nurse-educator   160
21. The trainer   166
22. Our dream team   171
23. The nurses – I   175
24. The nurses – II   187
25. A mother's testimony   199
26. Death summary revisited   203
27. Smokescreen   206
28. Solving the puzzle   211
29. The nurses – III   223
30. Closing addresses   241
31. The manner of her death   268

PART THREE: March 2000 – May 2003   277

32. Police investigation   279
33. Nursing investigation   289
34. Professional solidarity   294
35. Not wanted at the inquest   301
36. Passing muster   313
37. Appeals   317
38. Only one recommendation necessary   322
39. Nursing propaganda   325
40. Deep pockets   332
41. Preparing for trial – the Crown   335
42. Preparing for trial – the Defence   341
43. Legal manoeuvring   346
44. A mother's mistake   351
45. Death by a thousand cuts   356
46. Justice prevails?   360
47. No moral conscience   363

Epilogue   367

Endnotes   369

People	Position
	(at the time of their involvement in events)
Bauer, Stephan	Manager, Biomedical Engineering Technologies, Hospital for Sick Children
Berde, Dr. Charles	Anaesthetist, Director of Pain Services, Children's Hospital, Boston
Browne, Margaret	Assistant Crown Attorney, Ministry of the Attorney General, Ontario
Cairns, Dr. James	Deputy Chief Coroner, Office of the Chief Coroner for Ontario
Catre, Dr. Melanio	Orthopaedic resident, Hospital for Sick Children
Culver, Paul	Chief Crown Attorney for Toronto, Ministry of the Attorney General, Ontario
Davis, Michael	Detective-Sergeant, Metro Toronto Homicide Squad
Desparmet, Dr. Joelle	Anaesthetist, head of Pain Service, Hospital for Sick Children (and hospital in Montreal)
Deutsh, Sharon	Friend of the author, critical care nurse
Doerksen, Ruth	Nurse, Hospital for Sick Children
Douglas, Mary	Nurse-Educator, Hospital for Sick Children
Edwardh, Marlys	Lawyer, Ruby & Edwardh
Fuerst, Michelle	Lawyer, Gold & Fuerst
Gallant, Dr. Lee Ann	Paediatrician
Goldbloom, Dr. Alan	To Feb. 2001: Senior VP, Clinical and Academic Affairs, Hospital for Sick Children. Feb. 2001-Nov. 2002: Executive VP and Chief Operating Officer, Hospital for Sick Children
Gomberg, Frank	Lawyer, Teplitsky Colson
Goody, Hank	Assistant Crown Attorney, Ministry of the Attorney General, Ontario
Grief, Dr. Cindy	Author's sister, psychiatrist
Grinspun, Doris	Executive Director, Registered Nurses Association of Ontario
Hawkins, Patrick	Lawyer, Borden Ladner Gervais
Hedden, Dr. Douglas	Orthopaedic surgeon, Hospital for Sick Children
Hughes, Kate	Lawyer, Cavalluzo Hayes Shilton McIntyre & Cornish

Khawly, Justice Ramez. . . . . . Judge, Ontario Court of Justice
Krkachovski, Van . . . . Lawyer, McCague Peacock Borlack McInnis & Lloyd
Laxer, Dr. Ronald . . . . Rheumatologist, Associate Paediatrician-in-Chief, Hospital for Sick Children
Lucas, Dr. William. . . . . Regional Coroner, Office of the Chief Coroner for Ontario
MacKenzie, Gavin . . . . Lawyer, Heenan Blaikie
Mailis, Dr. Angela . . . . Director, Comprehensive Pain Clinic, Toronto Hospital
McIntyre, Elizabeth. . . . . . . Lawyer, Cavalluzzo Hayes Shilton McIntyre & Cornish
McMahon, John . . . . Regional Crown Attorney, Ministry of the Attorney General, Ontario
Posno, Anne . . . . Lawyer, Lenczner Slaght Royce Smith Griffin
Rang, Dr. Mercer. . . . . Orthopaedic surgeon, Hospital for Sick Children
Reeder, Dr. Jean . . . . To April 2000: Chief of Nursing, Hospital for Sick Children
Reingold, Dr. Morton . . . . . Coroner, Office of the Chief Coroner for Ontario
Rocco, Dr. Frederick . . . . . . Psychologist, Behavioral Medicine, Children's Hospital, Boston
Roy, Dr. Lawrence . . . . Anaesthetist-in-Chief, Hospital for Sick Children
Rust, Dr. Robert . . . . Neurologist, Children's Hospital, Boston
Schily, Dr. Markus. . . . . Anaesthetist, Hospital for Sick Children
Shore family . . . . Lisa, Sharon, William, Devon and Aron (and grandparents Barbara and Phil)
Soriano, Anagaile . . . . Nurse, Hospital for Sick Children
Stevens, Marian. . . . . Risk Manager, Hospital for Sick Children
Strofolino, Michael . . . . To July 2002: Chief Executive Officer, Hospital for Sick Children
Watt, Justice David . . . . Judge, Ontario Superior Court of Justice
Wedge, Dr. John . . . . Chief of Orthopaedics, Hospital for Sick Children
Wilder, Dr. Robert. . . . . Anaesthetist/Pain Service physician, Children's Hospital, Boston
Wright, Dr. James . . . . Orthopedic surgeon, Hospital for Sick Children
Young, Dr. James. . . . . Chief Coroner for Ontario

ACKNOWLEDGMENTS

I began writing this book in the summer of 2000, following the coroner's inquest into Lisa's death, and completed it over the next few years as events unfolded. I could not have done it without the strength and support of my husband Bill, my best friend and editor extraordinaire.

To my friends and family, who read version after version of my manuscript and offered invaluable suggestions and comments, I cannot thank you enough. Myriam, your extraordinary preface is moving beyond words.

And to all the "good guys"—Frank, Sharon, Jim, Gail, Mike, Hank, and many others: it is because of people like you who were not afraid to stand up for what you believed in that we were able to accomplish so much in the face of so many obstacles.

PREFACE

As a forensic anthropologist, I analyze human remains in the aftermath of a crime. This is the means by which recovery and some form of identification is made. It is always a difficult experience to recount and reconstruct criminal and oftentimes heinous acts, and it is especially traumatic when it involves a child. Those of us involved in death investigations, from police officers and homicide investigators to coroners and pathologists, know the psychological impact of the senseless and cruel death of a child. There is a myth that we eventually become desensitized to these sorts of crimes. This is entirely false. In the event that a child is murdered, whether intentionally or through neglect, we all lose a sense of hope, and our faith is profoundly shaken. The psychological impact never goes away. Finding answers, piecing together the events that led to the child's death, and bringing the perpetrators to justice are crucial, especially if these can prevent future tragedies.

In the case of Lisa Shore, I was not involved as a forensic investigator but on a more personal level, which made this tragedy even more painful. I was Lisa's grade school teacher shortly after my graduate year at teacher's college.

My memories of Lisa are very vivid because she left those sorts of impressions. In my especially rambunctious class of grade fours, Lisa was an island of quiet poise, with her flaxen gold hair and shy demeanour. She worked steadfastly to finish all of her assignments, despite the noise level and the good-natured teasing from other students. She would never raise her hand to ask or answer questions and was barely audible when called upon to speak. Most days she loved nothing better than to spend her free time piecing together large and intricate puzzles. On a one-to-one basis, however, Lisa was a very different little girl. Staying in during recess became a time when Lisa could be herself. A great sense of humour emerged as she showed me card tricks, giggled profusely, and lamented the condition of having only brothers at home. She was an A-student in the classic sense of the word.

The following year I left teaching to pursue forensic work and research, but I often visited the school. One day Lisa greeted me with an exuberant smile and told me that Grade Five was easy. I never saw her again.

I had heard, sometime soon after, that she had broken her leg and was recovering with some difficulty. Then one day the school called to tell me that she had died. The first thing I thought was that a child does not die from a broken leg. No one had any answers at that time.

Pregnant with my first child, I attended Lisa's funeral. I approached Sharon at her home shortly after but could not express my condolences or my grief adequately as I choked back a flood of tears. Sharon stared as if in a trance, grief-stricken and in shock. She shook my hand and moved on. In the kitchen I met Lisa's grandparents, Sharon's mother and father. Bereft, Lisa's grandfather talked about his golden little girl, how she loved art, and how he'd never hear her voice again. He passed away shortly after Lisa's death. To this day I believe that the amount of pain broke him completely and left him unable to go on living.

I continued to keep in touch with Sharon, and slowly the answers emerged. The place where our children should feel the safest and under responsible care proved to be the very place where Lisa would lose her life because of neglect.

Through the media, during various press conferences, and on the Internet, half-stories circulated; soon enough Lisa's death became a politicized event. Nurses were suddenly banding together, and the Hospital for Sick Children seemed more intent on protecting its staff than taking responsibility for the tragedy that had occurred within its walls. It was interesting throughout to witness the behaviour of lawyers acting on behalf of their clients, and the absolute inability of the hospital or the nurses to actually apologize for their 'mistakes'.

In the end there really was no justice, nor was there any justification. The worst part of all of this is that it should not have happened.

Lisa's death was entirely preventable. She was not ill; she did not suffer from a terminal disease. Her death was not an accident on the part of someone with good intentions; her death was the result of total negligence. Added to this was the entirely inappropriate and unacceptable conduct of a variety of people throughout the investigation and the subsequent inquest.

To say that Sharon Shore is brave and persistent is an understatement. To say that she is a grieving mother who has lost her only daughter is to understand the source of her strength and her persistence. I know that she has faced a constant uphill battle in taking on a reputable and renowned institution, nurses, doctors, lawyers, and lengthy proceedings and hearings. Where many of us would have been broken by now, Sharon has continued the fight and this time she is more readily armed. I know she has done this for Lisa.

–Myriam Nafte
September 2004

A child who is born is something to seek out, something to search for, a star, a northern light, a column of energy in the universe. And a child who dies–that's an abomination.

-Peter Høeg,
Smilla's Sense of Snow, 1995

INTRODUCTION

At 7:18 in the morning, three young doctors entered my ten-year-old daughter's hospital room on routine morning rounds. Lisa had been admitted just a few hours earlier after being brought to the Emergency Department to obtain some pain relief. She had broken her leg in a schoolyard accident several months earlier, and although the break had healed, it had left her with nerve damage that flared up periodically and caused unbearable agony. There was nothing life threatening or remotely dangerous about it; she only needed some medical help to make her pain go away.

As one of the doctors bent over towards her, he yelled, "Call a code!" Doctors, nurses, and technicians immediately rushed in, filling the tiny room beyond capacity. The nurses gently tried to lead me out. "No, no, I want to stay," I insisted. "I need to be here when she wakes up. She'll be frightened when she sees all these people!" The doctors performed CPR, frantically pushing up and down on Lisa's chest. They hooked her up to a large machine, attached defibrillator paddles, yelled "clear", and jolted her with electricity. "Again". "Clear". Jolt. "Again". "Clear". Jolt.

On TV, the doctors always manage to resuscitate their patient, who suddenly coughs and flutters her eyelids. We viewers become teary-eyed with relief, knowing that everything will be okay. But this time there was to be no "happily ever after". At 7:52 on the morning of October 22, 1998, at the Hospital for Sick Children in Toronto, Canada, beautiful, vibrant ten-year-old Lisa was officially pronounced dead.

Why did a healthy child in a major North American city, who went to a reputedly world-class children's hospital just for some pain relief, die within hours of being admitted? No one knew the answer. And for a long time, no one except us, Lisa's family, wanted to bother looking for one.

A year and a half after her death, to the stunned surprise of virtually everyone, a coroner's inquest jury found that Lisa's death was a homicide. Another year and a half after the jury's momentous finding, the police charged the two nurses who were responsible for her care on the night she died with criminal negligence causing death. It took almost two more years for court proceedings to begin, only to end abruptly as doctors and nurses changed their testimony, became less-than-forthcoming in the witness box, or refused to testify altogether.

When we claimed the hospital was responsible for her death, everyone thought we were so grief-stricken and overwrought that we were blindly grasping to find someone to blame. No one believed our allegations that health care professionals—nurses who take care of sick children!—had turned their backs on a dying child because they didn't think there was anything physically wrong with her, because they believed her problem was mental and not physical and therefore she wasn't entitled to the same level of care as their "real" patients.

Our allegations that Lisa's nurses were directly responsible for her death were ultimately borne out by the coroner's inquest, the findings of two nursing experts, and the professional misconduct charges laid by the College of Nurses of Ontario. Despite this, the Hospital for Sick Children never stopped trying to conceal the truth. When its efforts were unsuccessful, the hospital, its lawyers, and the nursing community marshalled their collective resources in an attempt to portray me as a demon bent on vengeance, who was single-handedly responsible for destroying the careers of two innocent and conscientious nurses.

While no hospital wants to trumpet its failures, how could the senior administration of this renowned children's hospital and research centre, the famous Hospital for Sick Children, go so far as to mislead and deceive the coroner's office, the justice system, and the family of a child who died a result of its employees' negligence? The hospital quietly paid us a small settlement and thereby avoided a medical malpractice lawsuit, so it didn't have to worry about any legal liability. Why would it subsequently go to extraordinary and very costly lengths to deny the truth and protect staff whose misconduct was so egregious that every doctor and nurse who learned the details and was not affiliated with the hospital or its nurses unanimously condemned it?

All referenced documents may be found at
www.lisashore.com

PART ONE

February 1998 – October 1999

∼

1

THE BEGINNING OF THE END

We—my husband Bill and I, our 10-year-old daughter Lisa, and our two sons Devon and Aron, then aged 9 and 6—were a typical suburban Toronto family. Bill designed software at a local high-tech firm, and I was an accountant. We worked hard, but our children always came first. Our marriage was strong, our extended families close, and as so many of us do, we took our health and happiness for granted.

Lisa was a well-liked and intelligent child, and an enthusiastic and bright student whom the teachers loved. Shy with most adults, she was bubbly and effusive with friends and family and had a perennially sunny disposition. She was good-natured and generous to a fault, and frequently squandered her allowance buying candies and trinkets for everyone around her. She delighted in drawing, painting, and working in clay, and every year on Mother's Day and my birthday I eagerly awaited the ornate cards she would design for the occasion.

Lisa eagerly tackled gymnastics, trampoline, folk dancing, choir, soccer, art classes, and as many other activities as she could cram in. Although she inherited most of the best qualities from both sides of the family, the maternal side's tendency to clumsiness was so overwhelmingly powerful that the paternal traits for agility and co-ordination never had a fighting chance. One family member per generation seemed destined to be afflicted with the dominant "klutz gene", and Lisa was the chosen one in hers. Anything that could be tripped on, knocked over or spilled invariably was. When playing ball, Lisa seemed to catch as many balls with her face as she did with her glove.

So when her school called on February 11, 1998, to say that Lisa had fallen and hurt her leg while playing in the schoolyard, I groaned and thought, "Not again!" Although the school attended to her quickly, she hadn't been able to get up on her own and staff had used a dolly to wheel her inside. I assumed this was going to be just one more of Lisa's many minor mishaps to add to the family lore.

When I came to pick her up, however, I could tell immediately that she needed to be seen by a doctor. She was in such severe pain that it was difficult to manoeuvre her into the car for the drive to the local hospital. Generally not a complainer, this time she had ample reason to whimper: her leg was badly broken. In medical terms, she had sustained "a non-displaced spiral fracture of the tibia". The tibia is the large bone that extends from the knee down to the foot, and non-displaced means simply that no surgery or pins were needed to fix the break. A spiral fracture is exactly as it sounds: a break that rotates down the leg in a spiral. It is usually indicative of great force and is often found in abused children who have been thrown violently.

The Emergency doctor set the break with a thick plaster cast that extended from the top of Lisa's thigh all the way down to the tip of her toes; it looked like it weighed more than she did. We made feeble jokes about those poor toes, the only part of her leg that stuck out of the cast. No one told us there were fibreglass casts that were lighter than the heavier plaster ones and which would have improved Lisa's mobility significantly. The klutzes in our family injure themselves frequently but never seriously, and we had no experience with broken bones and casts.

After we brought Lisa home, she continued to moan in pain. Unsure if this was normal, I called a hospital help line staffed by registered nurses who provide telephone advice to parents and caregivers of sick children. The nurse told me it was usual for a child to be in some pain after a fracture. "There's nothing to worry about, unless her toes start turning purple. If that happens, bring her in right away." Still thinking Lisa's discomfort was abnormally high, I contacted her paediatrician, who told me the same thing and prescribed codeine for short-term relief.

The next morning, after an uncomfortable night, Lisa's toes did look purple. Now that we were positive something was wrong, we brought her downtown to the Hospital for Sick Children, where we thought the care would be better than at the nearby general hospital where the cast had first been put on.

The Hospital for Sick Children, known fondly in the community as "Sick Kids", is a world-famous paediatric teaching hospital affiliated with the University of Toronto. It has almost 400 patient beds, a staff of 3,000, and more than 14,000 admissions annually.[1] It considers itself one of the top four children's hospitals in the world.[2]

A cast that is on too tightly can cause a dangerous condition called compartment syndrome, where, in layperson's terms, the muscles turn to mush. The orthopaedic resident who examined Lisa considered compartment syndrome a possibility, and called for a staff surgeon to come down to Emergency to examine her. Lisa lay quietly on the stretcher, in too much pain even to answer questions.

The resident sawed away at Lisa's cast to open it up, while the orthopaedic surgeon supervised. The moment the cast was split, her pain was relieved. As if a light had been turned on, the forlorn, despondent child we had brought in disappeared and was replaced by a happy, animated chatterbox. The surgeon took over from the resident and repaired the cast by putting spacers—they looked like wine corks—down the split. This enabled the existing cast to still be used, but with a bit more room inside. In order to hold the whole thing together, he slapped on more plaster, the equivalent of adding another plaster cast on top of the first. Still not finished, he then put yet another cast on top of the first two a bright pink fibreglass one. Poor Lisa now had the weight and thickness of three hip-to-toe casts on her leg, one on top of the other. She could barely move her leg, but she was so delighted to be out of pain she didn't care. The surgeon clearly enjoyed joking with his newly revitalized, cheerful patient. He looked over at me, grinned, and said, "You wouldn't know it's the same child, would you?"

We took Lisa home, relieved she was once again the personable, easy going ten-year-old we knew and loved. The next two weeks passed uneventfully. We rented Lisa a wheelchair because the triple cast's heaviness made walking with crutches difficult. She went back to school, proudly using the school elevator that was normally off-limits to students and collecting signatures and cartoons on the cast from her classmates and friends.

Almost two weeks later, on the morning of February 24, 1998, Lisa woke up screaming in agony with shooting pains surging through her leg like electric shocks. Frightened and worried, we immediately took her back to the hospital. Since it was a weekday when the hospital was at maximum staffing levels, and Lisa had a file on record as a result of the recent visit, we bypassed Emergency and were sent directly to Orthopaedics.

Dr. Douglas Hedden, a tall, earnest looking surgeon, examined Lisa and decided to admit her to the general surgery/orthopaedics floor, Ward 5A/B. He was unable to explain her pain, but could see it was severe and required intervention.

We waited expectantly for doctors to do something to make Lisa feel better. She was given Tylenol 3s, but they had no effect and she continued to moan in pain. She couldn't move the leg at all, and any attempt by others to do so only magnified the pain. She insisted on keeping her leg horizontal at all times, crying that it hurt even more if she tried to lower it. Only her toes stuck out of the cast, and she screamed if they were touched even lightly. Each time a nurse came in to see her, the nurses would wiggle Lisa's toes. When a new nurse came on shift, she would begin her check by wiggling even more vigorously than her predecessor had. Each time Lisa cried out in distress.

We were upset and bewildered. To watch one's child in excruciating pain is unbearable at any time, and our anguish was compounded by not understanding why it was happening or what could be done to alleviate it.

It is a frequent practice in teaching hospitals for groups of medical residents to visit patients on rounds. It was on one of these group visits that the term RSD—Reflex Sympathetic Dystrophy—was first mentioned in passing as a possible diagnosis to account for Lisa's problem, although I was told it was an unlikely possibility since it did not usually occur so soon after an injury. I subsequently learned this is completely untrue: each person is different, and RSD can develop immediately or over a period of several weeks following a precipitating injury.[3]

No one explained anything about this disease to me. I later learned why not: none of the orthopaedic surgeons or residents knew much about it. Desperate for information and guidance, and unaware that the physicians were nearly as clueless as I was, I believed everything they told me. Normally I would have done some research on the Internet, but I did not want to leave Lisa's side.

What exactly was Reflex Sympathetic Dystrophy? It was first identified during the US Civil War, in a doctor's description of the unusual, long-lasting pain of some injured soldiers as "the most terrible of all tortures".[4] It often arises from a trauma to the body such as a fracture, sprain, or bullet wound, and is thought to be the result of an associated injury to nearby nerves. Days or weeks after the original injury, the sufferer begins to experience relentless, out-of-proportion pain often described as throbbing or burning. The lightest touch on an afflicted area, even a gust of wind, can bring excruciating pain. The piercing, knifelike pains, like those that so tormented Lisa, can be one of RSD's symptoms, although they are described less frequently in the literature. Nonetheless, such lancinating paroxysmal episodes are an obvious indicator to most physicians of neuropathic pain—nerve pain—which ranks as one of the most difficult-to-treat symptoms of many illnesses, including diabetes, cancer, and AIDS.

Lisa's suffering continued. She complained of a constant burning sensation, with recurring and frequent waves of electric shock-like pains. My husband Bill likened these attacks to watching a pregnant woman in the worst throes of labour. Having been present for the deliveries of each of our three children, he spoke from experience. Lisa's pain would come quickly, shoot through her like a contraction, stop for perhaps fifteen or twenty seconds, and then start anew. In the seconds between the waves of shooting pain, Lisa could talk, eat, and even muster a smile.

The doctors ordered a bone scan, a test in which radioactive dye is injected into the body and monitored while it flows through the bones. As one of the more helpful residents explained, a bone scan is used mainly to detect bad things like cancers. He told me it would be better if they didn't find anything, and that the scan was being done to rule out the worst possibilities.

The bone scan took place the next day, without incident. Lisa had never been afraid of needles or medical procedures, and she accepted whatever was being done to her without complaint. She had faith the doctors and nurses were trying to help her.

Later that afternoon, Dr. Hedden came into the room to give me the test results. He said they hadn't found anything at all wrong. He explained that the radiologist "had more than twenty years experience" and pointedly emphasized that he had "specifically requested a very experienced radiologist look it over to make sure the results were accurate". It seemed he was being unnecessarily patronizing, but I was determined to remain polite and pleasant. I knew that objecting might result in my being labelled a troublemaker and could potentially jeopardize Lisa's care. Lisa needed the best medical treatment possible, even if some of her doctors were lacking in bedside manners.

It took a few moments to realize that Dr. Hedden was not just patronizing me, he was challenging me! He was emphasizing the radiologist's expertise to show me there was nothing wrong with Lisa, and if I argued otherwise his tone implied I would be disputing the findings of one of the hospital's best diagnosticians and demonstrating the extent of my foolishness.

In hindsight, he must have already assigned me that troublemaker label. Possibly I had asked him one too many probing questions or perhaps I had questioned one of his opinions or pronouncements. But this was the defining moment when it dawned on me that he didn't believe Lisa's pain was real. When Dr. Hedden said they hadn't found anything wrong with Lisa, he wasn't telling me they didn't know what was wrong with her yet…he was telling me there wasn't any problem at all. I remember staring at him in disbelief, shocked into uncharacteristic speechlessness.

How could he not see Lisa's pain? I did not want Lisa to know how he felt; a child should have confidence her parents and all the doctors and nurses believe in her and are there to take care of her and help her get better. All I could think to do was to find Lisa another doctor and hope he or she would be more open-minded. I asked if Lisa could be transferred to the care of the kindly staff surgeon who had changed her cast in the Emergency Department when her toes had started turning purple. No, that was impossible, I was told, but I don't recall anyone explaining why.

After Lisa's death, I obtained copies of all her medical records, including the fateful bone scan.[5] The "very experienced" radiologist had written that the images were inconsistent with RSD and that RSD was very unlikely, a diagnosis that Dr. Hedden and his colleagues accepted without challenge. Having ruled out the possibility that Lisa had Reflex Sympathetic Dystrophy, they decided that the only remaining possibility worth considering was that her pain was psychosomatic.

None of them realized the radiologist had made a diagnostic error. The acknowledged gold-standard research paper on paediatric RSD at that time was a comprehensive 1992 study by doctors at Children's Hospital in Boston, which was available at the Hospital for Sick Children library. It stated that bone scans should not be used to make a diagnosis of Reflex Sympathetic Dystrophy, only to rule out other conditions.[6]

The radiologist's expertise clearly did not extend to RSD, so she ought to have checked some of the reference material before she wrote up her report. And in spite of her error, Dr. Hedden and his colleagues were wrong to conclude that Lisa's problem was psychosomatic. They could not have done any independent research or they too would have read the Boston literature and understood RSD's varying presentations. They made a psychiatric diagnosis without consulting a psychiatrist, who would have quickly assessed Lisa and diagnosed her as a happy, well-adjusted child. They spread their opinion of Lisa as a malingerer—and their disdain for me, who steadfastly maintained that Lisa had a genuine physiological problem—to the other surgeons and the nurses on the orthopaedic ward. Their mistake, coupled with their attitude of smug superiority, set the stage for the events that were to lead to Lisa's death eight months later.

I tried to remain outwardly cheerful in Lisa's presence, although I was angry and frightened inside. What could I do to get proper care for her? Late that night, after Dr. Hedden had come and gone, an orthopaedic fellow[7] walked into the room. Visiting hours were over, everyone had gone home, and Lisa was sleeping. The ward was quiet and the room was dark, as I had already turned the lights down. The fellow sat down across from me, introduced himself, and bluntly said, "There's nothing physically wrong with your daughter. Her pain is clearly a product of her imagination, and you need to accept that." He then stood up, turned, and left.

I burst into tears and then hurriedly dried them, afraid a nurse would walk in and think I was overly emotional. Through the course of Lisa's stays at the Hospital for Sick Children, we would encounter stupidity, mistakes, indifference, incompetence and outright negligence, but this doctor took first prize for intentional and pointless cruelty.

Lisa was not a whiny child, and was more than willing to try to distract herself from the pain with television, books and puzzles. Those of us who knew her well could see this formerly happy, giggly little girl had become quiet and resigned. She was always polite and did whatever was asked of her, including allowing her toes to be frequently manipulated in spite of the pain it caused. It seemed to my husband and me, however, that most of the nurses were not interested in talking to Lisa–or me–any more than was absolutely necessary. Dr. Hedden and the other orthopaedic surgeons had obviously discussed their conclusion that Lisa's problem was psychosomatic with these nurses. On Ward 5A/B, a unit that dealt almost exclusively with post-surgical patients, a child who did not have an incision was obviously one who was not welcome.

As part of their patient check, the nurses had to ask Lisa how much pain she felt she was in on a scale of 0 (none) to 10 (worst imaginable). Most of the time she would respond with a number between 3 and 7, but since she lay quietly in bed and wasn't groaning, they would mark in their notes "patient in no visible distress". The cycles of shooting, stabbing pains which caused her to scream out in agony would start without warning, last anywhere from fifteen minutes to an hour and a half, and then subside almost as quickly as they had started. Half an hour to two hours would go by and then the pains would begin anew. If asked for a pain scale when these attacks started, Lisa would groan out a number between 9 and 10, but when they reached their peak intensity she would be in so much pain that she couldn't even hear the question.

The doctors came by twice a day, but the nurses were omnipresent and as a result far harder to cope with. They would do what was required–such as taking the aforementioned pain scale–but it was apparent they did so begrudgingly. While only the orthopaedic fellow had explicitly stated that he thought Lisa was making this all up, the behaviour of the rest of the hospital staff implied it. It seemed as if I were constantly justifying Lisa's right to be a patient at the hospital.

On one occasion, a nurse came by and said, "I've noticed that whenever I walk by and look in, Lisa doesn't seem to be in any pain, but when I come in the room she starts moaning right away." I tried to explain that Lisa's pain came like a quick electrical shock, followed by a twenty second or so break, followed by another shock. "When you walk by quickly", I told her, "you're much more likely to see the long break between the spasms than the lightning bolt of pain. But when you come in the room and stay for a few minutes, you can see the spasms happening. It might look to you like she's doing it for your benefit, but if you stand outside and watch her for twenty seconds or more, you'd see that her pains have nothing to do with your being here or not."

But this nurse did not intend to wait around. Despite my explanation, she wrote up her notes implying Lisa was putting on a performance.[8] None of the nurses took the time to try and talk with Lisa or make an effort to get to know her, preferring to take their cues from the orthopaedic surgeons.

Another nurse was so contemptuous of me that he made no attempt to conceal it, and Lisa fared little better. Whenever he came into the room he ignored me altogether unless I asked him something which demanded a response. One time he arrived when Lisa was in terrible distress, writhing and grunting and barely conscious of anyone or anything. He scolded her as if she was misbehaving, suggesting by his tone of voice that she should know better. He told her with disapproval in his voice to think about nice things to get her mind off the pain. I had been spending hours with Lisa each day talking about everything under the sun, trying to distract her, and knew he would never say anything like that to someone he really believed was in terrible pain. I tried to convey, in a non-offensive, joking sort of way, that his comment was foolish, by saying with a smile, "That's what they tell women in labour. It doesn't usually help them either!" Of course he wouldn't look at me, so he didn't see the expression on my face indicating it was meant at least partly light-heartedly. He practically spat out with disgust, "That isn't very helpful!" and wrote in the chart that I had "great anxiety" with respect to Lisa's pain and hospitalization.[9]

Confirmation of my accurate assessment of staff attitudes came from an unlikely source. As it happened, I met an old acquaintance from high school who was staying with his child on the same ward. He told me he had come to the nursing station one time just as I was leaving, and heard the nurse say loudly to her colleague about Lisa and me, "I wish they'd go home already and stop bothering us!"

Lisa had been treated at this hospital on another occasion, for a different condition. She had had an emergency appendectomy only a few months earlier, and had been an in-patient for over a week. Due to bed shortages, she had been sent to the plastic surgery/burn unit instead of the surgical ward where she was now. I have only praise for the nurses on that unit and the excellent care they gave Lisa. Why was it so different this time? Even when in pain, Lisa was gentle and soft-spoken. No matter how frustrated or angry I was, I never raised my voice to anyone; I even brought the nurses doughnuts on several occasions hoping it might make them think better of me.

I didn't know what to do, who to call, or what to say. All my life I had implicitly trusted doctors and nurses. Nobody had ever before accused me of paranoia, but I couldn't shake the feeling I was being "watched". It wasn't that anybody was doing anything surreptitiously, it was more that the nurses behaved strangely whenever they were in the room. Usually, nurses keep an eye on their patients even while they engage in casual conversation with the parents. Now, whenever I spoke they watched me with a keen intensity, probably hoping to find something they could document. They may have thought they were being subtle in their scrutiny, but they were painfully obvious. I wanted to cry, but was afraid to because I was sure the nurses would write about it and make it sound like I was an unstable and over-emotional mother. My instincts were right: The Feb. 27, 1998 nursing student's note states in part that the plan was to "monitor pain and psychosomatic correlationship <sic> of pain, and to continue to observe the mother-child interaction".[10]

Dr. Hedden came by and told me that Lisa was "over-reacting", a comment he did not add to the written record, and recommended she be evaluated by a psychiatrist. I was inwardly seething but tried to maintain, as always, a calm façade. Lisa's pain was real, and she was about as normal a child as could be. The orthopaedic surgeons and the nurses on this ward were fools and worse. I decided it was time to start a journal to record who said what, for Lisa's and my own protection.

Early each morning the orthopaedic residents came in to do rounds, asking how Lisa was and how her night had been. Since Lisa was usually up very late due to the pain, she was invariably fast asleep when the doctors arrived. I would consistently answer their questions with some variation of "she has two types of pain: the constant burning pain and the terrible shooting, stabbing pains which come in waves throughout the day. When she gets the stabbing pains, she's in terrible agony." They acknowledged what I said, but never commented or asked any further questions.

Lisa and I were fortunate to have a lot of support, at least from people outside of the hospital. Family and friends visited frequently to try and cheer up Lisa and to relieve me. My husband and my parents were there daily, with newspapers and coffee for me, and candy, books, and the scratch-and-win lottery tickets that Lisa enjoyed (except we called them scratch-and-lose tickets).

A friend went to the University of Toronto Medical School library and did some research on RSD. My sister Cindy, at that time a third year medical resident, tried to elicit more information from the doctors, expecting she would be treated with more courtesy as a fellow physician than I had been. Her specialty was psychiatry, and her words of encouragement to me—coupled with a compassionate medical perspective that was far different from what I had seen from the hospital's doctors and nurses thus far—helped give me strength.

On the fifth day of Lisa's admission, Orthopaedics finally called in the pain doctors. The Pain Treatment Service, as it was called, was a relatively new concept in paediatric medicine. It wasn't that doctors weren't trying their best to relieve children's pain before, but this was the first attempt to integrate each specialty's knowledge and research into a cohesive whole. Pain was a by-product of something else, and there was little focus on the study and treatment of the pain itself. The cardiologist, for example, would attempt to treat a patient's post-surgery pain, but if the patient's pain stemmed in part from other conditions, the cardiologist would need to consult with specialists in those areas rather than with a physician who would specifically concentrate on managing the child's pain. A child with a condition such as RSD whose primary symptom was intense pain was often ignored by the existing system. Not all that long ago, most doctors believed young babies didn't feel pain, and operated on them without anaesthetic. Nowadays they know better, thanks to the work of some dedicated researchers, and recognize that relieving or at least minimizing children's pain is an essential part of what paediatric medicine is all about.

The concept of a dedicated pain treatment service for children first developed in the mid-eighties, but was slow to spread. Pain treatment as a sub-specialty came to be considered the purview of anaesthetists, perhaps because they were already the acknowledged experts at monitoring patients' physiological responses to pain and trauma during surgery and other invasive procedures. However, as one physician so aptly explained to me, this meant that the same doctors who worked exclusively with unconscious or sedated patients were abruptly forced to deal with conscious, responsive people and their families. Those who chose to be anaesthetists often did so because they were not "people persons", and many were reluctant to leave the protection of their operating rooms. That, and the fact that treating pain was not considered a "glamorous" specialty, may have partly accounted for the specialization's snail-paced rate of growth.

By the late nineties, however, most major children's hospitals in North America had clinics devoted to relieving children's pain, comprised of anaesthetists, psychiatrists, nurses, and physical therapists. But the Hospital for Sick Children did not adapt to the times. More than a decade after the first pain treatment clinics began, Sick Kids still had no comprehensive pain treatment service. Dr. Joelle Desparmet, a Montreal doctor who specializes in paediatric pain, had been recruited by Sick Kids on a part-time basis to start such a service. However, she maintained her practice in Montreal and devoted only two days a week to Toronto. And even with her part-time presence, the hospital's Pain Service ignored chronic pain sufferers who lived with pain all the time; it existed solely to help children manage acute pain, the short-term pain caused by trauma, surgery, or medical procedures–the pain that goes away when the injury or trauma heals.

The deficiencies of the hospital's Pain Service team, as it existed when Lisa arrived, were numerous. It could not assume primary responsibility for patients; its function was limited to assisting other specialties like Orthopaedics. Even then, it only covered in-patients: if a child arrived with pain as the main symptom, as Lisa had, the child would be out of luck. If the child had a chronic disease that flared up periodically and caused intense pain, the Pain Service team was unavailable to him unless some other doctor admitted him. Once the patient was considered well enough to go home, access to the Pain Service was cut off no matter the residual level of the patient's pain.[11]

When the orthopaedic surgeons finally called Pain Service for a consultation, the team consisted of two full-time nurses and the part-time services of Dr. Desparmet and a psychiatrist. I was told so often by different doctors and nurses how fortunate the hospital was to have Dr. Desparmet, that I thought a deity had descended from on high. I felt hopeful for the first time in days; surely she would have the knowledge and experience to help Lisa, and would not treat us as if we were both suffering from mental illness.

Dr. Desparmet started Lisa on a course of oral morphine and a combination of over-the-counter and prescription drugs to sedate her at night and help her sleep.[12] However, in spite of the high and probably justifiable regard in which Dr. Desparmet was held, her expertise in the area of Reflex Sympathetic Dystrophy was questionable. On March 2, 1998, the Pain Service progress note stated that the possible diagnoses included RSD but that the time course was not consistent.[13] That was exactly what the orthopaedic residents had told me: Lisa's problem was unlikely to be RSD because the pain started too soon after the fracture. Yet a physician knowledgeable about RSD would have been aware that the time course varied from patient to patient and was consistent with RSD.

Over the next few days, Lisa was sent for an MRI and a spinal X-ray; both came back negative. The pain medications, including the morphine, proved wholly ineffective and did nothing to alleviate Lisa's suffering. The nurses' disdain for her and for me continued unabated. At the height of Lisa's pain, when she would cry out with each wave of electric-shock-like pain, she sounded eerily like a wounded animal. It was inconceivable to me how those horrible noises could have been construed as anything other than coming from a child in utter torment.

We were living a surreal existence. The two Pain Service nurses visited Lisa daily, and appeared competent and compassionate. Dr. Hedden, the orthopaedic surgeon, was polite on the surface even though I could sense his annoyance with me. I would occasionally run into the surgeon who had first treated Lisa in Emergency, and he was invariably cheerful and sincerely friendly; I always felt things would have been so much better had he been Lisa's doctor. The orthopaedic residents may have been sceptical about Lisa based on what their superiors told them, but they were too young and naive to be anything but polite. The nurses ran the gamut from nasty (one of them) to uncaring and unpleasant (most of them) to warm and compassionate (two of them).

After a few days of evaluation, Pain Service concluded that Lisa was genuinely suffering. Dr. Desparmet decided to give her a continuous infusion sympathetic block via lumbar epidural.

What did that actually mean in English? The autonomic nervous system is broken down into two divisions, the sympathetic and the parasympathetic. The sympathetic nervous system reacts to stress, danger, or pain with the "fight or flight" response. It is responsible for raising the blood pressure, the rapidly beating heart, dilation of the pupils, and increasing the rate of metabolism. The parasympathetic system takes over to cool the system down afterwards, to "rest and digest".

If you stub your toe, it hurts, and the sympathetic nervous system response will kick in. In a few minutes, the pain will subside. The pain of a surgical incision will likewise go away, although it will take substantially longer than a few minutes. If a nerve gets compressed or damaged, the nervous system doesn't send the correct message to the brain to shut off this fight or flight response, and the pain doesn't go away. This is "sympathetically maintained pain". Some people call it neuropathic pain, or simply nerve pain. Sciatica, where sufferers may be totally incapacitated as searing waves of pain travel along the sciatic nerve, is an example of the torment that nerve pain can cause. The excruciating pain of shingles, the re-emergence of the chicken pox virus from a dormant state in the nerve tissues, is neuropathic. Occasionally shingles pain can manifest as lancing, stabbing pains which can continue long after the virus becomes dormant again. Phantom limb pain, the term coined to explain the burning pain some amputees experience in a limb that has been removed, is also neuropathic. Neuropathic pain is very difficult to treat; morphine and other potent narcotics often have no effect. Just as anyone can get sciatica or shingles, so can they develop Reflex Sympathetic Dystrophy.

What can you do with a sympathetic nervous system that has gone haywire? One thing is to administer a sympathetic block, that is, to anaesthetize the sympathetic nerves. This is done by way of a spinal epidural, similar to what is given to pregnant women to relieve labour pain. It can be done in the form of a one-time dose that wears off quickly, or over a longer period of time by a continuous flow of medication.

On March 4, 1998, on Lisa's eighth day as an in-patient, she received a spinal epidural block. It was done in the operating room under a general anaesthetic, and she spent several hours afterwards in the recovery room. When she was finally brought back to her room, she slept for a long time, although she would waken momentarily if she was poked before immediately falling back asleep. I sat by her bedside watching the readings on two monitors she was hooked up to. Although I had no idea what they were measuring, as long as the numbers didn't change very much, I was reassured that everything was all right.

When Lisa finally awoke, she sat up and told me the pain in her leg was completely gone. I was finally able to cry openly and with joy, without worrying about how it would be misinterpreted by the nurses.

My happiness was short-lived. The pain in Lisa's leg had disappeared, but in its place, similar waves of paroxysmal pains began in her upper back near the site of the epidural. There were no problems with the epidural itself, but Lisa's pain increased over the next few hours until it was unbearable. When a nurse came in to ask her what her pain score was on the 0 to 10 scale, she shrieked, "12! 13! It's worse than the leg pain was!" The pain continued unabated until she eventually fell deeply asleep, exhausted. When she awoke the next morning, the unrelenting pain in her back continued and Dr. Desparmet ordered the epidural infusion turned off.

These strange pains that Lisa reported made no sense to the doctors; to them they were yet another sign that she did not have Reflex Sympathetic Dystrophy and a further indication of her "need for attention". When one part of her body was treated, they felt she simply made the pain "reappear" somewhere else.

Months later, in an on-line RSD support group, I read several anecdotal reports of people with RSD who had experienced similar responses to epidural blocks. Since there is no published research on this and few doctors have seen many RSD patients, it is not surprising that doctors would not recognize a rare symptom or side-effect, or that they might attribute it to psychosomatic causes.

But when the epidural infusion was discontinued, virtually all of Lisa's pain disappeared. She would still get occasional stabbing spasms, but they would last several minutes instead of several hours. Lisa felt wonderful!

Two new doctors came by to visit–a neurologist whom I had

previously asked to be called in to assess Lisa, and a psychiatrist from Pain Service—whom I had not asked for. The neurologist saw a healthy and extremely cheerful child, and wrote in the chart that he saw no neurological or psychiatric problems.[14] He suggested that if the pain recurred, aggressive pain management should be undertaken to prevent undesirable long-term consequences.

The Pain Service psychiatrist met with Lisa once, and spoke to me at length on another occasion when he found Lisa asleep and decided not to wake her up. He wrote in his notes that Lisa's pain appeared to have a physiological basis, even if the overall picture was not typical of any one pain syndrome. He also suggested that in light of her pain being described as paroxysmal, stabbing, and intermittent, some medications should be considered on a trial basis.[15]

Lisa was discharged later that day, eleven days after being admitted. She felt well, even though she still experienced brief episodes of pain. Because the pain had not completely disappeared, I asked if Lisa could be followed by Pain Service instead of Orthopaedics. The answer was no, since Pain Service only worked with in-patients.

Lisa was scheduled to come back to the orthopaedic clinic the following week so doctors could monitor how well the broken leg was healing. No one discussed any follow-up management for the pain that had brought her to the hospital in the first place, or what to do if it came back.

2

AMBUSH

Whatever it was that had caused Lisa so much pain had almost disappeared. We were optimistic the twinges that sporadically occurred throughout the day would decrease in frequency and eventually stop altogether. We were grateful to Dr. Desparmet, who had been responsible for giving Lisa the successful epidural block, and ecstatic at getting away from the hostile hospital environment. Although I had tried my best to protect and shield Lisa from seeing that hostility, she had been well aware of it.

Lisa was herself again, talking animatedly on the phone with her friends and trying to catch up with missed schoolwork. She still had on a heavy full-length cast and had difficulty getting around, but she was so happy to be almost pain-free that she didn't care. I kept her at home for a few days to be sure she was okay and to see if those spasms improved. Lisa wanted to go back to school so badly, however, that she decided that whenever she felt a spasm she would simply find a quiet place at school to rest until the worst of the pain passed.

The night before she was scheduled to return to school, my husband and I were watching television. I called out to Lisa that one of her favourite programs was starting and she should come watch with us. Unfortunately, she was still ungainly and awkward with the cast and crutches. As she came into the room, she lost her balance and went down heavily, smashing her broken leg against the hardwood floor.

She immediately started screaming in pain, the same cries of agony we thought we would never hear again. We dreaded the prospect of taking her back to the hospital, and hoped the pain was only a temporary setback that would soon subside. We waited several more days, and the paroxysmal pains did not go away; if anything, they got worse. We had no choice but to go back.

When Lisa and I arrived in Emergency, one of the more friendly orthopaedic residents was on duty. He saw Lisa shrieking in pain and knew she was genuinely suffering, so he gave her some intravenous morphine. The morphine had no effect, and Lisa continued to thrash and moan. The resident and I spoke a bit about RSD, and I told him how effective the epidural had been, at least until Lisa had fallen and hit her leg. Acknowledging that none of the orthopaedic surgeons had known how to treat her, he smiled and said, referring to the epidural, "Good to know we did the right thing!"

When a patient is admitted to the hospital, she must be assigned to a staff physician, even though she may receive most or all of her care from the residents. The orthopaedic resident asked if he could list Dr. Hedden as the responsible physician, since he had been Lisa's primary doctor on the previous admission. I asked if it would be possible to get someone else. I had unsuccessfully tried once before to get the doctor who had been so nice to us the first time Lisa came to Emergency; I asked for him again, to no avail. Since I was adamant Lisa be treated by someone other than Dr. Hedden, she was admitted under the care of Dr. Rang, an elderly physician who had seemed reasonably pleasant the one time he had visited Lisa. I was too naïve to realize that doctors always discuss difficult or unusual cases amongst themselves and Dr. Rang was already well-acquainted with Dr. Hedden's diagnosis.

Lisa was once again admitted as an orthopaedic patient, but due to a bed shortage was sent to the plastic surgery ward which Orthopaedics used for overflow. This was the same ward Lisa had been in months earlier for her appendectomy, where the nurses were far kinder and more compassionate than their colleagues on the orthopaedics floor. The ward included the hospital's burn unit, and children with severe burns frequently experience terrible pain, ironically because of damage to sensitive nerves. Perhaps these nurses were inclined to be more understanding of a child's pain, regardless of what they thought was its cause.

Although the nursing was better, we now had to deal with Dr. Rang. Talking to him was futile; I got the sense that instead of dismissing what I said as Dr. Hedden had, Dr. Rang never actually listened to me in the first place. One thing was constant, though: both doctors were equally convinced Lisa's problem was in her head and not her body.

Dr. Desparmet and her Pain Service team were back in the picture, too. I expected she would order another epidural block for Lisa since the first had worked so well, but she had now decided Lisa's pain was psychosomatic. She found it "interesting" that Lisa had reinjured herself just before she was scheduled to go back to school. I explained that Lisa was a klutz and tripping was a consistent and normal event for her, and how eager she had been to return to school, but Dr. Desparmet ignored whatever I said. She declined to do an epidural block, telling me the pain Lisa was experiencing had made her depressed and anxious, and this depression was making her pain much worse than it really was.

Dr. Hedden, although not officially listed as the admitting physician, still came by to look in on Lisa. The only reason he did so, I figured, was because he considered it his personal mission to get me to concede that my daughter was mentally ill. While Dr. Desparmet was telling me that Lisa was in pain because she was depressed and anxious, Dr. Hedden informed me that whenever he looked in on Lisa she seemed too happy, that children with real pain become terribly sad and depressed and therefore her pain could not possibly be genuine.

Our family, as well as our friends and Lisa's teachers, never doubted Lisa for a moment. She was a loving, loved, protected daughter in an intact, stable family. When Lisa was not experiencing the stabbing pains and did not feel too badly–those times that Dr. Hedden classified as "too happy", she would be found in the ward's playroom playing video games, or down in the hospital's teen lounge doing puzzles or drawing pictures. Her classmates sent her get-well cards and bought her a two-foot tall Tickle-Me-Elmo, which she would hug tightly and keep close to her whenever the pain became unbearable.

Why would someone with this background, who had been healthy her entire life and whose family was similarly healthy, make up an illness complete with symptoms neither she nor anyone around her had ever heard of before? Medical literature is replete with children who develop headaches and stomach aches as a cry for attention or a mask for depression, but how could any intelligent person come to the conclusion Lisa was such a child? If the doctors thought there were psychological issues at play, why didn't they order a psychiatric evaluation as soon as they first considered that possibility?

Lisa's pain was far worse at night. In the day, she always said her leg hurt but the burning pain was mostly tolerable. When trying to explain her symptoms to other people, I would compare it to someone who has a chronic headache yet manages to function in spite of it. But just like the killer headache that stops the strongest person in her tracks, Lisa's pain at night was uncontrollable and unbearable. Unfortunately, the doctors only saw her during the day. Contrary to their opinion, Lisa was *not* an attention-seeker. If she wasn't feeling too badly when the doctors came by, she was happy and cheerful; it would never have occurred to her to pretend otherwise. When we told the doctors how different things were at night, it was clear they didn't believe us. Out of desperation, we borrowed a video recorder from a relative to tape Lisa. We felt like heartless voyeurs, but hoped that a few minutes of watching Lisa in agony might somehow convince the doctors her pain was genuine. How were we to know this would become the last recording of her ever?

On one of Dr. Hedden's visits, he took me aside and told me about a former patient of his who had unexplained pain and would not leave his bed. One day, he said, the boy's father decided to stop catering to him and forcefully demanded his son get up and walk. Lo and behold, the child then got up and walked, thereby proving his illness had been psychosomatic. Dr. Hedden told me I needed to stop being so obstinate and understand my daughter's pain was not real and that her problems were largely my doing. If I would only stop catering to her and demand she immediately stop this nonsense, just as the father of his former patient had done, then her pain would go away. I told him that perhaps this other child's pain was psychosomatic, but Lisa's was real. His response was to order a psychiatric assessment of our entire family, almost certainly not as a diagnostic aid but to confirm his opinion we were all mentally unstable. Just as Dr. Hedden had waved the radiology test results in my face that stated–wrongly–that Lisa did not have RSD, he wanted to do the same with a psychiatric report to prove he was right and I was wrong.

The Pain Service psychiatrist had seen Lisa a couple of times, but he had told me his role was only to try to help Lisa manage her pain. What Dr. Hedden wanted was a clinical evaluation, not just for Lisa and me but also for my husband, whose belief in Lisa was equally considered part of the overall problem. The family psychiatric evaluation was not a request but an order: Bill had to take time off work and we had to take our two young sons out of school in order that the entire family could attend.

My sister, the third year psychiatry resident, explained that patients are frequently referred to psychiatrists after other doctors have concluded their problems were all in their heads. Psychiatrists pride themselves on being able to recognize patients who have real physiological problems that have been improperly diagnosed by other specialties, she told me, and they are very alert to this. She stressed I should have confidence in the upcoming assessment and that the psychiatrist would be able to make an intelligent evaluation.

For the first part of the assessment, a psychiatric resident came by to assess Lisa alone. He spent about half an hour with her, and afterwards said to me, "She's a nice kid, I really like her."

Out of curiosity, I asked Lisa shortly afterwards what the doctor had talked to her about. She characterized the interview as only a ten-year-old would: "It was really stupid, Mommy!" She gave me some examples of the questions he had asked: "Does anyone in your family hit you?" She told him no. "Who yells at you the most in your family?" Her six-year-old brother. "When your mother yells at you, what sorts of things does she say?" "I told you not to do that! You're going to hurt yourself, and you better not come crying to me!"

I was pleased that this psychiatric report would show Orthopaedics that Lisa was a normal child living with a normal family. There was only one problem, although I did not know it at the time: the doctor never wrote up a report of that visit. Months later, determined to find out why his report had not made any difference to the abysmal way in which Lisa was treated, I ordered copies of her psychiatric records. These records are kept separately from a patient's regular medical chart, and I had to fill out special authorization forms at the Department of Psychiatry to get them. The report I wanted was not included in the files I received, so I ordered the records a second time. Still unable to find it, I called the department and told them an important document was missing. I asked them to check everywhere for it, but nothing turned up. The only notes the psychiatrist made about this visit were "Lisa seen by myself (psych resident). Family to be seen tomorrow for assessment at psych clinic..."[1] and "In addition to meeting with Lisa alone on the ward, the family was seen by myself and Dr. G. on Wed., March 18th".[2]

I was nervous about the upcoming family assessment because I believed the orthopaedic surgeons would put more weight on it than on the positive report I assumed the resident had already given them about Lisa. Our assessors were the same resident who had interviewed Lisa alone and a senior staff psychiatrist, who explained that their role was simply to help us learn to cope with Lisa's pain and not to evaluate our family. We were completely bewildered, because Orthopaedics had been very clear this was to be an assessment. Nobody needed to pull a six-year-old out of his Grade 1 class in order for him to learn how to cope with his sister's pain.

During the session, Lisa had a short and relatively mild period of stabbing pains, not nearly as severe as the evening ones that routinely kept her up screaming until 3:00 in the morning. The senior psychiatrist demonstrated ways to distract Lisa and to keep her mind off the pain—exactly what my husband and I had already been doing for weeks. Rather than risk annoying her by telling her that, I tried to make myself look suitably appreciative and grateful for her advice.

These two psychiatric assessments had accomplished nothing. The resident failed to write up notes; had he done so, Lisa might have received better care. Had there been some communication between Orthopaedics, Pain Service, and Psychiatry, the latter would have known they were expected to do a clinical assessment, and Orthopaedics might have learned that psychiatrists found the Shore family—every one of us—to be healthy and functional. Because no one did their job properly, Lisa's doctors at the Hospital for Sick Children continued to maintain her pain was not real.

Lisa received almost no medical treatment during the ten days she spent in the hospital. She was given Ibuprofen (Advil) and Tylenol 3, neither of which had any effect on her pain. Only once did someone at least try to do something: One night as Lisa lay in bed groaning in pain, I requested that the nurses contact Pain Service. The resident who came up had never seen Lisa before and did not know the other doctors felt her pain was imaginary or at least highly exaggerated. He saw how much she was suffering and ordered a PCA morphine pump for her.

The PCA–"patient controlled analgesia"–pump is a device that allows patients to give themselves small doses of pain medication whenever they feel they need it. When the patient presses the button, the painkiller flows from the pump through the IV and directly into the bloodstream. Why is this a better way of getting pain relief? When one has a terrible headache or toothache and has taken painkillers, one has to wait four hours or so to elapse before one can take any more pills, even though the pain may have returned long before. What if each time the pain started to emerge, one could take just enough medication to beat it back down again? Everyone has heard stories where a suffering patient in a hospital begs for painkillers but has to wait in desperation until a very specific time to get the medication. The PCA pump prevents that needless suffering by giving the patient the ability to control the timing of his pain relief.

Lisa kept pressing the PCA button, trying to make the pain go away. Sadly, we had already learned that morphine did not affect her neuropathic pain, although Lisa could feel the drug course through her body. After a short while she asked that the PCA be removed.

One of the anaesthesia residents working in Pain Service was from France, and she was not completely at ease in English. Since I could get by in French, we had a number of conversations late at night by the nursing station, when things were quiet and Lisa had fallen asleep. She talked about "la douleur chronique"–chronic pain–and how difficult it was to treat, and explained there were medications that were sometimes effective. The only problem with those medications, she said, was that they took several weeks to take effect.

I was stunned. Chronic meant ongoing, something that didn't get better and go away. No one had ever referred to Lisa as having chronic pain. Did this mean she was always going to have it? And what were these medications that the doctor had spoken about? No one had mentioned that either, even though Lisa had been in pain for weeks now. How dare these doctors be so blindly convinced Lisa's pain was in her head that they refused to even consider any other treatment possibilities!

The next strategy the doctors devised was to hold a "family meeting", where we would be invited to meet with representatives from Orthopaedics, Psychiatry, Pain Service, Physiotherapy, and Nursing, in order to discuss and plan Lisa's treatment as a united group. This would have been a good idea were it to be conducted by well-intentioned health-care professionals, but considering the treatment given to Lisa thus far, I knew this meeting would be nothing more than an ambush. I anticipated there would be a united group, as they promised, but one united only to convince us our daughter's pain was psychosomatic. I knew I was right when all of a sudden everyone stopped talking to me. As hostile as they had been before, now all they would say whenever I asked anything was "we'll discuss it at the family meeting".

I called my sister Cindy. "I would never ask you to take time off from work unless it was really important. But they're combining forces so they can all tell me that Lisa's pain is in her head. They'll throw medical terms at me and I won't know enough to argue. If you're there, if they have to face another doctor, it won't be so one-sided." Cindy knew what had been going on, and instantly agreed to come.

The meeting room was full. Dr. Desparmet was there with one of the Pain Service nurses and the Pain Service psychiatrist. Dr. Rang, along with some residents and nurses, represented Orthopaedics. For the defence there was my sister, the medical resident, and Bill and I.

The ambush began. Not surprisingly, nobody had anything to say about Lisa's treatment or what their plans for her were. Instead, the doctors sat back and suggested I tell them what it was *I* expected them to do. I asked Dr. Desparmet why she would not give Lisa another epidural block when the first had worked so well. She answered that she doubted one would work. "How can you be so sure of that," I asked, "since Lisa had been in terrible pain which almost completely vanished immediately after getting the epidural?" She muttered that it had been a coincidence. "What?" I demanded incredulously, "You think that was a coincidence?" "Yes," she repeated.

Bill asked Dr. Rang why it was that every time Orthopaedics and Physiotherapy tried to get Lisa to do some weight bearing on her broken leg, her pain levels increased sharply for several hours afterwards. Did he not think there was some direct correlation between the weight bearing and the increased pain? "One swallow does not a spring make" was his clichéd non-answer.

How could I make these doctors believe Lisa's pain was real, if measurable physical responses were being totally discounted? I could see my sister out of the corner of my eye, looking shocked. Many people have had contact with a doctor whom they perceived to be arrogant or condescending, but physicians usually treat each other with great respect. Cindy was experiencing the patient's perspective and did not like what she was hearing. She spoke up.

She started quizzing the Pain Service psychiatrist, doctor-to-doctor. He had just returned from vacation and apparently had not bothered to review the psychiatric notes before he came, so he was unable to answer her questions. The doctors conferred among themselves, somewhat embarrassed, and decided they would call the psychiatric resident, the one who had evaluated Lisa but never written it up, to sit in on the remainder of the meeting. Once he arrived and saw who was present, he realized he was facing an audience who would challenge him no matter what he said. He apparently decided that the best position to take was no position at all, because he hemmed and hawed and ultimately said little of assistance to anyone in the room.

Cindy gave up trying to elicit anything relevant from him. She turned back to the Pain Service psychiatrist, who, although ill-prepared for the meeting, at least seemed competent and generally knowledgeable. Cindy suggested trying Lisa on a trial course of medication for her pain, at which point Dr. Desparmet took over the conversation. She said she didn't see any point in treating Lisa with medication since they didn't know if she even had RSD, and moreover, she doubted that medication would work. Cindy visibly bristled at these statements. She told Dr. Desparmet that if a patient has a fever he is given Tylenol even when it's not known what is causing the fever. "In psychiatry," she said, "we don't know the mechanism for schizophrenia but we still treat the psychosis. Lisa's symptom is pain. It keeps her awake at night. It's organic and therefore should be treated empirically." Dr. Desparmet was adamant that Lisa should not be given medication, to the point where she and Cindy were arguing with one another!

Dr. Desparmet's colleague, the Pain Service psychiatrist, agreed Cindy's suggestions were reasonable. Faced with that, Dr. Desparmet reluctantly capitulated and agreed to try Lisa on low dosages of two medications, Gabapentin and Amitriptyline.

Gabapentin is a relatively new drug, originally developed for epilepsy and subsequently discovered to be extremely effective in the treatment of neuropathic pain. It is considered very safe; people have taken extraordinarily high amounts—over 80 times the level that Lisa was prescribed—without any long-lasting adverse effects.[3]

Amitriptyline is an anti-depressant that has been found to relieve many types of chronic pain. It is a dangerous medication with occasional but serious side-effects, and overdoses can be lethal. It is also highly sedating, and is often prescribed to chronic pain patients for the dual purpose of relieving their pain and helping them sleep. Because the newer psychotropic drugs such as Prozac are so much safer and have fewer adverse effects, Amitriptyline has fallen somewhat out of favour with psychiatrists.[4] For those with chronic pain, however, it often helps where nothing else does.

I came out from the meeting feeling better than I had in a long time. At least something was being tried! Bill and I decided to take Lisa home since we could give her pills just as well as the nurses could. Two days after the family meeting, on March 25, 1998, we requested a full discharge. Although we had been told it would take at least two weeks for these medications to have any effect, Lisa was given only a one-week prescription. No one explained what we should do when the one-week prescription ran out, and nobody discussed any kind of monitoring or reporting to evaluate what effect, if any, the drugs might have. Just bring her back to Orthopaedics in one week to have the broken leg checked, we were told, and take her to the Pain Service psychiatrist so she could learn how to manage her pain.[5] The hospital was "cutting us loose".

At home, Lisa spent that night grunting and screaming as the electrical shock-like pains ran down her leg. The next day, Dr. Rang called to see how she was doing. I told him Lisa wasn't doing well and was in great pain, and he casually advised me that she needed to continue seeing the psychiatrist so she could learn to cope better. He also assured me that if we felt we could not "handle her" at home we could bring her back to the hospital and they would readmit her.

That evening was perhaps the worst ever. Lisa was in torment. We were in our own hell: wanting to cry but holding it in for Lisa's sake; angry at God for letting an innocent child suffer like this; pleading with Him to take her pain away and give it to us instead; offering to give up anything and everything if only He would stop her agony. She was screaming gutturally, inhumanly, incoherently. The next day was the same. As much as we hated the thought of being back at Sick Kids, we didn't know what else to do. "They have to see her like this,"

I said to my husband with tears rolling down my face, "then they'll believe this pain is real. They'll have to do something!"

I called Orthopaedics but was told there were no scheduled clinics operating that day and we should proceed directly to Emergency. We arrived there about 10:00 p.m. that evening. The triage nurse, responsible for making a preliminary assessment of patients to assess how quickly they should be seen, classified Lisa as an "ortho problem".

Lisa was in so much pain that we asked if she could lie on a stretcher so she could keep her leg extended horizontally. One was found, but it did not easily fit in the waiting room and we had to stay in the corridor. From that vantage point, we could see all the doctors and nurses passing by. I saw the orthopaedic fellow walking around attending to patients; he had been the one who had so bluntly told me right at the beginning that Lisa's pain was all in her head. Although I wasn't keen on having to deal with a doctor who I knew from experience was unpleasant and cruel, at least he wasn't in surgery or handling a trauma case and would be able to see Lisa fairly quickly. I anticipated no problems—even with him.

Four long and painful hours later, well after all the sore throats, stomach aches, and other minor problems had come and gone—including some that had arrived after us and had been seen by the orthopaedic fellow—Lisa's name was finally called. Because she was on a stretcher, we were moved to the corridor just outside of the examination rooms, where we could again watch the passers-by. A first year resident approached us, and I explained the story to her briefly. She murmured that she already knew it, saying that the fellow had "filled her in". The way she commented, "I understand she's seeing a psychiatrist..." and "I see she's taking Amitriptyline...", which most people know for its anti-depressant properties rather than for its effect on pain, left me no doubt as to exactly what she had been told. I explained Dr. Rang's promise of admission and insisted she go back and tell this to the fellow, who was standing just down the hall in plain view.

The fellow had no intention of speaking with us directly, and this unfortunate resident was forced to play the intermediary, going back and forth between us like a translator. We watched while he spoke with her, but he never once looked at us even though we were standing close by. She came back and told us his final words, "she's not an orthopaedic problem, she's a psychiatric one, and he doesn't want her taking up a bed in the orthopaedic ward. No admit."

Filled with rage and despair, we took Lisa home. I swore I would never bring Lisa back to such a horrible institution. Tragically, seven months later, on October 21, 1998, I would relent and bring her back—to her death.

3

SEARCHING FOR HELP

Where could we turn to get help for Lisa? Based on all I had read on the Internet and in research papers, I was convinced she had RSD. Most doctors and nurses had never heard of it, although estimates of sufferers numbered in the millions world-wide. Lisa's experience of being told the pain was all in her head was, sadly, the norm and not the exception for those with this disease.

A typical feature of RSD, I learned, is allodynia, meaning that sensitivity is so great that a waft of air or the touch of a tissue on the affected area can cause excruciating pain. Although the only exposed part of Lisa's affected leg outside of her cast was her toes, she could not bear to have a sheet or blanket covering them.

I tried to learn as much as I could about this disease. There had to be doctors in Toronto who treated people who suffered with it, doctors who were not affiliated with the Hospital for Sick Children. I kept hearing about Dr. Angela Mailis, director of the Comprehensive Pain Clinic at the Toronto Hospital, Western division. She was reputed to be the doctor in town for adults with RSD, but I also heard there was a six-month waiting list just to see her for a consultation.

My sister was friendly with one of Dr. Mailis's colleagues, who agreed to speak to Dr. Mailis on Lisa's behalf. This colleague was apparently successful in conveying the urgency of the situation, as Lisa was given an appointment for the following week.

On March 30, 1998, three days after being turned away from the Hospital for Sick Children, Lisa and I met Dr. Mailis. Her manner was stern and unfriendly, like the proverbial drill sergeant. Lisa, who was by nature very shy with adults when she first met them, was intimidated and terrified. Dr. Mailis sharply rebuked me for bringing Lisa in while she was still in a cast, saying she could not do a thorough examination and would not have agreed to see her had she known. Since we were already there, she relented and examined her as best she could. Lisa was moaning in pain, and Dr. Mailis chastised her and told her to stop. Lisa complied as best she could, gritting her teeth and trying to keep as quiet as possible.

In spite of her intimidating manner, Dr. Mailis did appear concerned. She told me the situation was quite serious and would take many months to improve. Without intervention, she went on to say, Lisa's pain would become permanent, her leg would atrophy, and she would likely remain in a wheelchair permanently. I burst into tears on hearing this, not because I was so devastated at her comments—although I was—but because I was so relieved that someone finally believed that Lisa had a genuine problem. I quickly wiped away the tears, told her why I had cried, and listened as she explained what she would try to do for Lisa.

Dr. Mailis normally admitted her patients to hospital for four days, and observed and evaluated them while trying several different treatments to gauge their effects. She proudly explained that no one else used her exact methods, and that patients came from all over expressly to see her. The only potential problem with treating Lisa was that her hospital had no paediatric beds, and she did not know if it would be willing to admit a child. Her youngest patient to date had been sixteen, and getting her admitted had been extremely difficult. I said I would sign a waiver relieving the hospital from liability, and she promised to follow up and get back to me as quickly as possible.

We discussed the medications that Lisa had been so reluctantly started on at Sick Kids. I was worried about having been given only one week's supply of drugs, and explained that no one at Sick Kids seemed to want to manage or monitor the effects of these medications. I told Dr. Mailis I hoped she would take over that role. She did, maintaining the Gabapentin dosage that Sick Kids had prescribed. When she heard that Dr. Desparmet had put Lisa on a dosage of 5mg of Amitriptyline per day, she scoffed disdainfully, "That isn't enough for an insect!" and increased it to 25mg.

I had no intention of allowing the Hospital for Sick Children any more opportunities to mistreat Lisa. She still had a broken leg, however, which needed to be watched. The orthopaedic surgeons were fully competent to treat that, so we brought Lisa back to the hospital's orthopaedic clinic for a follow-up visit two days later as scheduled. Nobody said a word about her pain, and no one bothered to ask about the medications they themselves had prescribed only days earlier. The only thing they told us was that Lisa was not walking enough, and if she did not increase her efforts the cast would never come off.

We tried everything to distract Lisa from her pain. I watched a lot of bad children's television for her sake—although she would have argued with that description. The best diversion we discovered was a passion for 1000-piece jigsaw puzzles. Lisa could spend hours assembling them. If she had a puzzle piece in her hand when the stabbing pains started, she would moan as the spasm hit, and when it passed would go right back to finding where the piece fit. It was also something the rest of us could join in and do with her. We went through puzzle after puzzle, always taking a photograph of each one when completed. We told her we would make a "puzzle photo album" for her, one of many promises her death prevented us from keeping.

Thirteen days after starting the Gabapentin, Lisa's pain decreased dramatically. Before she had kept her leg extended horizontally at all times because it hurt too much to move it. Now she began bending it and trying to walk as the doctors had ordered. The constant burning pain that never went away decreased in intensity from her rating of 5 or 6 out of 10 to 3 out of 10. The excruciating stabbing pains that occurred off and on throughout the day and for most of the night she rated as 8, 9, or 10, when before she had not been able to rate them at all because she had been screaming incoherently. Now she would grunt and cry but was still able to communicate with us. She began falling asleep around midnight, several hours earlier than before starting the medications.

Lisa continued her weekly visits to Orthopaedics. On her next visit, she limped in without crutches. The doctors were surprised and pleased, and Dr. Rang told Bill to bring her back in two weeks to have the cast removed. Even Dr. Desparmet came down to examine her. Lisa was cheerful during the examination—which of course led Dr. Desparmet to conclude she was completely pain-free. However, by the time Lisa and Bill returned to the car, she was crying in pain again, no doubt the result of the exercises the doctors put her through during their examination.

On April 13, 1998, secure in the belief that Dr. Mailis would continue to care for Lisa, I wrote a letter to Dr. Desparmet, with a copy to Dr. Rang.[1] I explained what had happened with the orthopaedic fellow in the Emergency Department, told her that Dr. Mailis believed Lisa had RSD and had increased her medication levels, and that Lisa's condition had improved two weeks after starting the drugs. There was no response to my letter.

Over the next two weeks, Lisa's pain continued in regular cycles, always much worse for the two or three days following her visits to Orthopaedics when the physiotherapists made her do a lot of walking and stair-climbing. The pain in the evening was still excruciating, but Lisa was able to manage the chronic daytime burning pain quite well. She began attending school part-time. The pain would increase as the day progressed and we would usually have to pick her up before noon, but at least she was getting out and seeing people and trying to keep up with her schoolwork.

A week after I wrote the letter, Dr. Mailis advised me that her hospital would not admit Lisa under any circumstances due to her young age. I remember her exact words to me, because they seemed so sincere: "I have never had to turn away a patient before. As a physician and as a mother, I am very upset about this." She said she would contact a colleague in nearby Hamilton to see if he might be able to admit her to his hospital.

Not only did she never get in touch with me about whether the other doctor could treat Lisa, she wrote a consult letter to Lisa's paediatrician, dated the following week but not mailed until a month later, that directly contradicted everything she had been telling me.[2]

At Lisa's next orthopaedic appointment, Dr. Rang said her leg was healing, but not as well as expected. Lisa had already had the cast on for ten weeks—the more-or-less standard amount of time for this type of fracture—but he told her she would have to keep it on for another three or four weeks. Dr. Rang recommended the cast be bivalved, split open and then wrapped closed with a tensor bandage so that it was removable. In addition, he ordered the bottom part of the cast cut away to expose Lisa's ankle and allow her to wear a shoe.

While undergoing this cast adjustment, Lisa began to experience acute pains, no doubt caused by the technician's manipulating and prodding her leg. She started crying silently. Since the technician had been told Lisa could wear a shoe—which we had brought with us, just in case—he tried to ram her foot into it. Lisa started screaming. I was furious, and demanded the technician stop immediately. I had to borrow a wheelchair from the hospital to get Lisa to the car, as she was in too much pain to walk. The next few days, as expected, her pain was much worse and she could not make it to school.

With Dr. Mailis unable to treat Lisa, we were left stranded yet again. I began searching elsewhere. I had been told of a pain clinic at the children's hospital in London, Ontario, and contacted the doctor who ran it. She explained that her clinic had no experience with RSD although it did have a graduate student studying it, and that the clinic primarily used psychological counselling to help patients manage their pain. I thanked her, but did not feel this was the right place to bring Lisa. I believed we still needed someone to first acknowledge Lisa's pain as real and start treating it appropriately before we added psychological interventions.

My desperation increased as each night was spent watching Lisa crying in pain. I went back to the Internet, to every RSD website and RSD mailing list in existence looking for suggestions and ideas. Everyone seemed to have only praise for Dr. Charles Berde of Children's Hospital in Boston. Bill's sister, a scientist and professor at Harvard University's School of Public Health, spoke to her colleagues and they recommended him too. *Time* magazine had run a cover story several months earlier entitled "Heroes of Medicine",[3] about a number of doctors who were pioneers or groundbreakers in their respective fields; one of them was subtitled "A Child's Pain" and was all about Dr. Berde and his world-renowned expertise in treating children in pain. Not only that, but the story opened with a child who had RSD and who was accused of faking by his doctors, until he came to Dr. Berde and was successfully treated.

This was where we had to go. Although the first available date for an assessment by the hospital's pain clinic was a month away, I took the appointment gratefully.

Knowing how expensive medical treatment in the US could be, we applied to the Ontario Health Insurance Plan—OHIP—to obtain funding for the Boston trip. According to OHIP rules, one is not allowed to go out of the province for medical treatment unless that treatment is either unavailable here or the treatment delay will result in permanent, irreversible tissue damage.[4] Treatments considered experimental are always denied. Second opinions with doctors at world-famous hospitals, such as the Mayo Clinic or Sloan-Kettering, are never funded. You may be bedridden and in terrible pain waiting for knee-replacement surgery, but no permanent tissue damage will result if you need to wait a year or longer to get it. Unless you can afford to pay out of pocket to get knee-replacement surgery in the US, you will just have to spend the next year of your life in bed and in pain.

The rationale for our request was that proper treatment was not available at the Hospital for Sick Children, and other local hospitals could not treat paediatric patients with this condition. Treatment was therefore not available on a timely basis, which met one of OHIP's two criteria. Lisa's paediatrician, Dr. Lee Ann Gallant, wrote a letter of support, calling this "an unfortunate situation of tangled bureaucracy".[5] We sent her letter as part of a package to OHIP that also included an RSD fact sheet from the National Institute of Neurological Disorders, Dr. Berde's 1992 research paper on RSD and children, and a copy of the *Time* magazine story about him.

Just after we prepared the application, a full month after Lisa had been seen and then discarded by Dr. Mailis, Dr. Gallant received Dr. Mailis's belated consult report. Dr. Mailis had written that Lisa's pain was primarily psychological and that the family psychodynamics had contributed to and perpetuated the problem. She even stated she had told me this and I was unhappy with her conclusion—which was completely untrue.

What was wrong with these doctors? Dr. Mailis had fed me those lines about how she understood, being a mother herself, and how Lisa would end up in a wheelchair if not treated promptly—and now had written something completely different in her report. I had become quite adept, I thought, at detecting when a doctor was patronizing or humouring me. Dr. Mailis would never win the prize for charm, but neither did I get the sense when we met that she was being dishonest with me. Bill and I figured there were two possibilities: either she couldn't treat Lisa and wanted to divest herself of responsibility for having turned her away, or what we thought the most likely, Dr. Desparmet had called Dr. Mailis after receiving the letter I had sent and told her that Lisa's problems were psychological and that Lisa's family was a large part of the problem, which in turn caused Dr. Mailis to retroactively revise her opinion.

With Dr. Mailis's letter on file, the likelihood that OHIP would approve our application for out-of-country funding was nil. Grateful that Dr. Gallant was concerned enough to send me a copy of the letter, I wrote out a response in which I attempted to address and refute the various statements Dr. Mailis had made.[6] However, with Lisa still in so much pain, I was demoralized and exhausted and did not feel strong enough to fight with Dr. Mailis. I never sent her the letter, although I did send it to OHIP in the hope it would favourably reconsider our funding request.

Lisa's cast was finally removed, but she walked with a pronounced limp and her pain seemed to be getting worse. When she wasn't experiencing the paroxysmal pains, she was able to wear a shoe. Each night, however, when the shooting pains returned, she would not allow anything to touch any part of her leg. She would fall asleep with her right leg extended off the bed, hanging in mid-air so as not to come into contact with anything.

I called Children's Hospital in Boston on May 8th to see if there had been any cancellations at their pain clinic that would enable us to get an appointment sooner. One had been received just an hour earlier, and Lisa was given an appointment four days from then. An OHIP bureaucrat called that same afternoon to confirm receipt of all the documents we sent. When I told him we were going to Boston sooner than anticipated, he said if we went before OHIP made its decision, our request would automatically be denied.

I had a choice between taking Lisa to Boston in a few days time with no chance of reimbursement, and having her wait in pain for several more weeks on the off chance the government *might* reimburse me. No loving parent would have found this choice difficult. We would do anything that might help take away Lisa's pain, no matter the cost.

We were going to Boston regardless, but the inflexibility of the OHIP bureaucracy rankled. I met with my MPP, a cabinet minister, told him the whole story, and asked for his help in obtaining OHIP funding. I explained that if Lisa needed to be admitted to the hospital in Boston, we would have to cash in our retirement savings to pay for it. He promised to do what he could to help, and I believe he really did try. Unfortunately, even a cabinet minister could not fight government bureaucracy.

We left for Boston two days later.

4

BOSTON

Children's Hospital in Boston is the primary paediatric teaching hospital of Harvard University. For the past fifteen years, *U.S. News & World Report* magazine has surveyed thousands of board-certified specialists to find out which hospitals they rate as the best in their respective fields. For each of those fifteen years, Children's Hospital has ranked number one or two in paediatric care in the U.S.[1]

The Hospital for Sick Children in Toronto also receives many accolades, yet it had provided terrible care. Because of that, I didn't trust any hospital and was afraid the doctors in Boston would say Lisa's pain was all in her head, just as the Toronto doctors had.

The Chronic Pain Management Clinic at Children's Hospital is an outpatient clinic that sees approximately 150 new patients per year. Although those patients are cared for primarily by pain specialist anaesthetists such as Dr. Charles Berde and his colleague Dr. Robert Wilder, it uses a multidisciplinary treatment approach which includes psychologists and physical therapists, and it draws on other specialties as needed.[2]

On May 12, 1998, Lisa, Bill and I arrived at the clinic, where we had been told to expect to spend most of the day. The assessment would include three separate components: a psychological evaluation by the Department of Behavioral Medicine, a detailed examination by the pain specialist, and an assessment by Physical Therapy, after which the people who had seen us would meet to discuss their individual conclusions. We would then see the pain specialist again, who would explain the group's findings and proposed treatment plan.

The psychological assessment began first. We were handed several written questionnaires to complete, some for Lisa alone and some for the adults only. Once they were done, the psychologist, Dr. Rocco, met with Lisa. After he finished with her, he met with Bill and me while Lisa waited outside, and finally, he met with all three of us together. We all felt comfortable with him, able to speak freely about our concerns, our hopes, and our fears, without the sense that someone was testing us and finding everything we said somehow wanting.

The second part of the day's assessment was spent with Dr. Wilder, the clinic's coordinator. We had expected to see Dr. Berde instead of a physician we had not heard of, but it quickly became clear that Dr. Wilder was the resident expert on RSD. He was very intelligent, serious, and soft-spoken, and we told him everything. He wondered out loud why the Hospital for Sick Children had not done an epidural block during Lisa's second admission when the first one had worked so well; I answered that it was because by that time no one believed Lisa's pain was real.

We discussed the Toronto orthopaedic surgeons' unwavering conviction that Lisa's pain was in her head. Dr. Wilder couldn't believe what I was telling him, saying, "We've got our orthopaedic surgeons so well-trained to look out for things like this, at the least sign of unusual pain they send the kids over to us right away." He took a detailed history and conducted an extensive physical examination on Lisa. Dr. Berde poked his head in the door to say hello, and stayed a while to chat and observe.

Next, we saw the physical therapist. She confirmed that Lisa's leg had some oedema, or swelling, around her ankle because of fluid accumulation under the tissues, and pointed out that there was a measurable difference in the circumference of each leg.

We ate lunch in the hospital cafeteria, daring to hope that maybe we had come to the right place after all. Dr. Wilder's exam had been thorough and professional. He had asked questions and listened to our answers without acting as if he didn't believe us. The psychologist had seemed to genuinely like Lisa. The physiotherapist told us that this hospital treated many, many children with chronic pain, and that physiotherapy was considered an active part of the pain team group.

After lunch, we returned to see Dr. Wilder. He had met with Dr. Rocco and the physiotherapist to discuss Lisa's case, and they had all agreed she had RSD.[3] While I had known this in my heart all along, it was difficult to keep from crying with relief. At last someone would do something to help Lisa get better.

Dr. Wilder explained that epidural blocks, like the one Lisa had in Toronto, were not offered as a matter of course but usually only when a child's pain was extremely severe. The doctors at Children's believed that regular physical therapy was the treatment of choice for children with RSD, although it frequently took many, many months until they improved. He stressed that most of the children they saw with RSD did get better. I wanted to press him for more information, such as what percentage was "most", and whether "get better" meant a full recovery, but decided the time was not right to ask. Lisa had been living with so much pain that anything had to be better than this.

Dr. Wilder upped Lisa's Amitriptyline dosage from 25mg per day to 40mg per day. He hoped the increase might help reduce the pain further since she had such a good response from the medication previously. He didn't want to increase the Gabapentin, saying it was better to change only one medication at a time to more effectively monitor what effect it had. This increase did not alleviate Lisa's pain, but it did make her fall asleep very quickly. Since her pain was always at its worst at night, being able to fall asleep just as the pain started increasing was a solution—of sorts—to the problem.

Dr. Wilder decided to admit Lisa to the hospital the following week and give her an epidural block to "kick-start" her recovery. The pain clinic's usual policy when dealing with a child in so much pain was to admit them for eight days, but he knew it would be a financial hardship and proposed a five day Monday to Friday stay instead.

In Canada, no one is ever turned away from a hospital or denied treatment due to inability to pay. Children's Hospital may have been one of the best places in the world to go for medical treatment, but it was still a business—and one that did not extend credit to its customers. We would have to prepay the estimated cost of the five-day stay. Dr. Wilder kindly volunteered to check with the business office to let us know the exact amount; when he called back the next day, he asked me—sounding very sheepish—if I was sitting down. I supposed he found dealing with the mercenary aspects of medicine a little embarrassing. He told me the hospital insisted on a prepayment of $16,000 (about $23,000 Canadian dollars), payable in cash, by credit card, or certified cheque.

I hastily arranged for my father to loan me the money, to be repaid when we returned to Toronto and could withdraw funds from our retirement plans. Bill drove back to Toronto alone to relieve the babysitter, and I stayed on in Boston with Lisa. I dutifully showed up at the billing office on Sunday, the day before Lisa's scheduled admission, certified cheque in hand.

What a difference between Children's Hospital in Boston and the Hospital for Sick Children in Toronto! It wasn't in the patient's room size or the decor, or even the quality of food (although Lisa would have happily told you the pizza in Boston was far superior to that at Sick Kids), but the unbelievable difference in attitude. The nurses on this ward routinely saw children with chronic pain. They treated Lisa as a patient with a legitimate problem, and every single one of them was outstandingly competent, caring, and compassionate, just as one imagines all paediatric nurses should be. The other little girl sharing the room with Lisa was rather cranky and petulant, and it was evident that the nurses really enjoyed and liked our uncomplaining, always-ready-to-oblige little girl. A bonus for me was that I was able to have friendly conversations with them without being made to feel like a bad mother. The doctors explained everything and answered all my questions without a trace of condescension.

Many children with chronic pain become invalids and lose touch with normal day-to-day routines. Sometimes, the parents become so overprotective of their children that they themselves unintentionally or otherwise become an impediment to the healing process. The Toronto doctors had obviously read some of those case studies and decided that those situations applied without exception to every family, including ours. Their eagerness to ignore the obvious in favour of something they had once read explained a lot about their attitudes towards me. In Toronto, the physicians simply assumed I was overprotective and a poor parent, whereas in Boston the doctors work with the whole family in a non-judgmental way to help speed the child's recovery. The team tries to maintain a semblance of "the real world" for their patients at all times, so the children wear regular clothes instead of pyjamas during the day and parents are asked to stay away while psychologists and others work with the child. Parents may call and are given information about how their son or daughter is doing, and they are free to visit or stay overnight. I tried to stay the night but quickly abandoned the idea because the other child's mother snored and kept me awake. Lisa was always a very sound sleeper, and coupled with the sedative effects of the Amitriptyline, it was likely she would sleep through the night without waking. If she did awaken, she knew to call me and I would be there within twenty minutes.

Lisa received an epidural block on her first day. My extensive research had taught me that blocks given early on in the course of this disease generally work well, but as time passes, they often stop working. Since the first block had resulted in immediate pain relief, I fully expected this one to do the same, but sadly, it had no effect. I was devastated, but tried not to let Lisa see. What would Dr. Wilder try next?

He changed the medications that flowed through the epidural catheter, but that did not help either. Lisa's pain increased significantly as the week progressed, probably due in large part to the daily exercises in Physical Therapy. Dr. Rocco, the psychologist, worked with Lisa every day, and the two of them developed a wonderful rapport.

Lisa's pain continued to worsen, and I grew more heartbroken. By the third day, she was suffering so much that Dr. Rocco decided the usual protocols about the parent not being there should be abandoned. He had a nurse call to tell me that instead of staying away during the day as I had been asked to do, it would be better to come down and be with her.

My parents decided to drive the ten hours from Toronto to Boston to cheer up the grandchild they so adored, and not incidentally to take care of me. When Lisa saw them, her grin stretched from ear to ear and she threw her arms wide for a big hug. I was grateful for their love and unbounded support. When the hospital clown visited and started his routine, Zaidy Phil (Zaidy is the Jewish word for Grandpa) couldn't resist. He and the clown immediately recognized each other's comedic talents. Soon a roomful of people was laughing—including nurses who had come in to check on their patients and ended up staying for the entertainment. The two of them were so quick and witty that the clown afterwards expressed admiration and told my Dad he should consider becoming a clown too.

During this time, I was also involved in ongoing long-distance conversations with the OHIP bureaucrat in Toronto regarding our application for out-of-country funding. The bureaucrat, ever mindful of his duties, told me at one point that he would "wait and see which way the wind was blowing" before making a determination as to whether OHIP would reimburse us for the Boston hospital costs. I called him daily to find out if the wind was blowing in the right direction. Finally, he confirmed that a decision had been made–except then he refused to tell me what it was. He said OHIP had sent a letter to Lisa's paediatrician and she was the only one who had the authority to tell me its contents. I could not believe that such a stereotypical civil servant archetype really existed, but we had found him. The paediatrician snorted when I explained the bureaucrat's pigheadedness, and faxed me the OHIP letter.[4] Funding was denied.

Why the denial? Not because we had gone to Boston in advance of getting approval, but because OHIP had contacted the Hospital for Sick Children for information about Lisa and her condition. Sick Kids had told OHIP that Lisa's problems were mostly psychological and it was able to treat her correctly in Toronto. The letter also maligned the Boston hospital–arguably the most renowned facility in the world for treatment of paediatric RSD–for not recognizing "possible psychological factors". It stated that it had spoken with orthopaedic surgeons, anaesthetists, psychiatrists, and rheumatologists. The last specialty was a surprise; where had Rheumatology come from? If rheumatologists were so willing to be consulted, why hadn't they seen Lisa when she was a patient in their own hospital for three weeks?

Dr. Wilder thought that having a rheumatologist follow Lisa when she went back to Toronto was an excellent idea. He said he would contact the OHIP doctor who wrote the letter and ask him which rheumatologist had indicated the willingness to follow Lisa. He did so, only to discover that the OHIP doctor had gone to the same school of bureaucrat training as the clerk. This doctor refused to speak with Dr. Wilder and told him he would only give the requested information to Lisa's paediatrician in Toronto. We concluded that he had likely not spoken to anyone in Rheumatology but had merely written down what the Hospital for Sick Children told him, which was why he did not have the names of any doctors to give.

Just as I had been forced to do from the beginning, I made my own inquiries of friends, family, and physicians until I found a rheumatologist at the Hospital for Sick Children, Dr. Ron Laxer. Dr. Wilder called him and Dr. Laxer said he would be happy to follow Lisa in Toronto. I also contacted Bloorview-McMillan Centre, a Toronto facility for children with disabilities and special needs, to arrange for the ongoing physiotherapy that Dr. Wilder felt Lisa required.

I thought ahead to the attitudes of the doctors and nurses I would be going back to at the Hospital for Sick Children, and asked Dr. Rocco to write an opinion letter on Lisa's "mental state" for me. He was happy to oblige, and wrote a wonderful letter saying Lisa had no psychological or behavioural problems and that he saw no evidence of any problems with the family dynamics.[5]

By Friday afternoon, Lisa's pain decreased somewhat. The intense physical therapy earlier in the week had probably made her pain levels increase, which in turn led to a reduction of the amount of therapy that could be done, which finally led to the decrease in pain. Knowing that none of the various blocks he had tried had worked, Dr. Wilder increased Lisa's Gabapentin dosage from 600mg/day to 900mg/day, and her Amitriptyline to 60mg/day. Having read the pharmaceutical compendiums, I knew they said the maximum recommended Gabapentin dosage for children was 600mg. When I questioned Dr. Wilder, he reassured me that many of his paediatric patients had had great success at higher dosages, and that Gabapentin was a very safe drug. Both Dr. Wilder and Dr. Berde regretted that they had not been able to relieve Lisa's pain, but felt that with time her prognosis was excellent and she would likely make a full recovery.

5

LISA GETS HER LIFE BACK

If there was ever a child who did not let her illness dishearten her, it was Lisa. Although she still spent her nights crying in pain, by day she was mostly able to bear it and would not complain. Only if asked would she answer that her leg hurt a lot.

Shortly after returning home, exactly four days after Dr. Wilder had upped Lisa's dosage of Gabapentin, the terrible evening pain sharply decreased. It was still quite severe, but she stopped grunting and groaning and now only grimaced. She rated the evening pain as 7 out of 10 instead of 10 out of 10, and the Amitriptyline we gave her around 9:00 p.m. made her fall asleep within the hour, before the pain could get any worse.

Even the daytime pain seemed to be more tolerable. On May 26th, Lisa was able to return to school full time. She was thrilled, telling me, "The teachers are so happy with me, Mommy! It's near the end of the year and everyone is goofing off, but I missed so much school that I'm practically the only one paying attention in class!"

Lisa resumed her social life too, at least in the daytime. Nights were still sufficiently painful that she stayed in and took her Amitriptyline "sleeping pill" as soon as the pain started to increase. Where she was able to walk with a barely discernible limp during the day, at night she would not put her foot on the ground and used her crutches to walk. When she went to bed, she still kept her leg extended off the bed to avoid the touch of the sheet or bedcover.

We had applied for Lisa to get physiotherapy at Bloorview-McMillan, but it would take several months until the facility could process all the paperwork. Knowing how important therapy was, we took Lisa to a private clinic. Although sometimes painful for her, the therapist was gentle and did not push her any more than she felt Lisa could handle. I called Dr. Wilder and told him how improved Lisa was and that it seemed to be attributable to the increased dosage of Gabapentin. Lisa had shown no side effects from this medication thus far, and Dr. Wilder suggested raising the dosage even higher, to 1200mg per day. Since Canadian pharmacies do not accept prescriptions from American doctors, I told him Lisa would be seeing Dr. Laxer, the rheumatologist at Sick Kids he had spoken with, in only a few days time and I would ask him to write the prescription.

On June 16, 1998, Lisa and I met with Dr. Laxer and a resident. His examination showed she had many of the classical signs of RSD. Her injured leg was purplish and mottled in comparison to the uninjured leg, she had severe pain in reaction to even the lightest touch, and the sole of her foot had lost all its wrinkles and become smooth, as if the area had undergone a facelift and had the skin pulled tightly back. Dr. Laxer agreed that Lisa had RSD. He told me that all his RSD patients had gotten better with aggressive physiotherapy, and explained that he did not believe in giving them any medication. In fact, he wanted Lisa to come off the drugs she was taking.

I knew that at one time it was thought that children did not need any pain medications for RSD, but I was flabbergasted to hear someone think that way in 1998. RSD was acknowledged to be a terribly painful disease. Although the prognosis was better for children than for adults, it took a long time even for children to recover. How could anyone who was up-to-date on treatments and protocols for RSD not believe in using medication to help relieve the pain? Why was it all right to leave children in pain but perfectly appropriate to use medication for an adult?

I told Dr. Laxer that these medications had given Lisa her life back, that she had previously been screaming in pain most of the time and thanks to the medications was now back in school full-time. I was emphatic that I was not prepared to have her go off them, and explained I had been planning on asking him to increase the dosage of Gabapentin from 900mg to 1200mg per day! I didn't think it was a good idea to mention that it had been Dr. Wilder's idea, since many doctors take offence to being told what another doctor recommends. Dr. Laxer was taken aback at my request and curtly told me he did not feel it was appropriate to have me making decisions about Lisa's medications, suggesting instead that Lisa see Dr. Desparmet in Pain Service as she was the one who knew about those types of drugs. Given his disapproval, I was very surprised that he agreed to give Lisa a prescription at the higher dosage I had requested.

I asked him for a letter confirming Lisa had RSD,[1] reasoning that the other doctors at Sick Kids would be inclined to believe it if the diagnosis was made by one of their own. On the way out, on a whim, I asked the resident how many RSD patients Dr. Laxer had seen. She said she didn't know, but assured me he had seen many. I asked how many he had seen recently, and she responded, "None this year."

I did not intend to contact Dr. Desparmet. She had not been helpful to us, felt that Lisa's pain was psychological, and had been unwilling to prescribe the medications that had made such a difference to Lisa's quality of life. The only doctors who had helped us were Gallant and Wilder, so it was only logical to continue taking Lisa to Boston to see Dr. Wilder whenever necessary. In the interim, I made arrangements with him that whenever Lisa needed a prescription renewal or change, he would fax a note to Dr. Gallant, who would then reissue it on her own prescription pad.

One week after Lisa started Gabapentin at the new dosage, her pain levels declined even further. During the day she rated her pain as 2 out of 10, with occasional increases up to 5. That night, instead of the shooting pains starting as they most often did between 6:00 and 9:00 p.m., they didn't start until 11:00 p.m. Instead of keeping her leg hanging off the bed so nothing touched it, Lisa rested it on her bed.

This meant that Lisa could enjoy her summer–and so could we. She biked, rollerbladed, and swam. She had been planning to go to sleep-away camp, but we had cancelled it for fear of pain-filled nights. She didn't understand why, since she told us she was now feeling "pretty good". We promised her she could go there next year, expecting that somehow by then the problems would be resolved. Lisa went instead to a local day camp for the whole summer, where she had a marvellous time and made many new friends. When she had the occasional pain spell, she went to the camp infirmary and rested until it passed.

At the end of June we drove to Boston for a follow-up appointment with Dr. Wilder. During the visit, Lisa sat in his chair and swivelled around in circles, ignoring us completely. I was a bit embarrassed at her behaviour, but Dr. Wilder said he was happy to see her acting like a well child who had better things to do than hang around a doctor's office. I told him what Dr. Laxer had said about taking Lisa off medications. He agreed that was the best policy long-term but said he would not stop anything until he was sure her pain was under control, at which time he would gradually taper her off everything.

We had many happy times that summer. We saw fireworks on Canada Day, visited Canada's Wonderland, bought cotton candy and lost money at the carnival booths at the Canadian National Exhibition, and visited Niagara Falls. Lisa still took her Amitriptyline every night as her pain levels increased, and she would be in great discomfort until the sedation kicked in, but there were no more tormented screams. Each morning she awoke cheerful and refreshed and with only a bit of pain in her leg, ready for whatever the day held in store.

At the end of the summer, the pain started increasing again. It was still tolerable in the daytime, and she started Grade 6 with all of her friends. She would go to bed crying in pain, but woke up each morning feeling well enough to go to school. So much for Dr. Desparmet's theory that her pain was due to a desire to avoid school.

All the visible signs of RSD cleared up. Lisa was no longer limping, her leg was not mottled and purplish, and there was no visible swelling; only the pain remained. I was glad I had obtained some medical letters attesting to her RSD, since the absence of physical manifestations of the illness would have made it far too easy for the doctors at Sick Kids to fall back on their "it's all in her head" theory.

I read an Italian research paper about a child who had a nerve entrapment that had been surgically corrected, which in turn had cured his RSD.[2] Since I felt that the stabbing pains that plagued Lisa were more indicative of nerve damage than was typical for RSD, I thought it would be a good idea to get a neurosurgery assessment. Once again Dr. Gallant was supportive, and she gave us a referral to a doctor at Sick Kids.

We saw the neurosurgeon in mid September 1998. By now wary of every doctor at the Hospital for Sick Children, I came prepared with a binder that included Dr. Rocco's letter stating that Lisa had no mental problems, Dr. Laxer's letter diagnosing RSD, and the research paper on the boy with the nerve entrapment.

The doctor examined Lisa briefly and said he saw no sign of RSD. I showed him the research paper on the 10-year-old, and he said, quite surprised, "I haven't read this one." He spent the next few minutes going over it, muttered how worthless it was, and gave it back to me with a curt dismissal. He told me, "These chronic pain things can take a long time to resolve. I wouldn't do anything for at least six months." No longer willing to let statements like that go unchallenged, I pressed him to suggest exactly what it was he suggested I do in six months. I had to ask the question three times before he realized that I was waiting for him to give me a real answer. After thinking about it, he finally recommended I bring Lisa in six months time to see Dr. Desparmet. Then he told me, "I'm not an expert on entrapments anyway," and our consultation was over.

I contacted Dr. Wilder in Boston about Lisa's increasing pain levels, and he recommended trying a slight increase in Gabapentin from 1200mg/day to 1400mg/day. This seemed to do the trick, and successfully brought her pain down to the level it had been before.

The Terry Fox Run, an annual charity run held every September in Canada, has been credited as being the largest, single-day fundraising event for cancer research in the world. The "Terry Fox Marathon of Hope" has raised over $340 million since Terry Fox first decided to run across the country in 1980.[3] Lisa's school held its own run annually, with its oldest students, Lisa's Grade 6 classmates, as the runners. The class discussed the implications and prevalence of cancer, and we told Lisa that her middle name, Celine, was given in memory of her great-aunt Celia who had died of breast cancer long ago.

Lisa was determined to walk or run the eight kilometres in memory of Aunt Celia, and resolutely went door-to-door on our street collecting pledges. The shy little girl, normally too timid to start conversations with adults she didn't know, got pledges from almost every neighbour on the street. I doubted she would be able to complete the entire course, expecting the pain in her leg would flare up, but she surprised us all. She successfully completed the run, collected her pledges, and received a certificate she was so very proud of.

Within the next couple of days, however, the pain in her leg grew worse and worse. By September 28th, the pain was so bad that even the Amitriptyline did not put her to sleep. She was up until about 3:00 a.m., moaning and crying, until she finally collapsed from sheer exhaustion.

We hoped that the next morning she would wake up with reduced pain levels as was usually the case. Instead, from the moment she opened her eyes in the morning she began writhing and screaming, with no letup. This was different from anything we had seen before.

Distraught, I called Dr. Wilder, only to discover he was away on a conference and not due back until the next day. I sat beside Lisa all day long and much of the night, trying to offer comfort. Those terrible times of unrelenting agony from earlier in the year were back. Every electrical shock that surged through her made her scream, and I wanted to scream alongside in anguish.

I got hold of Dr. Wilder the next day. He had been at a conference in Halifax, where he had met and spoken with Dr. Desparmet about Lisa. He suggested that if Lisa was in such bad shape, it would be better to avoid the long drive to Boston and have Dr. Desparmet see her in Toronto. I agreed, and Dr. Wilder offered to call her on my behalf. He called back soon afterwards to report that she would see Lisa on an emergency basis; all I needed to do was call Sick Kids' Anaesthesiology to arrange a time. But when I did, I was told Dr. Desparmet could not see Lisa until ten days later. Lisa was screaming in unremitting pain and I needed to wait ten days for an "emergency basis" appointment? I called Dr. Wilder back in a near panic and told him what she had said. He didn't believe me and said he would call himself. After he learned that what I had told him was true, he said he would see Lisa as soon as we could get her to Boston.

We left at 5:00 a.m. the next morning. Lisa moaned in pain for the entire nine-hour drive. We went straight to the hospital, where Dr. Wilder, true to his word, saw her immediately. He tried a number of different medications, sending Bill running down to the pharmacy repeatedly, but none had any effect. He asked one of his colleagues, an anaesthetist who was also an acupuncturist, to administer an acupuncture treatment, but it too was ineffective. Dr. Wilder suggested we return to our hotel and increase Lisa's dosage of Amitriptyline, in the hope it would sedate her. It did, and she finally fell asleep.

The moment she awoke, however, she began crying in pain again. We brought her back to the hospital, where Dr. Wilder decided to administer a single shot epidural in the hope it would break the pain cycle. He also suggested we consider trying to have Lisa get involved in some biofeedback and relaxation therapy when we got back to Toronto to help her manage her pain. We agreed, but said we had no idea where to find clinics that offered those therapies given we were inclined to exclude the Hospital for Sick Children from our consideration. He sent us to the Behavioral Medicine department, suggesting that the staff there could probably help with a referral. Although Dr. Rocco was no longer working there, the doctor we met with told us that Dr. Rocco had spoken highly of Lisa and had really liked her. She spoke with Lisa and with us, and agreed with Dr. Wilder that Lisa would be a good candidate for biofeedback and cognitive therapy. However, neither she nor any of the colleagues she checked with had any contacts in Toronto, so we thanked her and told her we would find a clinic on our own.

Lisa was given the epidural under a general anaesthetic. After the procedure was finished and she was taken to the recovery room, Bill and I were allowed to stay with her. She was still sedated and hooked up to various vital signs monitors, which I watched intently just as I had done when she received the epidural back in Toronto months earlier. I still hadn't learned what the readings meant, but I knew that consistency was important and if the numbers didn't change very much it was probably a good thing. Suddenly, one of the readings dipped quite a lot, at least to my uninformed eye, and I panicked and called out for a nurse to come quickly. The nurse said everything was fine, but I kept watching those monitors until Lisa woke up. When she opened her eyes, she rated her pain as a 5 or 6 out of 10–a vast improvement over what it had been, but still very uncomfortable. As the epidural began wearing off, she started crying in pain once again.

Dr. Wilder started Lisa on a new drug called Carbamazepine (Tegretol), and decided to maintain her on the new Amitriptyline dosage of 75mg/day. Carbamazepine is an anti-convulsant like Gabapentin, commonly used for epilepsy but also found to be effective in treatment of paroxysmal lancinating pains, which was exactly what Lisa had.

That evening, the intensity of the pain lessened slightly for a short while, and then resumed again in full force. We returned to the hospital the next morning, and I asked Dr. Wilder if we could get a consult from a neurologist. I knew that the constant onslaught of paroxysmal pains that Lisa was experiencing was not consistent with RSD, and thought that a neurologist might be able to suggest some other possibilities. Dr. Wilder made a phone call to a colleague and asked if he would see us right away because we were leaving shortly to go back to Toronto. Judging by the one-sided conversation we heard, the neurologist was not happy about the idea.

Dr. Rust did see us quickly. And just as quickly, we knew we had made a terrible mistake. Dr. Rust evidently had felt he couldn't say no to Dr. Wilder, but he was very angry about it and took it out on us. He was hostile and unpleasant, and scolded Lisa for moaning. He started to take a family history, and asked Bill and me whether we got headaches and if we took medication for them. When we both said we did, once in a while, like most other people, and took Tylenol for them, he turned to his resident who was taking notes and said something like "family history of headaches, taking medication". Bill and I looked at each other in chagrin. I knew he was implying there was a family history of pain problems, which was quite untrue.

Dr. Rust examined Lisa, commenting that when she moaned in pain, there was no change in her heart rate, and if she was genuinely in pain that wouldn't be the case. We told him it had been like that right from the very start, even in Toronto. His nurse came in approximately three times during our visit, looked at us with disgust, and told him each time that he was way behind schedule and there was a roomful of patients waiting for him. What she didn't say but obviously meant was "get rid of these people". That was exactly what he did, telling us he didn't see evidence of any neurological problems. We left there as quickly as we could, feeling as if we had landed back in the middle of the Sick Kids orthopaedic department, surrounded by doctors who felt we were wasting their time.

Secure in the knowledge that Boston was the one place where we could totally rely on and trust the doctors, we considered our visit to Dr. Rust to be a "bump in the road", and didn't worry about it. We did not know this unpleasant physician would write a report saying that Lisa's problem was psychological in origin, and that his report would one day be used by those responsible for Lisa's death as justification for their negligence.

We left for Toronto, discouraged by Dr. Wilder's apparent inability to reduce Lisa's pain. Although it was fall and the temperature was cool, Lisa kept one leg of her sweat pants rolled up so it did not touch her skin. She would not put on shoes or socks, and used crutches to go to the car. Once inside, she lay across the back seat with one leg hanging off so nothing could touch it. Every bump the car went over was agony for her.

As we drove the nine hours from Boston to Toronto, Lisa's pain began to recede. By the time we reached home she was feeling quite a bit better than she had been the last few days, and had stopped the continuous moaning. Her pain increased at night, as was usual, but the new, higher dose of Amitriptyline sedated her before things got too bad.

She woke up the next morning happy and cheerful, with the pain having settled back to its previous lower level. She went right back to school, as if the past week had never happened. She still reported burning pain if asked, but as always, did not otherwise complain. Each night she would cry in pain until the pills put her to sleep, but she would be relatively fine in the morning. We thought the flare-up of the past week must have been caused by the over-exertion resulting from Lisa's participation in the Terry Fox Run. After a few days of torment, the flare-up subsided on its own. Would it happen again? If it did, how long would it last? We had no idea what to expect.

We hired a lawyer to appeal OHIP's refusal to cover the Boston medical expenses. We thought we had a strong case, even though the lawyer said the odds were against us. We had medical records to prove the doctors at the Hospital for Sick Children had misdiagnosed Lisa and therefore no proper medical treatment had been available in Ontario. I attended a hearing with my lawyer, but nothing was resolved; OHIP wanted additional information before it would make any decision. The parties could have obtained the same results much more cheaply and efficiently with a five-minute phone call rather than through this quasi-court proceeding, I thought, but I apparently did not understand the legal subtleties that had unfolded before me. My lawyer said the hearing had been very successful and he was now much more optimistic about our chances of obtaining reimbursement than he had been before it started. He guessed that the odds of winning had increased from 25% to about 50%. When fighting OHIP, winning the battle apparently means one's case has not yet been thrown out.

I decided it would be a good idea to meet with Dr. Desparmet again. I still didn't like her, and I fully intended to keep Dr. Wilder in Boston as Lisa's primary physician, but I thought it would be smart to have someone in Toronto to fall back on. Since Dr. Wilder had spoken to Dr. Desparmet about Lisa genuinely having RSD, I hoped and expected a slightly better reception from her this time.

I discovered that Sick Kids' Pain Service was finally running a real outpatient clinic–of sorts. Every Friday, or sometimes every other Friday, for a couple of hours, or sometimes for less time than that, Pain Service saw outpatients. On October 9th, 1998, just a few days after we returned home from Boston, I brought Lisa to the clinic where we met with Dr. Desparmet, a resident, a nurse, and the team's psychiatrist.

What a contrast to the way we had been treated before! They seemed to really be listening to me. The psychiatrist said that the 75mg per day of Amitriptyline Lisa was taking was quite a bit higher than what they would have prescribed, and I explained that her night time pain was still very bad and this was the amount she required for effective sedation. I asked if Dr. Desparmet would take over prescribing Lisa's medications from this point forward, figuring it made more sense logistically to have her do it than Dr. Wilder faxing a prescription up to Toronto for Dr. Gallant to reissue. She was reluctant, telling me that Lisa's paediatrician should be the one doing the prescribing, not her. I thought to myself, "Why on earth does she feel it appropriate that Lisa's paediatrician do the prescribing, when she's the only one around who knows about these particular drugs and their use in treating chronic pain conditions?" Although technically more than qualified to treat Lisa, she was apparently unwilling to assume responsibility for Lisa's care the way Dr. Wilder had. What was the point of her seeing Lisa in this clinic if she wasn't going to manage her medications? I already knew I could not rely on her to see Lisa in case of emergency, based on our experience just two weeks earlier. I realized how essential it was that Dr. Wilder remain Lisa's primary doctor. Dr. Desparmet did give me a repeat on one of Lisa's prescriptions, stressing that she was doing so for this one time only, and ordered some blood tests and an electrocardiogram for Lisa to ensure the medications were not causing any adverse effects.

Lisa read a book during my conversation with Dr. Desparmet, oblivious to everyone around her. I think she felt that if she paid attention and acknowledged she had a medical problem, then it became real. As long as she did not think about it, as long as she wasn't in terrible agony, RSD did not concern or affect her. If this was how she coped, it was fine with me. She did look up on occasion, when required to answer a direct question. When Dr. Desparmet examined her, Lisa told her that her leg always felt like it was burning. She rated her pain at that moment as 3 or 4 out of 10, and then went right back to reading her book. When Lisa had ignored Dr. Wilder when we visited him in the summer, he had said it made him happy to see her acting like a kid with better things to do than pay attention to him. The psychiatrist who was there for the consultation, faced with a similar situation, wrote in his notes that Lisa was "sullen".

That night, Lisa's pain flare-up was not as bad as it had been the last few weeks. We attributed this to the new medication, the Carbamazepine she had started taking eleven days ago in Boston. It seemed as if all of the various medications that were effective with neuropathic pain took days or even weeks to start working. We measured our victories in small improvements; any decrease in pain was cause for celebration. Over the next few days her night time pain, always higher than in the daytime, became tolerable—a 4 or 5 on her pain scale instead of the 9 and 10 of the weeks past.

Lisa had the electrocardiogram and the results were normal. She had extensive blood tests, all normal. The various drugs she was taking caused no noticeable side effects. Lisa became her happy self again, attending school, playing with her friends, and going to birthday parties and to movies—all the usual activities of the normal 10-year-old she was. We started planning her upcoming eleventh birthday party. We began talking about our next summer's vacation. We began thinking to the future, something we had not done for a long time.

6

OCTOBER 21, 1998

Sunday, Oct. 18, 1998 was a very busy day for Lisa. We took her and her brothers to see the play "Goosebumps–Live on Stage", a professional production based on author R.L. Stine's horror books. Because I had purchased the tickets early, we had front row centre seats. The children had never seen a real stage performance from that close up before, and Lisa in particular really loved the show and all its special effects. Later that afternoon, she went to a classmate's birthday party where she partied and played indoor glow-in-the-dark minigolf.

The physical therapy we had arranged for her at the Bloorview-McMillan Centre was set to begin the next day. The Centre was starting a weekly group for children who had rheumatoid arthritis, an often-painful condition, and the staff felt Lisa would fit in well with the rest of the participants. The first hour of the two-hour session would consist of physical therapy custom tailored to each child, and the second hour would be spent in the facility's extra-warm pool. Lisa had been so active in the past few months that we didn't think she needed any therapy, but we believed in the philosophy of "it won't hurt, it might help, so why not try it?"

We had previously met with the woman assigned to be Lisa's therapist and explained to her that RSD was different from other conditions in one very significant way: The adage "no pain, no gain" does NOT apply. Therapy or exercise done to extreme can lead to severe and incapacitating pain and cause a major exacerbation of the RSD. It is imperative that new exercises get introduced gradually and activities that cause pain be avoided. We told the therapist Lisa was her own best judge of what she could and could not do, and if she felt it was time to stop an activity, then it was time to stop. We also discussed this with Lisa, making sure she knew it was all right to sit out any exercise that was painful or uncomfortable.

When we picked her up at the end of the first Monday night session, she was in tears because her leg hurt so much. She told us that the second hour in the pool had been spent walking back and forth, with none of the swimming or leg strengthening exercises we had expected. She hadn't wanted to make a fuss, so she didn't stop or tell anyone how much her leg was hurting.

The next morning, Tuesday, October 20, 1998, Lisa awoke in greater pain than usual. I knew she was uncomfortable when she complained her leg hurt, since she normally never complained during the day. She insisted on going to school anyway, but was crying by the time she came home. This was starting to sound just like the horror of only a few weeks ago, where even the doctors in Boston were unable to provide her with any relief.

Based on the much warmer reception Lisa and I had received when we saw Dr. Desparmet two weeks earlier, I felt I could now bring Lisa to the Hospital for Sick Children and she would be treated well. My rational side said that Boston hadn't been able to help relieve her terrible pain during the last flare-up and therefore Sick Kids wouldn't be able to either, and it would be a waste of time to take her to the hospital. The distraught mother side of me was desperate for something–anything–anybody–to stop Lisa's pain. I was afraid of spending another day listening to my daughter scream in unbearable agony without being able to help her in any way.

I wavered between calling the hospital and not calling, but Lisa's pain continued to grow worse. I had to do something. The next morning, on Wednesday, October 21, 1998, I called Sick Kids' Pain Service. I spoke to one of the nurses and discussed the possibility of bringing Lisa in. I said I would wait a few hours and see how things went, hoping against hope that her pain would miraculously recede.

The nurse and I spoke several more times over the course of the day, as Lisa's pain grew more and more intolerable. We eventually agreed we would bring her in via the Emergency Department, and the nurse would notify whoever was on call for Pain Service that evening to expect Lisa's arrival. I called a relative to stay with the boys and packed Lisa's and my bag for a stay of several nights at the hospital. Remembering from previous hospital stays that pillows were sometimes in short supply, at least for parents, I packed two pillows, one for Lisa's leg to rest on and the other for me.

Bill, Lisa, and I started preparing to leave about 8:30 that evening. Lisa's pain was so severe she could not walk or bear any touch on her leg. Moving an 85-pound preteen who could not stand on her own down the stairs and into a mini-van was a difficult undertaking, and we drove slowly so as not to jar her.

The last time we had taken her to the Emergency Department for help, the orthopaedic fellow had told us to leave. The possibility we might encounter a similar attitude again did not occur to me; after all, Dr. Desparmet and her Pain Service team were now working with us and not against us. I had become a much better informed advocate for my child, and would never again allow Lisa—or me—to be treated with condescension by doctors whose arrogance exceeded their common sense or diagnostic abilities.

Lisa was grimacing and grunting in pain. The Pain Service nurse had been true to her word, however, and Lisa did not have to see a resident for a preliminary assessment. We were ushered into an examination room very quickly, Pain Service was advised of her arrival, and the doctor was on his or her way down.

Lisa was by now taking three different medications: Gabapentin, Carbamazepine, and Amitriptyline. I gave her the usual evening dose of the first two but wanted to check with the doctor before giving her Amitriptyline, because that drug was so sedating I was afraid its effects could conflict with something the doctor might want to give her.

Dr. Markus Schily, an anaesthesia fellow and the Pain Service physician on call, came in. He knew a bit about Lisa already from the Pain Service nurse, and we filled him in on the rest while he examined her. In a heavy German accent, he told Lisa he was going to help her, and that he had a little girl at home about the same age as her.

I told him about Lisa's not having taken her Amitriptyline, and why, and he told me without any hesitation that it was perfectly fine to give it to her. Dr. Schily decided to put Lisa on a PCA morphine pump, which would allow her to push a button and self-administer a small amount of morphine whenever she felt she needed it for pain control. I had already mentioned to him that morphine did not have any effect on Lisa's pain, but I was afraid if I told him that giving her morphine was not a good idea, he would get angry. After our miserable past experiences with the hospital, I worried that the cooperation of the staff and their willingness to help would be very short-lived if I suggested they weren't doing the right thing. I told Lisa, "It might not help, sweetie, but who knows, maybe this time it just might. Let's give it a try, ok?"

Back then, I knew as much—or more to the point, as little—about morphine as the next person. It was a controlled substance and a highly addictive narcotic. Lisa had been given morphine seven months ago when she had first come to the hospital in pain, and hadn't had any problems with it other than a bit of itchiness. No one had ever discussed its dangers with me, and its lack of effect on Lisa had left me with the vague impression that it wasn't as frightening a drug as most people thought it was. I did not know that morphine has one potentially deadly side effect—respiratory depression—which if left untreated can lead to coma and death. This side effect, although not a common occurrence, is a known risk and necessitates that nurses monitor patients on morphine thoroughly and carefully. Certain factors can increase the likelihood of respiratory depression occurring, such as interactions with other drugs or pre-existing respiratory problems.

When a child is put on a PCA morphine pump, the doctor or nurse always emphatically tells the parents that only the child may press the button, never the adult. This seemed like common sense—why should a parent give a child any medication that isn't needed? If a child can't or won't press the button himself, he obviously does not need any more morphine. I have since learned that the reason parents are given this warning is to prevent them from overmedicating their child, which could lead to disastrous consequences.

In spite of its danger, morphine is considered quite safe when used in a hospital setting with appropriate monitoring. A morphine antagonist called naloxone (trade name: Narcan) can instantly reverse morphine's potentially deadly side effects, and this reversal drug is available on every ward at the Hospital for Sick Children that cares for patients who may be on morphine.

As each knife-like bolt of pain shot down her leg, Lisa moaned and grunted. Dr. Schily asked her to try and stop making those noises. Lisa tried so hard to comply, but just couldn't hold it in. Would anyone ask a mother-to-be in labour to be quiet? This is the eternal problem with painful conditions: if patients verbalize their pain they are perceived to be whiners and complainers, and if they grit their teeth and keep quiet, the doctor writes on their chart that they're in no apparent pain. I told Lisa that if she needed to make noise when the shooting pains came to just go ahead and do it.

Dr. Schily explained to Bill and me that we would have to wait to see if Lisa could be admitted. Anaesthesia and Pain Service at the Hospital for Sick Children still did not have any direct admitting privileges and could only admit patients if Orthopaedics gave permission. Not much had changed since last March, apparently, except this time Lisa's leg was no longer broken and I would not have to deal with the orthopaedic surgeons—even if Lisa was to be admitted to the orthopaedic floor.

Shortly before midnight, Lisa was put on an intravenous, or IV drip. The IV drip is given to a patient for two reasons: the sterile solution ensures the adequacy of fluid levels and prevents dehydration, and it also provides a ready access to administer medications quickly and directly into the bloodstream. To give Lisa a head start on pain relief, Dr. Schily gave her a 2mg dose of morphine directly through her IV. The effect of morphine given in this manner is felt almost instantaneously, but just as I expected, it did not reduce Lisa's pain at all.

Dr. Schily and the Emergency Department nurse together hooked Lisa up to the PCA pump, carefully checking the machine's settings. They both left the room immediately afterwards, but the nurse returned with a pulse oximeter which she attached to Lisa. A pulse oximeter is a device loosely resembling a high-tech clothespin, attached by cable to a monitor displaying a digital readout. The clothespin is clamped lightly onto a patient's finger and emits what looks like a red light. This light is actually two lights, one red and one infrared, which together measure what percentage of a person's haemoglobin molecules are carrying oxygen. A normal oxygen saturation level for a healthy adult or child would be between 97%-100%. If a patient on morphine began to experience respiratory depression, this percentage would start to decline and the oximeter would sound an alarm. The oximeter is thus a very valuable monitoring tool in that it warns of impending danger—decrease in blood oxygen levels—rather than sounding an alarm after the danger point has been breached and the patient may already be critical.

It would be unusual for a patient who was awake and alert to suffer any respiratory distress, particularly when that patient is a child with two concerned parents hovering over her. The nurse's act of putting Lisa on oximetry was merely an indication she was highly competent and had taken extra care to ensure that any adverse reaction would be promptly noticed and treated. The red glow the clothespin emitted made Lisa's finger look eerily transparent. In between the spasms of pain, Lisa waggled her finger and marvelled at the glow's strange effect.

Dr. Schily returned and saw that the morphine had not reduced Lisa's pain. He wanted to do something to help, so he gave her another 2 mg. of morphine through her IV. He also let us know he had received confirmation there was a bed available for Lisa on the orthopaedics ward. "You might as well go home now," I said to Bill once we heard Lisa would definitely be admitted. "I'll call you first thing in the morning and let you know what's happening." Bill kissed Lisa goodbye, telling her he'd see her tomorrow.

The nurse came back shortly after to check on Lisa, and told me Dr. Schily had left orders for her to be transferred up to the ward only when her pain score went down to a "5" (out of 10). I told her the morphine didn't do anything to relieve her pain, and the pain would not go down below what it was now, which was 8. "The only thing that would help," I said, "would be to get her up to the ward to let her get to sleep." She answered, "I can't do anything about it, these are the doctor's orders." "Then she's going to stay here all night," I responded.

In the meantime, Lisa kept pushing the PCA button trying to obtain morphine hits. I guess she was looking for the same kind of miracle as I was, hoping the morphine would suddenly and magically start working. I knew from experience that eventually she would fall asleep, exhausted. The orders not to let Lisa move upstairs to a real room and to a real bed until her pain decreased may have been made with the best of intentions, but they reflected a lack of understanding of her condition. I wondered whether I was still going to have to fight for Lisa in spite of the hospital's ostensible acceptance of her as a bona fide patient with a real medical problem.

Around 12:45 in the morning, Lisa needed to go to the bathroom. Unable to walk on the injured leg, unable to bear having anything touch it, and hooked up to an IV, this was a difficult exercise. The nurse removed the pulse oximeter, apparently satisfied that Lisa was in no danger. I got Lisa into a wheelchair and we finally reached the bathroom. She sat on the toilet, held her hands out to me to give me a big hug, and said, "Mommy, you take such good care of me."

As I wheeled her back to the examination room, I noticed she had suddenly become so sleepy that her head kept rolling forward. She would jerk her head back trying to keep awake, only to have it roll forward again. It was immensely difficult to get her out of her wheelchair in this condition and back on to the stretcher; she was fast asleep literally before her head hit the pillow. I had never before seen Lisa change so instantaneously from complete alertness to an almost comatose state, but I assumed it was the morphine added to the Amitriptyline she had taken earlier that was making her so sleepy. I was happy she was asleep and out of pain.

The nurse came back and told me she had contacted Dr. Schily about Lisa's pain not decreasing even with the morphine. He had agreed it was okay to send Lisa up to the ward even if her pain score was still high, and the nurse had already paged Transport. This is the collective name given to the purple-shirted hospital employees who move patients around the hospital. It is not unusual to have to wait a while for Transport to appear, and it took over thirty minutes before someone arrived, about 1:30 am. Lisa was sound asleep and did not stir. The nurse gave me the thin binder containing Lisa's Emergency Department paperwork and told me to give it to whichever nurse would be taking care of her.

The Transport woman and I brought my sleeping daughter up to a room on Ward 5A. At 1:40 a.m., the orthopaedic floor was eerily and unusually silent. There were no doctors or nurses anywhere in sight, no parents and children wandering the halls, and no audible beeps and hums of equipment.

Two nurses were already waiting in Lisa's room, but neither of them said anything to me. Although I remembered most of the nurses on Ward 5A from Lisa's previous admission, these women were both unfamiliar and had never been Lisa's nurses. One of them took the binder I had brought up from Emergency, and then they both rolled

Lisa over from the stretcher to the hospital bed. As Lisa was as limp as the proverbial sack of potatoes, I asked if they wanted me to help; the younger of the two nurses told me no, they didn't.

Both nurses checked Lisa's PCA pump, carefully going over the machine's settings together, and then took Lisa's vital signs. Neither of them introduced herself, gave me so much as a glance or said anything to me except to answer that they didn't need my help. It was as if I didn't exist. I thought to myself that these two would not be winning any congeniality contests in the near future, and that it was my bad luck to be stuck with them. There was no way I could know that these two nurses, complete strangers to me, already disliked and resented my daughter and me before we ever arrived on the ward and had chosen to express their resentment by deliberately ignoring me.

Lisa was still in her street clothes, so the nurses undressed her and put her nightshirt on. I asked again if they needed some help and was again rebuffed. I decided I had better make some small talk so these two discourteous women would at least realize I was a reasonable person and a competent mother. The nurses started arranging the two pillows I had brought from home around Lisa, and I smiled and told them that no, one of those was for me. At that, one of the two nurses—the younger one, again—looked up and acknowledged me. I told her I knew from past experience how hard it was for parents to get pillows sometimes, so I had made sure to bring my own. I asked some innocuous questions in an attempt to engage them in friendly conversation.

Only the younger one ever spoke to me. Assuming she was Lisa's nurse, I regarded her carefully. She was very tiny, looked to be Filipina, and spoke with just the barest trace of an accent. She seemed about sixteen years old, but I knew she had to be older because her badge identified her as a registered nurse. I was sure I had never seen her before, so I guessed she was either new to the hospital or had not been working on this particular ward when Lisa had been a patient seven months earlier.

The second nurse never looked at or talked to me, and since I assumed she was just assisting Lisa's nurse while the ward was quiet and I would not see her again, I did not pay her much attention. She waited for Lisa's nurse to finish speaking with me, and the two of them left the room together. A few minutes later, Lisa's nurse—the teenager, I mentally labelled her—returned with some sheets and blankets. I made up the couch, grateful I had the foresight to bring a real pillow. I knew the next few days would be emotionally difficult, and prayed the doctors could do something to alleviate Lisa's pain. I unpacked the few things I had brought, took off my jeans and socks, and got washed up and ready for bed. As was my custom when I washed up, I left the door open so I would hear if anyone came into the room. Before I turned off the light, I checked on Lisa again. She was sleeping so deeply and soundly that she had not moved at all.

Each bed has privacy curtains around it, which are normally pulled back out of the way. When a doctor or nurse performs an intimate examination or procedure, he or she usually pulls the curtains closed, but otherwise they are left open. I drew the curtains about one-third of the way, just enough to block the sight of the couch on which I slept from anyone standing at the door of the room. This served two purposes: the nurses would not be able to easily see me when they came in to check on Lisa, giving me the illusion of privacy, and when they did come in, the curtain would block a good portion of the hallway's light.

Neither of the two nurses had come back into the room after Lisa's nurse brought me the bed linens. At approximately 2:15 a.m., early in the morning of October 22, 1998, I closed the lights and went to sleep.

7

OCTOBER 22, 1998

The sound of the doctors talking in the hospital corridor woke me up. I glanced at the clock on the wall: 7:18 a.m. Standing behind the bed curtain I had drawn partially closed, I hurriedly put on my jeans so I would be presentable when the doctors walked in. I thought to myself how pleasantly surprising it was that there had been no alarms, buzzers, or nurses paging one another via the intercom all night long; it was the quietest night I had ever spent at this hospital.

Three orthopaedic residents walked in, trailed by a nurse who remained at the doorway. I said to Lisa, "Good morning!" hoping that today she would miraculously be in less pain than the night before. One doctor came over to me and asked how she had slept, and the second one walked over to Lisa. Just as I started to answer, the doctor at the bedside yelled, "Call a code."

This is a joke, right? No, not a joke, but a bad dream, from which I was going to wake up any second. No, it wasn't a dream, it was real, but the doctors will fix everything. Look at how they're doing all kinds of things to her. Lisa will wake up, and we'll tell her children the story of how she almost died when she was a child but they brought her back. No, no, no, this isn't happening! No, I won't leave! No, I'm staying. I need to stay. I need to be here, to hug her when she wakes up! Lisa!!

Can't get to her, too many people in the way. Telephone Bill. "Bill, come to the hospital. Lisa's in bad shape!" Telephone my sister. "Cindy, come to the hospital! They called a code on Lisa!" Call my parents. "Mom, something terrible has happened!" Call Bill again. "Bring the boys, don't send them to school!"

What's that nurse saying? "I checked her at 5, she was fine," she said. "I checked her at 6, she was fine," she continued. Who was she talking to?

Lisa, wake up!! I'm here, baby, wake up. Please wake up! No, I have to stay here! I don't want to go out! I have to be here with my little girl! My little girl needs me!! She's not waking up! They're jolting her with electricity, and she's not waking up! I have to get out of here! I need to run away! Now I can't get out, there's too much equipment in the way. A nurse sees me, she sees I want to run. She takes me outside. I have no shoes on, no socks. As I go out, I lock eyes with Dr. Hedden. I stare at him as I go out. He looks different from usual. He looks sad. The nurse leads me away, barefoot, to an empty room.

Cindy comes running. She looks in to Lisa's room, sees everyone busy in the resuscitation attempt. A nurse tells her she's not allowed in. Cindy tells her she's looking for me, and someone leads her to the room I am in. We hug and cry.

Soon, one of the doctors who had been involved in the code comes in to tell me they had worked on Lisa for about forty minutes but couldn't bring her back. She says they decided to discontinue resuscitation efforts because after this much time... I know she means that even if they could revive her, Lisa would be a vegetable. She means that Lisa is dead.

I am frozen, numb. Another unfamiliar doctor comes in. Down the road I will learn this is Dr. Wright, an orthopaedic surgeon who has the misfortune to be listed on Lisa's medical chart as the responsible physician. He tells Cindy and me they don't know the cause of death, but they think it might be an embolism, a blood clot. He explains this can happen without warning, and that I will have to wait for the autopsy results to be sure. He tells me to feel free to call him if I have any questions, but his demeanour conveys his fervent hope that I do no such thing. His words are devoid of warmth or sincerity. Thankfully, I will never see or hear from him again—at least not until one year later, when he will be compelled to testify at a coroner's inquest. When he testifies, he will claim he thought the PCA pump had malfunctioned, meaning that Lisa had received a morphine overdose. The hospital's eventual explanation of why it never conducted a thorough investigation was because it, too, believed the problem lay with the PCA pump. No one mentions this possibility to us. Why tell us it may be an embolism if everyone already thinks it's a morphine overdose?

Is it so we won't think the hospital may have done something wrong? Lisa's been gone for minutes and the cover-up has already begun.

Here come my parents. I collapse in their arms, all of us crying hysterically. This isn't real. She can't be dead. I'm never going to talk to her again? Never hug her? Never stroke her hair? Never laugh together? My little girl is gone forever? I don't believe that. It's not true!

Someone's taking me somewhere. Who? Where? I don't care. I let myself be led. Another room, this one bright and cheerful, with couches and chairs. A room for breastfeeding mothers. No babies here now. No happiness here now.

More people come in. My brother and sister-in-law. My friend Debbie. My friend Len. How did everyone find out? Where is Bill? Morning rush hour traffic from the suburbs is bad. Finally, finally, Bill comes in. Can't stop crying. Can't think. Everyone is crying. Everyone asks me what happened. I say I don't know. I tell them that the doctors don't know. All I know is I heard a nurse say she checked Lisa at 5 and she was fine, and she checked her at 6 and she was fine.

My father takes charge. Daddy always knows what to do. Talks to everybody. Keeps us talking. Keeps us going.

The chaplain comes in. Gives me a deep hug, almost smothering me with the strong smell of her perfume. I hate strangers who hug me. But she is sincere. She is trying to do her best to console and help. I hear afterwards she started to cry after she left the room.

My father talks to her about the autopsy. Jewish people normally don't approve of autopsies. Sometimes there is no choice, and there must be one. Like now, when we don't know why Lisa is dead. There are certain procedures and protocols to be followed. Daddy tells the chaplain and the coroner we don't care about halacha, about religious dictates. He says to do the most complete and thorough autopsy that can be done. We have to know why Lisa died. "Yes, yes," the rest of us vigorously agree. Please do everything to find out why she is dead.

A hospital social worker comes in. She also radiates compassion and sincerity, just like the chaplain. All we can do is cry.

The coroner arrived about 9:45 a.m. He offered his card–Dr. Morton J. Reingold, Coroner, Metropolitan Toronto, expressed his condolences, and explained about the autopsy and what was going to happen. My sister-in-law didn't think his explanation made sense.

She asked in disbelief, "But aren't you going to seize the morphine pump?" Dr. Reingold answered, "We're only interested in the body, not in peripheral devices." I begged him to call me as soon as the autopsy was finished, and he promised he would.

We were told we could go "say our goodbyes" to Lisa. As we walked towards the room, we passed the large chalkboard by the nursing station that showed each patient's name, room number, nurse, and doctor. Lisa's name was still there.

She looked as if she was sleeping. Pale and still, with yellow hair hanging loose around her. She was an enchanted princess waiting for a kiss to wake her up. How could we say goodbye and turn around and walk away? The pain was indescribable—physical, emotional, and spiritual. Why couldn't I have died instead of her? Please bring her back and take me! She's only sleeping, it's all a dream, wake up!

When we left, we walked out past that same large chalkboard. Lisa's name had been erased. She no longer existed. Why couldn't they have waited until we were gone before they did that?

Dr. Desparmet arrived, and the Pain Service nurses. I was in a macabre receiving line, as each of them came up and hugged me. No one spoke.

I called Dr. Wilder. He didn't believe it either.

We made it home somehow. Family members, themselves in shock, made the funeral arrangements. The autopsy was scheduled for that afternoon, so we waited by the phone for the coroner's call. And waited and waited. None of us could bear to make the call, so we asked Cindy's partner, also a physician, to call Dr. Reingold to see why we had not heard anything.

The autopsy had been completed; Dr. Reingold had just not bothered to call us. He wasn't too busy to take the call from Cindy's friend, however, and he told her matter-of-factly that the autopsy had not been able to determine any cause of death.

Why had Lisa died? She may have had RSD, but RSD was not a life-threatening disease. She had pain, but in every other respect we believed she was a normal, healthy 10-year-old. She did not have a blood clot, as Dr. Wright had suggested. What had caused her to die? Was it a coincidence she died in the hospital? Would she have died if she had been at home in her bed?

We had to start planning the funeral. For Jewish funerals, it is customary for people to make memorial donations instead of sending flowers. Families usually select a favourite charity and request contributions be sent there in the name of the deceased. We needed to choose a charity quickly so it could be included in the newspaper obituary notice. In a daze, the first thing that came to mind was to have donations sent to the Hospital for Sick Children. Thankfully, my father was adamant we do no such thing. "We don't know why she died. Maybe the hospital had something to do with it. Maybe there will be problems with the hospital. We can't let people donate to the hospital until we know for sure it had nothing to do with her death."

I honestly thought my father was crazy. The hospital had not always been very kind to us, but it having something to do with Lisa's death was the most ridiculous thing imaginable! My stubborn Dad: he was the only one with foresight. If only he had lived long enough to know just how right he was. Sadly, he died exactly one month later at age 65 of a massive heart attack. We know it was triggered by his immense grief at the loss of his beloved granddaughter. Thanks to him we set up the Lisa Shore Memorial Fund, where all the donations would remain until we decided which charities to contribute to.

In keeping with Jewish tradition of burying the dead as quickly as possible, the funeral was scheduled for the next day, on Friday, October 23rd. We needed to notify our synagogue and speak to our rabbi; we had to arrange for the cemetery plot; people would be coming back to our home after the funeral, and we would need coffee and cake for them. So many things to think about and to do, by the very people who were barely capable of managing a coherent thought.

Our salvation was a stranger named Sharon Deutsh. Sharon had joined our synagogue one year earlier, and had seen it had no resources in place to help members in times of bereavement or illness. On her own initiative, she had organized a dedicated corps of volunteers who could be called upon on short notice to help families in need.

Sharon came to our home immediately, and saw our tears, our confusion, and our stunned shock. She took charge, liaising between the funeral home, the rabbi, the family, and everyone else. She arranged to stay in the house while we were at the funeral and cemetery, to set out the coffee and desserts for all the people we expected to come back to our home after the funeral. She made sure members of the congregation would be at our home each morning and evening for the next week to lead prayer services. Everything that needed to be done was done, by Sharon and her Chesed Committee (the Hebrew word means "Acts of Kindness").

As one would expect from someone who had spearheaded such a committee, Sharon was an exceptionally compassionate and dedicated individual. Her background as an intensive care nurse in the trauma unit of one of the city's largest hospitals had exposed her to a great deal of tragedy, and she was experienced in dealing with families touched by sudden and tragic death. She listened to us, she hugged us, and she gave us the support we so badly needed. I did not know her before Lisa died, but she has now become one of my closest and dearest friends.

We needed to write Lisa's eulogy. We had been to too many funerals where well-intentioned ministers and rabbis had given eulogies for people they had not known very well, eulogies that did not convey a real sense of who that person was. We did not want that to happen for our little girl. All day long we talked about her, and all night long we wrote about her. Bill and I slept about one hour each that evening, but we finished the eulogy early in the morning on the day of the funeral.

All her classmates were at the funeral. Every substitute teacher in the community must have been called in, because almost every teacher in the school was there too. Family and friends came in from across North America, and a favourite aunt and uncle on a world trip caught an overnight flight from London. Hundreds attended. It was standing-room only, we were told afterwards, for we could not see anyone through our tears.

We were allowed to be alone with Lisa for a short time. We placed her favourite stuffed animal, Yum-Yum, in the casket. We put in her best Beanie babies. We gave her the baseball cap she wore day in and day out. The card from all of us telling her how much we loved her was tucked in beside her.

We wanted to die too, to be with her.

The funeral service began. I know two rabbis spoke and said prayers, but all I can remember is the eulogy that Bill read. Everyone wept. Bill's voice was steady, breaking down only at the very last sentence.

Thank you for coming to remember our Lisa.

I want to start at the end because it typifies what a loving, caring person Lisa was. Just before falling asleep for the last time Wednesday night, she gave Sharon a hug and said, "Thank you for taking such good care of me, Mommy."

One day when Sharon was picking up Lisa and Aron at school, a teacher she didn't know stopped her in the hallway and told her that she had often noticed Lisa when she was on yard duty at recess. This teacher told Sharon that Lisa was a wonderful child, always looking out for the younger kids, and said that we should be very, very proud of her. We were. We are. We will always be. Lisa gave so much more than she received. Any time Devon had school projects that needed illustrations or other visual arts, Lisa would do it for him. Lisa enjoyed helping her brother by doing something that she loved and he hated, allowing Devon to learn the fine "art" of delegation.

Lisa also often helped her youngest brother, Aron, with his homework—Hebrew and other subjects. Or she just read to him. Last year she helped make his Grade One Siddur cover, drawing a beautiful picture of a dove in front of the Western Wall. And just a few weeks ago, she helped Aron make a miniature shoebox succah for his school, with little clay figurines.

Lisa had a lifelong love and ability for jigsaw puzzles. When she was just three, she used to do 200 piece puzzles, upside down, from the middle out. It was another year before she figured out the concept of doing the straight edge pieces first, not that she needed the help. When she finished a puzzle, she made me take a picture of it before dismantling it. We will treasure the photo album containing the results of those hours of persistence and diligence. When Lisa and I did a puzzle together, she would always put one piece in her pocket as we neared the end. Once all the pieces but one had been put together, she would triumphantly produce the final piece and claim the "Glory".

At various times, Lisa wanted to be an architect and a cartoonist, but most recently she wanted to become a Veterinarian. Lisa loved all animals, particularly dogs. We all would have loved to have a dog, but then we couldn't have Sharon, who is severely allergic. We already tried that when Sharon and I first met. To compensate, Lisa and her inseparable pal Jenna, who lives next door, had staked out the entire neighbourhood. They knew where every dog within walking distance lived, the dog's name and breed. Our houses are just off Green Lane, a semi-busy street where people often walk by with their dogs. Whenever they spotted a dog being walked, a "Dog Alert" was sounded and they would rush out to ambush the dog and its owner. That was Lisa, doing everything with exuberance. Always having fun. In fact, Lisa managed to pack more living into just under eleven years than I have done in my forty. While there is no doubt that most of all she loved her family and all her friends, she still found time to love…

Animals

Baggy Sweatshirts

Her Crazy Bones Baseball Hat

Chocolate Chip Hamentashen – a Shore innovation we enjoy year-round

Chocolate Chip Pancakes

Chocolate Bars

Chocolate… Well, you get the picture

For meals - Pizza, Pizza, more Pizza. The rest of the time, she ate Pizza Bagel lovingly supplied by Bubbie Barbara.

She also enjoyed…

Our annual summer trip to the Laurentians to visit her Uncle George and Auntie Lorna

Junk Food

Green Apples

The Arrogant Worms

Nintendo

Reading

Playing in the Park – We moved so we could have one in our back yard

Sleep-overs – Let me stress that this is a list of the things SHE loved, not us

Eating Ice Cubes

Trampoline

Potching my tushie

The Simpsons

Riding her bike

Referring to New Hampshire as New Hamster

South Park

The words "Kookamonga" and "Flamingo" when spoken by Zachary

Swimming – as long as the water wasn't frozen, she went in

All kinds of arts and crafts:
-Drawing
-Silk Painting
-Making Boondoggle Bracelets
-The Super Hammie cartoon strip

Math—Yes, when asked what her favourite subject was, math even beat out recess

Stuffed Animals, her favourite being Yum-Yum

Yum-Yum is a stuffed lion that she got as a gift for her fifth birthday. She had it with her almost every night for most of the next six years, and it was with her at the end.

For a time, part of the ritual when putting Lisa to bed was the Hide Yum-Yum game. The rule was that Yum-Yum had to be hidden somewhere in Lisa's room. One of us would cover our eyes while the other person hid Yum-Yum. At first, I would hide Yum-Yum in drawers, on shelves, in her knapsack. But as time went on, in order to avoid using the same hiding place twice, I had to get more and more creative. I hid Yum-Yum on the ledge outside her window, in the garbage can, between the mattress and box spring, even on one of the wings of the ceiling fan (No, it wasn't on at the time). I was even considering the air return vent to see if I would be able to open it without her hearing me. Each day, as I was running out of unique hiding places, I kept threatening to mail Yum-Yum to Australia. Then one day, Yum-Yum was missing. Although I knew it had to be somewhere in the house, I teased Lisa and asked, "Do you know much it costs to mail a box about THIS big to Australia?" By this point in her life she had learned to question most everything I said, but this time she wasn't quite sure. By the time Yum-Yum was found, we invented a new night time game: Yum-Yum fights. One of us would throw Yum-Yum across the room, and then we would wrestle each other to be the first one to grab her, sliding across the floor and grabbing each other's arms just as the other one was about to snatch her. Lisa seemed to win about three out of every five matches. When Lisa started spending time in the hospital, she got an identification bracelet and had it put around Yum-Yum's neck. I told you that Yum-Yum was with her on the last night of her life. In fact, she's still holding Yum-Yum now and will forever. I like to think she'll be holding onto me too.

Lisa inherited the Grief Klutz Gene that seems to afflict one Grief per generation. First Zaidy Phil, then Auntie Cindy, then Lisa. If it could be spilled, tripped over, tipped over or dropped, Lisa found the way to do it.

Lisa liked the Animaniacs–those strange looking cartoon characters. I like the Animaniacs. They have catchy, clever songs that list things like the planets, the senses, movies, stuff like that. One of their songs lists every country in the world, or just about every country. Lisa and I memorized the song and would sing it together, in good times as well as when fighting through the pain. Once I sung the opening words "United States, Canada, Mexico, Panama", off we went for two minutes and 155 countries of joy.

We also memorized the Animaniacs song naming the US states and their capitals. I was suitably shamed into writing an additional verse covering the Canadian provinces and their capitals, which in time we also learned by heart. In fact, last year in school when Lisa had a test where she had to fill in a map with the provinces and their capitals, she got them all right because she sang this verse to herself.

One of the Animaniacs' songs goes on forever, listing all of the U.S Presidents sung to the tune of the William Tell Overture. Earlier this year, Lisa taught it to me. All of it. Not that it was all that useful, but it helped her get a Final Jeopardy question about the first president following Lincoln to wear a beard. Again, I felt shamed that we were being overly Americanized, and vowed to write a Canadian equivalent. I regret to say that I have not yet done it. If I had been Lisa, that song would be finished now. Lisa made the time to do everything she wanted to do. I, we, can all only hope to emulate her example. In case you haven't got it yet, the answer to the Jeopardy Question was Ulysses S. Grant.

In all her life, I don't think I ever saw Lisa frightened. From the time she was young, she was never afraid of the dark. She loved scary movies. She went off to sleep away camp knowing hardly anyone who would be there. She was an UM – an unaccompanied minor – twice, flying off by herself, once to visit Bubby and Zaidy in Florida and the other time to visit her Grandma and her cousins in Vancouver. When we went to help remove a dead mouse from a friend's house, Devon picked the mouse up, and Lisa said, "Let me see! Let me see!" No roller coaster was too scary for her. She longed for the day she would reach 54 inches so she could go on ALL the scariest rides at Canada's Wonderland. I don't know how many times I measured her, plotting the course to the magic height. She reached and passed 54 inches last winter, so when we went this summer, we let her and her cousin Shannon split off so they could tackle the rides that had been previously out of her reach.

The most amazing thing about Lisa was that she never feared the next onslaught of the terrible pain she suffered through much of the past few months. This brave little girl got through each onslaught and once on the other side, forgot about it. She didn't dwell on it, didn't anticipate the next wave, just dusted herself off and resumed doing the things she enjoyed.

In her life, Lisa lived in three houses and two countries, visited three provinces and twelve states, but the most important place she journeyed to was into the hearts of the people here to pay tribute to her today.

Lisa loved Hawaiian donuts, the ones with the multicolour sprinkles on top. She always ate the dough first, saving the sprinkles for last. I always kidded her that this was foolhardy. I told her that an asteroid could come down from the sky after she had eaten the dough but before she got a chance to eat the top part with the sprinkles. She would laugh at me, get up and open the door, go outside, look up and say, "No asteroids, Daddy," then come back inside and slowly savour all those sprinkles she had saved for last.

Lisa, honey, look out, asteroid.

8

MOURNING AND EVENING AND MOURNING AGAIN

The week following a loved one's burial is the time of shiva, the seven days of Jewish ritual mourning. Visiting the mourners, the ones who "sit shiva", is considered a good deed of the highest order. Even those whose relationship to the deceased or his or her family was peripheral at best will often visit and pay their respects.

Lisa's shiva was held at our home, and the house was filled with an endless stream of visitors. I was forced to talk, to be sociable, even to smile, although I have no memory of whom I spoke to or what I said. Against my will, I had to get out of bed each morning and get dressed, in order to be there for guests. I was practically force-fed because I didn't want to eat or drink.

My cousin and her fiancé had come in from out of town for Lisa's funeral and to be with us during the shiva. The fiancé's brother, Frank Gomberg, lived in Toronto and came to the house to pay his respects.

Frank took us aside and told us he was a civil litigation lawyer who specialized in helping victims of accidents and medical malpractice. He gave us his card and said we should call if we ever needed his help. Just as I had thought my father was crazy for not wanting memorial donations to go to the Hospital for Sick Children, I thought this man was equally insane. What possible reason could there be to need a lawyer? Luckily, others there were smarter than I. My father took Frank's card and put it in his pocket.

The shiva ended. The house was quiet except for the sounds of sobbing. I was still waiting for Lisa to come through the door. I still pretended every time I passed her room that she was bent over her desk doing her homework. In the morning when I awoke, for a fraction of a second I would think the family was intact and all was well—and then reality hit. I stayed up most of the night, and then cried myself to sleep. We loved Lisa so much, how could she not be here? This little girl had so many dreams and hopes, never to be fulfilled.

The following night was Halloween. Lisa's costume, which she had picked out only two weeks ago, lay on the floor in her bedroom. Devon went out trick-or-treating with a friend, but six-year-old Aron could not understand why we weren't happy about taking him out. My brother offered to take Aron out with my niece and nephew, so we went over to their place.

I did not realize that other children's joy could cause such profound pain. I did not anticipate that each time the doorbell rang and adorable little kids in costumes appeared, I would feel as if I had been punched in the stomach. We were not able to hide from Halloween after all.

Amid our tears was a fierce desire to know what had happened, and why. The autopsy showed nothing. Did Lisa have some strange disease no one knew about, that would have killed her even without the pain in her leg? Lisa was always so happy, so healthy, so full of life, that we couldn't believe that.

I ordered copies of Lisa's hospital records, from Toronto and Boston.

The coroner's office had not contacted us. We knew Dr. Reingold had been responsible for the autopsy, but since we had heard nothing further from him we did not know whether his office was still involved in the case.

My father called and met with Frank Gomberg, the lawyer who had given us his card. I wasn't sure what this would accomplish, but was more than willing to let my Dad take care of things. Frank explained he had a fair amount of experience in dealing with the coroner's office and had acted for clients on several coroner's inquests. He explained that Lisa's death was still a coroner's case and we would have to go to the coroner's office with any concerns and questions.

We never actually hired Frank, and we never talked about fees, but somehow he just "evolved" into our legal representative and official liaison with the coroner's office. He sent Dr. William Lucas, the Toronto regional coroner, a letter advising that I had requested Lisa's medical records, asking if this was all right or if it would impede the investigation in any way.[1] We assumed, wrongly, that the coroner's office, investigating a child's unexpected and unexplained death, would have immediately seized Lisa's medical records and removed them from the hospital. This seemed not only inherently logical but also the only way to ensure there was no alteration or backdating of medical records. On the chance there had been incompetence, negligence, or even foul play, how else could a proper coroner's investigation be conducted?

We were assured it was no problem for us to order copies of Lisa's records.[2] We did not discover until more than a year later that at the date of the letter, no one from the coroner's office had looked at Lisa's records or even asked for a copy of them.

Frank did learn that the coroner had seized the PCA morphine pump Lisa had been using. Maybe my sister-in-law's shock at hearing him say he wasn't interested in peripheral things had caused him to change his mind. According to Dr. Lucas, preliminary reports indicated the morphine pump was not defective, but it was going to be sent to a lab for further analysis. Dr. Lucas also explained that a toxicology screen would be done to determine which drugs were found in Lisa's body and in what quantities.

We could do nothing but wait. My parents decided to take a vacation in Florida. While there, Mom and Dad decided to attend a local synagogue for Saturday services—something they never did—just so they could say Kaddish (mourner's prayer) for Lisa. On November 21, 1998, at synagogue and in the middle of prayers, my father suffered a massive coronary, keeled over, and died instantly. Exactly thirty days after Lisa died, my father was gone too. He was sixty-five years old, and although not in perfect health, his death was an unexpected and devastating blow to the family.

We did it all over again. Another funeral, in the same place. Another eulogy, this one read by my sister Cindy. Another drive to the cemetery, where my father was buried right beside Lisa. We sat shiva in my home again and recited Kaddish once more.

Besides my all-consuming grief at my little girl's unexplained death, I now mourned my father, the family patriarch. Dad was the strong one, the one who always "took care of everything". It seemed that now I had to become the strong one and inherit that role. Like my father, I am also an accountant, and we had worked together for many years in the business he owned. I dealt exclusively with the clients, and he managed everything. Suddenly, at a time when I could barely concentrate, I had to do my regular job, handle my father's estate, manage the business and the employees, and worry about having sufficient cash flow to meet the payroll. If it weren't for my husband Bill's steadfast support and love, I would not have survived. If I hadn't had two children who needed their mother, I think I might have considered suicide.

9

RECORDS AND QUESTIONS

Boston Children's Hospital sent me Lisa's medical records right away; Sick Kids, just a few miles down the road from us, took weeks to send theirs. I was in a numb haze, and listlessly flipped through the Boston documents. There was nothing of importance there, or anything that would give me a clue about what had happened to Lisa. Then I saw the Boston neurologist's report: Dr. Rust had written that Lisa had conversion disorder,[1] a psychiatric diagnosis where the patient's psychological problems produce physical symptoms.[2]

Like the orthopaedic surgeons at Sick Kids, Dr. Rust belonged to that species of physicians who make instant diagnoses of mental illness whenever they find something they don't understand or can't explain. To say that a 10-year-old child, whom he had physically examined for at most thirty minutes, had a mental illness, when he had not evaluated her background, her family, her attitudes, or her life, was quack medicine at its worst. Dr. Rocco, the only psychologist who had ever taken the time to really assess Lisa, the only one who was therefore qualified to diagnose Lisa's mental state, said she had no psychiatric disorders. How many people had suffered, in addition to their legitimate medical problems, the torment of being told they were faking? How many lives had been ruined by physicians who were under the delusion they knew everything?

Boston had been our refuge, our security, the one place where Lisa was treated like the regular, normal little girl she was, and now this horrible man was going to destroy that with one sentence. Everything that doctors write in a patient's chart is considered sacrosanct, whether accurate or not, and irrespective of the doctor's qualification to make the diagnosis. This report would be Lisa's medical epitaph, forever engraved upon her tombstone. Here lies Lisa, mentally ill with conversion disorder.

All the suffering and torment she had endured was real. All of us who cherished and loved this sweet, innocent, carefree child knew it. Now she was dead, and I would not let anyone ruin her name and her memory, least of all this bastard. My daughter was gone forever, and I wanted this poisonous document to die with her. I took his report and ripped it into tiny pieces.

Weeks passed and we still did not know the cause of Lisa's death. One of the Pain Service nurses at Sick Kids sent an e-mail to an Internet mailing list to which I subscribed, populated primarily by health care professionals who specialize in paediatric pain. She wrote that her hospital was reviewing the monitoring policies for patients who were receiving narcotics. How did other institutions monitor such children? What mechanisms were in place to ensure nurses were competent in using monitors? How did they know the nurses were using the monitors correctly?

Did this have anything to do with Lisa? Had the hospital identified a problem with the way she had been monitored? We suspected the answer was yes. Our neighbour had mentioned that his sister's friend and her son had been on the same ward as Lisa on the night she died. This mother had said that right after Lisa's death, the nurses put all the children on the ward on monitors. Since Lisa hadn't been on any monitors, it sounded like the hospital had panicked and put emergency measures into place to make sure no one else died unexpectedly.

Frank kept in regular touch with the coroner's office so he could get the autopsy and toxicology results the minute they were ready. Dr. Lucas said the toxicology tests would take weeks to complete, and informed Frank a complete autopsy had not been performed because we–the family–had insisted it be done according to halacha, Jewish law, which imposed many restrictions. That was ridiculous! My father had loudly and repeatedly insisted a complete and thorough autopsy be done because we needed to know why Lisa had died, and I and everyone else in the room had heard him. We were frightened to learn that someone's incompetence might have cost us the chance to learn what had happened to our precious child. Little did we know that this was just the beginning of the mistakes, bungling, cover-up, and deceit we would encounter in our struggle to learn the truth about what had happened to Lisa.

Lisa's medical chart from Sick Kids finally arrived. I remembered that Sharon Deutsh, the woman from the synagogue who had been so caring and competent in the days following Lisa's death, was an intensive care nurse, and asked her if she would mind going over the medical records with me. She immediately agreed.

We spent many hours together poring over those records, as Sharon analyzed and explained them. Months later, she confessed that when she'd seen them that first time, she had known instantly that the nursing care had played a major role in Lisa's death, although she had to carefully work her way up to telling me because of my anguish.

I told her everything I remembered about the night of Lisa's death. I described Lisa's excruciating pain when we arrived, how she had finally fallen asleep around 1:15 a.m. in the Emergency Department, and how the nurses had so rudely ignored me.

We scrutinized Lisa's nursing flowsheet.[3] This is the spreadsheet-like form on which nurses mark down essential data each time they check on their patient, such as vital signs, observations on the patient's condition, what time a doctor was contacted and what the doctor said. This document is supposed to tell the doctors, nurses, and whoever else looks at it "at a glance" what the patient's condition is. At the Hospital for Sick Children, this document is hung outside the patient's door on a clipboard.

"There are some very strange things here," Sharon muttered. "Look at Lisa's vital signs. Her heart rate was 72 when she arrived on the ward at 1:45 a.m., which seems pretty normal. Look at how it increases over the course of the evening, up to 120, up to 130, up to 134 beats per minute. Something was obviously going on."

"What's the normal range?" I asked.

"In an adult, 60-90 beats per minute," she answered. "I'm not sure about children, but Lisa wasn't a baby, so it's probably almost the same.[4] But it's not just the heart rate itself you need to look at, but how much it changes over a period of time. An increase like this, when Lisa was fast asleep, means she was in trouble. See, look at her breathing. When she comes in, she's breathing 16 times per minute. Then it goes down to 14, then to 12, then to 8 and 10. After that it starts to go up and down all over the map."

"And what are normal breathing rates?" I asked.

"The average adult respiratory rate is 12 to 20 breaths per minute. I don't know the rates for kids,[5] except they tend to breathe faster. I would guess their average breathing rates would be higher, if anything. But it's just like the heart rate—you have to look not only at the absolute number, but at how much it changes. Lisa started out at 16 breaths per minute, and went down to 8 or 10 fairly quickly. It's pretty obvious she was in respiratory distress."

Sharon kept talking as she read. "This just doesn't make any sense! There's a blood pressure taken at 1:45 a.m. when Lisa arrived on the ward, but no more blood pressures are taken after that. The nurse was in Lisa's room, because she wrote down the increase in heart rate and the decrease in respiratory rate on the flowsheet. Why didn't she do a blood pressure? This has to be wrong!" Sharon explained to me that blood pressure was not only one of the basic vital signs, it was the one that allowed you to make sense of all the others. When a patient's vital signs are not stable, it is critically important to know what the blood pressure is.

"It doesn't look like they ever tried to wake her up. With vital signs like this, why didn't they assess Lisa's level of consciousness? Why didn't they take her blood pressure? Why didn't they get the doctor down there? Why didn't they transfer her to the ICU?" I watched Sharon grow angrier and angrier. "What the hell were they doing?" she railed. "Lisa was dying right in front of their noses!" She explained to me that the most dangerous side effect of morphine is respiratory depression, and Lisa's slower breathing should have made it evident that this was what was happening. Any competent nurse would do a complete and thorough assessment of her patient if she saw something like that going on, which would definitely include taking the patient's blood pressure and trying to wake the person up. If the patient can't be awakened or is unusually dazed and groggy, then it is a medical emergency that requires a doctor's immediate presence.

Sharon next pulled out the Emergency Department notes. These pages covered the period before Lisa was transferred up to the ward, and included several measurements of her vital signs. Sharon wanted to see how Lisa had been before she was transferred to the ward.

She explained what we were looking at. "Lisa's respiratory rate in Emergency, when she was wide awake and in a lot of pain, was 20 breaths per minute. By the time she got to the ward, her respiration had already started to go down. Even her blood pressure had dropped way down, from 106/84 in Emergency to 90/60 on the ward."

"I don't understand. Then why didn't they call the doctor?"

"According to this flowsheet, they did," Sharon said, "at 4:05 a.m. See the note on the side? It says 'very drowsy, Pain Service aware of decreased respiration and increased sedation'. But I don't see anything to show the doctor did anything about it."

"Why not? What did he say when the nurse told him that her breathing was so low? Why didn't he come to see Lisa? He was the one who gave her the morphine in the first place!"

This didn't make sense. Why did all these people let her die without trying to do anything about it? "Why didn't the coroner say anything about this?" I cried. "Lisa died almost two months ago—how could he have seen these records and not known right away that something was wrong? Why didn't he tell me this?"

Sharon and I started reading the nursing progress notes. These are the nurse's handwritten notes about the patient, and they are supposed to contain comments, observations, and important events in greater detail than found in the nursing flowsheet. The nurse will—or should—write down the patient's vital signs on the flowsheet immediately after checking the patient, but the progress notes are often recorded hours later, at the end of the shift or whenever the nurse has a bit of time. Ideally these notes should be written as close as possible to when the observations were noted, but in practice, a nurse often makes only one progress note at the end of her shift. Then again, I had once heard a doctor say in passing that it didn't matter what the nurses wrote, since no one ever read their notes anyway.

There were two nursing notes in the file, both written by the same person. There were no legible signatures on the notes or on the nursing flowsheet, but we found the nurse's name—Ruth Doerksen—by matching the scrawled initials to the names on the computerized records. I matched this name to the image and memory I had of Lisa's nurse, that tiny girl who looked like she was about sixteen. Doerksen's first note[6] was written at 1:50 a.m., only a few minutes after Lisa arrived on the floor. It was inaccurate, but the inaccuracy seemed fairly innocuous: Doerksen had commented that Lisa was "in no obvious pain when moving from stretcher to bed", and, as if to emphasize her point, she noted in the next sentence that Lisa had "no voiced complaint of pain". I snorted derisively, "What was she trying to prove? Of course Lisa wasn't crying in pain, she was fast asleep!" Having mentioned it twice, Doerksen belaboured the point a third time by adding that Lisa was "asleep on stretcher and settled to sleep as soon as moved over to bed".

"She didn't 'settle' anywhere, she was never awake to be settled!" I reiterated forcefully.

The second note[7] was not innocuous at all. I read it through, and read it again. Nurse Doerksen had written, "Child settled to sleep and was asleep all night except when woken by nurse for vital signs." That was wrong. Not only wrong, it was impossible. Lisa was one of the world's soundest sleepers, long before she had started taking the medication that so heavily sedated her. Even an alarm clock going off beside her ear wouldn't wake her up; she once slept right through when our burglar alarm accidentally went off, even though it awoke practically the whole neighbourhood! The only way any nurse would have been able to wake Lisa up would be if she had yelled at the top of her lungs, turned on the light, and poured a pitcher of cold water over her. That might have woken her up–maybe. I'm a light sleeper, and I knew there had been no attempt to wake Lisa up. "This nurse is lying! She's lying! No one ever woke Lisa up! There were no sounds in the room that night. If Lisa had so much as whispered 'Mommy' I would have heard her," I sobbed.

The room was spinning. We were still trying to come to grips with Lisa being dead, thinking that reading the records might give us some clues about what had happened. Instead of finding clues, we saw nurses and doctors who didn't do their jobs, who apparently neglected my daughter and let her die. Not only did they do nothing to save her, they had deliberately written untrue information in the records.

Sharon pointed out that this second note had been written several hours after Lisa had died, and suggested the nurse might have written the entire note "to fit the circumstances". In other words, if she lied about one thing, she might have lied about everything. Maybe she was trying to make it retroactively look like she had been doing her job properly.

Nurse Doerksen also made reference to a Corometric monitor, which she wrote had been "applied since arrival to unit".

"What's a Corometric monitor? What does it do?" I asked. "I don't know exactly," Sharon answered, "but it's probably some kind of vital signs monitor."

I called my sister, who called a friend who worked at the hospital. We learned that a Corometric monitor is a brand name for an apnea monitor, that is, a monitor that measures both heart rate and respiratory rate.

"Lisa was on one of those in March, the first time she stayed at the hospital because of her pain. But she wasn't on any monitors when she died!"

That second nursing note, written shortly after Lisa died, was a lie from beginning to end.

"Did any alarms go off when Lisa died?" Sharon asked me quietly.

"No, it was quiet. The doctors came into the room just like it was a normal day."

Lisa's nurse was lying, but who would believe me? I was a distraught mother. If I was having trouble accepting that a nurse from the Hospital for Sick Children could do this, why should Sharon Deutsh—a nurse who I barely knew—believe me?

Sharon replied, "Of course I believe you. It's obvious that Lisa wasn't on a monitor. If she had been, there would have been alarms going off like crazy." And in case I doubted her, she continued, "You're a mother. Your child is in the hospital, a few feet away. I know that if she had been awake, if she had so much as said 'boo', you would have jumped. I know this nurse is lying."

We kept reading. Dr Wright, the orthopaedic surgeon who was recorded as the admitting doctor because Pain Service had not been able to admit patients, had prepared a "Death Summary" report.[8] He had been the doctor who had approached me after Lisa had died and told me with patent insincerity to call him if I needed anything.

His summary contained more errors than accuracies. Lisa was admitted on Oct. 21; he wrote that it was Oct. 9. He said she received 11.5mg of morphine over 3 hours; the record showed it was 14.5mg in $1 \frac{1}{4}$ hours. He listed two of Lisa's three medications, but got the dosages wrong. He couldn't be bothered to check the chart for the third and primary drug, referring to it only as "another anti-convulsant medication", without name or dosage. He said Lisa was awakened at 5:00 a.m. (she hadn't been), her vitals were fine (they weren't), and that she responded appropriately (she hadn't woken up, so she could not have responded).

This letter was addressed to the coroner and purported to accurately summarize the care Lisa received on her last night. Why would Dr. Wright, who had never met Lisa, be the one responsible for preparing such an important document? Given all those errors, he evidently had not spent much time or effort in preparing it. I would learn that Dr. Wright's cavalier disregard for Lisa's life and death would be the norm and not the exception for many doctors, nurses, and administrators who cared more about damage control than they did for their patients.

I still didn't know exactly why Lisa had died, but I now knew for sure something very bad had happened. I called the lawyer, Frank Gomberg.

Frank met with us the very next evening. I explained to him what Sharon Deutsh and I had found in the records, and he put our questions down in a letter to the coroner's office. My sister and her partner, both physicians, reviewed and edited those questions and came up with a few more of their own. On December 11th, 1998, seven weeks after Lisa died, twenty-four questions about Lisa's care at the Hospital for Sick Children were sent to the Regional Coroner of Toronto.[9]

We had already learned that a Corometric monitor measured heart rate and breathing rate. We asked about it nevertheless—what it was, why the coroner had not seized it, who had ordered its use and where those orders were. We said that no monitor was attached to Lisa when she arrived, and questioned if someone had brought one in the room in the middle of the night. We asked how it could be that a monitor was in use and yet no alarms went off when Lisa died. If a monitor was brought in during the night, did someone remove it again?

We asked about the inaccuracies and discrepancies in Dr. Wright's death summary. Why did he so significantly understate the amount of morphine Lisa had received? How was it that he wrote about Lisa having been awakened at 5:00 a.m. and found to have normal vital signs when this was not documented anywhere?

Why had the nurses taken Lisa's blood pressure only once, when her pulse had increased from 72 beats per minute to 134 beats per minute while she was fast asleep?

We asked about hospital protocols—when is a Corometric monitor ordered, what the settings on the monitor should be, and when a nurse is supposed to contact a doctor if the patient's vital signs change dramatically.

We wanted an inquest—a public investigation into the events surrounding Lisa's death.

Dr. Lucas responded to our letter within days, stating that he had asked the investigating coroner—in whom we had little faith given our recent dealings with him—to pursue the concerns we had raised. He said it was too early to decide whether an inquest was warranted, and advised us the toxicology results we had been anxiously awaiting would not be ready for another six to eight weeks.

We still didn't know why Lisa died, but we were sure the hospital had something to do with it. Could it have somehow been a morphine overdose, even though everyone said it wasn't? Why did the nurse lie in her notes about waking Lisa up and using a monitor? Why was it going to take four months for the coroner's office to do toxicology testing, when they could do it in the United States in one month?

All we could do was wait. Just to get away, we went down to Florida over the Christmas holidays to stay at my parents' condominium. But it was a sad, lonely time; my father, whose presence had always filled the place with warmth and laughter, was gone. Our Lisa, the little girl who must have been part fish because of all the time she spent swimming, was gone. We took our boys to see many movies, but I spent much of the time unable to see the screen through my tears.

10

THE CORONER'S OFFICE

Six weeks after we sent our questions to the coroner's office, Dr. Wright called Dr. Gallant and told her he wanted to set up a meeting with us once the toxicology results were in "to see if they could get to the bottom of things". Was the hospital's newfound helpfulness attributable to our having hired a lawyer? We said we would be willing to meet after our questions were answered.

Frank waited until the time we had been told the toxicology results would be ready, and called Dr. Lucas once again. "They're not ready yet," he was told. He continued to call once each week for the next month, always getting the same response. The coroner's office did not seem to consider this case a priority, and it was not happy about Frank's calls. Someone needed to "light a fire", we thought, and wondered whether the media might be interested in our story. Frank contacted a reporter at the Toronto Star whom he knew from another case. The reporter was interested, but his newspaper wanted to wait until it had the toxicology results before doing a story.

Two weeks later, Dr. Reingold phoned to say he would be attending a meeting at the hospital to discuss Lisa's death, and I was welcome to come. I wanted to go, but I made it clear that I would like to bring my lawyer along. Dr. Reingold said lawyers are generally unwelcome at meetings like these because it makes the doctors feel uncomfortable. I guess no one cared about the unfair advantage a group of doctors and hospital administrators have over grieving parents who are neither knowledgeable about medical care nor aware of what sort of questions they should be asking. I told Dr. Reingold I would not attend unless Frank could come with me.

Dr. Reingold called me back two days later to tell me I was not invited after all, and that the purpose of the meeting was for the coroner's office to obtain answers to the questions. That they were our questions and not the coroner's seemed to have been forgotten. The hospital's previously expressed desire to meet with us to get to the bottom of things had quickly evaporated. I asked Dr. Reingold why a meeting was being held in the absence of any toxicology results, when that had repeatedly been used as the reason for postponing a meeting, and he answered that the coroner's office was just trying to expedite matters.

I remembered how Dr. Reingold had broken his promise to call us as soon as he had Lisa's autopsy results, and did not trust what he said. I guessed that he already knew what the toxicology results were or else he would not be having any meetings with the hospital. I not-so-innocently asked, "You have a verbal report on the toxicology results, don't you?" He reluctantly admitted he did, and said they were positive for the medications Lisa was on and nothing else. Although some of the levels were high, none were at lethal levels. My daughter was dead, we had been waiting and waiting for this information in the hope we could learn why–and Dr. Reingold was ready to meet with the hospital and discuss the results with them but not with us. Why did I have to back him into a corner to learn this?

I said *I* would call *him* after his meeting with the hospital to find out how it had answered *our* questions, since I knew he would never call me on his own.

Dr. Reingold met with the hospital on March 1, 1999. I waited a day before calling him so as not to seem too impatient, and left him a message; he waited a day and a half before returning my call. He said all the questions had been addressed, but there had been some conflicting information and "it was not clear what all the answers were". Because he was not completely satisfied with what he heard, he had directed the hospital to put its answers in writing.

I tried to get something more specific from him, but he told me little. He described the Corometric monitor and how it worked, which was about the only thing I already knew. He explained it had three alarms, for pulse, respiration, and lead disconnect. The hospital claimed Lisa had been on a monitor, and that "the resuscitation team noticed leads on her". When I said she wasn't on a monitor and there was nothing in the records that showed she was either, he answered, "I'm aware of that."

The nurse said she had called the doctor when Lisa's respiration went down around 2:00 a.m., but he didn't return her call and she didn't pursue it. She says she did speak to him around 4:00 a.m., but there were conflicting facts about that conversation. Dr. Reingold offered nothing further except to state that the nurse claimed she told the doctor certain information and the doctor denied he was given that information.

That was pretty much all anyone would ever be able to find out about the meeting, because the handwritten notes Dr. Reingold made were scanty and almost illegible, and he never formally wrote them up. He would remember little of the meeting when asked about it some months later, and no one from the hospital would ever be forthcoming about that meeting or anything else to do with Lisa's death. However, the conflict between the nurse's version of events and the doctor's had apparently served to elevate the importance of Lisa's death in the coroner's case queue. Dr. Reingold informed me that while they hadn't been sure before, his office had now definitely decided to present the case to the Paediatric Death Review Committee.

Dr. Jim Cairns, the Deputy Chief Coroner of Ontario, was to become involved in the case, and Dr. Reingold said we could call Dr. Cairns at any time for information. In keeping with the efficiency and competence Dr. Reingold had demonstrated thus far, he didn't bother to give us a phone number for Dr. Cairns, but since I had so little regard for the coroner's office by this point I did not expect to have any need for it.

We were thoroughly disgusted. It was apparent that the coroner's office had done no investigation whatsoever into the unexpected and unexplained death of my daughter. We had wrongly assumed that when a coroner was called to investigate a mysterious hospital death, all of the patient's records would be seized in order to protect the integrity of the investigation. Dr. Reingold had not even bothered to ask for Lisa's records until we started asking our questions. All indications were that the coroner's office would have taken no action whatsoever on this matter had we not become involved.

There were glaring irregularities in Lisa's records, which would have been obvious to any competent medical professional–including those at the Hospital for Sick Children–who actually reviewed the chart. We asked questions that raised very serious issues about the quality of the medical care she had received. I swore Lisa had not been on any monitors, directly contradicting what the nurse had documented in her notes. So how was it possible the coroner's office had not been sure until after it met with the hospital whether the case even merited further investigation by this Paediatric Death Review Committee? Obviously, the coroner's office was prepared to give the hospital the benefit of every doubt, no matter how suspicious or irregular things appeared.

While we were waiting for answers, the lawyers began their jockeying. Patrick Hawkins, from the blue-chip Bay Street firm of Borden Ladner Gervais (at the time known as Borden & Elliot), represented the Hospital for Sick Children and its nurses. Frank did not know Hawkins personally but told us that his law firm frequently represented hospitals. Another prominent law firm separately represented the doctors; they didn't fall under the hospital's protective umbrella because they were considered independent practitioners rather than employees.

A lawyer at one of the firms told Frank that the hospital knew that someone had "fucked up". Unfortunately, the hospital would expend vast amounts of time, energy, and money publicly denying what at least some of its staff and lawyers were willing to admit in private.

Both law firms–the hospital's and the doctors'–offered to set up a meeting for us with Sick Kids. We knew by this time that Dr. Reingold had already met with the hospital and requested a written response to our questions, so we told Frank to tell them we were agreeable to a meeting as soon as we got answers.

Hawkins informed Frank that the hospital's official response would be ready within a day or two, but Dr. Reingold had specifically instructed him to send it only to the coroner's office. Frank waited a week before calling Dr. Reingold to ask for a copy, only to hear it "wasn't yet available". Frank asked him the same question he had been asking Dr. Lucas for weeks: when would the final toxicology report be ready? Dr. Reingold told him the results were being printed up at that very moment, but we weren't entitled to them since we had never requested them formally and in writing. Frank expressed astonishment that Dr. Reingold had never mentioned this requirement in their many phone conversations, and immediately faxed him an "official" request for the autopsy and toxicology reports.

Dr. Reingold called him back the next day to tell him he had discussed Frank's request with his boss, Dr. Lucas, and they had decided not to give the reports to us because the investigation was still ongoing. Dr. Lucas's justification for his decision was that everyone had to have equal access and there had to be a "level playing field". He would not explain how withholding information from us about our daughter's death—information we had been waiting for months to get—would accomplish this objective.

Dr. Reingold also said he had not yet received the hospital's written response to the questions, but when he received it he would not release that to us either. We wondered how the coroner's office rationalized that as a level playing field. Dr. Reingold agreed we could ask the hospital directly for a copy, but when Frank called Hawkins for it, Hawkins said that Dr. Reingold had expressly forbidden him to give it to us!

I had been patient, polite, and reasonable, but this was beyond reason. On March 11, 1999, I wrote to the Solicitor-General of Ontario, the cabinet minister in charge of the coroner's office, and copied Drs. Reingold and Lucas.[1] For good measure, I also sent copies to the Chief Coroner of Ontario, Dr. James Young, the Deputy Chief Coroner, Dr. James Cairns, and to my own government representative. I described the incompetence of the coroner's office despite our having raised many questions about Lisa's death, and said that we wanted to know what was going to be done about it.

I sent the letter by overnight courier. The next morning I received a phone call from Dr. Young informing me he already knew about the case and had spoken about it twice that week with Dr. Cairns. Dr. Young reiterated that the coroner's office would not release the hospital's written response, the autopsy report, or the toxicology results, as they all formed part of the coroner's investigation. Remembering Dr. Reingold's comments about a level playing field, I answered that I had no objection to us and the hospital both getting copies. Dr. Young explained this was not the problem, it was that the coroner's office had released information in the past that had become public and prejudiced matters. I told him we would be willing to sign a confidentiality agreement. He said he would discuss it and get back to us, which was a euphemism for "my decision stands". When I asked why no one had told us we wouldn't be given this information when we had been calling for weeks asking about it, he could not give me an answer.

I asked why everything was taking so long. When would the investigation be completed and when could we expect a decision regarding an inquest? Rather than trying to give me a reasonable estimate or trying to provide a sincere explanation about what had caused the delays, Dr. Young rhymed off a list of excuses: it was a very complex case, they have many, many cases to handle, their department was very small, he hadn't read the file, these things can take a long time, and things can be very open-ended. When I questioned what kind of organization could not provide any estimates at all, and asked if there were any department policies and procedures that addressed this issue, he told me in a huff, "*I* make the rules around here!"

I made a great effort to speak cordially, although I felt like hanging up on him. I asked when he thought the toxicology and pathology reports might be released to us. He didn't know, he said. For someone who made the rules around there, he could be pretty powerless when it suited him.

Dr. Young had evidently been trying to placate me with soothing words and without the least intention of actually responding to our legitimate concerns, but the conversation did not go the way he had planned. He called Frank next, probably expecting to have an easier time with him. He assured Frank that the coroner's office was taking Lisa Shore's death very seriously and explained that Ontario was the only province where the coroner's office even attempted to "pull the matter together". Usually, he said, results are simply released to the family, and the family has to put things together itself. I imagined that other provinces would not be pleased to hear how little Dr. Young thought of their coroner's investigations.

He did at least give Frank one nugget of genuine information, which was more than he had been willing to give me: Lisa's file would be discussed at the next Paediatric Death Review Committee meeting, after which Dr. Cairns would meet with us.

A few hours after my frustrating, unproductive discussion with Dr. Young, I received another phone call from the coroner's office, this time from Deputy Chief Coroner Dr. James Cairns. When he began talking in his thick Irish accent, I sensed a sincerity and truthfulness that had been demonstrably lacking from his colleagues. I felt, finally, that I was speaking to someone of integrity. He told me he had only been aware of the case for the past two weeks, and was apologetic about the way things had been handled thus far. Dr. Cairns promised that at the end of the investigation he would answer all of our questions.

He explained the role of the Paediatric Death Review Committee, which had been formed to review all children's deaths investigated by the coroner's office. It was composed of paediatric specialists from various regions of the province. I later learned that a senior member of the Homicide Squad also attended meetings where the death was thought to be the result of a criminal act. I asked about the appropriateness of doctors from Sick Kids investigating a death at Sick Kids, and he told me that if members are related to an institution under discussion they do not sit in on the discussion. Dr. Cairns explained that the committee met monthly and reviewed about four to six cases each time. The review led to one of three recommendations: refer the case to inquest, no inquest was necessary and the case should be closed, or further information was required. He considered the committee's recommendations when deciding whether to call an inquest, but the final decision was his alone. Although things were very backlogged, Lisa's case had just jumped the queue and was going to be reviewed at the next meeting.

I asked Dr. Cairns what was taking the forensic lab so long to complete the toxicology tests, and this time I got an answer: The tests had taken longer than expected because some of Lisa's medications were relatively uncommon.

I told him we were not trying to be difficult, and we realized there was a process to be followed, but we were frustrated at the lack of respect we had received along the way. Dr. Cairns said that now that he was involved he would ensure we were kept informed. "You deserve full and fair answers," he told me.

My letter had worked. The investigation into Lisa's death was finally in competent hands. We still had no answers, but I was a little more optimistic about the chances of getting some in the near future.

11

THE ANONYMOUS LETTER

Because we had made an issue of it, the coroner's office agreed that the hospital could provide us with a copy of its official response to our questions.

It was a superbly crafted letter.[1] To someone unfamiliar with the details, it looked on first glance to be a thorough explanation of events. On second reading, one got the sense that something didn't quite add up. After the third and subsequent readings, it became evident that the distortions, inconsistencies, and creative wordplay made it look as if a question had been answered when it really hadn't. But for me, focussed as I was on learning why Lisa had died, it only took one reading to realize that people were lying about what had happened, and even worse, the hospital was not willing to admit that anything untoward had occurred!

I had been so positive that once the hospital properly investigated, it would not fail to see how truly negligent the care Lisa received had been; if we could see it, then the only way hospital staff could miss it would be if they were wilfully, deliberately blind. I had been certain an institution as renowned as Sick Kids would be appalled and horrified at the unequivocal evidence of horrific nursing care and that it would instantly fire those responsible. In my imagination, the hospital administration would be so distraught that a child in its care had died due to the negligence of its staff that it would be begging for forgiveness and doing everything in its power to try and make amends. But the institution I expected to be honourable and principled had, in an instant, revealed itself to be exactly the opposite. Lisa's death meant nothing to the Hospital for Sick Children except as a problem best dealt with by denying that any problem existed. I was devastated.

The very first thing I said after reading the letter was, "These nurses are lying." According to one nurse, the monitor Lisa had been attached to had given off repeated false alarms, so she claimed she had turned it off to silence it. "There was no monitor," I cried. "There were no alarms, not a single one, no noise at all."

Sharon Deutsh, the nurse who three months ago had helped me review Lisa's records, was gradually becoming a good friend. She called me often to see how I was doing, and she was so empathetic and caring that I felt comfortable confiding in her. We talked frequently over coffee, about Lisa, the hospital, and the nurses. I needed her help once again, to try and discern the truth hidden behind this deceptive letter.

The letter came with a covering note from the hospital's Risk Manager[2] stating that she and several other staff had reviewed and edited it, but there was no indication of who had actually written it. Frank's guess was that it was the hospital's lawyer, Patrick Hawkins. Along with the letter, the hospital enclosed a thirty-page document entitled "Patient-Controlled Analgesia, Nursing Resource Material".[3]

Sharon and I went through the letter line by line and made extensive notes. By the time we finished we had eleven typed pages of comments. It seemed almost everything the anonymous author had written was deliberately vague, implied something had been done even though it had not, or was simply untrue.

For instance, we had asked why no one took Lisa's blood pressure in response to an increase in her heart rate from 72 beats per minute to 134 beats per minute over the course of the night. The answer: "This was possibly an attempt not to awaken Lisa once she had begun to rest". That might have sounded sensible to someone who didn't know any better–the nurses were trying to be kind and considerate–except who had ever heard of a nurse not doing something she was supposed to because she wanted to let her patient rest? Everyone knows that one of the problems in being in a hospital is that you can never get a good night's sleep because the nurses keep waking you up!

We had also questioned why the Death Summary said that Lisa had been awakened at 5:00 a.m., when there was no indication of it in the records and it was next to impossible to wake Lisa up even if she had been healthy and not close to death. The hospital's answer: The nurse woke Lisa up at 5:00 a.m. to take her temperature.

This meant the hospital's official response to our letter, if you combined these two separate answers, was: 1) the nurse woke Lisa at 5:00 a.m. to take her temperature, and 2) the nurse didn't wake Lisa at 5:00 a.m. to take her blood pressure because she wanted to let her sleep. How could any hospital write something so patently ridiculous and expect to be thought credible?

There were more equally illogical "answers". The nurses "attributed <Lisa's> increasing heart rate to the fact that the patient may be experiencing pain. An increased heart rate is a normal response to pain." Sure it is–if the patient is awake. If she is fast asleep, sleeping quietly and peacefully, with no fever, chances are she's not in much pain. Lisa was never woken up while she was under the care of those nurses, so why would they assume she was in pain? When Lisa was awake and in terrible pain in the Emergency Department, her heart rate was significantly lower. And as Sharon Deutsh reminded me, it wasn't only the heart rate itself but the change in heart rate that was indicative of a potential medical emergency.

The letter said "the sedation scale and pain scales were not recorded although there is an assessment of level of consciousness in the patient record". "Not recorded" implies it was done but not written down, when in fact it was never done. An assessment of level of consciousness means that the nurse wakes the patient to see how alert and responsive she is. Simply marking down the patient is "asleep", which is what was written on the chart, does not constitute an assessment of level of consciousness by any standard. Why couldn't Sick Kids just be honest?

I said that Lisa had not been on any kind of monitor, although the nursing notes claimed otherwise. The monitor had two separate alarms, and the hospital said that a nurse claimed that one of them had given off several false alarms so she had disabled it. But even if that had been true—which it was not!—then what about the second alarm? If there had really been a working monitor, why hadn't any monitor alarms gone off when Lisa died? The hospital's answer: There was a monitor, but we have no explanation for the alarm not sounding.

We asked who had ordered this alleged monitor—was it the physician, and if so, where were his orders? The hospital's response was "the monitoring orders were placed on the hospital computer system". But there were no monitoring orders anywhere in Lisa's medical records! Where were they? If the orders had been placed in the system, had they "disappeared"?

We would soon learn that this was the single most deceptive statement in a letter filled with deception. Any reasonable individual would assume that orders placed on the hospital computer system meant everything had been done properly–just what the sly writer wanted everyone to think. Yes, the doctor had placed orders in the system describing how Lisa was to be cared for, but the nurses had never read them! Without a doctor's orders, it would be impossible for nurses to provide proper care to a newly-arrived patient whom they knew nothing about.

"The PCA pumps are used frequently on Unit 5A and the staff know the protocols, such as doing the respiratory rates and heart rates," the letter stated. The author was very talented at manipulating words: knowing the protocols was not the same as *following* the protocols. The anonymous author neglected to mention that doing respiratory rates and heart rates were the *only* part of the protocol the nurses had followed; the rest of it had been ignored.

Everything about this letter was contemptible, but most abhorrent of all was the knowledge that two paediatric nurses were deliberately lying and this hospital was actively trying to help them get away with it. Those who "edited and reviewed" this pathetic letter could not fail to be aware they were editing and reviewing a cover-up. I was struggling with Lisa's death, but could see there was a far more insidious problem than two negligent nurses: a world-renowned hospital that cared more about covering up and protecting bad employees than it did about protecting its young and vulnerable patients.

Had the Hospital for Sick Children done something like this before and gotten away with it? Was this why it was doing this now? Because it could? Who would believe me if I said the Hospital for Sick Children was responsible for Lisa's death?

I knew I could not allow the truth about Lisa's death to be covered up. I called Frank and told him about the in-depth deconstruction of the hospital's letter Sharon and I had done. I explained how the hospital was attempting to deceive us and the coroner, that the nurses were absolutely, positively, without a doubt lying about the false alarms, and that Lisa had not been on any monitors. Frank listened to me and agreed the letter was deceptive, but I could tell he did not really believe me about the nurses being liars. He knew he had a strong legal case, but what I was saying seemed completely unbelievable to him.

With Sharon's help, I put together a lengthy list of notes and comments and sent them to Frank to review. He gave me some excellent advice: "Go through everything and take your top four or five points, and send only those top five to Dr. Young, the Chief Coroner". When I complained there were so many things that were wrong or misleading, and how was I to choose only four or five, Frank said, "If you send someone pages and pages to read, his eyes will cross and you won't get anywhere. If you give someone a short letter where each point is a major one, he'll read it and pay attention. You'll just have to pick the ones you think are the most important."

Frank was right. I stuck to basic questions such as where were the monitoring orders that had been "placed in the computer", and how could the nurse both not want to wake Lisa up to take her blood pressure yet wake her up to take her temperature?[4]

While the coroner's office proceeded with its slow-paced investigation, we started making our own independent inquiries. I contacted Dr. Wilder, the doctor who had treated Lisa in Boston, and asked if he would review her records and give us his comments. He agreed, and I couriered copies down to him immediately. We asked the hospital lawyer, Patrick Hawkins, for information about the Corometric monitor's model number and manufacturer. Both of these avenues were dead ends: Dr. Wilder never called me back, and Hawkins ignored the request about the monitor.

Since we had not yet received the autopsy report and had no expectation of receiving it anytime soon from the coroner's office, we sought out our own expert. Frank spoke with a pathologist in Chicago who had given expert testimony at some high-profile American murder trials. This doctor had had his own dealings with the Ontario coroner's office, and held it in very low esteem. He agreed we were getting a run-around, and we should not have to wait as long as we had in order to get such basic information as autopsy results. Frank had already told us that retaining experts such as this pathologist would cost thousands of dollars, so we decided to wait to see what the coroner's office would come up with first.

The Toronto Star was sitting on the story, waiting for our OK to publish. We hoped some publicity would goad the coroner's office into moving a little faster, so we gave the paper the go-ahead. On March 24, 1999, the first newspaper article about Lisa's death appeared on page 2: "Probe sought into death of daughter".[5]

12

THE CORONER'S INVESTIGATION

My next-door neighbour again reminded me that his sister's friend had been on the hospital ward with her son on the night Lisa died. I hadn't thought much about it before, but now that I knew how dishonest the hospital was I wondered if this person might be able to help us learn what had really happened that night.

When I called, she was more than happy to speak to me. She and her eleven-year-old son had been in the room next to Lisa; he had been scheduled for exploratory surgery the next morning. He had been on morphine that night for pain control, but not hooked up to any monitors. She had heard Lisa and me arrive and get settled.

She was absolutely certain no alarms had sounded that night. I was overjoyed to hear her provide independent confirmation that proved Lisa's nurses were lying. It would no longer be a he-said, she-said between Lisa's nurses and me. Now everyone would know there had been no monitors and no monitor alarms, and that I was the one telling the truth. I asked if she would be willing to testify to that at a coroner's inquest and she said she would.

She told me that shortly after Lisa's death, a cart full of monitors had been left in the hallway just outside our rooms, and it had looked as if the hospital had rounded up every last monitor it owned and brought them all there. When she asked why they were sitting there and not being used, a nurse told her they were set for infants and the nurses didn't like to use them on older kids because they gave off too many false alarms. Nonetheless, a short while later a nurse brought in one of those monitors and attached it to her son; she believed that most or all of the children on the floor were also hooked up to monitors. In light of what she had just been told about the nurses' reluctance to use them, she questioned why and was told that until then the monitors had been used at the nurses' discretion, but now they had become mandatory.

She and her son stayed over at the hospital for a few nights following Lisa's death. So many false alarms kept sounding because of all the patients newly placed on monitors that the nurses were run ragged. Her son's nurse turned off the alarm on his monitor, complaining about the false alarms.

This woman also had the name and phone number of the mother who had been in the room on the other side of Lisa, because the two of them had been quite distraught about what had happened and had spent a lot of time together. I called the other mother, and she too told me she was sure no alarms had gone off that night. She said she was a light sleeper and the alarms were so loud she knew they would have woken her. She also confirmed what the first mother had said about multiple alarms going off over the next few nights.

Dr. Cairns called to tell me the toxicology tests had shown high levels of morphine and Gabapentin, but the forensics lab had been unable to determine whether the Gabapentin level indicated an overdose. I knew Gabapentin was not toxic no matter how high the level, and told Dr. Cairns we knew Lisa had taken exactly the amount she had been prescribed and nothing more. Our concerns had to do with the morphine, I said. Dr. Cairns had hired a paediatric pharmacologist, a former dean of medicine at one of the region's medical schools, to investigate. Normally the coroner's office would have retained an expert from Sick Kids, but under the circumstances Dr. Cairns did not feel that was appropriate.

He also wanted to let me know that all the questions we had asked were valid, and he and his colleagues had the same concerns as we did after they had reviewed the records. He told me I was most definitely not an overreacting parent; Lisa was a healthy 10-year-old child who was in pain and had gone to the hospital for treatment of the pain, but there was nothing life threatening about her condition. He and his colleagues believed the morphine had caused an adverse reaction, as evidenced by Lisa's respiratory depression. They felt her tachycardia—the rapid heartbeat—was also not normal and had been the result of a chain reaction set off by the morphine.

There were drug issues and monitoring issues, he told me. All the results would be given to us when we met, which would be soon. He apologized for taking so long, but said he needed that time to interpret and analyze all the information.

The Paediatric Death Review Committee discussed the case at its April meeting. Frank, Bill and I met with Dr. Cairns one week later, exactly as he had promised.

The office of the Chief Coroner is a drab building, complete with worn furniture and portraits of coroners past. It could have been any government office anywhere, if you ignored the morgue in the basement. On a wall near the entrance was a plaque inscribed with the office's motto: We speak for the dead to protect the living.

Dr. Cairns' first words to us were an apology for the way things had been mishandled to date. To our surprise, he stood up to say this and sat down only when he had finished. It was deeply meaningful.

We were given the documents that we had been waiting for: the autopsy report, the toxicology report, and the lab report on the PCA pump and IV equipment. I flipped the pages of the autopsy report, unwilling to read clinical descriptions of my daughter's body parts but feeling as if it were expected. I felt faint but forced myself to look at Dr. Cairns while he spoke.

Lisa's death was not the result of a morphine overdose. Yes, the level of morphine in her body was high, but it was still in the "therapeutic range", that is, not high enough to be toxic. The therapeutic range is broad and moveable, however; what works for one person may well kill another. Although Lisa did not get an overdose, morphine can cause adverse reactions in some people and stop their breathing even at lesser doses. To put it in context, one doctor told us "it may not be an overdose, but if you gave that much morphine to a grown man, he'd drop like a horse". The Committee felt Lisa's respiratory depression was directly related to the morphine she had received.

The Committee did not feel Gabapentin was responsible for Lisa's death, which only confirmed what we already knew. Lisa had been taking this medication for months with no adverse effects whatsoever, and it was a very safe drug.

It felt that the drop in Lisa's respiration and the increase in her heart rate were highly significant. The hospital's answer to our question about Lisa's pulse going up because "Lisa was in pain" made no sense. Lisa was sleeping; if anything, the heart rate of a person sleeping peacefully would be lower, not higher. Lisa's pulse in Emergency, when she was awake and in terrible pain, was lower than it was when she was asleep on the ward. The Committee believed Lisa's pulse increased so much because she was oxygen-deprived, and Dr. Cairns agreed.

As for the hospital's response that the nurse did not take Lisa's blood pressure in "an attempt not to awaken Lisa once she began to rest", the Committee dismissed this as ridiculous. The orders were to take blood pressure, regardless of whether Lisa was sleeping or awake.

The hospital had stated in its letter that the monitor the nurses claimed was used on Lisa was set to alarm if her heart rate reached 160–180 beats per minute. The Committee felt this was far too high and completely inappropriate.

In answer to our question as to why the coroner hadn't seized the monitor when he came to the hospital to investigate, Dr. Cairns said it was because the coroner wasn't aware that Lisa was supposed to be hooked up to one.

One of our questions had been whether there were any doctors' orders for Lisa, since there were none in the medical records the hospital had sent us. There were indeed some; Dr. Cairns handed us a copy.[1] They had been printed up by the hospital three months after Lisa died, and each line had the word "suspended" at the beginning. What did this mean, and why had the orders only turned up now?

Dr. Cairns said he had wondered the same thing and had gone back to the hospital to ask, only to encounter great difficulty in getting an explanation. He finally learned that the hospital's Kidcom system was an integrated, hospital-wide computer system, but a few departments such as Emergency were not directly incorporated into it. Doctors could access the system and enter orders from Emergency as Lisa's doctor had done, but those orders were not considered to be officially entered and remained in "suspended" mode until they were "activated" by the nurse on the ward. Activation occurred automatically when the nurse read the orders and printed them off.

Was Dr. Cairns really telling us that the nurses had not read the doctor's orders? How was such a thing possible? How does a nurse take charge of a patient who arrives on the ward in the middle of the night from Emergency, a patient she has never seen before and knows nothing about, without checking to see what the doctor has ordered? How can a nurse know what medications to give, when to give them, what kind of monitoring to do, what kind of things to watch out for—in short, how to take care of the patient? The answer is simple—she can't!

I asked about Lisa's nurses. Dr. Cairns told me that one of the two had about fifteen years of experience. "That must be the second nurse, the one who relieved Lisa's main nurse," I thought, remembering that Lisa's nurse had looked like she was about sixteen years old.

Why did the orders have a print date of January 1999 when Lisa had died in October 1998? Because the hospital claimed it had not realized the orders were missing until it got our letter asking about them. When it went looking, it discovered the orders in limbo in its computer system. The hospital had immediately printed them out and sent them to the coroner's office, hence their January date.

The hospital knew that a healthy 10-year-old child had died of no known cause and the coroner's office was investigating. It discovered orders lost in its computer system showing that the nurses responsible for this child's care had never read them. And what did it do with that important knowledge? It concealed it, or rather, it said nothing and hoped that no one noticed. Yes, the hospital sent a copy of the orders to the coroner as soon as it discovered them, but it did so in a stealthy manner designed to draw no attention or notice. Instead of sending out the orders on their own with an explanation of their significance, the hospital bundled them with several other records and sent everything to the coroner with a covering note that read, "Please replace the doctors <sic> orders for admit 10.21.98 with the final orders. I have a copy of what you have and a copy of what you should have".[2]

Further evidence that this was an attempt at deliberate concealment by the hospital was the misleading way it wrote up its response to our question about whether doctors' orders existed. The hospital had said that monitoring orders did exist and that they had been placed on the computer system. No one would normally include information about orders being placed in the computer system in a formal letter sent to people external to the hospital, unless the author wanted the reader to infer that orders entered were orders that were carried out. The letter writer had known that the nurses had not read the orders and was trying to ensure that no one noticed.

I already knew the nurses had lied about putting Lisa on a monitor. They had lied about false alarms sounding, and about waking her up to take her vital signs. I knew they had not followed standard protocols. Was it possible that not reading the doctors' orders had been a deliberate act? Had the nurses wanted Lisa to die? Why was the Hospital for Sick Children trying so hard to cover things up?

Another thought struck us. Why did it take three months and our questioning for the hospital to find out about the missing orders? If anyone there had looked at Lisa's chart following her death, he or she would have seen the very visible evidence of substandard nursing care and asked the same questions that we had. So did that mean no one had bothered to look at Lisa's records after she died, or had they seen them and intentionally said nothing and done nothing? Either way, the Hospital for Sick Children staff involved in this cover-up appeared to be immoral, unethical, and unscrupulous.

What was contained in those orders the nurse never read? Clear instructions on how to monitor Lisa, using two separate monitoring devices. "I told you Lisa wasn't on any monitors!" I said. Dr. Cairns called this a very significant care issue, and informed us that the Paediatric Death Review Committee was extremely critical of this treatment. If the nurse was telling the truth about there having been an apnea monitor, then turning the apnea alarm off was dangerous and negligent. If the alarm was sounding, the Committee felt it was doing so because Lisa's respiratory rate was too low.

If there is a problem with a monitor, one should never turn it off, but should call Engineering and get a monitor that is working properly.

Dr. Cairns demonstrated an apnea monitor for us. Its alarm was as loud as a smoke detector's; it was designed to be that loud so it could be heard by nurses down the hall even if the patient's room door was closed. We all jumped when the alarm went off unexpectedly during the demonstration. Bill, who can sleep through anything, remarked, "That would have woken even me!"

There are three different measurements the monitor checks for: breathing rate, maximum heart rate, and minimum heart rate. Two of the three alarms–the breathing and high heart rate–can be turned off, but the minimum heart rate alarm cannot be disabled unless the machine is turned off completely. This means if a patient's heart stops or slows down to dangerous levels, the alarm will automatically sound.

The alarm will also sound if the leads are accidentally disconnected from the patient, or if the machine is not plugged in and the battery runs low. The monitor performs a self-test when first turned on that includes several seconds of its very loud alarm.

No alarms sounded when Lisa died and her heart stopped, but the hospital could not explain why. The Paediatric Death Review Committee's conclusion was that no alarm had gone off *because Lisa was not attached to a monitor,* exactly as I had been saying all along!

Frank no longer doubted me; he realized that my claims that Lisa was never on a monitor and that the nurses were lying had not been exaggerated. He now shared my belief that the hospital was wholly responsible for Lisa's death.

Dr. Cairns said an inquest was warranted–if we wanted one. In case we felt it would be too difficult to endure, he would make recommendations on behalf of the coroner's office and give them to the hospital. I thought he was trying to convince me not to have an inquest, but Bill saw in his offer a genuine attempt to help us avoid the emotional and financial investment an inquest would require. I was adamant I wanted an inquest, and Dr. Cairns agreed one would be held.

I wanted to know if any consideration had been given to the possibility of criminal charges. I was convinced that what happened to Lisa was more than just a terrible mistake. Nurses who took charge of a patient who came in from Emergency and never read the doctors' orders were more than negligent; nurses who lied about what they did and then documented those lies in their notes were criminal. If a monitor had really been found in the room when Lisa died, I said, then one or both of the nurses had brought it in surreptitiously to make it look as if she had been following orders. I asked Dr. Cairns if the police would be investigating, and he told me a Crown attorney would look at the file. I could tell by the way he said that and by the look on Frank's face that neither of them thought this was a matter worthy of a police investigation.

13

WAITING FOR THE INQUEST

The inquest would not take place until the fall, because it would take months to coordinate all the lawyers' schedules. Dr. Cairns confirmed he would be the presiding coroner.

A coroner's inquest is a quasi-judicial hearing into the events surrounding a death. In Ontario, one must be held whenever anyone dies in prison, on a construction site, or in police custody, but these mandatory inquests are usually short-lasting and rarely generate any public interest. Inquests into other deaths may be called at the coroner's discretion, such as when they have raised broad social issues or concerns for public safety. A coroner, who in the Province of Ontario must be a medical doctor, presides over the inquest. A five member jury is selected from the regular jury pool, and it has two important responsibilities: to determine facts about the death–how it occurred, where, when, and by what means–and to make recommendations designed to help prevent similar deaths from occurring in the future.

Everyone who has a "direct and substantial interest" in the inquest proceedings may participate in it, meaning they or their lawyers may introduce evidence, cross-examine witnesses, and make an address to the jury. Most often, the parties involved in an inquest are institutions, unions, insurers, and other organizations, all of whom have access to high calibre legal representation, and the family of the deceased. If the family can afford the very significant legal expense, is poor enough to qualify for legal aid, or can find a lawyer willing to work for almost nothing, it is welcome to participate in the inquest. If not, a brave friend or relative may represent the family, but more likely than not the family will be unrepresented.

In our inquest, Frank assumed that the participants would consist of the Crown, the Hospital for Sick Children, the doctors, the nurses, and us. Hospitals are generally insured under The Health Insurance Reciprocal of Canada, or HIROC, which provides them with complete legal coverage. Doctors belong to The Canadian Medical Protective Association, or the CMPA, which supplies physicians with lawyers and has a reputation for fighting everything on principle regardless of whether it is in the best interest of the individual doctor it represents. Nurses who work in hospitals have access to lawyers through membership in their union, and other nurses usually join nursing organizations that offer legal assistance as a membership benefit. We had no organization or legal insurance to help us, and Frank warned it would be very expensive. Bill and I agreed we would sell our home if necessary to ensure we had someone at the inquest to look out for us and help learn the truth about why Lisa had died.

Like a regular court, witnesses are subpoenaed and testify under oath. Unlike a regular court, the jury can only make a finding of fact, not a finding of fault. In other words, if the jury finds that a death is a homicide, it cannot officially hold anyone responsible for that death—even if it and everyone else knows exactly who is at fault.

A witness's inquest testimony cannot be used against him or her in a subsequent criminal or civil case. The intent of this rule is to enable witnesses to speak truthfully without fear of being blamed or punished. However, the flip side of that same rule means that witnesses can lie or shade the truth with equal impunity, secure from any and all consequences. In theory, a witness who lies—assuming it can be proven beyond any doubt—can be charged with perjury, but the criminal justice system does not concern itself with matters such as coroner's inquests where there can be no finding of fault or liability. No one in Ontario has ever been convicted of perjury because of his or her testimony at a coroner's inquest.[1]

"Explain this to me," I said to Frank. "If someone gets up and testifies that he committed armed robbery and shot someone, does that mean he can't be arrested because his testimony can't be used against him?"

"Yes and no," Frank explained. "His testimony couldn't be used against him, but the police would work backwards to build a case and try to get independent evidence."

"So has something like this ever happened, where someone who testified at an inquest was arrested afterwards?"

"I've never heard of it happening. Generally speaking, if there's any possibility of a crime having been committed, the police do an investigation first. The coroner's office will only commit to an inquest once there is no likelihood of criminal charges."

∼

Lisa should not have died, we knew that for certain. But whenever Bill and I told people that Sick Kids had been responsible for Lisa's death, we could see their faces assume that fixed, polite look that meant they didn't really believe us. What could we do to get people to understand the negligence of Lisa's nurses and the hospital's attempt to cover it up?

"How about setting up a website?" Bill suggested.

What a fantastic idea, I thought. I had no clue how to go about it, but was sure I could figure it out. After all, I had been using the Internet for years, and much of what was out there was pretty low-calibre.

I registered the name lisashore.com, set up the site with my Internet provider, and figured things out by trial and error. After several late nights and a fair degree of frustration, I managed to get a picture of Lisa up on the site. The image was a bit lopsided, but it was there.

On April 30, 1999, the website went live. I tried to carefully stick to the facts: the doctor's orders were not checked, no monitor alarms sounded when Lisa's heart stopped, and standard hospital protocols were not followed. I also posted Lisa's eulogy.

As visitors to the site began to increase, so did my mastery of website design and maintenance. The site grew and became more complex, and I started receiving many e-mails. By the time the coroner's office officially announced an inquest five months later, the site contained information about Lisa, some of her artwork, all the newspaper articles that had been published to date, and specific information about the circumstances of her death. I grew progressively bolder about saying what I felt, and added this sentence: "We believe that the nursing care that Lisa received on the ward was substandard and negligent, and that had she been under the care of nurses who were minimally competent, she would still be alive."

In July 1999, I gave the opening speech at the Canadian Reflex Sympathetic Dystrophy Network's annual conference in Victoria, British Columbia. I told Lisa's story to an attentive audience, and explained how memorial donations made in her memory and in memory of my late father had been used to set up a fund to help other children with RSD. I ended my speech with "Lisa took everything that life had to offer with joy and happiness. Would that we could all learn to do the same."

∼

That summer, we received a phone call from a police officer asking us to come down to the station for an interview. "What's this all about?" I asked Frank. He replied, "These cops are assigned to help the coroner in his investigation. They want a statement from you to put in the inquest brief." Giving a statement to the police was not mandatory, he told us, but there was no reason not to give them one. I asked Frank if he would come with us, but he said it was not necessary since we had nothing to fear and nothing to hide.

The inquest brief was a binder containing important documents which would be distributed to all the inquest participants. Frank guessed that the brief for Lisa's inquest would include her medical records, the autopsy report, Bill's and my statements to the police, and "will-says" from the doctors and nurses—a short summary of what each witness was expected to say when he or she testified.

With some trepidation, we drove down to the police station. 52 Division was a downtown, modern building with lots of glass—on the outside, anyway. The city had splurged on the building's exterior but kept the interior nondescript and utilitarian. Bill and I sat in the waiting area, speculating about the other people sitting near us, feeling a little like tourists who didn't belong.

I was ushered into a small interview room with video recording equipment already in place. Bill waited outside, as we were to be interviewed separately.

The police officer asked me if I wanted to talk a bit about the kind of child Lisa was. I did, even though the tape had to be paused several times while I wiped my eyes. Things proceeded more smoothly once I started to relate the events of October 21-22, 1998. When I was done, I waited outside while Bill gave his statement.

We were a little nervous afterwards. Had we told our story coherently so it could be easily understood? Had we forgotten something important? Like so many other things we naively worried about, our fears were misplaced. A police transcriber dutifully types up the interviews, but unfortunately also faithfully reproduces the speaker's every hesitation and interjection. The resulting document is practically incomprehensible and nearly useless. Even the smartest person doesn't sound too bright when his written speech contains numerous "ums", "uhs", and "ers". That's one, er, small step for man, one, uh, giant leap for, um, mankind. Thankfully, court reporters omit these everyday interjections when they transcribe trials, unlike their police department colleagues.

The police interviews with Bill and me constituted the entire pre-inquest police investigation.

14

MEDIATIONS AND MEETINGS

In our legal system, those who are injured through the negligence of others are entitled to collect damages as compensation for the harm done to them. Everyone knows that money rarely compensates for one's suffering or loss, but no one has come up with a better way of doing things. While we waited for the inquest to begin, Frank began working to settle our civil case, which meant we would be suing the Hospital for Sick Children for Lisa's wrongful death. He had to spend a good deal of time trying to explain the dollars and cents aspect of the process to us. Like most people, we read American books, watched American TV, and heard American news stories about multi-million dollar jury awards. The hospital killed Lisa, and we expected our case would also be worth millions. We dreamt of how we could use that money to do something in Lisa's name—funding a clinic where kids with RSD would be treated properly, giving poor children art classes and supplies, building playgrounds…

The reality was bitter. Canada is very different from the United States in this arena. In Ontario, under the Family Law Act, the value of a child's life is generally less than the cost of a new car. The child has no dependants to care for and earns no income—the only things that matter in a case of wrongful death. The emotional pain and suffering of the child's family is worth virtually nothing in our legal system. If a car accident killed a child and left her middle-aged breadwinner father with a permanent limp, the father would receive far more money in damages for his limp than he would for the life of his daughter.

A father in our bereaved parents support group had told me that the average settlement in a child's wrongful death was about $25,000 to each parent. Frank sent me a pile of legal cases to read where a child had been wrongfully killed, and the figure quoted by that father was about right. The highest amount an Ontario court had ever allotted to a bereaved family was $100,000 to each parent,[1] and the circumstances of that case were exceptional. A teenager had died while using his school's faulty gym equipment, and his parents were poor and uneducated Vietnamese immigrants who had come to Canada after great suffering and hardship. This boy was their only son, and it was expected in their culture that the son would take care of and support his parents financially and emotionally when he was older. Frank cautioned us that this was an extraordinary amount of money for a child's wrongful death, and that Lisa's death was not worth anywhere near that much.

What a lesson to learn! This logic is applicable not only to children but also to the elderly. The ailing senior citizen who dies wrongfully, perhaps by a medication error in a nursing home, is not worth very much in legal terms either, no matter how loved she was. The lives of the very young and the elderly have such minimal value in this country that many lawyers won't even take on these cases.

Now that we had been educated about reality, Frank felt that a reasonable settlement would be about $50,000 each to Bill and me, and a lesser amount for the boys. Lisa had been healthy, she had a loving and stable family, and her death was entirely due to the substandard care provided by the hospital. There was nothing that would reduce Lisa's "worth", which was why Frank thought her death warranted this "higher-than-usual" amount.

The lawyer for the doctors advised Frank that an expert had been retained to review the records, and this expert had found no breach of the standard of care on the part of any doctor involved. He would be representing these doctors at the inquest, but would not accept any liability or pay any damages. He asked Frank whether we would forgo an inquest if a financial settlement could be reached. When I heard that, I wanted to scream. How could anybody think paying us off would satisfy us when we had been pushing for answers and an inquest for so long?

The hospital's position was that although Lisa's care might have been less than ideal, it was not the cause of Lisa's death. Hawkins said it was not the hospital's fault that Lisa had a cardiac arrest, and even if she had been revived, she might have suffered severe brain damage. He was making two separate points, I think: First, since the hospital was only partly responsible for what had happened it should only have to pay a part of the total damages, and second, regardless of what the hospital had or had not done, Lisa would probably have ended up in such bad shape that her life would be worth far less in damages than that of a healthy child. On behalf of the hospital, Hawkins offered $25,000 each to Bill and me, about half of what Frank felt was appropriate.

Hawkins' argument would not hold up in court, however. The Supreme Court of Canada had considered a case where a person with a pre-existing medical condition was subsequently made much worse as a result of two motor vehicle accidents, and it had ruled that as long as those responsible for the accidents had contributed to the person's injuries in a major way, they could be held fully responsible.[2] In order for the hospital to be held wholly liable, all we had to prove was that its employees' negligence was one of the materially contributing factors to Lisa's death. Frank told Hawkins that a coroner's inquest was going to be called and civil liability was going to be imposed on the hospital at 100%. On Frank's advice, we rejected the hospital's offer.

Frank recommended we try mediation. Far less costly than going to trial, a mediator tries to broker a settlement that all the parties can live with. Those involved in civil litigation often voluntarily agree to go to mediation in the hopes of avoiding a trial; in Toronto and a few other regions, when a case is scheduled to go to trial the parties are compelled to attend a mediation first.[3] No one is forced to accept the mediator's recommendations, but usually people go into a mediation prepared to negotiate and compromise. For example, a frequent kind of mediation is between an accident victim and an insurance company. The insurance company and the victim both know that some amount will be paid for damages, but the insurer tries to minimize the settlement amount while the victim's lawyer tries to maximize it. Sometimes there are a number of insurance companies involved, and the argument is not about how much money will be paid, but about who is responsible for paying it or in what proportion.

The idea of sitting down with the hospital to discuss a monetary settlement to compensate us for Lisa's death was morally repugnant, and Bill and I were sceptical. We thought a trial would be better, but

Frank advised against it. "What's the purpose of going to court?" he cautioned. "For most people, that's the only way they can question the people involved. It's the only way they have to obtain a measure of justice. You'll be able to do that at the inquest. If you go to trial, it will take a long time, and the process will be very painful. If there's any way to avoid it, you'll be much better off settling beforehand. Did you understand when I explained what a dead child is worth in our legal system? Maybe you'd get $50,000 at a mediation and $100,000 from a jury, but the hospital would appeal the jury verdict. A judge would eventually roll the jury's award back to $50,000 to keep it in line with what is usually paid out for a child's death. Plus, it would take years to see any of the money. Dollar wise, going to trial won't make much difference to the end result."

"And there's an even better reason to settle this case before the inquest begins: If there's any outstanding litigation, the hospital has an excuse not to be forthcoming when its witnesses testify. It'll be afraid that if it admits its employees did something wrong, that admission would be used in a lawsuit and it would end up having to pay out more money. If you take that excuse away, there's no reason for the hospital not to be completely truthful at the inquest."

Or so we thought.

Accordingly, a mediation between us and the Hospital for Sick Children was scheduled for September 30, 1999, at the downtown ADR Chambers. ADR Chambers is a for-profit business specializing in alternative dispute resolutions such as mediations, arbitration, and private appeals. Its staff consists of eminent lawyers and retired judges; our mediator was a former Court of Appeal judge, highly credentialed and well-respected, according to Frank.

Both sides in the mediation prepare an information package—a mediation brief—explaining the case from its own perspective, so the mediator can familiarize him or herself in advance with all of the issues. The hospital's position was that in spite of its nurses having made two "inadvertent" errors—not activating the doctor's orders and disabling the respiratory alarm on the monitor—they provided conscientious nursing care in every other respect. Lisa was perfectly fine all night long, the brief continued, and had normal vital signs. She died suddenly through no fault of the hospital, but it would nevertheless agree to accept 50% of the responsibility. The brief also described

Lisa's previous medical history at length, stressing how Lisa's pain was "non-organic", i.e. in her head.

Our inquest brief was much more to the point. Frank summarized the facts and then had a page entitled "Grossly Objectionable Discrepancies with Respect to Lisa's Care". It had two columns, the "hospital's version" and the "plaintiff's version". Under the plaintiff's column, Frank wrote things like "this is a complete and utter fabrication" and "the nurse is either mistaken or she is falsifying the records and lying". Patrick Hawkins strenuously objected to Frank's calling his nurses liars, but the mediation nonetheless went ahead as planned.

Bill and I didn't care about the money, and we didn't want to have to sit down and smile at people who we felt were responsible not only for her death, but for covering up the truth and protecting those who were culpable. We were hurting and I think we wanted the hospital to hurt too, so why should we settle and make it easier for them?

"I just want to let you know," I told Frank, "that I won't sign anything if they want me to be quiet and not talk about what happened." "Don't worry, they won't try that," he answered. "And if they do, you just won't sign."

He also warned me before we went in to let him do the talking. "No matter what they say, you have to be quiet." He was speaking to Bill as well as to me, but he knew I was the one who needed to be cautioned. I promised not to say anything.

We sat down at a boardroom table, Frank, Bill and I on one side, the mediator at the head of the table, and three strangers on the other side. Patrick Hawkins introduced himself and the people on either side of him: to his right was Dr. Jean Reeder, the Hospital for Sick Children's Chief of Nursing, and on his left was a representative of HIROC, the hospital's insurer. Hawkins seemed relatively pleasant, which surprised me considering how offended I was by his mediation brief. He expressed his condolences, although he did not apologize.

Jean Reeder began speaking first, explaining all the nursing area changes made at the hospital subsequent to Lisa's death. I disliked her the minute she spoke, finding her to be insincere and condescending. Her smile was forced and thoroughly artificial.

She read from a shopping list. Barely looking up, she recited that they—I wasn't sure which "they" she was referring to—had learned from their mistakes, improved the process, reinforced and strengthened Pain

Service protocols, reinforced the quality of documentation, decreased the ratio of nursing staff to patients... She went on at length, as if she were addressing a board meeting about financial reports. Not once did she say she was sorry or even extend her condolences.

Reeder agreed that the nursing care provided to Lisa had been substandard, but then proceeded to explain how it wasn't so bad after all. The nurses inadvertently neglected to check Kidcom, she said. They did fail to monitor Lisa's condition and vital signs, but there was selective monitoring. They didn't do a pain score or a sedation score, because Lisa was in pain and they wanted to let her sleep. In hindsight, that was a mistake in judgment, but for the most part, pulse and respirations were monitored.

She said, "Why punish people for innocent mistakes?"

I had been pinching myself to stay quiet as Reeder went through her notes. But calling what those negligent nurses did "innocent mistakes" was outrageous. My face and neck were beet red with anger. Bill and I will never forget or forgive those words.

She said the nurses had been assessed, but did not elaborate. Had they been fired? Disciplined? Suspended? After she finished her spiel and I calmed down a bit, I asked her what the results of the assessments were. Instead of answering the question, all she said was the nurses had learned from this and they now knew what to do. I was about to tell Reeder she wasn't answering my question, but the mediator was way ahead of me. He interrupted her and said I was asking what the results of the assessment of their work were, not what they had learned. Reeder mumbled the nurses were still working there, leaving me to understand that nothing had been done.

I asked her how much work experience Lisa's primary nurse had, and she answered that Ruth Doerksen had been nursing since 1984. Positive she wasn't being truthful, I shouted out angrily, before I had a chance to think, "That's impossible! You're telling me that Ruth Doerksen has been around for fifteen years? Lisa's nurse didn't even look old enough to have graduated!"

Patrick Hawkins spoke to Reeder, "She must be confusing Ruth with Anagaile." To me he said, "Anagaile Soriano has only been at the hospital for about six months."

This did not make sense. Could he have been mistaken? According to the records, Lisa's nurse was Ruth Doerksen, but the one who acted as if she was Lisa's nurse looked like she was sixteen years old and not a veteran of fifteen years. Hawkins had just told me the young one was not Lisa's nurse, and was not the one who claimed to have attached a monitor to Lisa when she arrived on the floor. If the other woman had been Lisa's nurse, why hadn't she ever looked at or spoken to me? I knew the answer as soon as I asked myself the question: she had been on the ward back when Lisa had been there months earlier. Although she never took care of Lisa, she knew her by reputation—the patient with the psychosomatic problem and her demanding mother. Although we didn't know Ruth Doerksen, she knew about us. She did not want to take care of Lisa and she did not want to have anything to do with me. That was why she hadn't read the orders. That was why she had deliberately neglected Lisa. And that was why Lisa was dead.

Hawkins took over from Reeder and outlined the hospital's position, going on at length about how the doctors found Lisa's problems to be non-physiological. He said that even the doctors in Boston had trouble discovering what was wrong with her, quoting part of a sentence from Dr. Wilder's report completely out of context. Frank once again saw my clenched fists and red face, and warned me to keep quiet.

Hawkins no longer seemed pleasant, he seemed hateful. It wasn't only the cruel things he was saying, it was the way he said them. He was not the experienced politician who charmed you even while making what you knew were empty promises, but the snake-oil huckster who made you shiver with suspicion and want to run away.

The mediator was not impressed with Hawkins's comments. He curtly told him that none of this had anything to do with Lisa's death and to get to the point. Hawkins got to the point, telling the mediator it was Dr. Wright's opinion that Lisa's vital signs at 5 and 6 a.m. were acceptable, and Dr. Schily was of the same view. Dr. Schily had said he got a report from the nurses, and there had been no need from his perspective for action.

Hawkins was skilled at twisting the truth. Dr. Wright had never looked at Lisa's chart when he wrote that her vital signs were acceptable and had relied exclusively on what Doerksen had told him. Schily didn't know that action was required, because the report he got from the nurses was both inaccurate and incomplete.

Again the mediator showed how astute he was. He had seen the flowchart showing the change in Lisa's heart rate from 72 up to 134, and asked Hawkins what he had to say about that. Hawkins answered that doctors Wright and Schily did not explain what accounted for the rapid pulse increase.

Hawkins told the mediator that they were unable to get any more information from Dr. Schily, since he had left the country; Hawkins thought he was in Israel. I was still sorting out which of the two nurses was which, but I was positive Hawkins was wrong on this point. Dr. Schily was German and had probably gone back to practice somewhere in Europe.

The mediator turned to Dr. Reeder for an explanation. She had no answer for Lisa's heart rate increase either. This was outside her scope of practice, she said; she hadn't been on the floor doing direct nursing in a long time.

She did say that she would have been watching the heart rate and would have continued to monitor the child, just as the nurses did. Not once did she ever refer to Lisa by name; it was always "the child". She would have called the physician, just as Anagaile did. She allowed that she might have been more assertive with the physician than Anagaile was.

Hawkins picked up the narrative. He discussed the Corometric monitor, stating there could be no dispute about Lisa being on one. The orthopaedic resident said he saw patches on Lisa's chest when he found her without vital signs, and the clinical nurse said there was a monitor in the room with its respiratory alarm turned off. Witnesses after the fact would confirm there was a monitor, Hawkins continued. It was not the hospital's fault that the monitor hadn't been kept so it could be inspected or studied, it was the coroner's fault for not telling anyone to set it aside.

Then Hawkins went into his main argument. Lisa was fine until sometime after 6:00 a.m., after which time something catastrophic happened. "We'll never know what it was," he said, "but all the research shows that once a cardiac arrest has occurred in a child, the odds of survival are very low."

Frank stated our position. Lisa's vital signs were not normal, and neither the doctor nor the nurses took appropriate action. Lisa's nurses did not read the doctor's orders, and did not follow standard hospital protocols. Notwithstanding our differences vis-à-vis the Corometric monitor, Lisa had not been placed on a pulse oximeter as ordered. The Corometric monitor—if there was one—did not alarm when Lisa's heart stopped, and the hospital was unable to provide a reasonable explanation. Had Lisa been monitored appropriately, she would not have died.

In addition, none of the research Hawkins was citing was relevant, because it all measured survival rates of children who had suffered traumatic injuries or had a terminal illness. There was no research into the survivability of healthy children, because healthy children did not have cardiac arrests.

The mediator did his work. We waited in another room while he spoke to the hospital and its insurer. Then he came and spoke to us, told us how much they were willing to offer, and got our response. After several hours of this, an agreement was reached. I started to cry, but wiped my eyes quickly. Now that my daughter's life and death had conclusively been reduced to dollars and cents, I was expected to sign documents to confirm it.

Bill and I had previously agreed we would not take a single penny of what we called the hospital's blood money for ourselves. One third of it would be set aside to cover what we estimated would be Frank's legal fees for the inquest, one third was put into a fund for the boys to receive when they were older, and one third was put into an annuity with a payment to be made each year for the next 30 years. The payment date would be November 20th, Lisa's birthday, and we would donate it all to a charity in her name.

We signed. When we were back in the conference room, Frank asked, only half-jokingly, if the hospital would also pay his fees for the upcoming inquest. Hawkins answered, "Why should we pay so you can beat us up?"

Frank asked me if there was anything else I wanted to say or have the hospital do. I said I wanted a meeting with the orthopaedic surgeons who had cared for Lisa after she broke her leg, not to complain but to discuss the abysmal care she had received and to work with them to improve things for the next patient with RSD. Hawkins initially said he could not arrange this since the doctors were not employees of the hospital,[4] but after a discussion with Reeder they decided such a meeting could be arranged after all. They probably hoped that by giving me what I wanted, I might consider calling off the inquest.

"How could that be?" I asked Frank afterwards. "Once the decision is made to hold an inquest, would the coroner's office call it off just because I asked them to?" "The hospital seemed pretty sure you could do it," suggested Bill. Frank told us, "Inquests are very expensive, and the government picks up the tab. If you didn't want one, the coroner's office would be very happy to cancel it."

Reeder's later recollection of the mediation was inaccurate and self-serving. In response to my subsequent complaint against her to the College of Nurses of Ontario, the nurses' professional regulatory body, she denied ever making the statement "why punish people for innocent mistakes".[5] As for the meeting the hospital agreed to arrange with the physicians after the mediation—in her view, that was entirely her idea. As she put it, "In an attempt to assure the Shores that the clinical leaders in the hospital had also taken this seriously, I offered to set up a meeting for them to meet directly with the Chiefs of Surgery and Anaesthesia."[6]

The next day, Frank got a phone call from Hawkins confirming that a meeting had been set up in four days time with Dr. Lawrence Roy, the Chief of Anaesthesia and head of the Pain Service, and with Dr. John Wedge, Chief of Orthopaedics.

"I guess they're really worried about me, aren't they?" I marvelled. "Children wait six months to see a specialist at the hospital, and I get to meet the department heads in a few days. They must be completely terrified about this inquest. If they knew I had no intention of calling it off, I bet they wouldn't be so accommodating."

Frank and Bill agreed.

Thinking about this meeting, I felt it was very important to come across as articulate and credible. If I were a high-ranking department head, what would it take to convince me that what was being presented had merit? The answer was simple—I would want to see logical arguments, well supported by facts.

I was determined to make an effective presentation. This meeting was not going to be about Lisa's death—I did not hold these doctors directly responsible—but about Lisa's life. I needed to show them the nature of the poor care that their staff had provided. If I could get them to understand that, then perhaps they would be willing to implement some changes to ensure Lisa's story would never be repeated.

I put together a binder. The first section contained the speech I had presented several months earlier at the Canadian RSD Network conference, which described much of the poor treatment Lisa had received at the Hospital for Sick Children. I added some medical records and doctor's letters to substantiate what I was saying: the radiologist's report that wrongly concluded that Lisa definitely did not have RSD, notes showing the Sick Kids' psychiatrist's failure to write up his assessment of Lisa, and the letter from the Boston psychologist stating that Lisa had no psychological problems. Finally, I enclosed several peer-reviewed research papers, including the one written by the physicians in Boston that showed why the radiologist's analysis was incorrect.

I asked Frank to come, just in case. On October 5, 1999, Bill and I went to the hospital for our meeting. We had arranged to meet Frank in the atrium, the airy open central area of the hospital. We were early, and sat on a bench to wait for him. I wanted to scream and run out of there, but instead leaned against Bill and started to cry. If Frank hadn't walked in just at that moment I would have called this meeting off.

Once we left the atrium and went to Dr. Wedge's office, in an unfamiliar area of the hospital that held no memories, it was easier to control myself. After a few minutes wait, we were shown into a nearby room. Drs. Roy and Wedge were already there, as were Hawkins and Reeder. I wasn't surprised at seeing Hawkins—after all, I had brought my lawyer along, too—but I had not expected Jean Reeder.

The silence was ominous, as everyone waited for me to speak. No one smiled or even nodded politely. Hawkins and perhaps Reeder had coerced or cajoled two of the most senior and busiest physicians in the hospital to attend, on short notice, a meeting they definitely did not wish to attend, in the hope I could be placated and would agree to call off the inquest. Drs. Roy and Wedge were not happy.

I began by thanking them for coming, and said I was not there to discuss the events of October 1998, Lisa's death, or the upcoming inquest, but to talk about the medical care Lisa received in February and March of 1998.

The silence continued. I gave everyone a binder and asked them to read my speech, which I told them summarized the care Lisa received in those two months. It had been a good idea to do it this way, I thought to myself, given the hostility of my audience. They might have tuned me out altogether if I started talking, but at least they would read the speech.

After they had finished, I then referred them to other documents in the binders which showed some of the errors in Lisa's care. I didn't know enough to understand how to fix these problems, I told them, but I hoped they could make some suggestions.

The doctors seemed to become less hostile after they finished reading. Perhaps my speech had given them a sense of the profound devastation Lisa's death had wrought, or maybe they had been afraid to face me because they thought I planned to blame them. I may have been different than Hawkins and Reeder had made me out to be. Whatever the reason, a genuine conversation ensued, or so it seemed.

Dr. Roy advised that the hospital had just submitted a proposal to the government to fund a paediatric multidisciplinary pain management clinic, and gave me a copy of the proposal. He said it could take a year for a decision, and spoke of the short-term difficulties of attracting people to practice in this area. "Chronic pain is not glitzy," he told me, although one of their doctors had gone down to Boston for three weeks to study with the Pain Service people there.

Having learned from my speech the high esteem in which I held the Boston doctors, Dr. Roy asked what it was I liked best about Boston. Was it the specific doctor or was it the infrastructure of the group? I had to think about it, but decided it was the infrastructure that made it what it was–the individual practitioners were only one aspect of a cohesive, integrated team. As an example, I explained that even the ward nurses were experienced in dealing with children who had pain but no other symptoms, and they were all compassionate and caring–in stark contrast to Lisa's nurses on the surgical ward at the Hospital for Sick Children. I looked over to Reeder as I said that, but in order to soften the impact of my words I told her the Pain Service's nurse-practitioners at Sick Kids had been wonderful.

I suggested to the doctors that based on Lisa's experiences, they needed to improve their protocols and their education for Radiology, Orthopaedics, and Psychiatry. They appeared to agree.

I criticized the system that had allowed Lisa to be discharged from the hospital with prescriptions for Amitriptyline and Gabapentin, with the only follow-up care assigned to Orthopaedics. I told Dr. Wedge I was sure I knew more about Gabapentin than his orthopaedic surgeons did, and he agreed.

In reference to my description of the condescending and arrogant attitude of his surgeons, Dr. Wedge admitted that a "disproportionate" number of complaints of this nature were about orthopaedic surgeons. He asked for the names of the doctors with whom we had had problems, and I mentioned Drs. Hedden and Rang, and the fellow who had treated us so cruelly. Trying to balance my criticisms with praise where it was due, I took pains to talk about the one surgeon we had met in the Emergency Department who had been friendly and kind.

I believed Dr. Wedge was taking me very seriously. The fellow had long come and gone, but the other two doctors were house staff. He asked if they were equally to blame, or if one was a little more responsible than the other. I had not been expecting that question, but answered, "Dr. Hedden was blunter and more forthright in his opinions, while Dr. Rang resorted to gentle condescension and trite clichés." In other words, both were pretty bad. Dr. Wedge said he would take care of this matter internally. I could not tell if he really intended to do anything, but he sounded sincere.

Dr. Roy asked how I felt about Dr. Desparmet, the highly-regarded pain specialist doctor who had worked at the hospital for a short period of time to help set up its Pain Service. She had been the one who had given Lisa the epidural which had been so effective in relieving her pain, then refused to do a second one because she came to believe Lisa's pain was psychological. Still striving to be tactful, I told Dr. Roy I was sure she was very knowledgeable about pain, but wasn't sure how much experience she had with RSD. I also mentioned I had found her to be very arrogant. Dr. Roy said they had been planning to work with her, but in light of my experience they might reconsider.

I suggested to both doctors that they discuss Lisa's case during Grand Rounds, the educational lectures given regularly to medical and other hospital staff on a variety of subjects. Dr. Wedge thought that was a good idea, and I said I would be willing to attend and speak if he thought it would help.

Reeder discussed the hospital's proposed "river guide" system, where a nurse would guide patients and families through the system from start to finish. I told her I thought the idea was good, but that nurses took their cues from doctors. Such a system would not have helped us at all, since the nurses had followed the doctors' lead and treated Lisa as poorly as or even more poorly than the doctors themselves did. In order for this system to be effective, the guide needed to be someone outside of the medical and nursing staff, so families could have a sense they were being treated with objectivity. Dr. Roy agreed.

I told the doctors I'd like to know what changes would be made as a result of this meeting. Dr. Wedge suggested they get back to me in one month's time, but I said it would be better to wait until after the inquest.

Instantly, the atmosphere in the room changed. Bill had been sitting quietly and observing, and told me afterwards that it was as if a black thundercloud had just blown into the room. All signs of friendliness and collegiality vanished and were replaced by coldness and hostility. This entire meeting had been for no purpose other than to get me to call off the inquest. The minute they learned I had no intention of calling it off, they wanted nothing more to do with me.

Nobody at this hospital gave a damn about Lisa Shore. Nobody gave a damn about fixing some very real problems. Why was I going to all this effort? If another child like Lisa appeared tomorrow, he or she would be treated just as badly as Lisa was.

I never heard from either Dr. Wedge or Dr. Roy again.

PART TWO

November 1999 – February 2000

15

PREPARATIONS

Our dispute with the Province of Ontario continued. We had filed a claim to recover the $24,000 it had cost for Lisa's medical care in Boston, the Ontario Health Insurance Plan had turned us down, and we had appealed. I suggested to our lawyer that he advise OHIP that the coroner's office had called an inquest to investigate Lisa's death at the Hospital for Sick Children, as additional proof that Sick Kids had "messed up" in the care it had provided to Lisa.

The lawyer agreed, and made the phone call. He reported back that OHIP wanted to wait until after the inquest finished before making a final decision, "in case there was any evidence of malpractice on the part of the Boston doctors".

"What?" I yelled. "Don't those idiots ever read the newspapers or anything? Sick Kids mistreated her, so we were forced to go to Boston. The Boston doctors were the only ones who helped her! The inquest was called because of what happened at Sick Kids, not what happened in Boston!"

The lawyer agreed it was ridiculous, but counselled me to wait until the end of the inquest as OHIP had requested. He promised he would put pressure on them at that time, and told me to concentrate on getting through the inquest.

I kept in regular touch with my cousin, a Canadian who had moved to Israel more than twenty years earlier. He and I had been good friends when he lived in Toronto, and we had remained close. He had cried with me over Lisa's death, and I gave him ongoing updates on what had been going on since. He had just married, and I did not know much about his new wife except that she was a native-born Israeli and a cardiology nurse. During one of our conversations, my cousin mentioned in passing that one of the doctors who worked with his wife had once been at Sick Kids. The comment didn't register as particularly noteworthy, since many doctors from around the world come to the Hospital for Sick Children to work there for a year or so.

The next time I spoke to him, he told me this doctor had said he had heard something about Lisa's death while at Sick Kids, and wanted to know what was happening with the case. I still thought nothing of it, and told my cousin he was free to pass on to him whatever information he wanted.

But on our next phone call, he said this doctor knew a lot more than he had originally been willing to admit. Could this doctor have been working at Sick Kids when Lisa died? I remembered Hawkins saying that the doctor who cared for Lisa had gone to Israel. Although I still believed he had been wrong about that, perhaps this doctor had been friends with Lisa's doctor and had some valuable information to give us. More out of curiosity than anything else, I asked my cousin to try to learn more.

The doctor in Israel who worked with my cousin's wife eventually admitted the truth: he was Lisa's doctor, the one who saw her in the Emergency Department on October 21, 1998, and the one who gave her morphine. Had this been fiction, it would have been a very bad and wholly unbelievable plot development. The doctor who treated Lisa—a complete stranger to us—had been working in Toronto for only a short time, and then had left to work somewhere on the other side of the world. I have only one relative who lives outside of North America. And yet this doctor and my cousin's wife worked with each other at the same hospital in the same mid-sized town in Israel!

Bill, Frank, and I debated about what to do for a long time. Once Dr. Schily was outside of the province, the coroner's office could not compel him to return to testify. Unless he testified at the inquest, we would never hear his side of the story. The medical records showed that the nurse had called him at 4:00 a.m., when Lisa was near death, but he had not gone to see her. How could I convince Dr. Schily to come to Toronto when I held him partly accountable for Lisa's death?

My cousin discussed the inquest with Dr. Schily and convinced him to return. Dr. Schily had only one demand: we send him a letter that we would not hold him responsible or go after him in any way for Lisa's death.

We were not happy with this option, but Dr. Schily was far away and would never be held accountable for his actions no matter what we did or did not do. We wanted to hear his explanation of the events, hoping it would fill in some of the blanks about what had really happened the night of Lisa's death. Ultimately, the decision was simple: we were better off giving Dr. Schily "immunity" in exchange for his testimony, rather than not hearing from him at all. Frank drew up a release absolving him from all liability, and Bill and I signed it. Dr. Schily would be coming to Canada to testify at the coroner's inquest.

I remembered how Hawkins had brushed off mention of Dr. Schily during the mediation. He had told us the doctor was in Israel, confident he was beyond our reach and would never come back to Canada. If it weren't for the coincidence of a lifetime, Hawkins would have been right. He was in for quite a shock.

I spoke again with the mother of the child in the room next to Lisa, who reiterated her certainty that no monitor alarms had gone off the night Lisa died. She had obtained her son's medical records and allowed me to copy them. I took the relevant pages to my friend Sharon for a nursing review, and she was highly critical of what she saw. She discovered there were several different documents where nurses could record the administration of medications. If it's not all recorded in one easy-to-find place, Sharon warned, medication errors are more likely to happen. Drugs may be given as ordered and recorded on one piece of paper, and then repeated by someone else who is looking at a different piece of paper and doesn't realize they have already been given. She was also upset that the woman's son had been given morphine without the nurse having recorded any of his vital signs. In her view that was unacceptable nursing practice, because there should always be a current baseline to measure against before narcotics are administered in case the patient suffers any adverse effects.

According to the boy's nursing flowcharts, his vital signs were taken at 4:05 a.m. on October 22, 1998, by nurse Anagaile Soriano. But at that exact time, according to what Soriano had written on Lisa's chart, she was in Lisa's room taking some of her vital signs. There was one important difference, however: Lisa was near death and her vital signs were fading, and the other boy was healthy and sleeping soundly. Soriano went to the boy's room and took all of his vital signs, including his blood pressure, but despite Lisa's abnormal heart and breathing rates she did not bother to take Lisa's blood pressure. The hospital had already advised us in its deceitful response to our questions that the nurse did not take Lisa's blood pressure at 4:05 a.m. because she did not want to wake Lisa up. How was it that Soriano had no compunctions about taking the blood pressure of the healthy, sleeping eleven-year-old in the next room at precisely the same time?

There was more. Hours after Lisa's death, when the boy was placed on a monitor, his nurse noted it on his chart and recorded the monitor settings. A child his age has an average heart rate of between 70 and 100 beats per minute, and the nurse set the monitor to alarm if his heart rate reached 120. Lisa's nurse claimed she had set the monitor to alarm if Lisa's heart rate reached 180 beats per minute. Even if there really had been a monitor—which there hadn't—Lisa's heart rate when she came to the ward was 72 beats per minute. An alarm setting of 180 was so inappropriate that even a lay person would have realized it, yet the hospital tried to justify it by stating in its letter that this setting was "appropriate for a child her age".

I sent the boy's records to Dr. Cairns and advised him that the boy's mother was prepared to testify.

The coroner's office informed us that Margaret Browne, an assistant Crown attorney with about twenty years' experience, would be working with the coroner at the inquest. Frank called her and introduced himself. Margaret told him she had read up on the case and she agreed that the nurses were lying. Frank said he planned to come down hard on them, but Margaret forcefully responded there wouldn't be much left for him to cross-examine by the time she finished with them. We were sure that with the help of lawyers like her and Frank, the truth would emerge.

Frank was upset to learn that Hawkins would be representing both the hospital and Lisa's nurses at the inquest, terming it a serious conflict of interest. Having one lawyer represent them all would be bad for us too, he said.

This did not make sense. The opposite should be true: if something was bad for the nurses then it should be good for us, right? Wrong: if the nurses each had their own lawyers, then those lawyers would be trying to protect their clients. A lawyer often protects her client by trying to deflect blame onto others. The nurses' lawyer would attack the hospital and the doctors; the hospital would blame the nurses and the doctors; and the doctors would say that everything was the fault of the nurses and the hospital. Better still, if each of the two nurses got her own lawyer, they would go after each other. What better way for the truth to be revealed? "It would make my job very easy," Frank said. "All we'd have to do is sit back and watch."

What was likely to happen if only one lawyer acted for both the hospital and the nurses? For one thing, we would probably never hear the truth from anyone. We already knew the hospital's primary objective was to keep things quiet and deny any wrongdoing. The nurses would be encouraged to stick to the party line and everyone's story would be suspiciously identical. None of the nurses would tell the truth to exonerate herself, because she could only do so by implicating the other nurse and/or the hospital. The hospital, who was paying all the bills, would never allow that to happen.

A second problem with having only one lawyer was what would happen if the nurses suddenly realized they weren't getting effective representation. If they decided to do something about it in mid-inquest, which they were rightfully entitled to do, a long adjournment would ensue while waiting for their new lawyers to prepare their cases. If the inquest was already well underway, the new lawyers would ask that it be cancelled and a new one called. Dr. Schily was coming to testify but only reluctantly; we doubted we would be able to get him to come back a second time.

Starting and stopping the inquest, only to start all over again at a later date, would be emotionally painful, and our legal expenses—we had put money aside from the settlement to cover approximately two weeks worth of fees—would more than double. We resolved to try and let the nurses know they would be better off getting their own lawyers. Frank contacted Margaret Browne in the hope that she might be able to pass this information on. We also spoke to doctors, nurses, and friends of doctors and nurses, thinking the hospital's internal rumour mill might help spread the word.

Every document that one party in a legal matter sends to another party must also be sent to every other involved party. When I sent the information about the mother in the next room to Dr. Cairns, a copy also went to Hawkins. If the mother testified that no alarms sounded the night of Lisa's death, it would prove that Hawkins' clients, the nurses, were lying. He could not allow this, so he told the coroner that since the mother was not a witness to any of the events, her evidence would be of no assistance to the jury and he would take action should she be called to testify. Hawkins must have hoped that in a he-said, she-said contest of credibility between his nurses and me, the jury would believe the nurses, as long as there was no third party to corroborate what I said.

Frank responded in his usual forthright manner. If the nurses were to tell the truth, he wrote to Hawkins, their testimony would not need to be impeached. If they stuck to their ludicrous story, they would be impeached and shown to be liars; the choice was entirely their own.

Dr. Cairns called a pre-inquest meeting for November 3, 1999, a few days before the inquest was scheduled to begin, to provide everyone with relevant documents and to address any administrative or other issues that had arisen. We asked Frank if we could attend the meeting with him, and he said that would be fine. However, judging by the glances thrown our way by some of the lawyers when they saw us walk in, this was not usual practice.

We already knew Dr. Cairns, Hawkins, and the two police officers who had taken our statement several months earlier. We were introduced to Margaret Browne, who we had only spoken to by phone, and to the lawyer representing the doctors.

Much of the meeting centred on the inquest's logistics. It was moderately interesting, but most of the conversation could have been distilled into a short memo. For example, the courtroom was booked for two weeks, but one day was a statutory holiday, and Dr. Cairns would be unavailable on another day, so did the parties involved think we could finish the inquest in eight days? (They did.)

Then the matter of the other mother as a potential witness came up. Hawkins repeated his position that her testimony was not relevant, adding that if she were to be called, we would have to call all the other people on the ward and get their medical records too. He told Dr. Cairns he would object if the coroner called her as a witness. Dr. Cairns decided to have the police interview the woman and deferred his decision until the inquest. If she was subpoenaed, Hawkins would have to make his objections in court and Dr. Cairns would rule on it at that time.

The contentious issue of Hawkins' representation of both the hospital and the nurses was also addressed. Dr. Cairns, Margaret, and Frank each told Hawkins he had a serious conflict of interest, but Hawkins said his clients were content to have him represent them all. The lawyers pressed the point and Hawkins became angry. He muttered something about going to Divisional Court,[1] which would significantly delay the inquest, interfere with everyone's schedule, and make things more difficult for all participants. The matter was dropped.

When the group began considering the order of witnesses, Dr. Cairns explained that Dr. Schily would be testifying right at the beginning as that was the only time he was available to come in from Israel. Hawkins immediately objected. If Dr. Schily was appearing out of order, then the nurses should also be able to testify out of order right after him.

Dr. Cairns politely but firmly explained that it couldn't be helped about Dr. Schily going first, but he wanted the jury to learn more about the various issues before he would allow any other key witnesses to testify. Hawkins did not take the hint and refused to drop the subject. He argued that like Dr. Schily, his nurses had busy schedules, other commitments, and so on. Dr. Cairns did not appreciate this attempt to circumvent the process and curtly told Hawkins that if the nurses were subpoenaed by the coroner's office, they had better show up exactly when and where they were told to.

I initially thought Hawkins was slow-witted, because he seemed unable to read the obvious and realize when it was best to be quiet. On reflection, however, there was purpose to his obstinacy: If the nurses testified after Dr. Schily but before the jury was "up to speed", the jurors would not be in a position to notice all of his clients' inconsistencies. With luck, the other lawyers would be similarly snowed, and the nurses would escape rigorous scrutiny under cross-examination. If Hawkins acted like an obstinate pain in the rear, then maybe the coroner or the other lawyers might give in to his demands, if only to shut him up. I figured Hawkins must have used this tactic successfully in the past. One thing was clear: he had not endeared himself to anyone in the coroner's boardroom.

16

THE INQUEST BEGINS

We didn't know what to expect from this inquest. We knew what we wanted: to learn the truth about why Lisa had been left to die. The medical reason was no mystery, at least in our minds; it was a reaction to the morphine. We wanted to know how the nurses would explain not following the doctor's orders, and how they would justify recording Lisa's deteriorating vital signs without doing anything to save her. Would they finally decide to tell the truth about the monitor or would they continue to lie?

One thing I was sure of: the hospital wanted as little publicity as possible. I, on the other hand, thought the best way to have the hospital be held accountable was to keep the inquest in the public eye. Just before it was scheduled to begin, I sent e-mails and faxes to every local television station and newspaper reminding them about it. I tried to get their attention by telling them that hospital employees would be exposed as liars. Although that was the truth, I'm sure I must have sounded like a crank. Frank, a veteran of several inquests, had warned me that the media was very fickle. They'll come on the first day, he said, and come back on the last day. The hard part is to get them interested enough to come back on the second, third and fourth days.

Coroner's court was a sad and dreary place, perfectly representative of its focus on death. The waiting area's 1960-era seats had permanent indentations from the posteriors of the countless lawyers, families, spectators, and reporters who had attended previous inquests. The potted plants—or what might have once been potted plants—would have made excellent kindling, since the only thing remaining in the pots was dried brown sticks. Fire trucks regularly emerged from the fire station across the street with sirens blaring, and the noise would momentarily block out all attempts at conversation. And if the building wasn't charmless enough, its architects must have designed it in the summertime and forgotten to compensate for the winter winds. Gusts of bitter November air blasted into the lobby area each time the front doors opened.

The sign on the wall announced bluntly that the Lisa Shore inquest was assigned to Courtroom A, a brutal reminder that the name of the child we loved was now a description of a legal proceeding. Courtroom A was the smaller of the two inquest rooms. It looked just as one might imagine a courtroom should, with a witness box, jury seats, and a desk for the court reporter. In front was the coroner's desk, higher than anything else in the room. Although the jury members are drawn from the regular jury pool, there are only five jurors at a coroner's inquest instead of the twelve required for a criminal trial.

We entered from the back of the room. There were several rows of worn, squeaky seats available for spectators, the kind found in the dingy, small town movie theatres of yesteryear. Directly in front of them were four tables for lawyers.

Hawkins brought an assistant with him. The lawyer for the doctors initially came alone but soon brought along someone to help her. Lawyers often do that, especially if the case is complex and the client has deep pockets and can afford to pay. This assistant may be anything from an associate who will actively take part in the proceeding, to a recently minted lawyer, articling student or law clerk; the person might cross-examine witnesses or be little more than a glorified gopher who carries the files. I was going to be Frank's assistant. As he later told me, he could have brought someone from his firm to help him, but aside from having to charge me more, who knew the case and the documentation better than I did? I sat down at the lawyers' table beside Frank, with my briefcase and notepad.

I could tell that having a client sit in the lawyers' area was unusual, but it wasn't against any rules or the courtroom constable, a stickler for decorum, would have disallowed it. Since I was sitting in clear view of the witnesses, the coroner, and the jury, I knew how important it was to appear calm and unemotional. I was determined that no one would see me cry publicly, a promise I was able to keep until I was in the witness box trying to talk about Lisa.

There seemed to be an unwritten rule that the deceased's family and supporters got automatic entitlement to the first row of spectator seats immediately behind the lawyers. Next behind my family sat many nurses and other hospital employees. For the first day of the inquest, the media had come out in droves exactly as Frank had predicted, and the reporters stood crowded along the back and sides of the courtroom.

I did not know coroner's court had very specific rules of conduct, administered by the aforementioned constable, who shouted out "all rise" whenever the coroner entered. We all dutifully rose, remained standing until the coroner sat and the constable told everyone to be seated. Each morning and evening we also heard him intone, "Oy-yez, oy-yez, oy-yez," court being either in session or adjourned for the day. The phrase seemed pretty silly, as if we were in Britain in the eighteenth century, but as time went on we became more and more used to the formalities. We became so well trained that we all stood up long before we heard the constable's "all rise".

The jurors filed in first. They were a diverse group in gender, age, and nationality, truly representative of our multicultural society. Dr. Cairns, the presiding coroner, followed the jury in. Although we knew him to be friendly and pleasant, he seemed very intimidating looking down at us from his raised desk.

I wasn't frightened, but I was tense. It didn't feel real; my daughter wasn't really dead. I was only dreaming that I was sitting in a courtroom at a coroner's inquest. I started negotiating with myself: What was this place? I didn't belong here! OK, maybe by some peculiar accident I did belong here, but only to watch, with no direct involvement. All right, I was here to do more than watch, but I was only peripherally involved. Then I would tell myself that Lisa was dead and forever gone, and I was here to find out why she had died. And then I would refuse to accept that and would start over feeling like it was all a dream.

Dr. Cairns began the proceedings by telling the jury about Lisa's background and her death, sticking to the facts that were known and accepted by all. He explained in general terms who would be testifying and what the role of the jury was. The inquest served three functions, he said: to ascertain the facts relating to the death—the who, when, where, cause of death and the manner of death; to initiate a community response to preventable deaths; and as a means to satisfy the community that no death would be overlooked, concealed or ignored.

Lisa's paediatrician, Dr. Gallant, was the first witness, and her testimony was brief and factual. She explained about Lisa contracting RSD, how she had supported our decision to go to Boston, and how she worked with the American doctors to ensure Lisa could obtain locally whatever medications she needed.

Expecting the hospital to put forward its previously expressed view that Lisa or I had psychiatric problems, I passed a note to Frank. He then asked Dr. Gallant, "In terms of dealing with the parents, that's Bill Shore and Sharon Shore, did you ever find them to be in any way unusual, overly concerned, in any way nuts or anything like that, in terms of the way they were concerned about their children?" She answered, "No. I found that this family was very appropriate in regards to when they called the office, if it were for a telephone question or for a visit; there were no inappropriate visits or over-reactive visits. Everything was really quite straightforward."

Dr. Markus Schily, the Emergency Room doctor who had come in from Israel expressly to testify, was called next. I wondered how he would try to justify his role in Lisa's care.

He had been born and raised in Germany, but had emigrated to Israel in 1989. He completed his medical residency in Israel and worked at a hospital there as a staff anaesthetist. He had come to Toronto for one year only to do a fellowship in Paediatric Anaesthesia at Sick Kids.

He explained how the anaesthetists, in addition to their usual duties during surgery, were also in charge of providing pain control for the hospital's patients. While doing these shifts, they were known as "pain fellows" working on the Pain Service.

Dr. Schily described the evening of Oct. 21, 1998 in the Emergency Department, and his recollection of Lisa moaning in severe pain. He explained that he put Lisa on a PCA morphine pump to try to relieve her pain, hoping this temporary measure would suffice until the doctors who had treated her in the past could assess her the next morning.

At Frank's request, in preparation for the inquest, I had taken the most important of Lisa's medical records and enlarged them to 3 x 4 foot cardboard blow-ups. Frank explained that he had done this before at another inquest, and it had been well-received by the jury and the coroner. As Dr. Schily started talking about the morphine pump and the instructions he had written on Lisa's Emergency Department chart, we put the blow-up of those instructions on an easel. The jury could see it easily, as could most of the audience. Was it ever impressive, and very effective!

Dr. Schily explained that the hospital computer system was not available for Emergency Department patients, and that any doctor's orders for those patients had to be handwritten. Only if the patient was officially admitted to the hospital would the doctor enter orders for that patient into the computer system.

Dr. Cairns ordered a twenty-minute recess. Cameras were not allowed in the building, and reporters were not supposed to conduct interviews there. The rules were strictly enforced for the camera operators, who were forced to wait outside in the cold, but the reporters conducted their business freely in the foyer. As we exited the courtroom, the waiting media surrounded us. I would eventually get used to the microphones, video cameras, and tape recorders thrust in my face, but it was quite unnerving at first. All along, we had wanted the media to pay attention to us. Now that we had their attention, we planned to be as helpful as possible so they would keep coming back. Dutifully, Frank and I said a few words; Bill preferred to stay in the background.

Among the many things we learned about the way the media works was that whenever one sees people on the news walking in and out of courthouses, those scenes are almost always staged, except where the accused is trying to hide his face from the cameras. Bill and I dutifully did several entrance/exit performances, feeling foolish but trying to look serious. No one from the hospital spoke to the press or posed for pictures, so we were the only game in town.

After the break, Dr. Schily went through his hand-written Emergency Department orders. It was just a single page with only nine lines of information, including the dosage, lockout period, and other safeguards for the PCA pump. The fifth line, right in the middle of the page, had only three words: "SEE KIDCOM ORDERS". Dr. Schily explained that nurses all knew to check the computer for orders, but he had wanted to be very thorough and therefore had added this extra reminder. He described the Kidcom system, stating that no matter where in the hospital a patient was sent, staff knew to check Kidcom and see what had been ordered for that patient.

He told the jury he ordered two monitors for Lisa: an apnea monitor, known in the hospital as a Corometric monitor, to measure heart and breathing, and a pulse oximeter to measure the amount of oxygen in her blood. The apnea monitor has leads which are attached to the patient's body, like an EKG machine, while the oximeter clips on to the patient's finger. Dr. Schily elaborated that he did not like using the apnea monitor, but resigned himself to it because that was the way Sick Kids did it. In his opinion, the oximeter was a much better tool as it would sound an alarm as soon as the oxygen levels in the blood started to drop, when problems were starting. In contrast, by the time the Corometric machine alarmed, it usually meant the patient was already in trouble.

What was Dr. Schily's explanation for not coming to see Lisa at 4:00 a.m. when the nurse paged him, a visit that probably would have saved her life? According to his testimony, the nurse never once told him anything was wrong!

He said that when he spoke to the nurse he had taken it for granted his monitoring orders had been followed and the nurse was giving him an accurate report of Lisa's condition. She had reported that Lisa's vital signs were okay and that she was arousable. To him, arousable was the most important word because it meant Lisa could be woken up, which in turn meant her brain was working and she was not suffering from any of the potentially life-threatening side effects of morphine. It was vitally important that a child on morphine be awakened at different times during the night to have his or her level of sedation assessed, he testified. It was better to wake the child rather than taking a chance on having, as he put it, "a disaster".

He told the jury he offered to come down to the hospital, but the nurse had replied it wasn't necessary. Dr. Schily said he told her to check Lisa's vitals, check her saturations, and keep a close eye on her, and that if the nurse changed her mind and wanted him to come in she should call him back.

He was determined to show that the nurse had not been frank with him, and pleaded for the court's understanding. "May I explain my side? I wasn't next to the nurse. I can assume many things. I was at home in the bed and I have my recollection of today, and my recollection is that I heard something global about vital signs, and I don't recollect anything else. You also have to understand that as I pointed out before, we have our certain reflexes. If I would have heard one of the vital signs is wrong, is outstanding, is pathological, I believe that even at 4:00 a.m., I would have asked more, and I would have asked how high the saturation was, what is the blood pressure. So this is my recollection, that I didn't get these details."

He admitted he had been shocked to find out afterwards that his orders hadn't been read and Lisa's vital signs had not been taken regularly. Frank said to him, "In fact, shocked may be an understatement, right?" Dr. Schily quietly answered, "Oh, yeah."

Court was adjourned for the day. Dr. Schily was directly behind me, alone, as his lawyer stood nearby chatting with another lawyer. I knew he was about to return to Israel, and I wanted to say something to him before he left. I whispered to him in my grade-school Hebrew, thanking him for coming and telling him he had done a very good thing. We were both near tears as we shook hands. He answered me in Hebrew, telling me how truly sorry he was, and that it had been very important for him to come back. He pulled his kipah—the Jewish skullcap worn by observant Jews—out of his pocket, put it on his head, and left the court.

17

THE SMALL STUFF

The two people who appeared to be in charge of managing the hospital's inquest strategy were Dr. Jean Reeder, the Chief of Nursing, and Marion Stevens, a grey-haired, severe-looking older woman who was the hospital's Risk Manager as well as the co-ordinator of its misleading letter. Hawkins frequently went off to confer privately with the two of them during breaks.

The same group of nurses that had attended the first day of the inquest came back the next day, but not one of them ever looked at me directly. I recognized Anagaile Soriano in their midst, the younger of Lisa's two nurses. I knew the other nurse must have been there too, but since she had never spoken to me and never registered in my mind I had no idea what she looked like.

I wondered if these nurses intended to show up every day. Were they all generously using up two weeks of their vacation time to be there for their friends, or was the hospital paying their salaries as well as the cost of hiring temporary replacements to cover for them while they were here? Dr. Reeder solved the mystery when she approached me that afternoon for a little chat. "I hope you don't mind that all these nurses are here," she said. I minded very much, but I only nodded brusquely. "I felt it was very important that the hospital show its support for our nurses."

"What about Lisa?" I thought angrily. "What about supporting us?" But I said nothing. In addition to the ten nurses who would eventually testify, about one dozen more would show up every day of the twenty-one day inquest, just one more expense in the huge sum of money the hospital would spend "to support its nurses".

Dr. Reeder would not speak to me again until almost two years later.

The hospital went to some bizarre extremes to keep its staff away from us. Although the lobby of coroner's court held about fifteen seats arranged in a square, no hospital employee ever sat down if so much as one member of our family or our friends were already seated there. Even more peculiarly, none of the women—and the hospital group was mainly female—ever used the ladies washroom at the courthouse. We guessed they might be going to the nearest other facility, across the street at the 'Y', but we couldn't understand the rationale. Were the strategists afraid we would somehow contaminate their nurses? I was the first to notice they were not using the bathroom during breaks, but once I pointed it out we all took perverse glee in imagining how much discomfort they must have been experiencing as a result of somebody's ridiculous idea.

The court reporter was good-natured and friendly, and we chatted frequently. There was coffee available to staff, but the rest of us had to trek in the bitter cold to the store down the street if we wanted any. The reporter felt sorry for us, and brought in coffee and cookies from home for everyone. She left them just outside the courtroom so you couldn't miss them as you walked out. They were for everyone, not only us; we saw hospital employees helping themselves, too. It was a thoughtful gesture that helped make the inquest experience just a touch less frigid, but some courthouse staff didn't like it and complained to their superiors. The court reporter was told in no uncertain terms to immediately stop doing this. Apparently some sanctimonious bureaucrat decided that the people attending a coroner's inquest—the friends and family of the deceased, witnesses, and lawyers—were not entitled to simple niceties such as coffee, even if it didn't cost the coroner's office anything. That petty act did much to cement my already low opinion of many of the employees of the coroner's office.

The court reporter was upset at what she felt was an unfair and arbitrary decision, but was even more concerned about the potential threat to her livelihood. Inquest court reporters are freelancers; there is no formal rotation system and they are hired at the discretion of the coroner. She was right to have been concerned, because even though she had done many inquests before, after that incident she was never called to work in that courthouse again.

18

A SURPRISE THEORY

The Emergency Department nurse was the next witness. She seemed to be the kind of competent nurse everyone would want taking care of them when they are sick.

Her testimony was straightforward and to the point. She was adamant that every child who left the Emergency Department to go to a ward had Kidcom computer orders input to the system. No doctor or nurse needed to call up to the ward nurses to remind them to check the Kidcom system, nor would a doctor be required to make a note in the file about it.

When she was asked whether nurses would know to automatically check the computer for orders in every single case, she tartly replied, "Well, they have no orders other than the Kidcom orders."

The nurse explained she had helped Dr. Schily set up the PCA morphine pump for Lisa in the Emergency Department, and then monitored Lisa's vital signs until she was transferred upstairs. She was still on duty when she heard the code called a few hours later. She ran to Lisa's room on Ward 5A with her resuscitation equipment, and noticed a Corometric monitor on a little shelf with its display turned inward facing Lisa. She distinctly remembered that the monitor was not on, although she noticed stickers—the patches which the monitor's leads are stuck on to—on Lisa's chest.

I was confused. She seemed like she was telling the truth, yet she had testified there was a monitor in the room. There couldn't have been! I relived that night over and over again, and I knew Lisa wasn't on any monitors that night. If she had been, alarms would have gone off before she died.

Before, I had been convinced that whoever said they saw a monitor in the room on the morning of Lisa's death was lying, but now I realized there had to be another explanation. We theorized that when the doctors found Lisa dead, Doerksen had rushed in with a monitor and left it on the shelf. That made sense except for one thing: with all the people who ran into Lisa's room when the code was called, it would have been easy for a nurse to bring a monitor into the room without being noticed, but virtually impossible for her to have attached the patches on to Lisa's body undetected. Our theory was flawed, although we believed we were getting closer to the truth.

As part of the resuscitation effort, an EKG monitor had been hooked up. That monitor is also attached with patches, and we thought the nurse may have simply been confused about which monitoring device the patches she saw were for.

Dr. Catre, the next witness, was one of the three orthopaedic residents who had come into Lisa's room on morning rounds, only to find her without vital signs. Since that was the extent of his involvement with Lisa, his testimony was brief. He too had seen a Corometric monitor in the room, he said, facing inwards towards Lisa, but it was not on.

This reinforced our conviction that Doerksen had managed to bring a monitor into the room without turning it on. But he also confirmed there were patches on Lisa's chest attached to the monitor leads for the Corometric, the one thing our theory couldn't explain or account for.

The reporters who attended had written feature stories about Dr. Schily and his claim that the nurses had not followed his orders. I was sure that once the nurses began to testify there would be plenty of revelations to hold the reporters' interest, but worried that the next few witnesses would prove so boring the media would disappear and never come back. The hospital's Director of Biomedical Engineering was scheduled next to explain about Corometric monitors. How would anyone get a story out of that, I wondered? We did not know this witness's testimony would be far from boring, and a harbinger of the many unusual and disturbing things that were to emerge from this inquest.

Stephan Bauer confidently strutted up to the witness box with an armful of diagrams and graphs. Hawkins requested he be the one to start off the questioning instead of the assistant Crown attorney who usually went first, as he was the most familiar with the Corometric monitor and could therefore best elicit appropriate information from the witness. It seemed fair and logical, and everyone agreed.

Hawkins helped Bauer run through his educational and employment background. Then he told the coroner that Bauer had a presentation ready, and asked if Bauer could be allowed to show it to the jury. Frank muttered under his breath to me, "I don't like this. There's something funny going on here."

Bauer launched into a detailed explanation of wave forms, standard algorithms, electrical signatures, ventricular contractions and block diagrams, pointing to his graphs to prove his points. He was unpleasantly smug, punctuating each sentence with a loud snap of his fingers. No one could understand anything he was talking about, but at least the annoying snapping kept everyone awake. Talk-SNAP! Talk-SNAP!

Frank was wary and growing angrier with each passing moment. I took Bauer to be a technocrat who loved his job so much he believed everyone else would find it as exciting as he did, but Frank was waiting for a bomb to drop, and it soon did.

Because Bauer's audience was dazed by his interminable, incomprehensible testimony and continuous finger snapping, no one except Frank noticed when he segued into a pseudoscientific theory that explained how a heart monitor could be fooled into thinking that it heard a heartbeat even when there was none. Bauer wanted the jury to know that the nurses' implausible version of events—that Lisa had been attached to a working heart monitor that inexplicably failed to alarm when her heart stopped—was indeed possible according to this new theory.

Frank leapt up and asked that the jury be excused. "This is outrageous!" he stormed, referring not to Bauer's well-rehearsed performance but to Patrick Hawkins, the lawyer who was responsible for it. "This is a theory that nobody has ever heard anything about. There are no expert reports that have been served on anyone. To come up with a theory that nobody, including the Chief Coroner's Office, the Deputy Chief Coroner or the Crown attorney has heard anything about in the middle of a coroner's inquest, for an experienced litigation lawyer like my friend, is outrageous." Looking over at Hawkins, he added, "Mr. Hawkins, we're in a courtroom, and that doesn't mean that we're in Alice in Wonderland or in Fantasyland. This is a sleazy, cheap trick."

The assistant Crown attorney spoke up. "I'm listening for the first time to this, but it's my understanding that an inquest should be helping to explain something, to lead towards recommendations; it's my understanding that it is different from a criminal or a civil trial because there are no adversaries. In my submission, Mr. Coroner, this looks like an adversarial tactic… We did not expect to be 'sandbagged' by this and I'm going to suggest also that if there's any more coming, could we please have that, too? … I would put on the record that the witnesses from Sick Children's Hospital, all of them, did not want to be interviewed by your officers. They did not wish to make a statement. They wished, instead, I guess, to come and sort of come up with something. We have no idea, yet, with the rest of the witnesses from Sick Children's Hospital what they intend to say, but I'm getting very worried now."

Hawkins was undaunted. "Following Lisa Shore's death, the coroner's office was given every opportunity to meet with staff at the Hospital for Sick Children, including staff at the Biomedical Engineering department. Every single question that was asked of them was answered; every single request for production that was ever made by the coroner's office was answered… Mr. Bauer is not under any circumstances offering an absolute answer to anything that happened, he was called upon to explain the Corometric monitor and that's what he is explaining, and if he takes you to the chart and if you look at the chart, that will explain exactly how this rhythm formation was interpreted by the monitor used during the cardiac arrest to show a heart rate. And so I repeat, I object most strongly to Mr. Gomberg's characterizations. I have complied with, my client has complied with all of its obligations under the *Coroners Act* in terms of providing information and answers to questions."

Dr. Cairns did not mince words. He was angry and told Hawkins, "What I do not appreciate is suddenly being absolutely bamboozled by something that we've had absolutely no indication, and this is not a trial, this is to try and look into a child's death, and as a result of looking into that child's death, make reasonable recommendations to try and prevent it in the future… If our office does not have the expertise to know of something that you know of, I would expect that an institution the size of the Hospital for Sick Kids and with their responsibility is at least going to make me aware of that information…

I must say, unless you've got a different explanation, I consider this an ambush of the process."

Dr. Cairns ordered that Bauer provide the coroner's office with a detailed written explanation of everything he wanted to testify about, including any and all theories on the Corometric monitor's functioning. Bauer would only be recalled when Dr. Cairns was satisfied his evidence would be understood by a jury and all the lawyers present.

Court was adjourned for two days. In the meantime, the hospital's theory that a heart monitor hooked up to a child might not work properly if the child's heart stopped provided good fodder for the press. This was a real dilemma for the hospital: it wanted to convince the jury that its nurses were telling the truth, but the only way to do this was to suggest that its equipment had malfunctioned. When parents of patients attached to one of the hospital's 133 similar monitors heard of their potential unreliability, they became frightened and angry.

Months earlier I had done some Internet research and found the manufacturer of the hospital's Corometric monitors, G.E. Marquette. We had hoped that upon realising that the upcoming coroner's inquest would be looking into the reliability of its equipment, it would want to become involved. If it were to review the records, it would surely come to the same conclusion that we had: the only reason the monitor failed to alarm was because no monitor had ever been used. It would want to protect its reputation, and by doing so, it would help prove that the nurses were lying. Our interests in this matter, although different, overlapped significantly.

A corporate press release from a year earlier had touted a multi-million dollar strategic alliance between the Hospital for Sick Children and G.E. Medical Systems, the pre-merger name of G.E. Marquette. Although the hospital was apparently willing to jeopardize this relationship rather than admit Lisa had received substandard care, the manufacturer did not seem overly concerned. After a lengthy conference call, it had declined to participate in the inquest. But that was before the introduction of a new theory by the Hospital for Sick Children that its Corometric monitors didn't work properly. We thought it was a good idea to contact G.E. Marquette a second time. Even though the inquest had already begun, court decisions have established that anyone whose conduct might be subject to implicit censure or criticism at an inquest is entitled to participate in it.[1]

We provided all the contact information to Margaret Browne and suggested that the coroner's office call the manufacturer, but based on our past experience with the coroner's office, we didn't wait for them to do it and made the call ourselves.

This time G.E. Marquette was much more receptive–and much more concerned. The newspaper accounts of Bauer's testimony were quite persuasive: The Toronto Sun wrote, "Coroner fumes over 'ambush'",[2] and the Globe and Mail reported, "Lawyer calls testimony 'outrageous' / Inquest into girl's death erupts at suggestion alarm may have been faulty".[3] The company decided to seek standing at the inquest.

The lawyer selected to represent G.E. Marquette at the inquest, Van Krkachovski, was a good lawyer and a decent person, according to Frank. This was great news, but like many good things, it came at a price. Several days of testimony had already been heard, and Dr. Schily had come from and returned to Israel. Would he need to testify again? Would the jury members be able to come back at a later date or would they have to drop out? Would we need to start all over again?

On Friday, November 12, 1999, we got our answers. G.E. Marquette's request for standing was granted. The inquest was postponed until January 2000 to allow the lawyer time to understand the issues, but he had agreed there was no need to call a new inquest. Each of the jurors was willing and able to return in January, and all parties were to be given transcript copies of the testimony to date. Krkachovski waived his right to cross-examine Dr. Schily, who would therefore not need to return from Israel.

19

IF THERE WAS A MONITOR

Stephan Bauer, much humbled after the dressing down he and Hawkins had received at the inquest, sent a letter to Dr. Cairns several days later listing three possible explanations for the monitor having failed to alarm: either someone had turned it off, an alarm failure occurred, or the monitor was receiving a sinus rhythm.

The first possibility was inconceivable. No one would dare suggest I had turned off Lisa's monitor. If Lisa's nurses had turned it off–which they denied–then they should be arrested and charged with manslaughter. Possibility number one was out of the question. There could not have been an alarm failure, because the hospital had tested each of its monitors within days of Lisa's death, and they were all found to be working properly. And Bauer himself had testified that if the machine's power was low, or if the leads came loose, the alarm would go off automatically. Since no alarms had ever sounded, the second possibility was eliminated.

The third explanation restated the crazy theory that had caused such a commotion at the inquest. We knew by now it really was a crazy theory, because Frank had spoken with his father, an internist in Montreal, and Dr. Cairns had spoken with other physicians. Everyone had roundly denounced it. In case there was any doubt, the matter was going to be discussed at the next meeting of the Coroner's Paediatric Death Review Committee, to be held on November 20th, on what would have been Lisa's twelfth birthday.

My friend Sharon pointed out that there is such a thing as "pulseless electrical activity" which can fool a heart monitor, but this could not be such a case. The EKG readings Bauer was referring to had only commenced about thirteen minutes after Lisa was discovered without vital signs. Even if she had died at the exact moment she was found, which none of us believed to be the case, her heart would not spontaneously give off any electrical activity thirteen minutes later.

The Committee decided the issue of the monitor was a "red herring", Dr. Cairns reported to us. Either the monitor found in the room was not attached to Lisa, or it was attached and not turned on. The Committee felt the cause of death was an adverse drug reaction, evidenced by the nursing flowsheet that clearly showed Lisa in respiratory distress at 2:50 a.m.

That left the nurses with a significant problem. I already knew they were lying, and now the evidence pointed to the same conclusion. It didn't matter if the monitor wasn't on or wasn't attached; both possibilities contradicted their version of events.

Frank felt Hawkins was protecting the nurses because he was afraid if they "came clean" and told the truth there might be criminal ramifications. I thought the hospital didn't really care about anyone except itself and believed that covering up the truth about a child's death was the best way to deal with the matter. Either way, it was abundantly clear why Hawkins did not want the nurses to have their own independent lawyer: it would be too risky for the hospital if it could not control the nurses' testimony.

The lawyers continued lawyering behind the scenes. The monitor's manufacturer considered withdrawing from the inquest, fully expecting the hospital would agree the monitor was not on when Lisa's heart stopped. If the monitor was not on, there could be no fault attributed to the equipment. After some thought, it decided that Krkachovski would attend the inquest but not play an active role unless necessary.

When Frank reported this to me, I told him he had better enlighten Krkachovski. Even if everyone agreed the monitor was off when Lisa died, it was still going to be attacked, just in a different way. The nurse had said she turned off the monitor's respiratory alarm because too many false alarms were going off; wasn't that an implied criticism of the equipment? Frank agreed and said he would let Krkachovski know.

As it turned out, Krkachovski took a surprisingly active role when the inquest resumed. Although he never actually said so, it was apparent he didn't like what the hospital was doing and he did his best to help us.

Before the inquest reconvened, another meeting was held at the coroner's office, this time to see if an agreement could be reached as to whether or not the monitor was on when Lisa died. Bill and I went but this time we were not allowed to sit in. We knew Frank would come out to discuss anything important, so we tried to wait patiently in the corridor.

Frank came and told us that he and the other lawyers had agreed on the following statement: "When Lisa died, the monitor was turned off".

I refused. "Absolutely not! By saying the monitor was 'turned off', the implication is that it was first turned on." Frank tried to downplay things, telling us that the crucial thing was the agreement the monitor was off. I stubbornly disagreed. "If the media report the monitor was turned off–and they will–then everyone who reads it will think there was a working monitor."

Frank got the message and said he'd see what he could do. The next time he emerged, the revised agreement was "the monitor was not on when Lisa died". I told him that was better, but not good enough. I still believed there had been no monitor in the room when Lisa died, and that the one found there had been brought in after her death.

The statement was amended again, and this time we accepted it: "If there was a Corometric monitor in the room, it was not on when Lisa Shore's heart stopped."

The parties also agreed that no alarms had ever gone off in Lisa's room, at least from the time the doctors had come in. Dr. Catre was prepared to swear to that. "Why is this even being discussed," I muttered when I heard. "Everyone at the hospital knew right from the start that no alarms had gone off. Why else did it test all its monitors to see if they were working properly?"

Dr. Cairns advised Hawkins that the Paediatric Death Review Committee had examined and thoroughly repudiated Bauer's theory about the monitor detecting electrical activity and being fooled into thinking there was a heartbeat, and suggested it would be best for Hawkins not to pursue it any further.

The inquest resumed on January 17, 2000, with Stephan Bauer testifying for the second time. Evidently chastened by his previous experience, he was very subdued.

He explained how the Corometric monitor worked. Attached to

the patient by three leads, it measured breathing and heart rate, and was designed to alarm if certain parameters were exceeded. Another witness would subsequently clarify how the monitor measured those parameters: it counted the seconds between breaths and not the actual number of breaths taken. If the respiratory alarm was set for 20, for example, the alarm would go off if the patient didn't breathe for twenty seconds. This concept was difficult for everyone in the courtroom to comprehend, but eventually we all understood the monitor was not measuring the number of breaths per minute but the time interval between those breaths.

The heart rate alarms made more sense. There were two alarm settings, high and low. If the heart rate went above the upper setting or below the lower one, the alarm went off. The breathing alarm could be turned off, as could the upper heart alarm, but the only way to disable the low heart rate alarm setting was to turn the machine off altogether.

The alarms could not be disabled accidentally. In order to change the settings or turn off any of the alarms that could be turned off, the monitor had to be turned upside down and a tool such as a key or scissors needed to be used to open a slot on its underside and access the dials.

The monitor's alarms would also go off if the leads become disconnected from the patient, or the machine was not plugged in and the internal battery ran low. Some people at the hospital believed Lisa had thrashed around in her sleep and become disconnected from the monitor leads, but they didn't realize that had that really happened an alarm would have gone off immediately.

And there was one more crucial thing. When the monitor was first turned on, it did a self-check and its alarm sounded for several seconds. I knew for sure the nurses had not attached Lisa to any monitors when she first arrived on the ward, but until then I couldn't be absolutely positive that they had not wheeled one in sometime in the middle of the night when I was asleep. Now I was certain that no one had ever turned a monitor on in Lisa's room. Even if I had been asleep, I would have woken up the moment the alarm sounded.

Had I learned anything of importance from the detailed explanation of how the monitor worked? Only that there was no logical explanation that could explain how a working monitor could fail to alarm when the patient's heart stopped. Everything that Stephan Bauer explained supported what I had been saying all along: Lisa was never placed on a monitor, and her nurses were responsible for her death.

20

THE NURSE-EDUCATOR

Mary Douglas, a Nurse-Educator at the Hospital for Sick Children, testified next. She claimed she had seen a monitor in Lisa's room on the morning of her death, and that she had checked its settings. Three weeks later, she wrote up a detailed recounting of, as she put it, the "5A Incident".[1] It stated that she had arrived at the hospital around the time the code had been called and had immediately gone over to see if she could help. She saw Ruth Doerksen crying, and listened as Doerksen asked, "why didn't the monitor go off"; "I left her on the monitor, why didn't it work"; "Why didn't I check her at 7, I always check all my kids at 7, I checked my other 4 but not her"; "I know I checked it, I set the heart rate limits to 50 and 160 <or 180, Douglas wasn't sure> and turned the apnea alarm off. I don't know why I turned the apnea off, I never do that, maybe I shouldn't have done that, I don't know, but why didn't it alarm? It was turned off when we went in the room"; and "I know I left it on because I checked her at 6 and it was on then."

Hearing Doerksen's concerns about the monitor, Douglas decided to go to Lisa's room "where the body still remained" to verify the monitor settings; she claimed they were exactly what Doerksen had said they were. Afterwards, she sat with Doerksen while Doerksen wrote up a post mortem nursing note, and reviewed the note to make sure it was clear.

Although I knew Lisa's two nurses were liars, we had all hoped they were two "bad apples" and that the other hospital employees would be honest, truthful, and willing to help determine exactly what had happened to Lisa. We were so naïve.

Mary Douglas had many years of nursing experience, but had

evidently decided that protecting her nursing colleagues was more important than her integrity or her credibility. Throughout her testimony, she would not admit that Ruth Doerksen or Anagaile Soriano had made any mistakes in the care they gave Lisa, no matter how strong the evidence was. She refused to concede that either of the nurses had done anything the least bit wrong, even if she had to make outrageous and preposterous statements to prove her point. Whoever had coached her must have mistakenly thought that her seemingly authoritative responses would fool the jury into believing her implausible comments.

To Douglas, there was nothing wrong with the nurses not having checked or read the doctor's orders. According to her faulty logic, the nurses were instead to be commended for doing such a good job and skilfully using their clinical judgment, *because* they had to work without doctors' orders.

Doerksen and Soriano had only taken some of the vital signs the doctor had ordered to be taken, but according to Douglas and Hawkins this was indicative of "heightened monitoring". The erratic and failing vital signs that had marked Lisa's dying hours–those few that the nurses had bothered to take–were all mild and not worthy of any special concern. Douglas proudly boasted that the nurses had checked Lisa's respirations more frequently than ordered, calling it "exceptional". As soon as she uttered the word, however, loud guffaws of laughter erupted from the audience where my family and friends were seated.

I was not the only one angered by Mary Douglas's duplicity. Krkachovski asked Dr. Cairns if he could show Douglas the report prepared by the Paediatric Death Review Committee. It was to be presented and discussed at the inquest by a later witness, but Dr. Cairns granted permission to enter it as an exhibit now. The Committee's expert paediatricians had done a detailed analysis of Lisa's death, including one chart showing the vital signs the doctor ordered to be taken versus the vital signs the nurses actually took, and another graphically depicting the dramatic rise in Lisa's heart rate and the equally dramatic drop in her respiratory rate.[2]

Douglas disagreed with the graphs. Krkachovski asked her, "As I understand it, this chart is intended to compare what was ordered for Lisa on the orthopaedic ward versus what was actually done, and if I read the chart correctly, the solid black boxes or squares are what was supposed to be done and the tick marks are what was actually done. And would you agree with me that looking at this chart, it seems to indicate that a great many of the orders were not followed, if I can put it that way?"

Douglas answered, "Well, I think we're assuming, first of all, the nurse saw the orders and I think we know that that didn't happen, so that would -- the oximetry column therefore doesn't necessarily apply because that's at the physician's discretion."

"I'm not trying to be unfair to the nurses. I think the evidence will be that they, in fact, did not see the doctor's orders. My question simply is if you compare what was supposed to have been done on the basis of the doctor's orders and what the nursing staff did, there seems to be quite a difference between what they were supposed to do on the basis of the doctor's orders and what they actually did. Would you agree with that?"

"I don't agree with all of it, no. I mean, this is the first time I've seen this. My -- what jumps out at me right away is the 5:00 and 6:00 slot where there are dark spots indicating there should have been a blood pressure, sedation scale, pain scale and oximetry. I don't see that that was part of the protocol. I mean, I really -- I'd have to look at this more carefully, but I don't agree with all of it, no."

"Well, would you agree with me that there are an awful lot of black boxes that don't have checkmarks in them?"

"There are some."

"You wouldn't agree that there are an awful lot?"

"Well, I haven't counted. I think we know based on my evidence what was not done according to policy. I'm not sure why we need to repeat this in a chart form."

"Because I think it has a tremendous visual effect to actually report in a visual way what was supposed to have been done and what was actually done. I find it striking, maybe you don't. What I'd ask you to refer to is the second chart, which is a graph. This simply grabs two vital signs, respiratory rate and heart rate and the dotted line is the heart rate, which sometime after 1:00 a.m. seems to take a dramatic rise up to about 4:00 a.m. You would agree with that?"

"The heart rate did rise. Yes, I think we've talked about that."

"My characterization was a significant rise. Would that be accurate?"

"I believe I described it as mild, a mildly elevated heart rate and I would still say that. This graph's -- the scale on the graph makes it look like it's a significant rise. I think it's still a mildly elevated heart rate when you look at the actual numbers."

"And then the solid line is the respiration rate which seems to start tumbling in a significant way some time between 1:00 and 2:00? Does that seem right?"

"Again, we know that it went down to 8 and 10 at 2:50 and that prior to that, it was 14 and 16. Again, I'd describe that as mild respiratory depression; I maintain that statement."

"And it would seem that from 3:00 until about 5:00, the respiratory rate is very erratic; would you not agree with that?"

"The respiratory rate was taken a number of times between 3:00 and 5:00 and they found varied numbers between 3:00 and 5:00. The numbers were not significantly -- I wouldn't describe it as erratic, they changed. Overall they improved from 3:00 in an overall scale."

"But you don't find the peaks and the valleys in this narrow time period to be troubling in any way?"

"As I say, they changed a variety of times and they took them a variety of times. As I say, this scale I find deceiving because it makes it look like huge changes happened and when you look at the actual numbers, I don't see the same picture in my mind."

"Does this, in your opinion, reflect a child that is stable?"

"I don't see any huge, immediate -- I'm not sure of the word I want to use. As I said, that's a mildly elevated heart rate and a mild depression, respiratory depression. I wouldn't have a great fit over that, I would take note of it and want to notify the physician."

"Otherwise there's no cause for distress?"

"I don't see immediate distress here."

Bill, Frank and I could not believe what we were hearing. How could someone lie so brazenly? We were afraid the jury members, who did not have medical backgrounds, would think she was giving an expert opinion. This was undoubtedly exactly what Hawkins wanted, and he had found a willing accomplice in Mary Douglas.

Douglas frequently threw in the term "clinical judgment" when praising the nurses' actions, using it as both explanation and justification for everything a nurse did. A nurse used her clinical judgment when deciding whether to use monitors, or whether to turn monitor alarms on or off. It was perfectly appropriate clinical judgment in her view for Doerksen to set a monitor's high heart rate alarm to sound only if Lisa's heart rate went up by 250%.

The jury did believe Douglas—for a while. But by the end of the inquest, it was so upset about hearing the term "clinical judgment" used to justify the unjustifiable that it recommended the Hospital for Sick Children strike a committee to define the term, its parameters, and its limitations.

As various doctors testified over the course of the inquest, the jury members learned about proper protocols, procedures, and standards of care. The more the jury heard witnesses who were not affiliated with the Hospital for Sick Children testify that Lisa's vital signs were indicative of a child in extreme crisis, the more it understood how Douglas had been trying to deceive them. Eventually, it demanded that Douglas be recalled so it could challenge her on her earlier testimony.

Bill and I were so angered by Douglas's testimony that we decided to post excerpts of it on our lisashore.com website for the public to read. The website had been getting more and more visitors as media coverage of the inquest grew.

Since we no longer trusted anything Douglas had said, we sceptically reread her incident report. Why had she waited until three weeks after Lisa's death to write one up? It was convenient she had been there to listen to Doerksen tell her how upset she was at the monitor's alarm not having gone off, particularly since Doerksen neglected to mention it anywhere in her notes or discuss her distress with anyone else. Why did Douglas, upon hearing Doerksen cry about a monitor not working properly, a monitor that was supposedly attached to a child who had just died unexpectedly, do nothing about it except go to Lisa's room and check the monitor's settings?

Picture yourself in Mary Douglas's place. You have postgraduate nursing training and are responsible for the education and training of nurses on your ward. You come in to work one morning and learn that a child has just died mysteriously. A weeping nurse tells you that for some reason, medical monitoring equipment that was supposed to warn of impending danger to this child had failed to work. You decide to go into the dead child's room, knowing this is a coroner's case where no one is supposed to touch anything. Once in the room, you open the underside of the monitor to check its settings, then close it up and leave. You don't examine the monitor for signs of malfunction. You don't consider malfunctioning medical equipment to be very important, since you say nothing to anybody about it and don't document it anywhere. You read the notes the child's nurse has written about the incident, and although she cried hysterically about a monitor that failed to alarm, you see the nurse did not mention it anywhere in her notes. This is all perfectly acceptable to you, even justifiable.

It wasn't plausible. This was our theory about what had really happened: Expecting that her care of Lisa would be closely scrutinized, Doerksen knew she had a problem and enlisted her friend Mary Douglas to help her out. When Doerksen brought the monitor into Lisa's room, she had never turned it on and therefore did not bother to check its settings. Because no alarms ever went off, Doerksen realized that people would ask what settings she had used. If she didn't know, it would look suspicious. If she guessed and someone had already checked the monitor settings, her deception would be discovered. Doerksen sent Douglas into Lisa's room to get the missing information, to fill in the gaps in her story. That was why the monitor settings Douglas reported, where the upper alarm was set to go off if the heart rate exceeded 160 or 180 beats per minute, was way too high for a child of Lisa's age: it had been the setting used on another child, one who was much younger. Douglas may have been able to check the monitor settings without attracting notice, but if she had tried to change them she might have been challenged. Doerksen and Douglas were stuck with the highly unsuitable settings. Douglas was forced to testify that they were perfectly appropriate or else she would be explicitly criticizing Doerksen's actions.

We thought our version made much more sense.

21

THE TRAINER

The next witness was a hospital employee introduced as an expert on the Kidcom computer system. If there had been any doubt the hospital was actively striving to conceal the truth, there was no doubt left after she finished testifying.

The woman was responsible for demonstrating the system and training new employees. She had no technical expertise per se, which meant she probably would not have the answers we were looking for. As it turned out, the little she did know was of no help to anyone, since she was unwilling or unable to answer even basic questions. She would look around in bewilderment as the exasperated lawyers repeated their questions and tried to rephrase their words so she would understand. We thought at first she was incredibly slow-witted; listening to her testimony brought to mind the famous Abbott and Costello "who's on first" routine. However, there was much more going on than was immediately apparent. The Kidcom trainer had obviously been sternly instructed as to what she was or was not allowed to say. She was terrified of making a mistake and saying something the hospital did not want her to.

Even the jury was frustrated with her. At the conclusion of her testimony, the forewoman began questioning her, as jury members are allowed to do at a coroner's inquest. She asked the trainer whether there were ever any patients admitted to a ward without Kidcom orders. The answer was no, of course, but for her to admit that would have been a tacit acknowledgement that Lisa's nurses erred in failing to check for orders. Evidently this was one of the questions she wasn't allowed to answer truthfully. The juror, after repeated failed attempts at getting a straight answer from her, grew visibly exasperated, and said, "Do you know where I could have my question answered?" Hawkins attempted to step in and help his witness, and the forewoman snapped at him, "Oh, I quite understand that, Mr. Hawkins. I quite understand that. That wasn't my question. I'll have to try to make myself clearer to one of the nursing staff."

The Kidcom trainer had conclusively demonstrated the hospital's inquest strategy: Cover up, confuse, and mislead. Douglas's intransigence was not an isolated instance of one friend protecting another but an indication of what the hospital expected all of its witnesses to do. How could so many people be so willing to help the hospital cover up the facts in the death of a ten-year-old child?

The trainer's largely incoherent testimony did bring out two of the themes the hospital would use in its continuing efforts to deny any responsibility for Lisa's death: First, it attempted to point a finger at the doctor and away from the nurses, and second, it claimed there had been a missing step in the computer system which accounted for all the problems, and now that the system had been tweaked, all the problems had been fixed.

The original Kidcom documentation for admissions from the Emergency Department was presented as evidence to support the "blame the doctor" theme.[1] It was dated August 1994, shortly after the date of the original systems implementation, and stated that the resident, meaning the doctor caring for the patient in the Emergency Department, was to notify nurses on the admitting ward that they should check the computer system orders for their soon-to-be arriving patient. Dr. Schily had not done this, a fact of which Hawkins would keep reminding the jury.

We had friends who worked as residents at the Hospital for Sick Children, and my sister Cindy had once done a rotation in Emergency as part of her residency requirements. Every physician was unanimous on this point: doctors did not call up to the ward to tell the nurses to check the orders. Cindy was adamant she had never been told to do so as part of the Kidcom training she herself had received.

We surmised this documentation was the original instruction from 1994, and this step was necessary in the system's early years when staff were just becoming used to the idea of a computer system replacing the paper one. Once it became instinctive to check the computer for orders when a patient was admitted to the ward, the instructions became obsolete. No one wanted or needed to waste time making or getting a phone call telling people to do the obvious. Overworked Emergency paediatricians rarely called up to the ward nurses, delegating this task instead to competent nurses. On the night of Lisa's admission, the Emergency nurse had called up to the ward and given a detailed report about Lisa's condition. It would never have occurred to her to advise the nurse to check the computer system for orders, for, as she testified, "There's always Kidcom orders every time a kid goes upstairs".

The hospital had not updated its computer manuals, and its written instructions no longer conformed to the accepted practice. Now it was using its own inefficiency and failure to maintain up-to-date manuals to scapegoat the doctor, who had only been doing exactly what he had been taught by the hospital's Kidcom instructors. In the absence of a credible witness from the hospital who would tell the jury what the usual hospital practice was–and it didn't appear there would be any of those forthcoming–the jury might be fooled into believing Dr. Schily had erred. Since Dr. Schily worked in another country, he was unlikely to complain about what the hospital was doing. Moreover, he had already testified and would be unable to respond to or defend himself against any insinuations of culpability.

The second "theme" the trainer brought up was the improvement to Kidcom that ostensibly solved what the hospital pretended was a major system flaw. Formerly, when a doctor in the Emergency Department entered orders into the system, the orders remained suspended until the ward nurse went over to the computer and printed them out. Now, the trainer explained, the orders automatically printed out on the ward even though they remained suspended until officially activated by the nurse.

The trainer implied this would ensure a nurse could no longer forget to activate orders. Just in case she forgot to check the computer, she would see the orders on the printer and would therefore be reminded to activate them in the system. It did not take a genius, however, to realize that a nurse who could "forget" to read doctor's orders on the computer would be just as likely to "forget" to look at a piece of paper on the printer.

Systems improvements designed to eliminate specific errors have to make it impossible for those errors to occur, such as when anaesthetic gases in an operating room come with different sized connectors so that incorrect tubing will simply not fit together. The Hospital for Sick Children made no systems improvements or design changes to Kidcom as a result of Lisa's death. It didn't need to, since the system wasn't broken; the problem was the nurses who deliberately flouted the rules and violated procedures. By touting the printing of an extra sheet of paper as a panacea to solve the problem of dangerously incompetent nurses, the Hospital for Sick Children showed its utter disdain for the inquest process and its disregard for the death of Lisa Shore.

We knew how to make the system error-proof, and it wasn't by printing off a piece of paper, it was by the use of automated warning technology. If suspended orders from Emergency were not activated within a pre-defined reasonable time, an audible alarm could sound or the supervisor of the unit could be automatically paged.

In one of the hospital's more blatant efforts to mislead the coroner and the jury, the trainer presented a flowchart that outlined the steps in the hospital's "new and improved" Admissions from Emergency–Kidcom Orders.[2] The flowchart included the new step where suspended orders print on the ward, and stated that this step had been implemented one week earlier. This was untrue. Over a year later, the hospital would issue a status report in response to the inquest recommendations in which it noted that the implementation date had occurred after the inquest had concluded. Not satisfied with only one lie, the flowsheet process also included the following non-existent step: "If orders are entered in Emergency, physician phones nursing unit as to existence of suspend orders".

This flowsheet was a wholesale fraud, and would never form part of any official Kidcom documentation. Doctors didn't need to phone the nurses if orders were entered in Emergency, because orders were always entered. Nor did they need to remind the nurses to check for orders, because every competent nurse in every hospital everywhere knew to do it. It would be like adding a warning siren to a red traffic light, just in case the driver forgets that red means stop. With grim humour, we called the phoney physician instruction "the Dr. Schily step", because its sole purpose was to make Dr. Schily look bad. The new step where the orders supposedly printed out on the unit even though they were still suspended we said was "the Lisa Shore step", because it had no value other than making the hospital look better at the inquest.

Driving home that evening, Bill and I discussed the questions about the Kidcom system that the Kidcom trainer's less than impressive testimony had left unanswered. We didn't believe anything she had told us, reasoning that she had been so over-coached that even she didn't know what was true and what wasn't. Although Frank was not especially computer literate, Bill and I were. That night and over the next few days, we put together a list of questions about the more technical aspects of Kidcom.

What kind of audit trail existed in Kidcom? Who had looked at Lisa's medical records, and when? Who had printed out the doctor's orders after Lisa's death, and when? What kind of log existed?

Did suspended orders remain suspended and accessible in the system indefinitely, or did something happen to them after a certain period of time? Was there a length of time after which suspended orders could no longer be activated?

Had the hospital ever investigated automated warning technology to ensure that suspended orders were activated in a timely way?

Frank realized our questions were good ones. He puzzled over the best way to get the answers: should he ask the coroner privately to get the information, or should he make the request of the hospital in open court? We did not want to run the risk our concerns would be ignored, so Frank read our questions in the court, on the record.

Dr. Cairns thought they were good questions and directed Hawkins to obtain the answers. We hoped that by forcing the hospital to produce its computer records, we might learn who had been directly involved in the cover-up. We set a trap, not knowing who would be caught in it.

22

OUR DREAM TEAM

Our inquest team was outstanding. Every night, Bill, Frank, and my friend Sharon and her husband gathered around our kitchen table to discuss the events of the day and to decide what questions to ask the next witnesses. Each of us had different strengths and skills, and all of us were intensely committed to finding out the truth and obtaining justice for Lisa.

As a nurse with over twenty years of clinical experience, and with high standards for her own and for others' practice, Sharon often looked at a document or dissected the day's testimony with a perspective that was vastly different from ours. What would she or her colleagues have done in a certain situation? Given that some event or incident had occurred, how would she have charted it? Without her nursing expertise, the hospital would have been successful in many of its attempts to mislead and misdirect us.

Sharon's husband was a computer engineer who had gone back to school to become a counsellor. His technical expertise helped us thoroughly understand the Kidcom system and its limitations, and his insistence that we look at the underlying motivations for everyone's actions gave us yet another perspective with which to analyse and plan.

Bill saw the things that everyone else missed. He instantly picked up any inconsistency in testimony, no matter how small. If someone said something that did not correspond to what someone else had previously testified to, he remembered it and brought it up for us to mull over.

I was the organizer and co-ordinator, the one who knew the detailed history, the contents of every document, and where to find everything instantly.

Frank sat and listened, and frequently played devil's advocate. He often didn't agree with or understand our conclusions, and continually challenged whatever we said. He forced us to explain and justify everything, which seemed frustrating at the time but ensured our ideas held up under strong scrutiny. Once the rest of us could convince Frank of something, we knew we were right. Frank would then take our ideas, make his notes and prepare his questions. The next day, those notes and questions would translate into masterful cross-examinations.

We worked together each night long past midnight, all of us so caught up in the intensity of what we were doing that we barely noticed how exhausted we were. This group was the ultimate "dream team"–and also the dearest friends anyone could hope for.

Frank and I had established a good relationship with the media. It wasn't particularly difficult, since we were willing to talk on the record and the hospital wasn't. Hawkins would exit the courthouse and hurriedly walk past whichever reporters or photographers were congregated there. Hospital witnesses would not only ignore the media, they would often stay cloistered in a small office and not leave until all the reporters had gone away. We, on the other hand, gave the media lots of sound bites. It was nerve-wracking at first, trying to figure out what to say and sound calm and intelligent at the same time, but it got easier as we went along. The reporters saw for themselves the stunts the hospital was pulling, and even though they attempted to write balanced and fair articles, their off-the-record comments made it clear where their sympathies lay. As time went on, we even felt comfortable enough to joke with them. When the reporters like and respect you and you treat them with courtesy, if you tell them a comment is off the record, they keep it that way. If you say something you want to "take back", they won't use it in their stories. Once, when a male reporter asked me my age, the other reporters–all female–started chiding him on my behalf.

Bill preferred to stay out of the spotlight, so Frank and I did the interviews. Frank had previously warned me to be careful of what I said. He worried that if he said something inappropriate, a complaint might be filed against him at the Law Society, and if I said something too outrageous, I could be sued. I was circumspect, sort of, at least at the beginning. I made sure never to openly call the nurses liars, saying instead that "their version of events differed from mine". And *I* was telling the truth, I would hasten to add.

Of the two of us, I took Frank's warnings much more to heart than he himself did. He was far more outspoken than I and could always be relied upon to say something interesting. Once he ranted that "Lisa Shore would have received better care from a small hospital in Sudbury than she got at the Hospital for Sick Children!" I inwardly cringed at his politically incorrect reference to a smaller city that probably had perfectly fine hospitals, but everyone understood his point. He was so effective an advocate, and so sincerely outraged at the travesty unfolding around him, that he began getting phone calls from people who had seen him on TV and were so impressed they wanted to hire him.

Margaret Browne was on our side too. We had moved to the second inquest courtroom, which was larger and contained extra rows of seats off to the side behind the Crown attorney's table. My friends and family sat behind Margaret, as did the press, completely segregated from the hospital staff who continued to sit in the main area. During the proceedings, Margaret would often turn around and make comments to Bill. We knew her heart was in the right place, but wondered if it was appropriate that she showed her partisanship so openly.

The inquest's expert witnesses began to testify. I expected to hear graphic descriptions of my daughter's autopsy results along with other scientific information, so I decided to sit in the audience with Bill instead of in the lawyer's section with Frank. Frank didn't need my assistance to cross-examine these witnesses, but I needed Bill's strength and support to maintain my composure.

The toxicologist's evidence was as expected; Lisa did not have any toxic drug levels in her body and there was no evident toxicological cause of death. The pathologist's testimony was much the same–there was no anatomic cause of death. However, he did reveal one important and sad detail: in describing the swelling of the brain that is a usual part of the process of dying, he explained this had happened to Lisa over a relatively short period of perhaps five to fifteen minutes. "Was it reversible?" asked Frank. The pathologist gently answered that in his opinion, it was reversible right up to the moment of Lisa's death.

Had either of Lisa's nurses taken any action at any time during the night, Lisa would still be alive. Had they called the doctor and reported her vital signs, tried to wake her up, done anything at all, she would have been revived with no brain damage or other ill effect—right up until virtually her last dying breath.

The pharmacologist was also a physician and a former medical school dean. He testified that the nurses' failure to check the orders was unacceptable and shocking. He called Lisa's heart rate of 134 beats per minute "quite extraordinary", not just the rate itself but the magnitude of the increase. When her respiration went down to 8 or 10 breaths per minute, he termed it abnormal, saying that any observer would have said the same thing. The jury members started visibly squirming, remembering the hospital's nursing expert Mary Douglas's testimony of a few days earlier where she called Lisa's elevated heart rate "a mild elevation" and her drop in respiration "a mild depression". Finally, I thought, this jury is starting to understand the extent of the hospital's deceit.

Did he think that giving the morphine reversal drug to Lisa would have saved her life? Since he couldn't absolutely determine the cause of death, he could not say definitively, but he felt that had she received this drug there was a very high probability she would still be alive.

23

THE NURSES – I

The inquest was delayed for several days, but no one told us why. Thanks to some injudicious remarks, we learned it had something to do with Hawkins representing both the hospital and the nurses–the very matter he had been so strongly cautioned about before the inquest began. We thought that one or both of the two nurses at the centre of events had decided to get their own lawyers, but we were also pretty sure the hospital would not let that happen. Whatever the reason, Hawkins and his clients worked things out and the inquest resumed three days later with no change of counsel.

The late-night meetings around my kitchen table continued, because Hawkins routinely gave us important documents pertaining to his witnesses just before they were scheduled to testify. Most lawyers condemn this as a sleazy tactic designed to put the opposing parties at a disadvantage. Our little group had to go over each new document to try to understand its implications and figure out the appropriate questions to ask the witnesses, and we didn't have much time in which to do it.

Ruth Doerksen was scheduled to testify the following week. At 7:15 p.m. on Friday night, after most people have left their offices, Hawkins faxed Frank copies of her and Soriano's personal notes.[1] They were apparently written a few days after Lisa's death, and purported to be the nurses' best recollection of what had happened that night.

Doerksen's notes described how she had placed Lisa on a Corometric monitor when she arrived on the ward at 1:45 a.m.; how the monitor's respiratory alarm had gone off a short time later so she went into the room to reset it; how it had alarmed again and she reset it again; and she then went into the Constant Care Room to relieve another nurse but the monitor alarmed again so she returned to Lisa's room to permanently disable it.

At 5:00 a.m., Doerksen wrote, she awoke Lisa to take her temperature, and checked her breathing to see that it correlated to the monitor. She did the same at 6:00 a.m. At 7:00 a.m., when she was supposed to check Lisa again, she checked her other four patients, but "in the confusion of a sick call, the new staff coming on and MD's <sic> rounding", she somehow missed Lisa. She said she then entered Lisa's room about fifteen minutes later with the doctors on their rounds, and they found Lisa dead. She checked the Corometric monitor, "but it was turned off".

It was a work of fiction.

Lisa had not been put on a monitor, and no alarms had *ever* sounded. Doerksen never came back into the room to check on Lisa, at least not during the time the alarms were supposed to have gone off–which was when I was still awake. Doerksen never woke Lisa up to take her temperature. As far as her reasons for checking on her other four patients at 7:00 a.m. but somehow missing Lisa in the confusion, that was patently absurd. With fifteen years of experience, she was not likely to forget to check on a patient who had just arrived a few hours earlier from Emergency. The patient load was light, nurses check their patients every morning before their shifts end, doctors round every morning, and the next shift always starts at the same time. Sick calls, when a nurse phones in to say she's sick and won't be in that day, are always made well before 7:00 a.m. so the charge nurse has ample time to call in a replacement. The sick call Doerksen received that morning was made at 5:30 a.m. and not at 7:00 a.m., according to the later testimony of the nurse who made the call, thus conclusively exposing as a lie the statement Doerksen made as to why she didn't check on Lisa.

Because she had missed checking Lisa at 7:00 a.m., Doerksen wrote that she had decided to do it when she went in the room with the doctors on their rounds. But I clearly remembered that when the doctors came in the room, the nurse that accompanied them stood just inside the doorway and never went near Lisa–hardly the actions of someone planning to check on a patient.

Doerksen had not only tried to cover up her negligent care of Lisa immediately after it had occurred, she sat down two days later and with forethought put her lies in writing. Now she was going to testify.

Would she tell the truth under oath or would she compound her deceit by continuing to lie? Would she show any remorse or accept any responsibility for Lisa's death? If she told the truth, nothing she said could be used against her in any other legal proceedings. We had already been given a financial settlement from the hospital so she would not be sued. This was her chance to confess without any repercussions. If she expressed deep remorse, explained how she had panicked and done a foolish thing, she might elicit some sympathy from the jury and emerge with her reputation only slightly tarnished. On the other hand, if she continued telling lies, Frank would go on the offensive when he cross-examined her.

A nondescript middle-aged woman approached the witness box—a complete stranger. I realized that not only had I not known what she looked like, but never having heard her voice before I also hadn't known how she sounded. She spoke with a slight accent, and she seemed very nervous.

Krkachovski asked Doerksen why, when she was attaching Lisa to a monitor, she hadn't explained to me—the child's mother—what she was doing and why. Hadn't I asked? Most parents did, she agreed, but she claimed she didn't see me when she came back into Lisa's room with the monitor. "She must have been sleeping or in the bathroom," she said. What about after the three or four false alarms went off, didn't Mrs. Shore ever say anything to her then? Doerksen gave the same answer: she knew I was in the room, but she never saw me.

Dr. Cairns asked her the same question. "I seem to remember that you indicated you weren't sure exactly where Mrs. Shore was when you went into the room to put on the Corometric monitor. She may have been in the bathroom, she may have been somewhere else, but you didn't see her?" Doerksen answered, "I didn't see her, no."

He then referred her to her own notes, where she had written that after she put Lisa on the monitor, 'Mrs. Shore was at the door and was about to settle to sleep, I asked her if there was anything I needed to know about Lisa's medical history...and whether she had any allergies.' He continued, "That, to me, reads that when you put the Corometric monitor on, you knew exactly where Mrs. Shore was."

Doerksen decided that she remembered seeing and talking to me after all, but could not explain why she hadn't spoken to me about the Corometric monitor.

"I know she had come out to the door and was either closing the door or getting ready for bed. I don't know if it was at the moment when I put the monitor on or not, but I know she was at the door... I think I remembered asking her about anything more, if there was allergies, and that was it. I don't know if I was doing that at the same time."

"But that's the way it <the notes> reads here."

"Yeah."

She testified she went into the Constant Care Room around 2:15 a.m. to relieve the nurse on duty there. The Constant Care Room holds up to four patients–infants and children who must be continuously monitored because they have potentially life-threatening conditions. Most are babies who are apneic, meaning they can stop breathing at any moment. A nurse must be in the room at all times, and has to get another nurse to replace her if she needs to leave for any reason. According to a nurse who testified later, nurses cannot leave the patients in the Constant Care Room alone under any circumstances, not even if a Code Blue emergency is called in the room next door. That nurse said that leaving the Constant Care Room was such a serious transgression that someone who did it would probably have to face a disciplinary hearing before the College of Nurses, the nursing regulatory body that sets the standards for the profession.

Doerksen testified that while in the Constant Care Room, she heard the alarm sound on Lisa's monitor again, and went to Lisa's room and disabled the alarm. How could Doerksen have left those babies unattended? She replied that she believed she had asked Soriano, whom she thought was at the nursing desk, to keep an eye on them.

Since there had been no false alarms, we knew Doerksen had not broken the fundamental rule about never leaving the Constant Care patients. But her web of lies had grown so tangled that she had to confess to a wrongdoing she hadn't committed in order to get the jury to believe her lies about the monitor. We already knew the Hospital for Sick Children cared more about itself than about its patients, so it was not surprising that it seemed completely unconcerned that Doerksen, had she been telling the truth, had jeopardized the lives of its tiny patients merely to attend to a false alarm. Or was the reason it acted as if it didn't care because it knew the whole thing was made up, and that Doerksen had never in fact left the Constant Care Room?

Doerksen's story didn't hold up in another key area: the time. Lisa and I arrived on the floor about 1:45 a.m., and no one disputed that. The hospital's computer system showed that Doerksen had entered data into the computer from the Constant Care Room at 2:05 a.m., which meant that she had already relieved its nurse by then and therefore was no longer looking after patients on the ward. In the twenty minutes between 1:45 and 2:05 a.m., Doerksen claimed she had taken Lisa's vitals and checked the PCA pump; got information from me about Lisa's medications; left the room again to get bed linens for me; left the room again and returned with the monitor; attached multiple leads to Lisa's body and then set the monitor; wrote up a 21-line nursing note for Lisa's file; made up a nursing flowsheet; searched the ward, unsuccessfully, for a pulse oximeter for Lisa; went back into Lisa's room two or three more times because the monitor's alarms kept going off; checked Lisa's breathing each time to make sure she was okay and reset the monitor; gave a detailed verbal report to Soriano about all her patients so Soriano could take over their care while she went into the Constant Care Room; went into the Constant Care Room and received a detailed report from the nurse in there about those patients; sat at the computer terminal and organized her charts; and then signed on to the computer and entered data about Lisa.

I went to sleep at about 2:15 a.m., well after Doerksen was in the Constant Care Room. Doerksen had been in Lisa's room when we arrived onto the floor, but had left within minutes and did not return at any time while I was awake. It had been Soriano who had come back into the room to bring me bed linens, not Doerksen. No one brought in a monitor, and no alarms went off anywhere within earshot.

How could she wake Lisa to take her temperature at 5:00 a.m. and another time say she didn't take her blood pressure at 5:00 a.m. because she didn't want to wake her?

"I don't know."

Did she read the doctor's nine-line note that he wrote in Emergency, one of which said to check the computer system for orders?

"I don't recall that I read each line."

"Well, do you remember specifically which lines you didn't read?"

"Well clearly, I didn't read 'See Kidcom orders.'"

"Were there any other lines that you didn't read?"

"Not that I recall. I don't know."

Who did she speak to after Lisa's death? Who did she talk to about the monitor not having gone off?

"I can't name people. I don't know who asked me. Many people asked me about it. I don't know who they were."

Did she not think it important to note anywhere that she had turned off the apnea alarm?

"I didn't think of it at the time."

Why didn't she tell anyone or write down that she had unsuccessfully tried, as she claimed, to find a pulse oximeter?

"I didn't think of it at the time."

None of us believed anything she said. Neither did the jury, apparently, as one juror whispered to the other, unaware that I was watching her lips move, "She's lying." The reporters made it quite clear that they too believed she was lying. We didn't know what Dr. Cairns thought, but even he asked Doerksen some pretty pointed questions.

We thought the hospital had already descended as low as it could possibly go, but we were wrong. Douglas, the nurse-educator who had previously testified that the nursing care was exceptional, was "coaching" Doerksen from the audience while Doerksen testified. Before Doerksen would answer a question, she would pause and look at Douglas. Douglas would nod or shake her head vigorously to signal how the question should be answered, and Doerksen would respond accordingly. It was so overt the jury noticed and complained to the coroner. As the forewoman later stated when interviewed by the College of Nurses, "Ms Douglas's head was in continual motion. It was either nodding up and down, or back and forth... <the forewoman> found that the witnesses did not answer the question until Ms Douglas had given her head nodding. There were often long pauses before Ms Douglas completed her head nodding and the witnesses gave their answers...Ms Douglas appeared to be coaching the witnesses on the correct answer to be giving. She was very clear on what she thought the answer should be."[2]

The coroner sternly cautioned the audience. He did not specify anyone by name, but some of my family and friends had seen Douglas in action and we all knew exactly to whom he was referring. Douglas stopped, and put her head down.

In order to communicate successfully with a witness on the stand, the method of communication has to be worked out between the parties in advance. This signalling could only have been done with careful planning. Douglas was sitting in the middle of the audience, close to Jean Reeder, the chief of nursing, and Marion Stevens, the Risk Manager. It would have been impossible for them not to notice what she was doing. What kind of people could conceive of or at least condone such a bizarre strategy?

There were still more surprises to come. In answer to a question from Frank, Doerksen explained about patient care plans, sometimes referred to as nursing care plans. These are nursing documents that automatically print out each morning and evening on the wards for the nurses' use. Each patient has a separate plan that contains important information such as required medications, type of diet, and doctors' orders. Doerksen denied having seen Lisa's care plan when it first printed off, but admitted to having seen it after her death.

Frank asked her, "I want to talk to you briefly about the suspended orders. Did you ever see those suspended orders before January 26th, 1999 <the date the hospital claimed it first learned about them>?"

Doerksen answered, "I saw it the morning after Lisa's death on a care plan. The care plan had been printed out automatically at 6:15 <a.m.>. Someone had seen it and showed it to me."

"The suspended orders that Dr. Schily wrote in the Emergency Department, you saw the next morning?"

"I saw it after Lisa died. They were on a set of care plans that prints up automatically, and someone had pointed out or showed me Lisa's care plan for that morning, and I saw them there."

"You saw those Kidcom orders. Did you talk to Nurse Soriano about that?"

"No."

"Well, who was with you when you saw them?"

"I imagine the person putting the care plans together for the day had seen them and showed them to me. They were on the computer and somebody was sorting them out and showed them to me."

"Who showed them to you?"

"Another nurse would be normally putting them together and -- so that the next set of nurses could have a set of care plans."

"Well, do you remember the name of the person who showed them to you?"

"I can't recall who did it."

Even when Doerksen was ostensibly telling the truth, she only told half-truths. She admitted that the patient care plan printed out at the nurses' station around 6:15 a.m., a fact confirmed afterwards by another witness. She would not admit, however, that it was her job as night charge nurse to sort and staple them so they were ready for the nurses coming on shift at 7:15 a.m. Instead, she denied seeing them and said that someone else had got them ready. Soriano, the only other night nurse on duty aside from the one who could not leave the Constant Care Room, would soon testify that she hadn't prepared the plans because it was the charge nurse's job to do that. A nurse who arrived that morning at 6:45 a.m., half an hour before her shift started and before the other nurses arrived, would testify the patient care plans were already sorted and stapled when she arrived.

Doerksen had obviously seen Lisa's patient care plan before Lisa was found dead, somewhere between 6:15 and 6:45 a.m. No wonder she told the court she "couldn't remember" who had shown the orders to her. Had she truly accidentally forgotten to read the doctor's orders when Lisa first arrived—which was virtually impossible—she would have seen them listed as "suspended" on the patient care plan at 6:15 a.m. and immediately realized the enormity of her mistake. She would have rushed to the computer to unsuspend the orders, and she would not have "forgotten" to check Lisa at 7:00 a.m. when she checked her other patients. If, on the other hand, she had knowingly and intentionally neglected to read the doctor's orders, if she hadn't cared in the least about checking the doctor's orders for Lisa, then she would have performed her normal duties and sorted and stapled those care plans without a second thought. In order to maintain the fiction she had *accidentally* forgotten to check the doctor's orders, she could not admit to having seen them on the patient care plan at 6:15 a.m.

Frank was furious at Patrick Hawkins when Doerksen admitted to having seen those orders, and didn't hesitate to let him know. "... I'm taken completely by surprise on this evidence... This is shocking. It's no less than an absolute outrage. It's ridiculous. It's a hijacking of the process and it's outrageous that I should have to ask these questions and do what amounts to a police investigation in the context of a courtroom. And Patrick Hawkins knows it very well."

Doerksen couldn't remember the name of any nurse she had spoken to or interacted with. Although she claimed to have been surprised to learn about the suspended orders, she did not tell anyone about them, much the same way she neglected to tell anyone about the allegedly malfunctioning monitor.

The coroner asked her who else saw that vitally important patient care plan. "I recall just one person showing it to me," Doerksen answered.

"Do you know who that person is?"

"No, I can't tell you which nurse."

"Well, is it someone that works on that floor on a regular basis?"

"Yeah, it would have been somebody that worked there."

"So it's impossible for you to remember who it is, if we get the list of nurses who were on that day?"

"It could have been anybody. I don't know who it was."

"So that even if there were four nurses on and you were to stand in front of those four nurses, you could not say which one it was?"

"I'm sorry, I can't. I don't know who it was. I'm sorry."

"Well, to make it clear, then, it's your evidence that the only people that knew about this were yourself and one other nurse?"

"Yeah. And I didn't think it was important to tell anybody. I just thought it was on the chart. It was there on the record."

Frank quizzed her on this too. "All right," he asked. "So you have the care plan, and embedded or included in that care plan are the Kidcom orders. What did you do with the care plan?"

"I looked at it briefly to see if the PCA orders that I had was the same as the ones on the care plan on the -- in the suspended orders, and I looked for medications to see if I'd missed any medications. And that's it. I left it and left. "

"Just a minute. You saw the Kidcom orders for the first time?"

"Yes."

"Well, did you say to yourself something like, 'Holy cow, I haven't seen these before. This is kind of surprising?'"

"Yes, I did."

"And did you then go and speak to your supervisor and say the same thing, 'Holy cow, I never saw these before. This may be a problem?'"

"No."

"Did you ever discuss those Kidcom orders with anybody in the hospital?"

"No."

Frank had taught me that a good lawyer does not ask a question to which he doesn't know the answer. He asked her this next question on a whim, thinking he already knew the answer. "Now, let's just get back to something that I forgot to ask you about before, and that is these Kidcom orders which we've heard about, which you saw on the Nursing Care Plan that morning, October 22nd. We don't know what happened to those. Did you ever see those orders again?"

"Yes, I did."

"You saw those Kidcom orders again?"

"Yes."

"When did you see those Kidcom orders again?"

"It was two or three days later, after Lisa died, I was on shift."

"So just a minute now; you're on shift on October 25th or 26th, something like that, two or three days later. And you see those Kidcom orders yet again. Where did you see them?"

"In a care plan that I had printed up of Lisa Shore."

"Did you go and print out that care plan again?"

"I printed it out the day that I was on, two or three days later."

"We've already heard about the care plan where you saw it the first time and that's on October 22nd. And we don't know what happened to that care plan. You've testified that you didn't destroy the care plan. You left the hospital and you don't know what happened to it. You don't know if anybody saw it, you don't know anything about what happened to it."

"Right."

"Now, you're saying that two or three days later, you printed up the care plan, the same care plan from a printer which was attached, presumably, to the computer?"

"Yes."

"When you printed up the Nursing Care Plan, the Kidcom orders came out?"

"Yeah, they all print out together on the care plan."

"Right. And why did you do that?"

"I wanted to look at it again to make sure that there was anything in detail that I - that I'd missed."

"And we're not going to go through it all over again, the things that we talked about that were missed, but the point is this, you printed that up again. Did you discuss that, now you have another hard copy, with anybody?"

"No. I wanted to keep it just to look at sometime and go over it and -- just for my information to see if there was anything that I'd missed."

"So you wanted to keep it, and you've printed it up and you took it home, as I understand it?"

"Yes."

We were stunned. No one at the hospital claimed to know about the suspended orders until months after Lisa's death, but now Doerksen was freely admitting that she printed them out only a couple of days later and took them home with her without telling anyone!

One thing puzzled us about this confession. Doerksen lied about everything else, so what had made her admit she hid important evidence? She could easily have told Frank she never saw the orders except for the morning of Lisa's death. Once we thought about it, the answer became obvious. It was just the preceding day that we had asked the coroner some pointed questions about the Kidcom system, because we hadn't been able to get a straight answer out of the hospital's Kidcom expert. One of our questions was what kind of audit trail was generated when an employee printed out patient records. The coroner had ordered the hospital—in Doerksen's presence—to answer our questions, but the hospital had not had enough time to get the answers. The hospital's doctors and nurses knew in a general sense the hospital could track whoever printed out patient records; that was one of the tools the hospital used to ensure its employees didn't violate patient confidentiality. Doerksen believed there would be an audit trail of her having printed out the patient care plan, and she did not want to risk us being able to prove she was lying. She and Hawkins did not yet know that the computer log that recorded this information had been deleted long ago.

The hospital went into the inquest convinced no one would doubt the word of an experienced paediatric nurse over that of a distraught mother. Doerksen had been trapped into telling the damning truth because she thought there was corroborating evidence, and if we could prove she was lying then her credibility would evaporate.

At the end of Doerksen's testimony, the jurors began asking questions. The forewoman had not spoken much to this point, but she must have been watching Frank very closely as he conducted his cross-examinations. The more she spoke, the more she sounded like him!

"Could you tell me what the distinction is between your caring for Lisa that night and caring for a surgical patient on morphine?" she asked.

"The distinction is probably that the child would have had an anaesthetic, as well, from the surgical procedure, as well as the morphine or whatever medication was being used."

"But why you would distinguish between her and your surgical patients on morphine?"

"She had no anaesthetic, which makes it easier for her to settle to sleep and less monitoring might be required, because often the anaesthetist will order the SAT monitor because the child has just come out of an anaesthetic, as well as the medication, which makes it clear to him that they need to have more monitoring, and I think that's the only distinction that I can make."

"Well, I fail to understand the distinction. I guess I'll just have to leave it at that. I don't understand the distinction that set Lisa apart from your other patients in your care and your close monitoring of her. I don't understand that distinction. You told Mr. Hawkins that you had given a lot of thought to what happened that night. You wondered what you could have done, what you did do, what you might have done. Could you tell us now what you could have done differently that would have altered the outcome?"

"When I look back, I don't know what there is that I could have done differently, that I would have done."

Doerksen would not admit she had done anything wrong, even under oath.

24

THE NURSES – II

Anagaile Soriano, the next scheduled witness, had also written extensively about her memory of the night Lisa died. Like Doerksen, she wrote that she, too, could not think of anything she might have missed or could have done differently. Curiously, her notes contained no mention of a monitor at all. Was she perhaps going to tell the truth?

Those hopes were quickly dashed. Maybe the monitor story had not yet been concocted when Soriano wrote her notes, or maybe she was not prepared at that time to commit to paper any large-scale lies. But by the time she entered the witness box, almost $1\frac{1}{2}$ years after Lisa's death, she was ready to say whatever was necessary.

Her willingness to lie was almost understandable in a sad way. The Hospital for Sick Children was one of only a handful of large hospitals in the entire province where the nurses were not unionized. Non-unionized nurses, if they were smart, paid their dues and joined a nursing association such as the Registered Nurses Association of Ontario, or RNAO, a powerful advocacy group which also provides legal assistance to members. But the Hospital for Sick Children had positioned itself as a champion and defender of its nurses, leading many of its staff to believe that joining a nursing organization such as the RNAO was an unnecessary expense. At the time of Lisa's death, Soriano and Doerksen did not belong to the RNAO, and their only access to legal representation—other than what they could pay for out of pocket—was through the hospital. Soriano was a new graduate just embarking on her nursing career. A child died on her shift and there were some serious questions about her nursing skills and conduct in connection with the death, but the hospital was ready to defend and protect her. Soriano had two choices: She could throw her lot in with the hospital, continue covering up, lie under oath at the coroner's inquest, and keep her job. Or, she could tell the truth, admit she had given Lisa substandard care, that Lisa had not been put on a monitor, and that the whole false alarm story was a fabrication. If she did that, she would humiliate herself, open up the possibility of losing her nursing license for discreditable conduct, show that the hospital and some of its senior employees were devious and unethical, and undoubtedly lose her job. As a nursing novice who confessed to bad nursing, without a job and without good references, her budding career as a paediatric nurse would be over—or so she would have believed.

Soriano had an answer for every question asked of her, although most often it was "I don't know", "I didn't think of it at the time", or "it didn't come to mind". At the end of her testimony, one of the newspaper reporters had been counting and told us the exact number of times she had used those phrases. What she did say was mostly irrational or absurd. When asked to whom she spoke or remembered seeing at any particular time, she invariably couldn't recall, except for one nurse we had never heard mention of before. Doerksen had suffered from the identical memory lapse; she, too, forgot everyone except this one person. After we heard this heretofore-unknown nurse's name mentioned so many times by both nurses, we deduced that the hospital was hoping we would call that nurse as a witness, which we declined to do.

Soriano told the doctors' lawyer that when she telephoned Dr. Schily at home at 4:00 a.m., she had said to him Lisa was fine and he didn't need to come in. Then she explained how he should have come to the hospital to see Lisa anyway.

The lawyer asked, "Did you consider Lisa was stable at that time?"
"Yes."

"At no time during the evening did you suggest to Dr. Schily that Lisa Shore was anything but stable?"

"I believe I indicated to Dr. Schily her vital signs and that she was arousable and for me that she had stabilized."

"Dr. Schily testified that near the end of that discussion, he asked whether you wished him to return back to the hospital, and he indicated that you had said no."

"That discussion didn't take place."

"If it had taken place, if Dr. Schily had asked you if you were concerned enough for him to come back to the hospital at 4:05, what would your answer have been?"

"I would have said, 'Yes, you can.'"

"Why?"

"So he can assess the patient himself and maybe give other treatments."

"But at that time, at 4:05, you've already indicated to us you were not concerned with the stability of the patient."

"Yes."

"And you wanted the doctor to come back in the middle of the night, at 4:00 in the morning?"

"Yes."

"Did you indicate to him at that time at all that you required his assessment?"

"I didn't speak to him that I required his assessment."

"Why not?"

"I didn't think of it at that time."

"And you're telling us now today that if it had been offered to you, you would have wanted him to come back, even though you didn't ask him?"

"Yes."

"Even though the patient was stable?"

"Yes."

"Why didn't you ask him to come back at that time?"

"I didn't discuss anything with him with regards to coming to the hospital."

"So if he had asked you, you say you would have wanted him."

"Yes."

"So why did you not suggest that? Why did you not indicate to Dr. Schily that you had sufficient concern that you needed a physician to assess the patient at 4:05 in the morning?"

"I didn't need him to assess the patient at that time."

"So why are you telling me you wanted him to come back?"

"If he had suggested it. At that time, I wasn't thinking of it."

Although Soriano spoke to Dr. Schily at 4:05 a.m., she claimed she had paged him $1\frac{1}{4}$ hours earlier, at 2:50 a.m., because she was concerned about Lisa. The 4:05 a.m. call was her second page, she said. Dr. Schily had testified he only received the one page at 4:05 a.m., which he answered right away. If a nurse calls a doctor in the middle of the night, it's a fair assumption she is concerned about her patient. If Soriano had really called Dr. Schily earlier out of concern for Lisa, why didn't she page him again soon after or contact someone else when he didn't answer? Most nurses document every time they call a doctor, if only to protect themselves and prove they were doing their job.

Why would Soriano lie about calling the doctor and his not answering? Because anyone reviewing Lisa's chart could see that 2:50 a.m. was the first time her significantly deteriorating vital signs were recorded on the chart; 2:50 a.m. was when the doctor should have been called. Soriano and the hospital hoped the jury would infer that Dr. Schily was at fault for not responding to his page, rather than Soriano being at fault for not contacting the physician when she should have. Dr. Schily's lawyer produced a note from the Pain Service department where the contents of his pager, i.e. the record of calls received, had been documented when he returned to the hospital on the morning of Lisa's death. There was only one page from Ward 5A/B, at 4:05 a.m. Had Soriano really made a 2:50 a.m. call to Dr. Schily, the hospital would assuredly have produced the telephone records to prove it.

Frank asked Soriano, "You paged Dr. Schily at 2:50 for a reason, right? And the reason wasn't to tell him that the Yankees had just won the World Series. You paged him for a reason that had something to do with your concern about Lisa."

"Yes."

"And yet you hadn't taken any pulses?"

"No."

"Well, what's your explanation for that?"

"I made that phone call, and while waiting for that phone call I would have done a full assessment on her."

"Well, a full assessment, you didn't take her temperature."

"I didn't take her temperature, I didn't take her heart rate, I didn't take her blood pressure. I did my respiratory assessment on her."

"Well, that's not a full assessment, is it?"

"No."

"As a matter of fact, it's a very, very substandard assessment, isn't it?"

"I don't know what you mean by 'very substandard assessment'."
"You didn't take her temperature, right?"
"No."
"You didn't take her pulse?"
"No."
"You didn't take her blood pressure?"
"No."
"You didn't do a pain scale?"
"No."
"You didn't do a sedation scale?"
"No."
"That's a very substandard assessment, isn't it?"
"Yes."
"Now, you paged Dr. Schily at 2:50 because you were concerned, right?"
"Yes."
"You didn't re-assess Lisa five minutes later at 2:55, did you?"
"No."
"You were still concerned, weren't you?"
"Yes."
"You didn't assess Lisa at 3:00, five minutes later?"
"No."
"You were still concerned, weren't you?"
"Yes."
"You didn't re-assess Lisa at 3:05 or 3:10 or 3:15, did you?"
"Yes."
"You did?"
"I didn't."
"And you were still concerned?"
"I had taken the PCA morphine away from her already."
"You were still concerned, I suggest, at those times and didn't go back to record any vital signs for half an hour."
"Yes."
"Why was that?"
"I have no answer."
"You didn't page Dr. Schily at 2:55 or 3:00 or 3:05 or 3:10 all the way through to 4:05, did you?"
"No."

"Why not?"

"I paged him at 2:50 and I called him again at 4:00. In between those times, I went into Lisa's room. I was taking care of the other patients on the floor."

"Why didn't you page Dr. Schily again in that time frame, from 2:50, when you paged him, to 4:05 when you paged him again?"

"I believe I said I paged him at 2:50. I checked on Lisa, I checked on my other patients. I didn't realize it was already 4:00 and I had to call him again."

"So you didn't realize that the time had gone by?"

"Yes."

"And yet you were back in seeing Lisa at 3:20 and she had a respiration rate of 12 and a heart rate of 120?"

"Yes."

"Why didn't you page him at 3:20 when you were in the room?"

"I was waiting for the call back from Dr. Schily."

"Well, he'd already -- you'd already not gotten a call back for, as I do the arithmetic, from 2:50 to 3:20, that's 30 minutes. Why didn't you pick up the phone if you had to right in the room and page him?"

"Right in the room?"

"Right in Lisa's room."

"The phone that I was using was at the nursing station."

"I know that, but at 3:20 in the morning when you were in the room, she was the only patient on your mind when you were in the room dealing with her, wasn't she? Why didn't you page Dr. Schily right then and there?"

"I don't usually use the phones in the patients' rooms."

"Why didn't you leave the room and go to the nursing station and page Dr. Schily right then and there?"

"I don't know."

Hawkins got to question his own witness after the other lawyers had finished. He tried to repair the damage caused by Soriano's unconvincing testimony, but only managed to make things worse. He tried to show how busy Soriano's shift was, to explain how she could lose track of time and forget to call Dr. Schily back after he didn't answer her alleged page. Hawkins asked Soriano to describe all the nursing activities she might be doing at that time of night. But the litany of things she rhymed off—helping children to go to the bathroom, feeding a baby, attending to children who couldn't sleep–could hardly make a genuinely concerned nurse forget she had a patient whose vital signs were deteriorating. Had there been any real emergencies or other legitimate distractions occurring on the ward that night, the hospital would have brought them up in its nurses' defence long before this.

Soriano was no more honest with the coroner than she was with the lawyers. When Dr. Cairns asked her why she didn't follow the mandatory monitoring protocols, she answered, "I believe this was my first experience with an admission from Emergency with a child who had a PCA morphine. It didn't occur to me right away because usually I would get patients from the recovery room who have had surgery, post-operatively, they would have had PCA morphine, they would have had anaesthetic and when we receive them in the ward, this would have been the critical time. It just didn't come to mind that this was a different situation."

Dr. Cairns responded, "But it wasn't any different. The patient was on a PCA pump." "Yes, it was different," Soriano maintained. "So your reason for not following is?" persisted Dr. Cairns. Her answer: "I just didn't think of those."

What did Soriano have to say about the monitor? Yes, she definitely remembered helping Doerksen bring it in and attach it to Lisa, but after that her memory became extremely vague. Krkachovski questioned her about whether she heard any monitor alarms and she allowed she might have heard one but didn't know what room it came from. She ignored it anyway, since she was busy doing something else. Eventually the alarm stopped, she said, and she never asked Doerksen about it. Why didn't the hospital just throw out all its monitors, I thought to myself, since the nurses had no qualms about ignoring monitor alarms that might signify a child had stopped breathing?

That night, in the midst of our usual evening review of the day's testimony, Bill expressed his belief that we could prove the nurses were lying about the monitor alarms. Soriano's story didn't arouse any suspicion on its own; she said she had only heard one alarm go off while she was busy elsewhere and had let Doerksen take care of it. The problem was that we were all so focussed on whichever witness was in the stand that it was easy to lose sight of what other witnesses said about the same subject. And the pace was so rapid that nobody could take thorough notes.

The more we talked it out, however, the more we realized Doerksen and Soriano were telling two mutually exclusive stories. Doerksen had said she left the Constant Care Room to respond to yet another false alarm in Lisa's room. Knowing she wasn't supposed to leave the constant care patients unattended, Doerksen had claimed Soriano had been at the nursing desk and that she had asked Soriano to keep a lookout on the patients for her. Now Soriano was testifying she only heard one alarm go off while she was in another patient's room, and had not known where it came from. She could not have been at the nursing station as Doerksen claimed she had been. Had an alarm from Lisa's room really gone off, the nurse at the nursing station—a nurse who was not busy attending to patients—would have known exactly where it was coming from and would have been the one to respond to it. Had there really been an alarm sounding, no nurse would leave the Constant Care Room and run right past a nurse sitting at the nursing station. And even if you accepted this incredible account, once Doerksen had left the children in the Constant Care Room unattended, why wouldn't Soriano—supposedly still sitting at the nursing desk—go into that room to ensure the safety of its forgotten patients?

Was this deliberate strategy, having each nurse tell a complicated story that might be considered believable on its own and hoping she could get away with it, or did they accidentally forget to co-ordinate this part of their story? We needed to know exactly what Doerksen had said so we could challenge Soriano on it the next day, and ordered a rush transcript of Doerksen's testimony from the court reporter.

When Frank tried to cross-examine Soriano about whether or not she had heard an alarm coming from Lisa's room around 2:00 a.m. as Doerksen claimed had happened, Soriano stubbornly refused to answer his question. He asked her, "When Ruth left that Constant Care Room to turn off an alarm that she says she heard, that patient was your primary responsibility?"

"Yes."

"And yet you can't say whether you heard an alarm coming from Lisa Shore's room?"

"Yes."

"Don't you think that if there was an alarm coming from the room of a patient who was your primary responsibility at just after 2:00 in the morning, that you would have heard it?"

"Yes."

"And you didn't hear it?"

"I heard one alarm when I was giving my medications at that time -- at the same time."

"Yeah, but you can't say whether that came out of Lisa's room or whether it came out of any room?"

"No, I can't say that."

"And yet, Lisa's room was your responsibility?"

"Lisa and all the other patients were my responsibility."

"And you can't testify whether an alarm was alarming in Lisa's room that morning at just after 2:00 in the morning?"

"I heard that one alarm."

"You can't testify whether there was an alarm alarming that morning, just after 2:00 in the morning, coming out of Lisa's room?"

"I heard that one alarm when -- and the intravenous beep, and that was the alarm that I heard."

"Well, let me ask the question a third time, and I'll keep asking it until I get an answer. You can't testify whether there was an alarm coming out of Lisa Shore's room just after 2:00 in the morning on October 22nd, 1998?"

"I believe I said I heard an alarm with an intravenous beep at the same time."

Dr. Cairns interjected in exasperation, "No, the question is - it's a straightforward, clear question, and all it needs is a 'yes' or 'no' answer."

Soriano would not budge. She responded to the coroner's request with, "Yes, there is an alarm that I heard at the same time with the intravenous beep."

Frank said he would keep on asking the question until he got a straight answer. Hawkins tried to help his client, saying, "She doesn't know where that alarm was coming from."

The coroner wanted an answer and was not dissuaded. "The question was a valid question and all that the witness has to do is answer the question that Mr. Gomberg has put. And if you just listen to the question, it's clearly a 'yes' or 'no' answer."

"I said, yes, I heard an alarm."

Frank wouldn't give up. "Let me ask it yet again. You can't testify whether an alarm was alarming on the Corometric monitor in Lisa Shore's room at 2:00, or soon thereafter, on October 22nd, 1998?"

"I can't say for sure that it was coming from Lisa's room."

"Thank you. And Lisa was your patient at the time?"

"Yes."

Frank next tried to pin Soriano down on how implausible Doerksen's story about leaving the Constant Care Room while leaving Soriano behind at the nursing station was. He told her, "I want to ask you something that deals with the Corometric monitor, and I just want to read you something from the testimony of Nurse Doerksen, and then I have a couple of questions to ask you."

He began reading her the relevant portion of Doerksen's testimony.

> Mr. Krkachovski: You left the Constant Care Room to get some paperwork or something when you heard the alarm?
>
> Ms. Doerksen: Yes.
>
> Mr. Krkachovski: You then went to deal with the alarm?
>
> Ms. Doerksen: Yes.
>
> Mr. Krkachovski: Were you supposed to leave the Constant Care Room?
>
> Ms. Doerksen: No.
>
> Mr. Krkachovski: At all?
>
> Ms. Doerksen: No, I was not.
>
> Mr. Krkachovski: Did you tell Ms. Soriano that maybe she should look after the monitor while you stayed in the Constant Care Room?
>
> Ms. Doerksen: Well, generally what we do is say, 'Keep an eye on the -- or listen, keep an eye, an ear out for the Constant Care Room while I go and do something quickly'.
>
> Mr. Krkachovski: Did that happen?
>
> Ms. Doerksen: I believe I did, yes.
>
> Mr. Krkachovski: Before leaving the Constant Care Room to deal with the monitor, did you tell Ms. Soriano to keep an eye out for the patients in the Constant Care Room?
>
> Ms. Doerksen: I think Anagaile was probably at the desk, and I would have said to Anagaile, 'Could you keep your ear out for monitors in the Constant Care Room while I go and do this?'

Having reminded Soriano and the jury about Doerksen's version of events, Frank asked Soriano to explain the discrepancy in their stories. "Ms. Doerksen believes that you were sitting at the desk when that alarm went off. That's what she believes. Is that correct?"

"I don't remember specifically if I was sitting at the desk. I don't think I was at the desk. I was around the area near the desk, but I wasn't sitting at the desk."

"Well, if you were around the area sitting at the desk, I suggest to you that you would have heard the alarm, if there was an alarm coming out of the Shore room."

"If I was sitting at the desk, but I wasn't sitting at the desk."

"Well, if you were around the desk, then you would have heard the alarm coming out of the Shore room if there was an alarm coming out of the Shore room?"

"Yes."

"And you didn't do anything to go to the Shore room to check out the alarm?"

"No. I wasn't at the desk."

"You were around the desk?"

"I was around the desk, but I wasn't physically in the nursing station."

"I don't care whether you were in the nursing station. You were around the nursing station."

"Yes."

"And you didn't go in to check the alarm that was allegedly going off in the Shore room?"

"I didn't check the alarm that was going off."

"Nurse Doerksen did that after coming out of the Constant Care Room?"

"Yes."

"And you didn't go to the Constant Care Room to watch the patients there while Ms. Doerksen did this in the Shore room?"

"I was outside the Constant Care Room."

"Now, I suggest to you that that's highly unusual, that there's an alarm going off in the room of a patient of yours, Ms. Doerksen's coming out of the Constant Care Room and you're either at the desk or near the desk and you don't go and do anything about the alarm? Isn't that unusual?"

"I don't know if I have an answer for that."

"And I suggest it's highly unusual that when an alarm is alarming or allegedly alarming in a room of a patient who is on a PCA morphine pump, a patient that is under your care, I suggest that it's highly unusual that you don't even engage Ruth Doerksen in a discussion to find out what room that alarm is coming out of?"

"I can't answer that question."

We were not the only ones in the courtroom who were angry and upset about Soriano's testimony. A very elegant, dignified woman who had not previously attended the inquest sat in our section of the audience watching her testify. Dr. Robin Williams was the paediatrician who had reviewed Lisa's records for the Coroner's Paediatric Death Review Committee. She was scheduled to testify in a few days and had wanted an opportunity to quietly observe the proceedings so she could prepare herself. As she listened to Soriano, she held her hand to her cheek and repeatedly shook her head in dismay and disbelief.

25

A MOTHER'S TESTIMONY

The newspapers were giving the inquest extensive coverage. Some of the headlines read: "Girl's doctor says orders not followed",[1] "Girl's breathing alarm turned off",[2] "Inquest evidence suggests monitor wasn't turned on",[3] "Records withheld, inquest jury told",[4] and "Hospital contradicted at inquest".[5] We were glad the public was learning what the hospital was trying so hard to cover up.

In spite of all the public support we received, nobody from the hospital, the government, or any nursing organization contacted us. No one made any official comments. Although the people with whom we had been dealing appeared to be lacking in scruples, I had truly believed that when the hospital's higher-ups or its board of trustees learned more about Lisa's death, they would be disgusted at the cover-up, at the nursing care, and at the way its own institution was acting.

So where were they? Where was the head of the hospital, where were its trustees, and where were its senior physicians? Where were the hospital's good nurses, who should have been ashamed and angry to have been associated with two such bad nurses? Weren't any of the hospital employees who sat through the inquest day after day angry and betrayed at their colleagues' deceit? Didn't anyone at the Hospital for Sick Children have the integrity to stand up and say, "Why are we protecting nurses like these? What the hell are we doing?"

Apparently not.

Lisa's death had been devastating and inexplicable, and we wanted to find out why she died. Based on the hospital's actions, all it wanted was to pretend her death had never happened. Was this the hospital's usual and preferred mode of handling bad outcomes? How many other problems had it handled similarly, where parents spoke a language other than English, or lacked the education, the medical contacts, and the financial means and wherewithal to hire an excellent lawyer like we did? Maybe the hospital and its lawyers had been so successful in the past using the same techniques that they had grown arrogant and unable to conceive of any other way of doing things. But even given boundless arrogance and low ethical standards, what accounted for its inability to belatedly realize that its strategy at this inquest was failing profoundly and needed to be changed? Everybody could see the jury was unhappy with the hospital's witnesses, and the media was scornful and disgusted. One female television reporter said to me, "This is really frightening. I've got small children, and from what I've seen here, I'm afraid to take them to Sick Kids."

I was the next scheduled witness. The courtroom was more crowded than usual; a full house of television and print reporters was waiting expectantly to hear me contradict the nurses. Frank and I met with Margaret the day before, so she could explain the sort of questions she was planning to ask. No one told me what to say, nor did we discuss my answers. In the middle of our meeting, Hawkins called Frank, wanting to know what I was going to say about the monitors. Frank said I would testify there were no monitors attached to Lisa when she was came to the ward, but I could not say one way or the other whether there was one in the room the next morning when Lisa was discovered dead.

Frank told me not to be too nervous, because Hawkins would not be overly aggressive. Lawyers knew they had to tread very carefully when cross-examining sympathetic witnesses. I was a mother who had lost a child, and if Hawkins did not go easy on me, the jury would not like it. I was nervous regardless, but after several weeks of sitting in the courtroom listening to lies and evasions, I was also angry and determined the jury hear at least one person tell the truth about what had happened.

I described Lisa's visit in Emergency, the transfer to Ward 5A at 1:45 a.m., and the encounter with nurses Doerksen and Soriano. I was adamant that Lisa had not been placed on any monitor, at least not before 2:15 a.m. when I went to sleep. I was equally sure there were no alarms or other noises in the room at any time because I am a light sleeper and they would have woken me up. I did concede it was possible nurses came into the room in the middle of the night, but if they did it was very quietly.

Doerksen had testified she never saw me when she came into Lisa's room each of the three or four times the monitor allegedly emitted a false alarm. Krkachovski asked me if, hypothetically, Doerksen's evidence about the monitor's alarm sounding had been correct, would I have asked her any questions about what was happening. I told him, "Not only would I have asked some questions of her as to why this machine was alarming, I would have been in the hallway screaming for a nurse long before anybody made it to the room."

Frank was right about Hawkins. He kept his questions low-key, mostly trying to raise possibilities to account for the differences between what I said and what the nurses had said. Where it seemed reasonable I would allow the possibility, but I would not concede about the monitor.

He asked, "Would you agree with me with what Ruth Doerksen and Anagaile Soriano said, that they brought a Corometric monitor into the room and hooked it up to Lisa?" I was still reluctant at that time to call the nurses outright liars because I thought the jury would disapprove, so I tried to couch my words. "I would say that they are wrong, to be charitable."

Hawkins tried to imply that due to the shock of Lisa's death, I might have forgotten what had happened earlier. "You've seen and you've heard the demonstration of the Corometric monitor when it cycles or when it turns on. My recollection is that there is a single beep?" He was trying to downplay the piercing three-second long alarm by characterising it as a "single beep". I wasn't going to let him. "A beep that lasts for several seconds, but yes, you're right."

"Is it possible that you would miss or you would forget in the confusion after your daughter's death hearing that single beep?"

"You were talking about the confusion after my daughter's death, referring to a beep at 1:45 a.m.?" I looked at him scornfully, as if he was asking something completely absurd, and paused for effect. "No."

"Is it possible that the machine did beep once as we know it does when the machine is turned on and that's simply a detail that you've forgotten?"

I was losing patience. "Mr. Hawkins, there was no machine in the room, therefore there could be no beeps!"

"No beeps from your perspective; you're saying there were no beeps at any time at all?"

"That's correct."

Hawkins's junior had been watching the jury while he questioned me, and she could see them squirming. He was ready to keep going but she whispered to him and he wisely decided to end his cross-examination.

The jury had a few questions for me, and they were good ones. They asked if I had been taking any sedatives that night. I explained that I had never taken any sedatives in my life until after Lisa died. They wanted to know about one of the medications that Lisa was taking for her pain. "I wonder, Mrs. Shore, if you have any concerns and interest with the drug Gabapentin, just generally speaking?"

I told them I did. "Before Lisa died I contacted the drug company to find out more about the drug. I was told that it was not officially used for pain relief, that it was an <anti> epileptic drug. Even though hundreds of thousands of people use it for pain relief, it's not the official use, and therefore they would not give me any information."

Outside the courtroom afterwards, I faced a barrage of microphones and cameras. I was still hedging my words, afraid of getting sued, but I was getting bolder. I told everybody I was glad that *I* had the opportunity to get the truth out. Only one television outlet was brave enough to go with that, stating in its broadcast that I had called the nurses liars.

26

DEATH SUMMARY REVISITED

Dr. Reingold, the investigating coroner, was up next. Although we felt he had done a shoddy investigation, we did not plan to give him a hard time. He wasn't responsible for Lisa's death or for covering it up, and attacking him wouldn't help us get any closer to the truth.

The jury, on the other hand, was not inclined to be so charitable. One juror asked him how many years of experience he had as a coroner and if he believed he had done a good job in this case.

The forewoman quizzed Dr. Reingold about whether he had seen Lisa's nursing flowchart the morning of her death, when he arrived at the hospital. When he said he had, the juror asked him to look at the flowchart that was on exhibit in the courtroom. "I wonder, looking at that flowsheet now, if you could tell me if the same information is on that flowsheet today as was on that flowsheet at 8:30 or 9:00 when you looked at it, when you arrived at the hospital that morning?"

We had never before considered the possibility that the records had been doctored. This jury did not trust the Hospital for Sick Children either.

The hospital witness who had previously testified about the Kidcom system had not done a stellar job in explaining how it worked, so the jury wanted to learn more about it. Dr. Cairns asked the hospital to provide a demonstration. The hospital could not do one in the courtroom, so the inquest resumed the next morning at the Hospital for Sick Children.

The Kidcom expert was there again to do a "walk-through" for the attendees, but this time her boss, the system manager, was there to explain and answer questions. To our great surprise, this woman was articulate and truthful. She agreed that no matter how many prompts were placed in a system, they would all be ineffective if someone decided not to follow them. She thought it would also be common sense that where a patient had died inexplicably, to retain the various papers and printouts instead of throwing them out as the nurses claimed they had done.

I later heard that the hospital had extensively coached her on what to say when she testified, just as it had done with its other witnesses. The difference between her and the others was that she refused to be a party to this deception and had decided to answer all the questions honestly. I also discovered that she left the hospital's employ not long after the inquest concluded.

Dr. Wright, the orthopaedic surgeon who we had met on the morning of Lisa's death, was the next witness. He was the author of the inaccurate Death Summary and also one of the editors and reviewers of the hospital's anonymous letter, and we wanted to confront him about both documents and learn why he was party to such misleading information.

Dr. Wright was an accomplished physician, and well aware of it. He appeared arrogant and egotistic, at least initially, but by the time he finished testifying he was subdued and humble.

The afternoon before, at the typical last minute we had become so used to, we had been handed a different Death Summary, one that had somehow only just been discovered.[1] This one had been written by the resident who worked for Dr. Wright—another doctor who had never met Lisa—and was dated a week earlier than the one that had been sent to us as part of the medical records. The two documents were markedly different, as we discovered by comparing them line-by-line.

Dr. Wright explained that his resident's version had contained so many mistakes that he felt compelled to correct it. But rather than looking at Lisa's chart to make those corrections, he did it by memory, relying exclusively on what Doerksen had told him. The revised Death Summary contained even more mistakes and inaccuracies than the original version, even though it was much shorter.

Regarding the hospital's unsigned letter, he would not take any responsibility for it and claimed he hadn't really been involved in drafting the responses. Frank persisted, until Dr. Cairns suggested that Dr. Roy would be in a better position to answer his questions.

Dr. Roy, another one of the letter's editors and reviewers, was head of Anaesthesia and Pain Service and one of the two doctors who had met with me a few months earlier in an attempt to get me to call off the inquest. He was scheduled to testify in a few days, so we agreed to postpone our questions until then.

Dr. Wright had not been coached by the hospital and was not part of the hospital's cover-up. However, he was definitely part of the problem. His rationale for having prepared an inaccurate and sloppy Death Summary was that he didn't know Lisa and wasn't the one responsible for her care. Instead of doing the right thing by speaking to the people involved in Lisa's care, or at least asking them to review what he had written, he did a shoddy, substandard job and tried to justify it at the inquest.

The jury did not approve of Dr. Wright's actions. One juror asked, "The information that you have now about the charts, the protocol, what was done, what wasn't done; do you feel that there was negligence on anybody's part?" Dr. Cairns quickly advised him that inquests could not comment on whether or not negligence had occurred, so Dr. Wright was saved from having to answer.

Another juror asked him why he hadn't called the police. Dr. Cairns interjected that the doctor had done the right thing by calling the coroner's office. Left unsaid was the implication that the police should have been called—by somebody.

27

SMOKESCREEN

Dr. Robin Williams, the highly experienced paediatrician we had seen in the audience shaking her head in dismay when Soriano testified, was an impressive witness. Everyone in the courtroom, on our side of the gallery at least, liked and respected her. During her testimony, to her great embarrassment, her cell phone went off. Frank joked, "They put lawyers in jail for that sort of thing," and she quipped back, "Oh, good!"

But there were no jokes when explaining the Paediatric Death Review Committee's analysis. The Committee was critical of the nursing care that Lisa had received, and said there were many "red flags" that should have prompted the nurses to take action which might have saved her. As Dr. Williams put it, "So the Committee did feel that intervention earlier, you can never say for sure, but my goodness, here was an 11-year-old who came into hospital basically healthy on some medications who dies on the ward with her mother beside her. My goodness."

She was a wonderful witness who ably summarized the substandard nursing care and the missed opportunities to save Lisa. Hawkins knew that he could not undermine her testimony, so he tried to diminish it by deflecting blame elsewhere.

He attacked the composition of the Committee, saying that it was unqualified to judge nursing issues without having any nursing experts. It was a valid point, but there was a corollary to the accusation that he neglected to mention: had there been such an expert, he or she would undoubtedly have condemned the nurses in even stronger terms than Dr. Williams had.

Hawkins attacked Dr. Schily's actions in the Emergency Department, implying that he was negligent. He asked Dr. Williams, "We've heard an awful lot about nurses forgetting to check the Kidcom orders on the ward. Would you agree with me that a physician forgetting to write orders for care in the Emergency Department is an error or is a mistake of about the same magnitude as failing to check orders?"

Lisa received excellent care in Emergency. Dr. Schily did not forget to write orders and he had not been in any way negligent, and Hawkins knew it even though he was hoping to convince the jury otherwise. Dr. Williams tried to explain. "It doesn't feel equivalent to me, but, I mean, my view of even a busy Emergency Department is that the kids are there, awake, the parents are awake, they're waiting for transition to the ward, the nurse is in and out, there's easy accessibility to physicians. He may have been actually there. They don't feel equivalent to me."

Hawkins would not let it go. "So while it's reasonable to expect a physician to write orders in the Emergency Department, forgetting's okay? Is that what you're suggesting?"

Now I could better understand exactly what Frank meant when he said lawyers have to be very careful when dealing with sympathetic witnesses. Dr. Williams radiated competence and poise, and here was Hawkins trying to browbeat her. If it made me angry, it must have infuriated the jury. One thing was sure: no one was buying what he was trying to sell.

Mary Douglas, the nursing-educator, was recalled to testify again. The jury had become quite knowledgeable by now about what constituted normal and abnormal vital signs and knew that Douglas had been trying to con them, so they had demanded another opportunity to question her.

Juror number three asked her, "Did you help Ms. Doerksen write her testimony?"

The forewoman had a lot to say, but they were rhetorical questions. She didn't expect real answers from Douglas and didn't get any, but she wanted the chance to make a statement about some of the things that bothered her most. "I really don't have very many questions. We have clinical judgment and we have good clinical judgment, don't we? But we also have poor clinical judgment. How do we address poor clinical judgment?" "Is it reasonable to draw assumptions when a child, a healthy child, lost her life, is it reasonable to draw any assumptions but rather not to take all precautions? You yourself say you assume, that you trust these nurses, you expect them to tell you the truth, so therefore you assume. Why should we be assuming anything at that point of crisis?"

The forewoman was on a roll. "I also wanted to comment on the fact that to date, Ms. Soriano does not understand the Kidcom system clearly enough to access the doctor's orders that night, and to operate on the doctor's orders rather than her clinical judgment, yet she has been working, employed with the hospital 18 months, I believe. And somehow it has not surfaced that Ms. Soriano was ignorant of the -- that's not a good word, that she was 'less informed' than I, a lay person, as to how that Kidcom worked that night, how she should have accessed those doctor's orders for that little girl. And it hasn't surfaced in her review and so she's had one employee review. And she continued working an additional six months and, I mean, we heard it here, folks. She did not understand. That's very disturbing."

But those comments paled beside what Juror #4 had to say. He had not spoken to this point, but now he exploded.

"Am I permitted to give my thoughts as to what I figure happened that night?" He wasn't, but the coroner allowed him to speak hypothetically. "I guess if a patient is sent up to an orthopaedic ward from the emergency ward for the first time and she's in pain, just pain, now the nurses on 5A are accustomed to working with patients with broken limbs... Now understanding the fact that she's sent up, somebody might question the fact as to why this person is being sent up, she has a pain in her leg. They take her in, assuming that, gee, put her into a room, give her an aspirin and she'll be gone tomorrow without realizing how critical that patient is, that no care was, in fact, given or very little care was given to that patient."

Douglas answered, "When Lisa came in, she was a child with chronic pain who lived with pain every day and who functioned quite well in between times of pain. She's a child that in any nurse's mind, would not be considered critical; in fact, she may have been the healthiest child on the floor that night. Her status, as you described, as being critical is one that I don't agree with. That's one where, you know, in hindsight we look back and say this..."

"No, no, I didn't say it was critical, she has a pain in her leg. We'll put her into a room and basically forget her."

"Well, I would disagree that they forgot her. Certainly they did extensive checks on her with her respiratory status because of the morphine and their assessment of her was that she hit a point when she had mild respiratory depression that was dealt with appropriately. The physician was informed and then she stabilized and improved through the night. She had no more morphine in her system at that time, according to the nurses, it had been given many hours before and I'm sure that's what was going through their mind. The intent of Lisa coming to the floor was to allow her to sleep the night so that they could start an epidural in the morning."

"So regardless of why she was sent up, she would still get as much care as what any of the other patients would have had that night?"

"Oh, no. The care for every patient is individualized according to their diagnosis, their status, their medications, their treatments. Every child that has an intravenous is checked hourly just to see that the intravenous is -- that the site is okay and it's functioning and dripping correctly. Some children need one nurse in the room at all times for constant nursing observation because of their status. Some children, just depending on their recovery stage, their stability at the time, it varies with every patient and a nurse uses a great deal of judgment to do that, to decide how often to go in, what kinds of other monitoring needs to be done and things like that."

The juror didn't agree. "Might it have been possible that the nurses decided that she didn't require as much attention?"

"I'm not sure I can answer that on their behalf," Douglas said, although she had not had any difficulty in her previous testimony doing precisely that. "I think that the flowsheet is indicative of how often they went in and how closely they watched her. Yes, there were some vital signs missing, the two blood pressures, as I testified earlier, but they kept an extremely close eye on her respiratory status, which is the primary concern in a child receiving morphine."

The juror was blunt. "The testimony that we've heard by the nurses telling us what was done, what we find wasn't done, filling in flowsheets with parts of what should have been filled in... We've heard of instances supposedly where people have lied to one another, or errors being made in certain documents. And I'm not sure if I'm allowed to ask this but to me this sounds like a cover-up. We've been given a smokescreen. I realize Sick Children's Hospital is well known and unblemished, and I hope that this situation is just an isolated case and it covers the whole iceberg and not just the tip."

The next day's front page headline read, "Sick Kids cover-up charged, inquest juror points finger at Toronto hospital".[1]

28

SOLVING THE PUZZLE

We wanted the mother who had been in the hospital room next to Lisa to testify so she could tell the jury that no alarms had gone off that night. However, we knew Hawkins would do everything he could to prevent it, because her testimony would prove beyond any doubt that Lisa's nurses were liars. Although we were confident we would win a legal argument if Hawkins appealed, momentum had been building in this inquest and we didn't want to slow it down by fighting with him. We were pretty sure the jury did not believe the nurses' testimony anyway, so we agreed not to call the mother as a witness. Dr. Cairns was pleased we were so reasonable.

We were not inclined to be so reasonable about Dr. Roy, who was scheduled to testify next. When Dr. Wright testified, he had denied having any part in writing the hospital's letter. That left three remaining reviewers and editors: Dr. Roy, a senior nurse, and the Risk Manager. Of these three, Dr. Roy would have been the most familiar with PCA protocols and treatment of pain. Dr. Schily was one of his staff, and we felt Dr. Roy had to have been instrumental in the crafting of that misleading document.

Dr. Roy suddenly became unwilling to testify.

We could do in reverse what Hawkins had threatened to do about the mother: file a formal protest and demand Dr. Roy be subpoenaed. We badly wanted to hear from him, but we also sensed that compelling a respected physician like Dr. Roy to testify against his will would not be well-received by the jury. We reluctantly agreed to let him avoid testifying.

But during the lawyers' discussions about Dr. Roy we learned something else about the Hospital for Sick Children that was very disturbing: It had never held a Morbidity and Mortality review to discuss Lisa's death. Virtually all major hospitals, including Sick Kids, regularly hold such reviews to review deaths that occur in their facilities. Some hospitals review every death, whether due to trauma, disease, or health care mismanagement, while others review only those where doctors feel that something about them can be used as a teaching tool to help improve doctors' practices. The review is non-threatening, non-adversarial, by doctors and for doctors, and its objectives are to learn from previous experiences and to prevent errors from recurring. In disciplines where deaths are infrequent or unexpected, such as Anaesthesia or Obstetrics, Morbidity and Mortality conferences are taken very seriously and generally all deaths are reviewed. We had asked about this review knowing that those records were confidential, thinking the coroner's office might want to subpoena them as part of its investigation. We had not realized that Anaesthesia was just as eager as Orthopaedics, Nursing, and Risk Management to pretend Lisa Shore had never existed. We were bitterly disappointed we would not have the opportunity to question Dr. Roy about his department's glaring oversight.

There were other new witnesses we wanted to call. Before the inquest began, we had argued that the hospital had not provided information about other nurses on the ward so we were unable to determine if any of them should be subpoenaed. The coroner agreed this was problematic, so Hawkins submitted short will-says from several nurses. Although we did not trust they were complete or even entirely accurate, we saw nothing that hinted that any of these nurses had potentially useful information to contribute.

In light of everything we had learned, however, I decided to re-read those will-says. Originally, we had looked at whether the nurses had interacted with Doerksen or Soriano or had visited Lisa's room before she was found dead, but we had not paid much attention to whatever else the nurse claimed to have been doing. This time I noticed that one of the will-says stated that when the nurse came on duty in the morning and heard the code called on Lisa, she had been in a conference room listening to a taped report. The intent of that statement had been to show that this nurse had nothing to do with Lisa, but this time I questioned what taped report she had been listening to.

28

SOLVING THE PUZZLE

We wanted the mother who had been in the hospital room next to Lisa to testify so she could tell the jury that no alarms had gone off that night. However, we knew Hawkins would do everything he could to prevent it, because her testimony would prove beyond any doubt that Lisa's nurses were liars. Although we were confident we would win a legal argument if Hawkins appealed, momentum had been building in this inquest and we didn't want to slow it down by fighting with him. We were pretty sure the jury did not believe the nurses' testimony anyway, so we agreed not to call the mother as a witness. Dr. Cairns was pleased we were so reasonable.

We were not inclined to be so reasonable about Dr. Roy, who was scheduled to testify next. When Dr. Wright testified, he had denied having any part in writing the hospital's letter. That left three remaining reviewers and editors: Dr. Roy, a senior nurse, and the Risk Manager. Of these three, Dr. Roy would have been the most familiar with PCA protocols and treatment of pain. Dr. Schily was one of his staff, and we felt Dr. Roy had to have been instrumental in the crafting of that misleading document.

Dr. Roy suddenly became unwilling to testify.

We could do in reverse what Hawkins had threatened to do about the mother: file a formal protest and demand Dr. Roy be subpoenaed. We badly wanted to hear from him, but we also sensed that compelling a respected physician like Dr. Roy to testify against his will would not be well-received by the jury. We reluctantly agreed to let him avoid testifying.

But during the lawyers' discussions about Dr. Roy we learned something else about the Hospital for Sick Children that was very disturbing: It had never held a Morbidity and Mortality review to discuss Lisa's death. Virtually all major hospitals, including Sick Kids, regularly hold such reviews to review deaths that occur in their facilities. Some hospitals review every death, whether due to trauma, disease, or health care mismanagement, while others review only those where doctors feel that something about them can be used as a teaching tool to help improve doctors' practices. The review is non-threatening, non-adversarial, by doctors and for doctors, and its objectives are to learn from previous experiences and to prevent errors from recurring. In disciplines where deaths are infrequent or unexpected, such as Anaesthesia or Obstetrics, Morbidity and Mortality conferences are taken very seriously and generally all deaths are reviewed. We had asked about this review knowing that those records were confidential, thinking the coroner's office might want to subpoena them as part of its investigation. We had not realized that Anaesthesia was just as eager as Orthopaedics, Nursing, and Risk Management to pretend Lisa Shore had never existed. We were bitterly disappointed we would not have the opportunity to question Dr. Roy about his department's glaring oversight.

There were other new witnesses we wanted to call. Before the inquest began, we had argued that the hospital had not provided information about other nurses on the ward so we were unable to determine if any of them should be subpoenaed. The coroner agreed this was problematic, so Hawkins submitted short will-says from several nurses. Although we did not trust they were complete or even entirely accurate, we saw nothing that hinted that any of these nurses had potentially useful information to contribute.

In light of everything we had learned, however, I decided to re-read those will-says. Originally, we had looked at whether the nurses had interacted with Doerksen or Soriano or had visited Lisa's room before she was found dead, but we had not paid much attention to whatever else the nurse claimed to have been doing. This time I noticed that one of the will-says stated that when the nurse came on duty in the morning and heard the code called on Lisa, she had been in a conference room listening to a taped report. The intent of that statement had been to show that this nurse had nothing to do with Lisa, but this time I questioned what taped report she had been listening to.

My friend Sharon knew right away. Many hospitals have a system whereby the nurses on shift record information about their patients onto a tape. When the next shift starts, the arriving nurses sit together and listen to the tape made by the previous shift. Since one nurse's four patients may be re-assigned to four different nurses on the next shift, the nurse doing the taping saves time by making one recording and not having to speak to four separate people. Another advantage is that the nurse can prepare the tape over the course of her shift, starting and stopping it whenever she finds the time instead of giving all her reports verbally at shift change when she might be very busy.

This was astounding. Neither Doerksen nor Soriano had ever mentioned making a tape. If they did make one—and according to this nurse's will-say they had—then the nurses coming on shift had all heard Doerksen's report on Lisa as part of the daily routine of getting reports on their patients. What had Doerksen said about Lisa? Did that tape still exist? Both Doerksen and Soriano's failure to mention the existence of this tape made it crucial we find out more about it.

Lisa had died on Ward 5A, which was adjacent to Ward 5B and connected to it by a common corridor. Although they were two separate units with each having its own nursing station, both saw the same kinds of patients; shorter admissions such as overnight stays went to 5A and longer admissions went to 5B. Nurses could be assigned to either unit for the duration of their shifts. A nurse assigned to 5A worked her entire shift there, but might be assigned to 5B on her next shift. Bill made up a spreadsheet and slotted in all the will-says Hawkins had given us, and we discovered they came from three night nurses on 5B, three day nurses on 5B, and two nurses who were not directly involved in patient care. Only one 5A floor nurse will-say had been provided—and it was from the one who said she had listened to the taped report!

We demanded this 5A nurse be subpoenaed to testify. The coroner and Margaret Browne were quite disturbed to learn that such crucial information had been withheld, and they told Hawkins to comply. He was told on a Friday afternoon to make sure this nurse showed up in court first thing Monday morning. Hawkins turned towards the wall, but his dejection was evident by his body language, even from behind. We knew how much time and effort he and the others had been putting in to prep their witnesses, and just when he thought things were winding down he had a new witness to coach and not much time in which to do it.

He didn't know we also wanted to hear from every nurse on Ward 5A who had arrived for the morning shift and listened to the tape Doerksen had made, and that we wanted Doerksen and Soriano recalled so they could tell us what they had said on it.

Trying to make sense of the bits and pieces of information that had been extracted with such difficulty from the hospital's witnesses was like assembling one of Lisa's 1000-piece puzzles, but we had been doing it for a while and were getting much better at it. Now that we had heard from doctors, nurses, and Kidcom system experts, we thought we knew the essence of what had happened at the Hospital for Sick Children on October 22, 1998.

Lisa had arrived on the floor at 1:45 a.m., fast asleep. Her vital signs were already starting to decline in comparison to what they had been in Emergency, but Doerksen did not read the Emergency chart and did not notice. She was not happy about getting Lisa as a patient, since she remembered Lisa from her admission eight months earlier. She had never been assigned to Lisa's care, but the nurses all talk amongst themselves and she knew the orthopaedic surgeons had concluded that Lisa was perfectly healthy and just needed psychiatric help. The nurses disliked Lisa, and they disliked me, and Doerksen shared their dislike even though she didn't know us personally. She intentionally did not check the doctor's orders that night because she resented Lisa's presence among her "genuinely ill" patients, and her refusal to talk to me at 1:45 a.m. when we arrived on the floor was a manifestation of her anger. It was irrelevant to her that Lisa had received a very significant dose of morphine and that she was on a number of different medications, since Doerksen considered her a well child who did not require nursing care. And if Lisa wasn't worth checking the doctor's orders, Doerksen certainly wasn't going to waste any time hunting down monitors to hook her up to.

It was simply not possible for a fifteen-year veteran nurse like Doerksen to accidentally forget to read the doctor's orders. Would a long-time police officer who had spent years on patrol in a high crime area, one day and for no particular reason accidentally forget to strap on his gun when he went to work, when the gun was stored in the same place it always was? Would that officer then go on patrol and not once on his whole shift ever realize his gun wasn't by his side? Even if one were foolish enough to believe this, Doerksen would have been reminded of her accidental oversight when she saw the 6:15 a.m. care plan. Having forgotten to do something so essential, she would have thought to herself, "Oh my goodness, I forgot to activate those orders! I had better do it right away and get those monitors the doctor ordered for the patient!" But she didn't activate the orders, and she didn't behave like someone who had made an accidental error and was taking pains to correct it. Her decision to not tell anyone that she hadn't checked the orders was exactly what one would expect of someone covering up a misdeed, not to mention her having printed another copy out a few days later and taken it home.

Around 2:00 a.m., about fifteen minutes after Lisa and I arrived on the floor, Doerksen went into the Constant Care Room and left novice nurse Soriano in charge. Soriano came into Lisa's room several times, at 2:30, 2:45, and 2:50 a.m., each time checking and recording Lisa's steadily declining breathing rate. She did not take any of her other vital signs, even though the doctor's orders, hospital protocols, and minimally competent professional judgment all mandated she should. There were no monitors; had there been one it would have displayed Lisa's heart and respiratory rates, and Soriano would have recorded both vital signs on Lisa's chart instead of only her respiratory rate. By 2:50 a.m., Lisa's breathing was markedly abnormal, and Soriano took away the PCA morphine pump. This was a pointless exercise, since Lisa had been fast asleep when she arrived on the floor and had not used the machine at all. What Soriano should have done instead was to take a full set of vital signs, attempt to wake Lisa up, and immediately call the doctor.

Around 4:00 a.m., Soriano went around and checked on all her patients. She went to the sleeping boy in the next room and took all of his vital signs including his blood pressure, proving she knew that blood pressure was one of the vital signs she was supposed to check. She went into Lisa's room, and according to the chart did not take a blood pressure, a blood pressure that would have shown Lisa was near death.

Sharon said this did not make sense. In order to take blood pressures, Soriano would have toted a pole with a blood pressure cuff from room to room as she checked on each patient. If she had the pole with her in the room next door, she would have had the pole with her while in Lisa's room. If she took one patient's blood pressure, she took all the patients' blood pressures. Sharon was positive that a novice nurse, a recent graduate, would have adhered to the rules and protocols even more closely than an experienced nurse and would have carefully taken all her patients' vital signs.

Sharon managed to convince us Soriano had to have taken Lisa's blood pressure at 4:00 a.m., and that was why she paged Dr. Schily then: she knew what Lisa's blood pressure was and realized she had a medical emergency on her hands. Why wasn't the blood pressure recorded on the chart? She had an answer for that, too.

"Soriano didn't enter anything on the flowsheet when she did Lisa's vitals. The nurses testified it was their practice to write things on a paper they kept in their pocket and then refer to it when they entered the information on the flowsheet. Soriano saw Lisa was in trouble and ran to call Dr. Schily, so for sure she wasn't thinking about completing the flowsheet at that moment. Now flash forward: they find out Lisa is dead. Doerksen and Soriano know they're in big trouble. What can they do to protect themselves? Not knowing why Lisa died, they couldn't take a chance on falsifying the records. They didn't know what the autopsy would show, and if they made up something that didn't agree with the autopsy results their deception would be discovered."

Sharon was frustrated we couldn't see what was so obvious to her. "The sin of commission is much worse than the sin of omission, don't you understand? If Soriano wrote down what Lisa's blood pressure was at 4:00 a.m., anyone looking at the chart would know in a second that Lisa was dying. What could the nurses say when they were asked why they hadn't done anything about it? Instead of writing down the proof of their negligence, they thought it would be better if they just 'forgot' to record the blood pressure. Yes, some of the other vital signs looked bad, but not so bad they couldn't talk their way out of it. About the missing blood pressure they could say, 'Oops, we just didn't get a chance to take her blood pressure, sorry we missed it, just one of those things, if only we had known her blood pressure was so low, but since we didn't, oops, how could we have known she was dying, we're very sorry.'"

It was better to be seen as a careless nurse who forgot to do something like take a vital blood pressure than for others to learn that a nurse had seen her patient near death and done nothing about it. Mary Douglas had implied as much when she testified, as if it was of no consequence, that the nurses "just missed a blood pressure or two".

Each time we figured out something we were left with another quandary to resolve. If we accepted that Soriano had taken Lisa's blood pressure and knew Lisa was in crisis, why hadn't she told Dr. Schily the truth when he answered her page? That one was easy, Sharon said. Doerksen must have come back from break—or was on break but nearby—and learned that Soriano had paged him. Maybe she scolded Soriano for waking the doctor up for no reason and told her to say everything was okay, or maybe Doerksen told Soriano to go on break and she would take care of things, and it was Doerksen who actually spoke to Dr. Schily. Whatever the veteran nurse told the novice nurse to say or do, the novice nurse did. When Dr. Schily returned Soriano's page, he was told Lisa was stable and arousable and her vital signs were fine, even though none of those things were true. Dr. Schily, assuming his orders had been followed and Lisa was on oximetry which would have indicated any problems, told whomever he was speaking with to keep a close eye on Lisa and call him if she wanted him to come down to the hospital.

Doerksen made entries on Lisa's flowsheet at 5:00 a.m. indicating she had taken Lisa's respiratory rate, pulse, and temperature. There was no recording of a blood pressure, which at 5:00 a.m.—if Lisa was even alive—would have been approaching zero. She charted that she took Lisa's temperature by mouth, meaning Lisa would have to have been awake enough to keep the thermometer under her tongue, yet she glibly told the coroner at the inquest the reason she didn't take Lisa's blood pressure was because she didn't want to wake her up.

It was nearly impossible to awaken Lisa in the night, even when she wasn't drugged and near death. Either Lisa's temperature was never taken and the entry on the flowsheet was false, or her temperature was taken using an ear thermometer and Doerksen did not try to wake Lisa up. It was possible that some or all of the 5:00 a.m. entries were false. Dr. Wright testified Doerksen had told him that Lisa's vitals at 5:00 and at 6:00 a.m. were normal, but that was patently untrue; she hadn't taken all of Lisa's vitals, and those she took were not normal.

What if Lisa had already died by 5:00 a.m.? We did not know what the actual time of death was; we were told there was no way to tell for sure. Every television show we had ever watched indicated the time of death could be determined quite accurately, but apparently not this time.

Dr. Catre, one of the doctors who had tried to resuscitate Lisa and who had testified earlier, eventually admitted to a Crown attorney that when he touched Lisa she had been very cold, and in his opinion she had been dead for quite some time. He said there was no way the vital signs recorded on the flowsheet at 6:00 a.m. by Ruth Doerksen could have been accurate. He did not speak about this at the inquest, and refused to repeat his comments on the record when asked to do so while testifying in court.

So where had the monitor come from? Too great a number of people to disbelieve had said that Lisa had stickers on her chest for the monitor's leads and that they had seen a monitor in the room. That meant that someone—and there was only one plausible possibility as to who that someone might be—had brought the monitor into the room while Lisa and I were asleep, put stickers on, and attached the leads. When was that done? Could Lisa have been alive then and could she have been saved?

The Kidcom people had explained in detail how the patient care plans printed off at the nursing station between 6:15 and 6:30 a.m., and that it was the responsibility of the night shift charge nurse—Doerksen—to sort and get them ready for the nurses arriving for the next shift. Soriano, the only other nurse on the floor on night shift with Doerksen, had denied doing it. Doerksen also denied having done it, but we knew she was lying because another nurse had said they were ready for her when she came in early to start the next shift.

At first we thought Doerksen might have brought the monitor in when she saw the suspended orders on the patient care plan that had printed off around 6:30 a.m. But that didn't make sense, since it implied that not activating the orders was an oversight she was trying to remedy instead of a deliberate act. Had it been an oversight, Doerksen would have activated the orders, printed them off and left them in the file, and she would have brought in both of the monitors that were ordered, not just one. Had she been unable to find the second monitor, the oximeter, she would have documented that on the chart to protect herself. She would have notified someone that she couldn't find a monitor that had been ordered. Had it been an oversight she would have been devastated—as any caring nurse would have been—to think that she might have in some way been responsible for Lisa's death.

No, Doerksen saw the patient care plan, and her failure to activate the doctor's orders had been deliberate. Nothing she saw on the plan made a difference to the nursing care she failed to provide to Lisa. Doerksen sorted and stapled the patient care plans exactly as she was supposed to, and got them ready for the nurses coming on shift that morning.

Which brought us back to the obvious question: when did she bring the monitor in? There were two possibilities. In her handwritten notes, her supposedly honest accounting of events, she had written she "somehow" forgot to check on Lisa at 7:00 a.m. An experienced nurse would never forget her newest patient, the one who had arrived only a few hours earlier from Emergency and whose respiratory depression had prompted a 4:00 a.m. call to the doctor. Doerksen testified she planned to check on Lisa while accompanying the doctors on their rounds, yet she stood by the door when the doctors entered the room and never came near her.

The first possibility was that she did check Lisa at 7:00 a.m., just like she checked on her other patients, and found her dead. She knew she was in serious trouble because she hadn't bothered to activate the doctor's orders or put Lisa on any monitors. She assumed she would be blamed for Lisa's death and her career would be finished. In her panic she came up with the idea of bringing the monitor into the room, to make it look as if she had been doing her job. She couldn't say she had checked on Lisa at 7:00 a.m. and found her dead, since she hadn't called a Code Blue. Nor could she say she had checked on Lisa and she was fine, because the doctors were going to find out she was dead as soon as they started their rounds. Her best bet, she felt, was to pretend she hadn't yet been to Lisa's room, and to act as shocked as the doctors when they went in and found her.

Doerksen needed to devise an explanation for why she had gone into everyone else's room at 7:00 a.m. except Lisa's, but the best she could come up with was "I somehow forgot". She also added the little notation "po", meaning by mouth, to the temperature she charted or concocted at 5:00 a.m. A temperature taken by mouth would indicate that the patient had been awakened, notwithstanding Doerksen's claim that she did not take Lisa's blood pressure because she hadn't wanted to wake her.

By the time Doerksen found Lisa dead at 7:00 it was too late to activate those orders, since they automatically printed out with a time stamp. If Lisa was discovered dead around 7:15 a.m., it would have been very suspicious if the orders had shown they were printed at 7:05 a.m. It would be best, Doerksen figured, not to mention the suspended orders to anybody and hope no one noticed.

That was why no alarm ever sounded when Lisa's heart stopped; Doerksen had only brought the machine in a few minutes earlier. She could not turn it on, because the monitor's alarms would have gone off when it was not able to detect a heartbeat.

The second possibility we considered was that Doerksen found Lisa dead at 6:00 a.m., the last time she made a notation in the flowsheet. She brought the monitor in at that time, attached it to Lisa, and wrote down non-existent vital signs on the flowsheet. That would tie in with what the doctor later told the Crown attorney about the 6:00 a.m. vital signs not making sense. If Doerksen had found Lisa dead at 6:00 a.m. and done nothing about it, that would explain why she needed to "forget" to check Lisa at 7:00 a.m.

Both of those two possibilities led to the same inexorable conclusion: Doerksen brought a monitor into the room and attached it to a little girl who was dead. She had already decided not to call a code, and she couldn't turn the monitor on because it would not detect a heart beat and the alarm would sound and wake me; all she could do was wait until the doctors found Lisa without vital signs on their morning rounds.

Doerksen knew she would have to say she hooked up the monitor when Lisa first arrived because nothing else would make any sense. The nursing note she wrote shortly after Lisa's arrival at 1:45 a.m. made no mention of any monitor, because there hadn't been any. However, it became very important afterwards to prove a monitor had been in the room all night, which was why the nursing note written after Lisa's death with the help of Mary Douglas contained several monitor references: "Corometric monitor applied since arrival to unit and in situ throughout the night", and "when checked patient at 0600, monitor on and functioning".

Doerksen testified that when she came in the room with the doctors on their morning rounds, the monitor was off. How could anyone make multiple references in her notes to the monitor functioning properly, without ever mentioning the monitor was either off or malfunctioning when the child attached to that monitor had died?

Douglas said she went into Lisa's room to look at the monitor. Doerksen sent Douglas in to check the settings because she knew she would be asked about them. Douglas knew the room was supposed to be sealed off for the coroner and nothing touched, but her loyalty to Doerksen outweighed other considerations. That also explained why the monitor settings Douglas reported were so inappropriate for a child of Lisa's age: the monitor had been programmed for a much younger child and Doerksen had not had time to change anything. The hospital had said in its letter the settings were appropriate for a child of Lisa's age, yet another misleading statement it expected would be accepted.

Over the next few days and weeks, Doerksen and Douglas refined their stories to fill in some of the gaps. For instance, if the monitor had been working properly, the alarm should have gone off when Lisa's heart stopped. How could she get around that? A competent nurse would have been upset to find out that a monitor used on one of her patients, a monitor she relied upon, didn't work and her patient had died. A good nurse would have been horrified at what had happened. She would have immediately reported an apparent equipment failure to her superiors and to Biomedical Engineering. She would have completed an incident report and spoken about what had happened to everyone who would listen. She would have blamed Lisa's death on the equipment malfunction, which would have had the added benefit of deflecting any concerns anyone might have had over the quality of her nursing care.

Doerksen hadn't done that. But she thought of a way to pretend she had: with Douglas's help. Three weeks after Lisa's death, Douglas wrote up her recollection of that morning, taking particular care to record how upset Doerksen had been over the monitor not working. Douglas was conveniently the only person in the hospital Doerksen expressed her dismay to, and Douglas in turn mentioned it to nobody else.

Soriano was an unwilling accomplice, at least at first, we thought. Had Doerksen made Soriano go along with her story? Had she implied that if she didn't, no one would believe her anyway and she would lose her job?

Whatever the motivation, Soriano cooperated with Doerksen and said nothing. When she wrote up her personal notes several days later she never mentioned a monitor, because she wasn't prepared to commit such outright lies to paper. By the time she testified at the inquest, however, she was more than willing to back Doerksen.

We honestly believed this was what had happened. Everything fit. Why had it taken us so long to reach these conclusions? Because it was inconceivable that a nurse—any nurse, never mind one who cared exclusively for children—would go into the room of a child who had just died and attach a monitor to the child's body. It was unthinkable that a nurse would walk away from a dead child without calling a code and without raising an alarm, in order to save her own skin.

We had said from the start Lisa had not been put on any monitor when she arrived on the ward, and that the monitor had been brought in sometime in the middle of the night. But we had consistently refused to think about the details, because the details were unthinkable.

Frank refused to believe our conclusion at first. It wasn't the logic with which he had difficulty, it was the reluctance of an ethical person to conceive of an act as heinous as this. We spent hours and hours sitting around the kitchen table trying to convince him, but by 3:00 a.m. he not only believed, he was ready to explain it all to the coroner.

29

THE NURSES – III

The nurse whose will-say mentioned the taped report was so edgy and nervous in the witness box that she looked ready to faint. She was the day shift charge nurse, also known as the resource person, who took over from Doerksen. She arrived at work before her shift was due to start, before the doctors discovered Lisa was dead, and found out that Lisa had been assigned as her patient. The first thing she did was reassign Lisa to someone else, because she assumed a patient from Emergency would be too time-consuming to care for given her heavy responsibilities as charge nurse. What did she know about Lisa that made her reach that conclusion? She didn't remember. Did she have any other patients, and did she also reassign them? She didn't remember. Had she seen Lisa's patient care plan? She didn't remember. Her memory was conveniently vague on almost every count but one: she clearly remembered seeing the Corometric monitor in Lisa's room.

Frank got her to concede that a nurse needed to have her patient's care plan with her when she made the audiotape. This was more indirect evidence that Doerksen had seen Lisa's patient care plan at 6:30 a.m., since this was the only document she could have used to refer to when preparing the tape. Had the witness listened to the tape and had she heard anything about Lisa on it? No, she only had time to listen to the first few sentences before the code was called, and then she went to see if she could help. She couldn't recall if she ever went back and listened to the tape again. Whatever was on the tape was erased at the end of the next shift and the tape was rewound so nurses could prepare the next set of taped reports. Why didn't anyone think to give the tape to the coroner? Because he hadn't asked for it.

Frank suggested to the witness that she had seen Lisa's care plan, discussed it with Doerksen, and learned from Doerksen that Lisa was dead. She denied it, and Hawkins strenuously objected, "That is a completely improper question to come 16, 17 days into the inquest, and for Mr. Gomberg to suggest that at this very late date in the inquest is highly improper and highly inappropriate. To put it to this witness at this stage of the inquest, not having put it to any other witness and simply to make a suggestion, not calling any evidence to the contrary, is completely improper in my view."

Frank disagreed with Hawkins just as forcefully. "It's a perfectly proper question, and he's now making speeches for the press and for the jury. I'm entitled to put questions to witnesses. He knows full well that there were two other nurses on day shift that day; he's not given us statements from them. I suggest that they should come in, too, and that Ruth Doerksen should retake the box. I'll put the questions that I propose to put to her, the jurors can put the questions that they propose to put to her, and we can get to the bottom of this right here in this courtroom instead of all of the confusion and all of the other stuff that's been coming from Sick Kids from day one. Let's get to the bottom of it."

The jurors were also not impressed with the nurse's inability to recall anything of significance. "It was a long time ago," she told the jury forewoman. The forewoman responded, "Yes, it's a long time ago, but I'm sure it's an event that isn't forgotten. Lisa's death was a rather remarkable event, wasn't it?" The nurse did not understand. "Okay," the juror said, "we'll just leave it that it was a long time ago and you have vague, vague memories of many of the instances that occurred that day."

Dr. Cairns agreed that Doerksen and Soriano should be recalled. Since they were both present in the courtroom this did not pose a scheduling problem. Dr. Cairns told Hawkins the other Ward 5A nurses would also be required to testify the next day. We knew the hospital would be unable to coach the rest of the 5A nurses on such short notice, and hoped their testimony might be more reliable as a result.

Soriano took the stand, but we were only allowed to ask her questions to do with the tape recording. Witnesses may not be questioned on things they have already been questioned on because it is inherently unfair and would theoretically allow proceedings to drag on forever.

Soriano explained the types of things she would usually record, such as changes in a patient's vital signs or if a doctor had been called during the night. She said she did not use the care plan that printed out in the early morning near the end of her shift, but the earlier one that printed off just before her shift began.

With the first nurse's testimony about how one needed a patient care summary to make the tape, and Soriano's statement that she used the older care plans from the start of her shift, we hoped we had backed Doerksen into a corner. How could Doerksen have made a tape on Lisa without any orders and without any care plans? But lying was preferable than self-incrimination, and Doerksen seemed quite adept at it.

Doerksen said she made the tape immediately after finishing her 6:00 a.m. rounds, without checking the patient care plans that automatically printed off only minutes later. Did she make a tape on Lisa? Yes. Did she at any time realize she had no care plan for her? No, of course not.

This was Frank's only opportunity to bring up our theory of what Doerksen had really done with the monitor. He would not be allowed to introduce it in his closing address unless he first put it to Doerksen in the witness box. She did not have to agree in order for him to present the conclusion to the jury, but the jury had to hear the witness answer and then decide on its own whether the witness was answering truthfully. Frank was afraid to propose that Doerksen had attached the monitor to Lisa when she was already dead, because he worried the jury would be too aghast at the thought to believe it. The jury so clearly disliked the nurses that we did not want to risk jeopardizing matters.

Frank questioned Doerksen as bluntly as he dared. "I suggest to you that you saw that patient care summary sometime between 6:15 and 7:00 in the morning."

"Mr. Gomberg, you may suggest whatever you wish. I told you I saw it after Lisa died, and that's when I saw it."

"I suggest that at some time after you saw that summary, you went into Lisa's room and saw her dead."

"You may suggest whatever you wish. I have told you the truth."

"I suggest that you turned around, walked out of the room, got a Corometric monitor, walked back in the room and put it on a shelf."

"Mr. Gomberg, you may suggest whatever you wish."

The next day, Hawkins reluctantly produced the rest of the 5A nurses who had worked the morning shift when Lisa was found dead. We had already heard from the one assigned to be the charge nurse, and there were three others: one from the Constant Care Room and two of the three regular floor nurses. Hawkins told us the third floor nurse had left the hospital and was in England, leaving us wondering if, beyond the reach of the hospital's tentacles, she might have been the most forthright witness of all.

Hawkins told us that the nurse who was about to testify next had just completed a twelve-hour night shift, implying she might be tired and we should go easy on her. It was surprising, therefore, to see that after she finished testifying, this supposedly exhausted young woman chose to sit in the courtroom audience for the rest of the day to listen to three more witnesses.

This nurse was surly and sullen, and watching her testify taught me a valuable lesson: when you have a bad attitude, you offend everybody. The lawyers don't like you, the coroner doesn't like you, the jury doesn't like you, and no one will be the least bit inclined to give you the benefit of the doubt on anything at all. We surmised her twelve-hour night shift might have been spent on things other than patient care—such as being prepped on what to say.

Her belligerence and her steadfast devotion to the hospital mantra were evident to all as Frank conducted his cross-examination. "So you listened to the tape report with regard to your three patients?"

"Yes."

"But there were four taped reports on that tape, as I understand it; your three patients and your fourth patient who is not going to be a patient, because she's dead?"

"Yes."

"Now, my understanding from other evidence is that the reports on those four patients would be 'interspersed' with the reports from the patients of your colleagues, because there were nine or ten patients. I'm not sure how many patients there were, but they're not segregated so that your patients are all in one part of the tape, is that right?"

"Yes."

"So you'd have to at least listen to the name of the patient before you start fast-forwarding, isn't that right?"

"Yes."

"In other words -- you'd have to know Frank Gomberg is not your patient, so you'd have to hear the name and say, 'I don't need to know about that'?"

"Yes."

"How do you know how far to fast-forward?"

"Well, I'd be guessing, I'm not a hundred percent sure, but I believe that my patients fell later on into the report, so I knew to fast-forward to the end part of the tape, which was where my -- the review of my patients was."

"No, but I thought we just agreed that in terms of the eight or nine or ten reports or whatever the number is that's on the tape, you don't know where in that group of seven or eight or nine or ten you may find the report with regard to any one of your patients, isn't that what you said?"

"If I recall, the other patients I had were kind of together, so..."

"And you remember that?"

"Not a hundred percent, but I'm pretty sure, yes."

"Well, where was Lisa's report in terms of the seven or eight or nine or ten that you were listening to on the tape?"

"I don't know, because I didn't hear it."

"How do you know you didn't hear it?"

"Because I didn't stop for her name. Like, I just don't remember hearing it when I was fast-forwarding."

"That would be something that you would have to intentionally not listen to, isn't that right? Wouldn't you have to hear the name 'Lisa Shore' and then say, 'I don't have to listen to that'? Otherwise, you'd listen to it naturally and you'd listen to all the other ones, too."

"I don't stop the tape in between each patient to hear if the next one was mine, just fast forward it and I happen to come across my patients, the patients I had for that day. I did not hear her report at all."

"Well, did you hear her name?"

"No, I didn't."

"So you don't know whether her name was on that tape or not?"

"I don't know, no."

Margaret Browne also could not understand how this could be accomplished, and asked, "Can you tell me how you can fast-forward something to a specific point without listening to it? I don't understand how you can do that without listening to all the patients' names."

The nurse replied, "Well, I was just listening to where my patients -- I don't remember if they were towards the beginning of the tape or the end of the tape, I just fast -- I would stop in between to hear if it was my patient; if not, then I just fast-forwarded toward the end, but I didn't hear Lisa's name come up, no."

Frank had taught me that a good indication of a witness's credibility is her willingness to concede a point that appears to be true. Conversely, the witness who refuses to concede the obvious makes listeners disbelieve everything the witness says. This nurse refused to concede the obvious.

"Now, with regard to the patient care plans, they were stapled and segregated when you arrived so that your four patients, including Lisa, were in a stack together?"

"Yes."

"And where was that?"

"That was on the front counter of the nursing station."

"Do you know who put them there and when they were put there?"

"No, I don't."

"What's the normal practice?"

"Usually someone from the night shift staples them together and piles them."

"By someone from the night shift, do you mean a nurse?"

"Yes."

"So is it your belief that those things would have been put there either by Nurse Doerksen or by Nurse Soriano?"

"No."

"Well, who else was on the night shift who could have put them there?"

"Some of the other nurses. I don't recall who was on that night, but it could have been another nurse."

"Well, there's a nurse in the Constant Care Room; she wouldn't put them there, would she?"

"Probably not."

"Well, there were only the three of them, the Constant Care nurse on 5A, Nurse Doerksen and Nurse Soriano. Who else would have put those nursing care plans, taken them out of the printer, stapled them and put them in a pile for you to review?"

"I don't know. I don't know how many were on that night."

"Well, if you accept my hypothesis that the only people who were on were Nurse Doerksen and Nurse Soriano and the nurse in the Constant Care Room, and if we eliminate the nurse from the Constant Care Room as the organizer of those nursing care plans, we're left by the process of elimination with Nurse Doerksen and Nurse Soriano. Does that sound reasonable so far?"

"I can't assume that, though, I can't say it was either one of them."

"Well, give me another assumption, then, since you work on that floor."

"Like, I don't know how many nurses -- I can't answer that question, because I don't know ---."

"Well, we'll go back to my hypothesis and if somebody disagrees with it, they can jump up and start yelling that I don't know what I'm talking about, all right? There's Nurse Doerksen, there's Nurse Soriano, there's the nurse in the Constant Care Room; forget about her, because she didn't do it. So we're left with Doerksen and Soriano. I don't hear anybody yelling in the courtroom. Who else could have segregated those nursing care plans and put them on the desk?"

"If it was just the three of them that were on that night, then maybe it was one of them, but I don't know, I can't say for sure."

"So you would agree with me that it's not unreasonable to assume that it was either done by Ruth Doerksen or by Anagaile Soriano, right?"

"Sure."

The jurors did not like this nurse at all. One juror, fed up with hearing her say over and over that she never discussed Lisa's death with anyone at all, asked her why, after it was all over, wasn't she the least bit curious about what had happened. And why hadn't she been curious about what had been said on the tape, knowing that Lisa had died?

She answered, "I didn't feel that looking at the care plan, it would tell me anything different than what I already knew."

"What did you know?" the juror asked. "Just that she died?"

"Yes."

The hospital staff doing the witness-coaching had evidently been caught short by the last-minute request for the 5A nurses' testimony, and their work wasn't up to their earlier standard. All the nurses sounded like trained parrots. No, we never discussed Lisa's death at all, ever, with anyone. No, we didn't see Lisa's care plan. No, we didn't hear her name on the tape. No, we don't remember any of the people who were there that morning. Yes, we saw the Corometric monitor in Lisa's room.

The jury forewoman questioned the nurse with thinly veiled sarcasm. The nurse didn't notice. "So really you have very little to offer in terms of discussion regarding Lisa and the events that occurred that night during her care, but you do recall, however, the Corometric monitor was in the room?"

"Yes, I do."

"I would have thought that reading the patient care summary, inquiring of other nurses who were caring for a little girl that you seemed to indicate you remembered fondly, that you would have taken one step further for closure to inquire into the events surrounding her death. I do find that interesting. How does one get closure?"

"Well, at that time, I knew the basics, you know, how she had died, but at that time it didn't cross my mind to want to know the full details of ..."

"How did you know the basics, Nurse? Who told you the basics as to how she had died?"

"We had just, like I said, a group of us at the nursing desk were just discussing when she was admitted and that she was having this pain, which I knew about before, and that her death was unexpected, unexplained, a surprise in the morning, that's it."

"And can you remember who those nurses were that you just had these discussions with?"

"No, I can't."

The hospital made a crucial miscalculation about the next witness, the Constant Care Room nurse that came on duty on the morning of Lisa's death. The witness-coaches assumed that because this nurse had to spend all her time in the Constant Care Room, she would not have been involved in any of the morning's events nor would she have had the opportunity to discuss Lisa with the other nurses, and they therefore decided to spend their limited prep time working with the previous witness instead of with her.

The Constant Care nurse appeared to be genuinely untainted and answered all questions directly and honestly. When she got to the hospital that morning just before 7:00 a.m., her patient care plans were sorted and stapled and ready for her. This confirmed that whoever had prepared the care plans had done so before the next nursing shift started, meaning it could only have been Doerksen or Soriano. Since it would have been Doerksen's responsibility as charge nurse to do it, the testimony proved Doerksen had seen and prepared the care plans for the oncoming shift exactly as she was supposed to and exposed Doerksen's denial as yet another lie.

This witness also explained how nurses are not allowed to leave the Constant Care Room for any reason whatsoever, not even for a code, and most definitely not to retrieve papers from the desk or tend to a false alarm as Doerksen claimed she had done.

The final Ward 5A nurse to testify suffered from the same memory gaps as her colleagues. Yes, she had listened to the tape, but no, she had never heard Lisa's name mentioned. Frank, exasperated, gave a courtroom demonstration showing how ridiculous this was.

"Let's assume for the minute that there are nine patients that are being cared for by two nurses, okay, and we'll call them patients 1, 2, 3, 4, 5…and then 6, 7, 8, and 9. So taping is done by two nurses on those nine patients. So let's say Nurse Doerksen is taping on 1, 2, 3, 4, and 5 and Nurse Soriano is taping on 6, 7, 8, 9."

"First of all, we agree that the organization, just for purpose of analysis, is that the new nurse may be looking after patients 1, 2, 4, 7 and 9… Do you accept that proposition just for the purpose of this little analysis?"

"Sure."

"So somebody is going to have to listen to the tapes, one of the two nurses, we'll call her Nurse P. for the minute, just by way of example, would have to listen to the tapes on patients 1, 2, 4, 7 and 9, if you use my example?"

"If you use your example and your example is…"

"Well, let's just use my example for the minute, okay, because I don't think it's that far-fetched an example. Now, those tapes would not be in order unless something unusual happened, right? In other words, they wouldn't be in that order unless the nurses who were taping said to themselves we're going to go in and specifically tape so that 1 goes first, 2 goes second, 4 goes third, 7 goes fourth and 9 goes fifth, right? All right, and they'd have to advertently, those two nurses, say we're going to co-ordinate that taping to make it easy or easier for Nurse P, right, so that Nurse P can now can listen to those in one block, right?"

"Sure. But you can also have that you've got one patient from, say, 1 or 2, and then the rest of your patients happen to be 7, 8 and 9. So if 1 or 2 happens to be something that you may not need, you know, then you just need to listen to 7, 8 and 9."

"But my point, though, is this: it would take a fair degree of co-ordination between the two outgoing nurses to save the two ingoing nurses a bit of work, right?"

"But sometimes it has been done, it has been done, for say -- I mean, that would, your example would be a lot of work, yes."

We discounted everything she said, just as we did the other nurses, with one exception: She recollected that Doerksen had called her around 5:30 a.m. to ask her to come in to replace someone who had called in sick. We figured the hospital had not predicted we would ask this question, and therefore did not remind her that this was an answer she should "forget". The witness had no idea how incriminating her answer was, but we knew it conclusively proved yet another lie of Doerksen's. Doerksen had said one of the reasons she missed checking Lisa at 7:00 a.m. was because of a sick call, but the sick call had been made $1\frac{1}{2}$ hours earlier.

We tossed around the idea of calling other witnesses. We were still upset about not getting a chance to question Dr. Roy, and we really wanted to hear from the Risk Manager, another of the unsigned letter's editors. Knowing how close we were to the inquest's end, we decided not to press the issue. The hospital, however, decided it wanted to add a witness, and insisted she be the last to testify: Dr. Jean Reeder, the Chief of Nursing.

We had earlier discovered that Reeder recorded taped messages of support for her staff, and updated them every few days. Although intended for the hospital's nurses, anyone who knew the extension number could call in and listen. A former nurse at the hospital felt it was important we hear what Dr. Reeder had to say, and had given us the number.

Reeder's messages were unrehearsed train-of-thought monologues.

Maybe she thought this informal style conveyed warmth and intimacy, but it also made her sound highly unprofessional. Regardless of her style, however, her position was manifestly clear. After Doerksen's first day of testimony, Reeder's message was "...Our staff that have testified thus far have done—you'd be very proud of them in terms of their clarity, the poise with which <sic> they have maintained under duress and the information that they're sharing in the courtroom regarding the circumstances around Lisa Shore's death..."

We wondered which inquest she had been attending, because the clarity, poise, and credibility of the hospital employees who had testified to this point, with one or two exceptions, had hovered around zero.

By the time Anagaile Soriano finished testifying, Reeder was starting to feel some pressure over the continuous media coverage. Headlines like "Sick Kids' staff rapped at inquest"[1] and "Girl could have lived, inquest told"[2] made her job much more difficult. She recorded a new message of support for her nurses, sounding harried. "Hi, there. This is Jean Reeder on Friday, Feb. 4th at about 5:30 in the afternoon. I haven't recorded a message in several weeks because I have been focused day after day after day after day on the coroner's inquest around Lisa Shore's death. This has consumed about twelve to fourteen hours of my time each day as it has for many other people from the hospital involved in supporting the inquest. I'm tired, I know that all the individuals involved in this are very tired for different reasons. I know several nurses have expressed to me their frustration and sadness at the public media portrayal of nursing, or nurses and nursing care at Sick Kids during this inquest. I share your frustration in no uncertain terms. I sit in there and I listen to what's being said, and that's not exactly what's being portrayed in the media. When I testify I will be talking about a lot of the things that we have done here at Sick Kids to improve the practice and care of children on monitors, improve the Kidcom, improve nurses' communications, many things."

On the day Reeder was to testify, she made sure many senior hospital staff attended. None of them had ever shown up before, but they all turned out to hear her sing the hospital's praises.

We should have been able to predict the hospital's next move. After weeks of terrible publicity, it decided on a last-ditch attempt to improve its public image—by offering us an apology. In order to make sure the public knew about it, Reeder made the apology in the courtroom while sitting in the witness box, with all those senior hospital employees and many reporters present. It was too bad that it was one and one-half years after Lisa's death and nothing but a public-relations ploy, devoid of any sincerity.

"Mr. and Mrs. Shore and your family members, I have sat here throughout the inquest, we've met on two previous occasions, and on behalf of our institution, let me say how terribly sorry we all are, because we failed you as an institution. We are terribly sorry."

Reeder had been at that lengthy inquest every single day, as had we. She had never come over to us to apologize. We had met her twice before the inquest, as she correctly pointed out, both times to discuss the death of my daughter. She did not apologize either of those times. No one from the hospital ever had. But day after day of the hospital being portrayed in the media as party to negligence and cover-up had forced it to do that which it had so strenuously avoided until now.

Reeder told everyone the hospital had failed us. She didn't admit there had been any mistakes made. She didn't say the hospital had accepted responsibility for Lisa's death. Just what did "the institution failed you" mean anyway? I angrily dismissed her apology, leading to the next day's front-page headline of "Apology rejected!"[3] I told the reporter the apology was insincere, and that I had no use for it if it took a coroner's inquest and 15 months of lies and cover-up to get it. The only way to satisfy me, I said, was to fire the two nurses.

Having done her rehearsed sound bite, Reeder began her testimony. Hawkins took her through a well-prepared recital of the many improvements the hospital had made in the wake of Lisa's death. Although they were all changes for the good, none of them addressed the real issues.

For instance, the hospital had purchased a number of new oxygen saturation monitors, or oximeters. But that had nothing at all to do with Lisa. The hospital never introduced any evidence to prove oximeters were in short supply and that this shortage resulted in the lack of one being available for Lisa. Rather, Lisa's nurse had never bothered looking for one, in spite of the fact the doctor had ordered one to be used. One thing had nothing to do with the other, but the hospital must have hoped people would be fooled into thinking it did.

Another new improvement was that use of these oximeters was

now compulsory when a patient was on a PCA pump. That had nothing to do with Lisa's death either. The doctor had ordered an oximeter for her, and a nurse had testified it was the usual practice to use one for PCA patients. So how would making the oximeter compulsory have altered anything? Nurse Doerksen did not apply an oximeter to Lisa even though the doctor ordered it. She did not follow the hospital's then-existing monitoring protocols, so what would have made her follow this new one? Lisa died because the nurse broke the rules that were already in place. What would adding new rules to the existing ones have accomplished for Lisa?

Giving Pain Service admitting privileges was also a long overdue improvement. But if another child like Lisa were to come to the hospital, she would still end up on the same ward, attended to by the same nurses. It would not have made any difference to Lisa whether she had been admitted by Pain Service or by Orthopaedics; she would have still been assigned to the same nurses and she would still have died.

The litany of beneficial but wholly irrelevant changes went on. We didn't know it at the time, but the last "improvement" cited by Reeder was nothing more than another hospital subterfuge. She showed the court a set of three simple pamphlets, telling everyone that pamphlets like these had been developed to assist parents with the Kidcom system, PCA devices, and not surprisingly, Corometric monitors. She and Hawkins chose their words carefully, leaving everyone with the erroneous impression these pamphlets were now being routinely given out to parents. We later discovered these pamphlets were never distributed to anyone and were likely produced especially for this inquest to placate the unsuspecting public, the jury and the coroner.

We even found some grim humour in them. The fabricated pamphlet for the Corometric monitor told parents "it is important that you do not turn off the monitor"; we called that "the Sharon Shore instruction". It would never occur to sane parents to turn off a monitor attached to their child, just as loving parents would never tamper with their child's intravenous lines or their medications. The hospital wanted to imply to the jury there had been a monitor attached to Lisa and I had shut it off, which would explain why no alarms sounded when Lisa's heart stopped. It knew, or at least Hawkins did, that making the accusation outright would be a grave mistake that would backfire badly. But what if the suggestion was made indirectly, in an official, important-sounding pamphlet? If the pamphlet warned parents not to shut off the monitor, the hospital hoped the jury would subconsciously believe one explanation for the monitor not alarming was that a parent—me—had turned it off.

Frank had previously suggested to us that the hospital might stoop to this, but we had not seen any evidence of it until now and had assumed the hospital had realized how foolish it would be to try it.

When Frank began to cross-examine Reeder, she was barely able to hide her contempt for him. She added his name disdainfully at the end of many of her answers. "No, Mr. Gomberg." "Yes, Mr. Gomberg." In contrast to the many improvements she had already mentioned which were completely unrelated to Lisa's death, Frank inquired if she had made any that were related.

He asked, "Has something gone out on the Internet or in writing or something to the nurses saying when patients come up to the ward from Emergency, I want you to very carefully read the doctor's orders, because we had a disaster in the Lisa Shore case because nobody read the Kidcom instructions?"

Reeder answered, "I can't say it has been provided in the manner that you have described. However, this has certainly been discussed on this unit and several other units. However, we will continue to provide education so that everyone is clear around this and with our Kidcom policy taskforce, that will be even more explicit."

Frank persisted. "But, you see, I'm asking a very specific question and I'm not sure that I have the answer. In this particular case, a child came up to Ward 5A with orders made by Dr. Schily. There were orders inputted into the Kidcom system and in addition, the Emergency room orders specifically say 'See Kidcom orders'."

"Yes."

"We also agree that we've sat here now for 15 or 20 days, hearing that nobody and by 'nobody' I mean either Nurse Doerksen nor Nurse Soriano read that. That seems to me to be either a personal problem that these two nurses have, in other words, they didn't read what was there to be read, or it's an institutional problem in the sense that they didn't read what other nurses might not have read. Do you understand the question?"

"I believe I do, Mr. Gomberg."

"So I'm asking about the perception that you have as the head of nursing at the hospital as to whether this is an individual issue or an institutional issue."

"It is my view that this was a one-time occurrence that happened."

"Can you be sure about that?"

"I can never be sure about anything, Mr. Gomberg, but I am fairly confident this was a one-time event and it was an unintentional oversight."

"Well, I never suggested that it was an intentional oversight, but what I am suggesting is that if you're not sure whether it's an individual issue or an institutional issue, that one errs on the side of caution and sends something out to everyone to say, look, this may not be an institutional issue, but on the off-chance that it is, they better read these things very carefully because we had a child die when they weren't read. So that's why I'm asking you as the Head of Nursing whether that's something that might usefully be done."

"It will be useful and we will happily do that tomorrow."

"Now, in terms of the flowsheet -- first of all, I take it we could agree that because these Kidcom orders never made it up to the floor, the Kidcom orders themselves weren't followed. We can agree on that?"

"Yes."

"And that surely is an institutional problem, isn't it, in the sense that orders are made, put into the computer, if somehow they're not opened or they're opened and looked at but they're not activated, that's an institutional problem?"

"Do you mean institutional in terms of generalizing that this happens everywhere?"

"No, what I mean is institutional in the sense that we know it happened at least here --- and without pointing the finger at whether that's a problem from Emergency or that's a problem from upstairs, it's a problem that had consequences in this case because the child didn't have monitoring done."

"That's correct, and the institution takes responsibility for errors in judgment made by many staff in this particular situation."

"Okay, and my question is has a directive gone out or an Internet or whatever gone out dealing with the mandatory nature of not only reading what's written in Emergency, but of activating the Kidcom orders?"

"I don't know that, Mr. Gomberg."

Frank was incredulous. "Now, without being mean-spirited about it, isn't it surprising that you as the Head of Nursing are here on the last day of evidence of an inquest and you don't know the answer to that question?"

"No, Mr. Gomberg, it's not."

"Well, I guess the jury will decide that. Well, has an Internet directive or message gone out or a memorandum gone out or anything gone out to anybody—and by 'anybody' I mean the nurses, I'm not talking about the janitor, now—in the hospital? Has anything gone out to the people who deal with PCAs saying there may be a problem here; we had some people who for one reason or another didn't follow the monitoring in the manual and we want you to know from the head nurse on down that you've got to pay attention to what's in the PCA manual. Has that been done?"

"I don't know if it has or has not, Mr. Gomberg. I can't answer that question."

"Didn't you ask?"

"Pardon me?"

"Didn't you ask before you came here to testify before Dr. Cairns and the jury whether that's been done?"

"No, I didn't."

"I guess it would be a good thing to find out, wouldn't it?"

We glanced at the senior hospital staff who were there to hear Reeder testify. They looked distinctly uncomfortable.

The jury was not about to let Reeder off lightly. One juror asked, "So would you say that the care that Lisa received that night was not adequate?"

Reeder agreed. "I would say that the care Lisa received that night was not adequate."

The juror didn't believe her sincerity. "Not adequate care? Because some of the nurses and nursing educators feel that her care was, indeed, adequate when they've been asked that question."

As the juror continued questioning her, Reeder explained how what happened wasn't the nurses' fault at all, but Dr. Schily's! "From the perspective that there was incomplete monitoring and subsequent incomplete documentation and from the perspective that there was incomplete communication by Dr. Schily in the conversation that he had with Anagaile, that there was incomplete communication on the part of Dr. Schily with respect to providing more detailed information about Lisa's condition, about the multiple medications -"

The juror disagreed. "He provided everything on the orders, which were not accessed. Everything was there. And even in Emergency, he said in his testimony, 'I did more than that. I said see Kidcom orders.' And he wrote that on his Emergency orders."

Reeder continued, oblivious. "...So all these things together I would say yes, there was substandard care."

The juror was growing angrier. "And as Mr. Gomberg said a little while ago, there were three prompts. I don't think you agreed with the prompts, but whatever they were, they were opportunities for the nurses to get the orders and there were further prompts to that, because nurses know generally that you cannot treat a patient without orders unless you use this clinical judgment."

"Yes, that's correct."

"And, golly, it's a good thing there weren't–I mean, if there were medications–if I was being treated by a nurse on pure, sheer clinical judgment, I would find that very frightening --- because perhaps the doctor has ordered medications for me and I'm not getting them because a nurse is deciding on her clinical judgment what she's going to treat me, how she's going to monitor me and so on." The juror demanded to know, "You claim that you can speak to the veracity of these nurses. How can you do that if you weren't involved in this until February, many months after the incident? How can you sit there and say that you can speak to the absolute truth, honesty and veracity of these nurses when we've had such conflicting testimony and so many errors made? I don't understand that."

Reeder answered, "Well, all of us are called to judge other individuals and in my capacity of Chief of Nursing with my professional values that are widely shared by most registered nurses at Sick Kids, I have also gotten to know these two individuals throughout the course of this inquest. It's my professional judgment and in my years of experience that I do believe they are telling the truth."

If the nurses were telling the truth, then Reeder was calling me a liar. Little wonder I felt her apology was hypocritical drivel. She had sat through every single day of that inquest, listening to all the nurses' lies, inconsistencies, and evasions, and yet she could say with a straight face she believed they were telling the truth. Reeder was so deeply involved in the cover-up that she had lost all claim to honesty and integrity.

30

CLOSING ADDRESSES

After watching brilliant jury addresses on television and at movies, written by paid writers and expertly delivered by trained actors, one expects to see the same thing in a real courtroom. Real life is not like that. Lawyers prepare their speeches under severe time constraints. Immersed in a real inquest or trial, they frequently work nights and weekends preparing their closing arguments, drafting and redrafting them as the case progresses and changes. When they finally deliver their addresses, they may read them verbatim or at least refer extensively to their notes. A good courtroom presence may be diminished by a mediocre speech or a mediocre performance saved by a masterful close. Except for the judge's instructions to the jury, the speeches are the last thing the jury hears before it retires to deliberate.

An important factor in the effectiveness of an inquest closing address is the order in which it is given relative to the others. According to Frank, the best slot to have was the last, going first was second best, and being in the middle was the worst. By custom, Frank was entitled to go last as the representative of the deceased's family. Hawkins demanded the hospital get that position because, as he termed it, the hospital was essentially the victim in this matter. Frank magnanimously agreed to let him have it.

Inquest jurors decide the deceased's cause of death and the manner of death—whether homicide, suicide, accident, natural causes, or undetermined—and come up with recommendations designed to prevent a similar death in the future. The lawyer who addresses an inquest jury may summarize the evidence, give an opinion on the cause and manner of death, and suggest recommendations for the jury to consider adopting.

We had one of our regular late-night-around-the-kitchen-table discussions. Frank would write his own speech, but we had prepared a long list of recommendations for him to include. When we began talking about "the manner" of Lisa's death we planned to ask the jury to select, we encountered some resistance from him. "Lisa died because she went to Sick Kids. If she hadn't gone there, she would still be alive. Her death was a homicide," we said, "and that's what you have to ask the jury to find." Frank did not think that was a good idea. "I've never seen or heard of a medical inquest where the jury came back with a homicide finding. Juries just don't want to do that when they're talking about doctors or nurses. If you ask for homicide, at most you have a 10% chance of getting it." He suggested we ask for a finding that Lisa's death was accidental, explaining that such a finding would be almost as bad in the public's eyes. "An accident, at the Hospital for Sick Children? Don't you think that sends a pretty strong message?" We didn't. "Ask for homicide," we persisted. Even a 10% chance was better than no chance at all. Reluctantly, Frank agreed. And in typical Frank fashion, once he agreed, he became the most ardent proponent of Lisa's death having been a homicide.

The morning of the speeches, Frank told Hawkins and the other lawyers as a courtesy that he was going to the jury with a request for a homicide finding. Hawkins was shocked and angry. He must have figured that even though his client had gone through a difficult time in terms of bad publicity, everything was pretty much finished. He assumed the jury would come back with a finding of accidental death or unknown causes and the public would quickly forget what had happened. Now Hawkins had to consider the possibility that the worst was far from over.

Krkachovski was the first to address to the jury. He decided to stay away from the brewing controversy of asking for a classification for Lisa's death and did not ask the jury to make any specific findings. Instead, he summarized much of the testimony that had been given, and in a diplomatic, lawyerly way, called Ruth Doerksen a liar. We wanted to applaud when he was done.

> Good morning, ladies and gentlemen. As you know, I represent the manufacturer of the Corometric monitor, G.E. Medical Marquette Medical Systems, and I in fact will be relatively brief in my

submissions for a number of reasons. First, I plan to confine my submissions to the monitoring equipment, namely the Corometric monitor and the pulse oximeter. While it's clear from the evidence that the care that Lisa received left a lot to be desired, I have no doubt that Mr. Gomberg will cover that in detail, and I see no need for me to go over that ground as well.

The second reason for my brevity is, as Dr. Robin Williams from the Paediatric Death Review Committee agreed, this inquest isn't about the monitoring equipment. It's about the failure to properly use that equipment, and even Nurse Doerksen acknowledged there is no suggestion that the equipment malfunctioned in any way. And, of course, as we all know, the monitor was not even turned on at the time of Lisa's death, so there is not a heck of a lot of need to talk about the Corometric monitor.

And the last reason for my brevity is, to its credit, the hospital is in the process, as you heard yesterday, of implementing virtually all of the recommendations that I would have made to you, and what I'm referring to is Exhibit 68, the electronic monitoring guidelines.

So that I only have one recommendation that I would make to you, which is that these guidelines be implemented because they effectively set out what I would propose be implemented with respect to monitoring equipment.

Let me talk about the Corometric monitor now. As you know, there is a serious issue as to whether Lisa was on a monitor at any time. You've heard the evidence of Nurse Doerksen and Nurse Soriano, and you've heard the evidence of Mrs. Shore. I would suggest to you that on any reasonable interpretation of the evidence, that Lisa was not attached to a monitor that was on and functioning at any time during the course of the night. It seems to me that it makes little sense that a monitor of any kind would sound up to four alarms in 5 or 10 minutes, without there being any dialogue whatsoever between the nurse and the child's mother.

It seems to me that Mrs. Shore's evidence is far more credible on the point that, had she heard an alarm, she would have been after the nurse before the nurse even got to the room. That of course, didn't happen. Mrs. Shore heard no alarms. There was no dialogue about a monitor, because Lisa was not on a monitor. Had she been on a monitor, common sense dictates that the nurse would give some instruction to the parent about the monitor.

If you go to a hospital and your child is attached to a piece of equipment, if the parent doesn't ask the question, I suggest it's natural for the nurse to explain what the equipment is for, particularly in this case, because the equipment is intended to alarm. One would expect the nurse to say to the parent, 'Look, during the night this machine might go off', and as we heard the beep, it's a very alarming alarm. 'Don't be concerned, I'm going to come and deal with it.'

Again, there was no dialogue. That didn't happen. And I suggest it's simply not credible that Lisa was attached to a monitor, the monitor was turned on, it cycled with the alarm sounding, and then subsequently followed by up to four alarms, and nothing is said in the room. You heard Mrs. Shore's evidence that, for all intents and purposes, she was a stranger in the room. No one seemed to have any dialogue with her whatsoever.

We also have the evidence of the two day nurses, Sian Phillibert and Han Nguyen, that you're not supposed to leave the Constant Care Room, even for a code, let alone a Corometric alarm. And yet we have the evidence of Nurse Doerksen, that she left the Constant Care Room when she relieved Maureen, to attend to what I understand to be the last false alarm from this monitor and at the same time, as I understand the evidence, disabling the apnea alarm. Again, I find that inconsistent, where we have two nurses who say 'even for a code, we can't leave this room'. And yet, Nurse Doerksen, rather than asking Nurse Soriano who is now in charge of Lisa's care, going and looking after the alarm herself. Also, how did she know what room the alarm was coming from.

The lack of documentation, of course, doesn't help the nurses' cause. There is no mention whatsoever of the monitor in Lisa's chart prior to her death. Even something as significant as turning <off> the apnea alarm is not recorded anywhere, despite the fact that obviously, different nurses look after the same patient.

Nurse Soriano, if she had checked the chart, would have had no notation that the apnea <alarm> was not turned on. We don't know what might have been said on the audio tape about the Corometric monitor or the apnea alarm, but we do know that in the absence of any recording, had nothing happened through the night, there was nothing in the chart which would have indicated to the day nurses that this child is attached to a monitor in which an alarm will not sound for respiration, which is the very problem with morphine.

The side effect of morphine is respiratory depression. It strikes me that it makes no sense to disable the very alarm which would tip you off that there's a problem, bearing in mind again that she's not on a pulse oximeter. So that on Nurse Doerksen's evidence, there is nothing to indicate that something might go wrong with this child's respiration, even though she was on the morphine.

And I think it was Dr. MacLeod who acknowledged that respiration <distress> in terms of its onset, may be delayed or even may continue for a longer period of time than the administration of the medication. So that we have a situation where the very problem that might occur is not being monitored, in the way of equipment.

Oddly enough, at least to me, there is mention of other equipment in Lisa's chart, such as the IV and the PCA pump. There is also mention as we saw in another patient's chart, of a recording of a monitor. So that we know that some nurses, at least, do have a practice to make mention of the monitor when they apply it to a child. In this case, there is no such notation whatsoever. So the chart, the documentation, unfortunately for the nurses, doesn't back them up.

In terms of the notes that were made after Lisa's death, again I find it puzzling that Nurse Soriano in three pages of notes makes no mention of the monitor whatsoever, even though her express purpose in making the notes is (A), to record as best she could what happened, and (B), to come to terms, or to try to understand why it happened.

It strikes me that, putting myself in her place, if a patient is attached to a piece of equipment that doesn't sound an alarm and is ultimately discovered to be turned off when the patient is found dead, one would expect a good deal of anger, resentment, whatever you want to call it, from that nurse. Yet, I didn't see that in the testimony of either Nurse Doerksen or Nurse Soriano. There was no outcry. There was no 'who could have done this' and 'why was this done', coupled by the fact that no one seemed to investigate this in the days or weeks that followed.

Again, one would expect -- if I did everything I could to look after a patient, particularly putting that patient on a piece of equipment and somebody, for no good reason it would seem, turned it off, if you pardon the expression, I'd be mad as hell. And we didn't get that.

In terms of Nurse Doerksen's actions, conversations, notes, what have you, there's a good deal of inconsistency. I find it puzzling that she didn't take note of the monitor as she entered the room when Lisa was discovered dead, even though that was her practice on each of the prior visits. You may recall her evidence that as she walked into the room, she would glance at the monitor, then do her -- take her vital signs manually, and then correlate to the monitor. Inexplicably, she didn't glance at the monitor on this occasion. One must ask why, because it wasn't until she entered the room that she realized there was something unusual about this trip to Lisa's room.

But again more importantly, she sees the child dead in her bed. She says at 6:00 a.m. 'I had her on a monitor.' A natural, expected reaction would be to look at the monitor and say, 'Why didn't that alarm?' Yet her evidence is it's not until she goes away, comes back with the equipment, the crash cart, I believe, that she actually takes note of the monitor. That to me makes no sense. If you have a patient on a piece of equipment that's supposed to warn you, to me, an instant, automatic, expected reaction is to look at it and say, 'Why didn't that tell me there was a problem?' It didn't happen.

As the code is taking place, Nurse Doerksen pulls aside Mary Douglas and tells her that she doesn't know why she turned the apnea alarm off. In the note that Nurse Doerksen made after the fact, there is no mention of false alarms; there is no mention of Lisa being kept awake by the alarms; there is no mention of Mrs. Shore being kept awake by the alarms. She simply states, 'I don't know why I turned off the alarm.' And that might explain why there's no mention of the monitor for some time, to either Dr. Reingold or even Dr. Wright. Dr. Wright acknowledged in his testimony that no one said anything about the monitor.

I come back to the point that I made a few minutes ago. Why

not? If they had the child on a piece of equipment that was turned off by somebody, why would not have something been said by the nurses to the powers that be, that 'Hey, we've got to find out why somebody did this'.

Again, bearing in mind, Lisa's not the only child on this ward. You've got another eight patients on the ward, and I think the evidence was four in constant care. All of them are there in some way, for pain management. How do we know that what happened to Lisa may not happen to one of the other kids? None of that type of inquiry, investigation, curiosity, even, seemed to have taken place.

In her added nursing note which is in her chart, there is no notation about false alarms, or Lisa being kept awake, or any reason for the apnea being turned off. In fact, she states in the note: '... Corometric monitor applied since arrival to unit and in situ throughout the night. Child settled to sleep and was asleep all night, except when woken by nurse for vital signs. Mom at bedside, settled to sleep...' Now, this is made at, according to the note, at 9:00 a.m. after Nurse Doerksen has her conversation with Nurse Douglas. One would expect, given that these two events take place within a very short time frame, some level of consistency in what she's saying. Yet in the verbal conversation with Nurse Doerksen, she's saying one thing about the apnea; in the added nursing note, she's saying something completely different.

I also find it interesting, as you know, in the end of the added nursing note that Nurse Doerksen goes out of her way to indicate that the monitor was not simply in the room, but on and functioning. You will recall that she crossed out the words 'in situ' and specifically substituted -- she writes in the word 'error', and specifically substitutes 'on and functioning'. Why?

She uses the term 'in situ' before in the added nursing note. She uses the term 'in situ' in the progress note that was made at 1:50 a.m. What does it matter now to specifically state in the added nursing note, made after the fact, that it's not just there, but it's on and functioning.

To me, that suggests some level of anticipation of some questions that may be asked down the road. And, of course, it's not until she prepares her private notes, which is a day later, and in terms of recording, there is first mention made of turning off the apnea alarm because of false alarms, because of Lisa having trouble getting to sleep, et cetera. And of course, these notes don't get to Mr. Hawkins for some period of time, and don't get to us for an even longer period of time.

There is also the all-important question, if the monitor was on, why would anybody turn it off? And seemingly not someone responsible for Lisa's care, because Nurse Doerksen and Nurse Soriano testify they didn't turn the monitor off. Mrs. Shore says there was no monitor to turn off anyway. Maureen is in the Constant Care Room. There is no evidence to suggest that a doctor came into Lisa's room, particularly after or in between 6:00 a.m. when Nurse Doerksen states that she last saw the monitor on, and 7:15 when Lisa is found dead. Nurse Doerksen testified you can't inadvertently turn a monitor off, which would mean that a stranger to Lisa's care came into the room and turned the monitor off. Why? I don't have an answer.

Irrespective of what conclusions you might draw regarding the Corometric monitor, I suggest to you it's clear from the evidence that it was wrong equipment anyway. She should have been on a pulse oximeter. It's a more sophisticated piece of equipment. You've heard that now they're mandatory, when used -- or when a patient's on a PCA pump. You heard Dr. Schily's testimony that in his mind, a pulse oximeter is a better tool for detecting the side effects of morphine. In his mind, a Corometric monitor is a good secondary tool, but the first thing that should be applied is the pulse oximeter.

You also heard from Pauline Matthews that using clinical judgment, she had Lisa on a pulse oximeter in Emergency. You also heard the evidence of Jennifer Stinson that the majority of physicians order a pulse oximeter when they have a patient on medication such as morphine. So that I suggest to you it's clear from the evidence that what Lisa should have been on was a pulse oximeter. Now, Nurse Doerksen says, 'I looked, I couldn't find one.' But she doesn't do anything more.

And the evidence of Jennifer Stinson was that if you need a piece of equipment like a pulse oximeter but you can't find it, you call the Pain Service, and as you'll see from the electronic monitoring guidelines, there is a whole protocol now as to what a nurse ought to do if she needs a piece of equipment and can't get it and as Dr. Reeder agreed with me yesterday, it's inappropriate to do nothing. Again, this inquest is not about medical equipment; it's about medical care.

Lisa did not receive the care that she deserved, and it's up to us as a group to make sure that the same fate doesn't befall another child. Now, Mr. Gomberg will be putting to you some recommendations that the family have drafted. I'm not going to comment on those, except to say that I fully endorse those recommendations and they include implementing the electronic monitoring guidelines.

The lawyer for Dr. Schily spoke next. Her jury address was a dry recitation of the evidence as it pertained to her client, with some elaboration on how his actions were acceptable and met every standard of care. But where Krkachovski had spoken frankly, she refused to take any kind of position. In spite of the fact that she was mildly critical of the hospital for trying to suggest that Dr. Schily had done anything wrong, overall she was pretty much a hospital apologist. Her categorization of what had happened was "...the PCA protocol orders and the vital sign monitoring, I'm going to deal with those two issues together, because in my respectful submission, these failures occurred due to poor judgment calls, and anyone can make them". She recommended to the jury that when deciding whether Lisa's death was a homicide, suicide, accident, natural causes, or undeterminable, they choose accident because "...these human errors did not cause the death".

After listening to her, we weren't quite sure if she was representing Dr. Schily or the hospital. Her firm frequently represents physicians, and physicians and hospitals are usually on the same side of a malpractice case, so we concluded she did not want to say anything to offend a hospital with which her firm had a good business relationship.

Frank began his speech.

On October 21st, 1998, Sharon Shore and Bill Shore made a decision that will haunt them for the rest of their lives. The decision that they made was to take their beloved daughter, Lisa, to the

Hospital for Sick Children in order to stop, or at least reduce, her pain. Lisa was crying out in pain, and she looked to her Mommy and her Daddy to help her. Sharon and Bill did what any loving, frantic parent would have done. They did what you would have done, what I would have done. They took Lisa to the Hospital for Sick Children, reputedly the best children's hospital in the world.

Sharon and Bill placed Lisa's care and her life in the hands of the doctors and the nurses at the hospital. They put their trust in the hospital. That trust was cruelly betrayed, and Lisa is dead forever. There is nothing that anyone here can do that will bring Lisa back. There is not enough morphine in the world to stop Sharon's pain, and Bill's pain, and their son Devon's pain, and their son Aron's pain, and grandmother Barbara's pain, and grandmother Mary's pain.

What can you do about all of this? Why are we here? Well, I suggest that we're here to help ensure that a human tragedy like this never happens again, so that five jurors like you don't have to look into the pain-filled faces of grief-stricken parents again some day. You're here to help prevent another tragedy like this one, and I know from listening to the questions that you've asked over the last 15 or 20 days, that that's exactly what you're going to do.

Now, I'm not going to review the evidence at any great length, although I could do that. I'm not going to do it because I'm thoroughly convinced that you know it as well as I know it. I don't want to bore you or waste your time. If I do reiterate some points that are already firmly entrenched in your minds, then I apologize for that in advance.

I will also briefly talk to you about your fact-finding function, which is a little legalistic, and somewhat boring. I will warn you before I do that, so that at least you will know that it's coming.

This case is not a difficult one. The facts should have been easy to figure out, particularly to anyone at Sick Kids, if they wanted to figure them out. Once the facts are laid bare, the conclusions which emerge are fairly obvious. Unfortunately, what happened here was that the Hospital for Sick Children embarked on a campaign of deception, confusion, and outright corruption of the truth.

To call what went on here a 'smokescreen' and a 'cover-up' is exactly right. If it looks like a duck, and it quacks like a duck, there's a very good chance that it's a duck, except if you ask Ruth Doerksen, Anagaile Soriano, Mary Douglas or Carol Warren. They would have you believe that a yellow, quacking, winged bird is something other than a duck. And I know that you haven't been fooled, not in the least.

Witnesses like Jennifer Stinson, the pain nurse, and Susan Anderson, the Kidcom expert, and Pauline Matthews from the Emergency Department, were clearly truthful and forthright. Contrast that with the evidence of Anagaile Soriano and Ruth Doerksen. The difference is like night and day.

Examples of the hospital's morally bankrupt attempt to mislead and tell half-truths are the answers to the questions that I asked on behalf of the Shore Family in my letter of December 11th, 1998, which you have as an Exhibit. I signed my letter, and as I stand before you, I am proud to say that when I sign something, I take full responsibility for it.

The hospital's abject failure to take responsibility is a theme or a subtext that runs through this inquest. My letter of December 11th, 1998 was necessary because no answers up to that point had been forthcoming from Sick Kids. Sick Kids shouldn't have needed my letter to provoke an investigation into Lisa's treatment.

Surely, the highly unexpected death of an otherwise healthy ten-year-old should give rise to some curiosity on the part of the medical and nursing hierarchy at Sick Kids, particularly since nurses Doerksen and Soriano continued caring for other kids, and continue to do so to this very day.

But Sick Kids waited for a letter from me, and then waited some more after getting my letter from the coroner, Dr. Reingold... Sick Kids then spent over a month drafting and crafting a very lawyerly anonymous response to our questions. And I invite you to read the Exhibit. Not only were the answers carefully constructed, but they were cleverly sent with a letter from Marion Stevens. This covering letter talks about reviewing and editing, and I'm quoting, the responses. But doesn't say who is responsible for the answers. The author of the grossly inaccurate answers is the prolific 'anonymous'. Well, the shirking of responsibility for the authorship of the answers to the family's questions is directly in keeping with Sick Kids' attempts to shirk responsibility on most issues in this case.'

Frank proceeded to review the letter and how misleading it was.

> I suggest to you that the hospital engaged in a cover-up in a misguided orgy of deception which was intended to disguise, distort and bend the truth so that it would remain forever hidden from you. What the hospital did before you was to continue the campaign of deception that began when I was trying to deal with them.
>
> If the hospital really wanted to answer the family's questions truthfully -- remember, I wrote a letter, they wrote a response -- you have my letter, you have their response. I suggest to you that if they wanted to respond truthfully, they could have written a letter something like the one I'm putting before you here.

Frank put up a 3 x 5 foot display of this sample letter. It followed the same format as the hospital's actual letter, but attempted to answer the questions as honestly as possible rather than as dishonestly as possible. For example, where the hospital wrote "the blood pressure was taken on admission and not taken for the remainder of the shift. This was possibly an attempt not to awaken Lisa once she had begun to rest", Frank's imaginary letter said, "Lisa's blood pressure should have been taken as ordered, even if she was asleep".

The original letter offered "sincere condolences", but Frank's imaginary version was stronger.

> 'It is clear that Lisa Shore did not receive appropriate care while at the Hospital for Sick Children in the early hours of October 22, 1998. On behalf of the hospital, I apologize to the Shore family for this unspeakable tragedy. I enclose a list of the changes we have made, or are in the process of making. I hope that the changes we have implemented and will continue to implement as a result of our thorough investigation will ensure that a tragedy like this never happens again.'

If a picture is worth a thousand words, as the saying goes, then this case can be summarized by three pictures, in my submission.

Number one, the doctor's orders in Emergency; number two, the lost-in-space suspended Kidcom orders that Nurse Doerksen saw as part of the patient care plan on October 22nd, 1998; and number three, the flowsheet from October 22, 1998.

So let's spend a few minutes talking about the three pictures. Number one, the doctor's orders. I'm not going to go through them at length, other than to say to you that it is pretty apparent that Dr. Schily wrote 'see Kidcom orders'. We've been through that a million times. The Kidcom orders required a pulse oximeter and a Corometric monitor, and lots of other manual monitoring.

You see, Lisa was on morphine, and as Dr. Schily said, morphine is a potentially deadly drug. It's a very good painkiller, but it has potentially lethal side effects. Dr. Schily knew that only too well. That's why he made detailed and appropriate orders at 11:48 on October 21, 1998. No one, not one person who testified had suggested that there was anything wrong with Dr. Schily's orders. Nor could they. The orders were bang on correct.

You see, Dr. Schily knew that Lisa was being exposed to a danger. He was prepared in his medical judgment to expose her to that danger, knowing that she would be carefully watched. If she got into trouble, then the effects of the morphine would be reversed, and the danger would be eliminated.

The owner of the parachute school knows that jumping out of an airplane is a very dangerous thing. He tells the instructor to pack the main parachute, and to pack a backup chute in the parachutist's jumping equipment. The main chute was like the oximetry device, the backup chute is like the Corometric monitor. The new parachutist jumps out of the plane relying on the instructor, and relying on the school. Unfortunately, there are no parachutes in place. Who would jump out of an airplane without a parachute? Who would have their child go on morphine with no oximetry, no Corometric monitor, if they knew what this was all about? To ask the question is to answer it. No one.

Mr. Hawkins, I'm sure, will suggest to you that what happened here was a terrible series of very human errors. And that's one way of characterizing it, but I completely disagree. I'm not suggesting that anyone set out to kill Lisa; that's crazy. Or that anything sinister was done to cause her death; that's equally crazy. What I am suggesting is that there was a callous disregard for protocol and procedure, and an almost inconceivable disregard for the prompts that we've heard so much about, any of which, if reacted to, would have saved Lisa.

When the nurses failed to activate Dr. Schily's orders and when Nurse Soriano failed at 4:00 or 4:05 to convey the seriousness of Lisa's condition to Dr. Schily, they signed Lisa's death warrant. There were still opportunities for a reprieve, however. Both Dr. Smith and Dr. MacLeod testified that Lisa would probably have survived and would probably not have had any brain damage if Narcan had been administered, even as late as 6:00 in the morning. There was no reprieve for little Lisa Shore, though, because the nurses weren't doing their job.

Let's talk about driving a car for a minute. Have you ever driven through a stop sign by mistake? Even though Constable Culleton is here, I have to confess to having gone through stop signs many times in my life. I've never gone through two in a row. For sure, I've never gone through three in a row. Four in a row would be impossible. Five in a row would be outrageous.

At 12:00 in the morning, Nurse Doerksen took a call from Emergency, saying that Lisa would be coming up to Ward 5A. That was prompt number one to eventually activate the Kidcom. Well, they went through that stop sign. At about 1:30 a.m., Nurse Soriano took a phone call from Emergency, saying that Lisa would be coming up to Ward 5A. That was prompt number two to activate the Kidcom. Well, they went through that stop sign, too. At about 1:45 a.m. Lisa arrived on Ward 5A. That was prompt number three to activate the Kidcom. Another missed stop sign.

When Lisa arrived on Ward 5A, her Emergency chart arrived with her, including the Emergency flowsheet, including the detailed Emergency progress notes and importantly, Dr. Schily's specific, targeted, very pointed note, 'see Kidcom orders'.

That was prompt number four to activate the Kidcom. Well, they went through that stop sign, too. Now Lisa's on Ward 5A and there are apparently no orders. Not to worry, don't worry about it, there's a PCA nurses' manual to follow. The nurses failed to follow the mandatory orders in the manual. Unbelievably, they also went through that stop sign. Lisa's vital signs, and in particular, a highly elevated pulse rate from 3:20 a.m. was a stop sign. They went through that stop sign, too, attributing a high pulse rate to pain. Pain. Do you remember we spent some time on that?

Without going back to really figure out how much pain she was in, in the Emergency Department when she was in excruciating pain, her pulse, by the way, was stable at that time at 90. That's another stop sign. Well, they zipped right through that stop sign, too. Failing to figure out why Lisa was so cold at 5:00 a.m. was another stop sign. They went through that stop sign.

And on and on it goes.

You can probably identify other stop signs that I have missed. I suggest to you that this was no accident. This was neglect. It was intended to be benign neglect, because the nurses, in fairness to them, didn't think that Lisa had a problem. However, the benign neglect had very malignant consequences, because too many stop signs were violated.

Let's talk about the lost-in-space suspended orders. Do you think that the orders were really lost in space to the hospital for three months? Do we really have to paint by numbers here? Nurse Doerksen saw the orders as part of the patient care plan on October 22nd, 1998. Marta Papa told you yesterday that she saw them.

They then conveniently disappeared, and no one else saw them that day, even though Lisa had died. Obviously, whoever threw them out should have been on high alert to retain them. Can you believe it? The nursing care plan for a recently dead patient who died most unexpectedly was tossed out.

Five days later, Nurse Doerksen prints the suspended orders up and takes them home, where they remain for 15 months until I ask for them in open court, in front of your eyes, and she went home and got them and brought them in the next day. Come on, does that seem reasonable to you?

And yet, until January 26th, 1999, no one at the hospital thought to look carefully for doctor's orders that were obviously made, because someone at the hospital had to reverse at least the medication orders made by Dr. Schily. Those orders had to be reversed. Well, to reverse something, there has to be something to reverse. No one at the hospital thought to try to find the orders. The question is, did they want to find the orders, and the answer in my submission is a resounding no.

Sitting on the Kidcom orders for three months, and hiding them from the coroner, from the family, is just one more example of the moral bankruptcy of those who ought to have been getting to the bottom of this tragedy.

Let's talk about Coroner Reingold for a minute. I agree he didn't do a great job. His notes were lousy, and he should have asked more questions. There's no question about that. However, nothing that Dr. Reingold did caused Lisa's death, and his failure to sequester a Corometric monitor had nothing at all to do with anything, because there was no Corometric monitor ever used, in my submission. Pointing the finger at Dr. Reingold is just another example of the ethical malaise that afflicted and continues to afflict Sick Kids in this case.

The orders were the game plan for taking care of Lisa. They were the game plan. Because the nurses say they never saw the orders, and because there was no adherence to the PCA nursing protocols, Lisa was truly jumping out of an airplane with no parachutes on her back. They gave her the morphine, and they pushed her out of the airplane, and she had no parachutes. That's what this is about.

Now, the flowsheet. I'm not going to go through the flowsheet line by line, as I'm sure you can see it in your dreams, or nightmares. Certainly, Sharon and Bill do.

Dr. Robin Williams testified about that, and I suggest that she was really the moral conscience of the inquest, if I can put it that way. She looked at the flowsheet and at the treatment, and she was highly critical of both. And she has no affiliation to anyone. I didn't hire her. Mr. Hawkins didn't hire her. She just goes down the middle, and calls it the way she sees it, like an umpire.

Dr. Williams said that there were many, many signs of problems, including a significantly elevated heart rate, and a low blood pressure at 1:45 a.m. compared to what it had been in the Emergency Department. The respirations were also depressed. 'These were all red flags,' and I'm quoting her now, 'that ought to have gone up, that ought to have alerted the nurses to what was going on, even with the vitals they took. Even with the vitals they took.'

In a nutshell, Dr. Williams was highly critical of the monitoring that was done. In other words, according to Dr. Williams, much more ought to have been done. However, even what was done ought to have sounded the proverbial alarm. It didn't.

And Dr. Cairns is going to talk to you about the law, and I'm not going to get into that, as that's his responsibility. But I will talk to you briefly about what lawyers, judges and coroners call 'findings of fact'. And this is the part of my address that is somewhat boring, and I warned you that I'd bore you for a few minutes, but there's nothing I can do about it.

Dr. Cairns will tell you that a fact is only a fact when you, the five of you, find it to be a fact. I am perfectly entitled to express my opinion to you about what a witness said, and I haven't been bashful about doing that. Ms. Browne, Mr. Hawkins, Mr. Krkachovski, Ms. Posno and Dr. Cairns himself can also express their opinions to you about what witnesses have said.

With the greatest of respect to Dr. Cairns, it doesn't matter what Dr. Cairns thinks about the facts, any more than it matters what I think, or what Ms. Browne thinks, or what Mr. Hawkins thinks. That's up to you; the facts are up to you. What is crystal clear is that Mr. Hawkins and I agree to completely disagree about the facts. You have to determine the facts, and there are ways to do that. You do that by looking at a witness and assessing her demeanour in the witness box. Was she being candid? Was she trying to be helpful to you? Did she concede obvious points under cross-examination? Did it look like she was being truthful? How does her evidence or his evidence accord or diverge from the evidence of other witnesses? Does the evidence make sense? Is it logical? Is it internally consistent?

One example of what I say is an internal inconsistency is Nurse Doerksen's evidence that she woke Lisa at 5:00 to take her temperature, while at the same time saying that she didn't want to awaken Lisa to take her blood pressure. That's an internal inconsistency. You have to struggle with that.

Another example of an inconsistency is the completeness of Nurse Soriano's personal notes and her failure to mention a Corometric monitor in them. Nurse Soriano didn't add her own nurse's note to the hospital record. We talked about that. There's an added note by Ruth Doerksen but not by Anagaile Soriano. Nurse Soriano didn't do that because, in my submission, she wasn't prepared to lie on that point, in the hospital record. She did say in her evidence that she heard one alarm from a Corometric monitor, but she doesn't know if it came from Lisa's room. Does that make sense? Lisa was Nurse Soriano's patient at that time, and the alarm sounds just as Ruth Doerksen comes out of the Constant Care Room to pick up some papers.

Well, you heard on Monday of this week from Nurse Phillibert and yesterday from Nurse Nguyen that a nurse cannot even come out of the Constant Care Room to respond to a code, which is the most serious thing that can happen. But Ruth Doerksen comes out to pick up some papers. Doerksen would have you believe that she goes to Soriano's patient, Lisa, abandoning the three kids in the Constant Care Room. And she does all of that to turn off an alarm and in doing so, disables 50 percent of the Corometric monitor. She turns off an alarm designed to be loud enough to be heard by nurses in other patient rooms and down the hall, at the nurses' station. Does that make sense to you?

Sharon Shore is sleeping, and she sleeps right through the initial start-up cycling sounds of the monitor, plus three or four loud alarms. Doerksen hears all of the alarms from outside Lisa's room, but Sharon hears none of them. As Mr. Krkachovski put it, does that sound right?

Sharon and Bill take Lisa to the hospital for pain relief, and now Sharon sleeps through piercing alarms, and she told you and I submit, was honest, that if she had heard any alarms at all, she'd have run into the hall, screaming for a nurse. Isn't that what you would do if it was your daughter? Isn't that what you would do if it was your granddaughter? Either the breathing or the heart of your daughter, or your granddaughter, or your son, or your grandson may have stopped, and it's evidenced by a shrill alarm, what would you do? You'd go running into the hall, yelling and screaming, because you'd be scared out of your mind.

What the hospital would have you believe is that Sharon simply kept sleeping. That, ladies and gentlemen, is the craziest thing that I've heard in my 20 years around the courts. And if you can believe all, part or none of what a witness says, that's up to you. You can believe it all, you can believe part of it, or you can believe none of it.

In making your determination, I told you that you can consider what other witnesses have said. In other words, do you believe what Nurse Soriano said, or what Dr. Schily said about their 4:05 telephone conversation? Ms. Posno dealt with this a bit. I'm going to deal with it, too.

I suggest that Dr. Schily's version is much, much more credible. Once you find that Nurse Soriano is not to be believed on her version of what took place with Dr. Schily, you may choose to disbelieve her evidence about hearing one alarm coming maybe from Lisa's room, and maybe not. You can disbelieve her evidence about hearing cycling sounds from the Corometric monitor while she was standing near the door. You can disbelieve her evidence that there was a Corometric monitor attached and functioning during the night.

Let's just deal with that head-on for a minute. If there was a Corometric monitor, then why didn't the apnea alarm sound? Well, of course, because it was turned off. That's a convenient explanation.

Why didn't the cardiac part of the monitor sound when Lisa's heart rate went below 50 or 60? Well, the hospital has variously had three answers for that. The first answer is in the letter that they wrote me. Their answer there is, and I'm not going to go into it right now, 'We don't know, we have no explanation'. That's what they said initially.

Then Mr. Bauer came before you, and he tried to concoct an explanation. That was in November. And that's what got my friend, Mr. Krkachovski involved in this inquest. This Bauer-Sick Kids theory which was later dropped in favour of the agreement that we now have, the agreement being, quote, 'If there was a monitor in the room, it was not on when Lisa died'. But that, in November, Sick Kids brought Mr. Bauer in to offer some explanation as to why the heart part didn't alarm; pure unadulterated nonsense.

The third possibility is the whole monitor was turned off by persons unknown. I think Mr. Krkachovski dealt with it. Persons unknown. Doerksen didn't do it; Soriano didn't do it. There was somebody in the Constant Care Room, and surely my client didn't do it. Lisa didn't do it, so who did do it?

Well, I have a better explanation, and a much more credible

one. Ruth Doerksen and Anagaile Soriano were not very concerned about Lisa. They had no reason to suspect that anything bad would happen to her. A Corometric monitor was never attached to Lisa while she was alive. That's my explanation, and I would urge you to adopt it.

Some time between 6:30 a.m. and 7:00 a.m., after sorting and stapling the nine patient care plans which you heard about yesterday, Nurse Doerksen, in my submission, went in to check Lisa and found her dead. Nothing could be done for Lisa because she was gone. But Nurse Doerksen could make a bad situation a little better for herself. She ran and grabbed a Corometric monitor and put it on the shelf near the door. She ran out and did rounds with the doctors. The doctors found Lisa dead. Nurse Doerksen could not have saved Lisa at 6:45 or 6:55 or 7:05, whenever that happened. But she could save her career, and that's exactly what she tried to do, in my submission.

Where there's a conflict between Nurse Soriano and Dr. Schily, I'd ask you to accept Dr. Schily's evidence and to reject Nurse Soriano's evidence. It makes absolutely no sense to believe that Dr. Schily would just go back to sleep if he was told even half of what Anagaile Soriano says that she told him. Dr. Schily says that he was told that Lisa's vital signs were good, and that her respiration rate was just above 10 per minute. That's what he says. She was arousable. He told Nurse Soriano to look up saturation and carefully check sedation, respiration and all other vital signs. That's what he told you. Doesn't that make sense?

I asked Dr. Schily whether he'd have rushed to the hospital if he thought his orders hadn't been followed. He said yes. Doesn't that make sense? Nurse Soriano paged Dr. Schily at 2:50 in the morning and didn't page him again for an hour and 15 minutes. Does that make sense? Is that what you would do, if you were worried? If you were a nurse on a ward, you page a doctor in the middle of the night, and don't page him again for an hour and 15 minutes? In my respectful submission, you should reject Nurse Soriano's testimony in favour of Dr. Schily. Her testimony is simply, in my submission, not credible. In the same way, you should reject Nurse Doerksen's testimony where it conflicts with Sharon Shore's testimony.

Nurse Doerksen, in my submission, was highly evasive, and might even have been coached from the audience. What she said made very little sense. I would urge you to conclude that no Corometric monitor was ever turned on that night. No Corometric monitor was ever turned on that night, just as Sharon Shore said. That means a lot to Sharon and Bill, because it would vindicate what Sharon has been saying for 15 months, and in my submission, put the lie to the hospital's disgraceful cover-up, once and for all.

Now, you do have to answer five questions prior to making your recommendations and I'd like to go through those with you very quickly. Number one, the name of the deceased is pretty apparent, Lisa Shore. Number two, the date and time of death. There's some controversy about the time of death. I say October 22nd, 1998, and I'd suggest the time of death as somewhere between 6:30 a.m. to 7:00 a.m., is the best that I can pinpoint it. The place of death is the Hospital for Sick Children, Toronto. The cause of death is drug interaction, leading to respiratory and cardiac arrest.

And then I move to the 'by what means' area. And my submission to you -- and Dr. Cairns will deal with this, and I'm sure Mr. Hawkins will, too -- that the means of death, and this is not used in the criminal context, I caution you -- is homicide caused by the administration of a large dose of morphine without appropriately monitoring the life-threatening consequences of morphine, including increased heart rate, decreased respiratory rate, decreased blood pressure and decreased temperature.

Frank then read out our thirteen recommendations and the rationales behind them. Although normally the jury is not entitled to transcripts, an exception was made in this case and we were allowed to give our recommendations to the jury members for review and consideration.

Now, before I conclude, let me say this: Mr. Hawkins will make some points in his closing with which I completely and utterly disagree, just as I've made points with which he completely and utterly disagrees. The rules are such that I cannot stand up and respond to Mr. Hawkins after he finishes and sits down. When Mr. Hawkins does make these points with which I completely and utterly disagree, you have to respond in your minds as you would expect me to respond, had I the opportunity to stand up and respond on my own. You, in essence, have to furnish my responses to Mr. Hawkins because I can't do so.

On behalf of Sharon and Bill, I want to thank the jury members for paying such close attention to the evidence. It's truly been an honour to appear before you on behalf of the Shores.

Lastly, I want to briefly address a point that Mr. Hawkins made earlier in the inquest when he was cross-examining Sharon. Before Lisa died, I'd never met Sharon or Bill, or Lisa. In March of 1999, my brother married Sharon's first cousin, and they travelled from Montreal today to be here, last night, so that they could support the family. I was asked to get involved in this case by Sharon's father, Phil, immediately after Lisa died. I had a few meetings with Phil and the family before Phil himself had a fatal heart attack in November, 1998, about 30 days after his most beloved granddaughter Lisa died.

I don't think Sharon and Bill are relatives of mine, by way of a strict definition, but I'd love it if they were. They've become my friends, and I'm truly proud to have been their lawyer. They pursued the truth with integrity, great courage and tenacity. They've been helped by Dr. Cairns and Ms. Browne, and they're now turning the story of Lisa's last night on earth over to you. I know that you won't fail them. On behalf of Sharon and Bill, I thank you, and if Lisa were here, she would thank you too.

That was one of the most powerful speeches I had ever heard. I could see how moved the jurors were.

Patrick Hawkins gave his closing, the last of the day. He was a skillful writer; if one hadn't sat through the entire inquest and heard all the lies and evasions, one would have thought by listening to his speech that no one had done anything at all wrong.

Let's not blame the nurses, he said.

Different things and different people combining, of human errors and system errors, and to fix the problem, we do have to look at all of those issues. What I'm suggesting and what I'd like to go through in a moment, is that if we are to learn from the death, and if we are to ensure that this doesn't happen again, we cannot focus on particular people or particular nurses. The focus has to be on the whole system, the broader picture, everything and everybody that was involved in the care provided to Lisa, and that is what I and my clients have been trying to talk about and have been trying to demonstrate.

It was the system that was flawed, he said.

> Mistakes were made. There were errors in judgment by the people involved in Lisa's care. There were also gaps in the systems that provide care, in the systems at the Hospital for Sick Children such as Kidcom. The hospital and its staff, particularly the nurses involved in this case, accept responsibility for those mistakes and for those errors, and they are not in any sense trying to deny the errors, to back away from them, to hide or to in any way do anything other than acknowledge that errors were made.

We never heard any nurses accept even the least bit of responsibility for their mistakes and errors. We hoped the jury wasn't going to fall for this.

Hawkins disagreed with Frank's and our opinion that the hospital's letter was misleading and deceitful.

> Mr. Gomberg commented at length a few moments ago about the hospital's response to the Coroner's office. It's not something that has been referred to in any great detail at the inquest, and I think that's very significant. I'd urge you to read the letter, read the questions and read the response.
>
> All of the people, all of the facts that are reflected in that letter, they relate to the evidence, they relate the versions of events offered by various people who've been witnesses at this inquest. Dr. Schily, Nurses Doerksen and Soriano, Nurse Douglas, Pauline Matthews, Dr. Catre; all of these people, the facts that they have to offer, the factual background, that's what's written up in the letter.
>
> Each and every one of these people testified, with the exception of a couple of questions to Nurse Doerksen, the letter came

up with nobody. A couple of questions to Dr. Wright. It wasn't addressed, the facts of the letter weren't addressed with anybody, with any of the witnesses to say this is wrong, that's wrong. All we have is a global allegation that it's a sham, or a global allegation that it's misleading. What I would suggest you do is read the letter, read the questions, and read the answers. If you compare the questions to the answers, you'll find, I believe, that it is accurate and it is complete. It is an honest attempt at answering the family's questions.

Dr. Schily was criticized for not writing more detailed instructions for the nurses. I was confident the jury would realize how absurd this assertion was given that the nurses had not managed to read the nine lines he did write.

I think in these circumstances where there is little knowledge about Lisa's condition and what's going on, I think it is reasonable to expect, and this is what Dr. Williams said, it is reasonable to expect a physician to make a note of his examination. Absolutely, we have his orders, but that's not the point. The point is a note or a communication of his history of the patient, his assessment, his examination, and what he feels are the issues, something to document that interaction, or to communicate that interaction that he's had with the patient.

And that is a progress note or a consultation note. It's the type of information that he put the next day in his letter to his lawyer. That's the type of information that, in my view, and in the view of a number of people who testified, should be communicated somehow to the receiving nurses, either in writing or verbally.

Dr. Williams agreed that it's reasonable in these circumstances for there to be a progress note. Jennifer Stinson said that especially in unique circumstances, you've got to be careful about your communications, either verbally or in writing. Ms. Posno even quoted Dr. Schily who says that he believes in writing things down, and my suggestion is that a note by Dr. Schily, findings, assessment, examination, may have helped.

And that's certainly something that as a reminder, it's not an extra step, it's a reasonable expectation as a reminder to nurses and physicians to carefully note (inaudible). I think that is a good thing to do, and a reasonable way to try to move forward.

And in particular, we've heard lots of criticisms of nurses for making incomplete notes. The same standard, the same expectations have to apply to physicians and others involved in patient care, particularly when there are no notes, and particularly when you're dealing with a unique and unusual situation.

Hawkins blasted Frank.

…One of the truly unfortunate things is that this insinuation and this innuendo that there's hiding and that there's covering up is placed on the shoulders of Ruth and Anagaile and the suggestion that there was an intentional attempt on their part to hide things… We hear more of that same blame and pointing the finger in Mr. Gomberg's summation, suggestions of lying, failing to meet standards, disregarding basics of nursing practice, covering up. All of these, in my view, are a distortion of this process, and a distortion of why we're here, and an abuse of the fundamental principle of what an inquest is about, to try to prevent similar tragedies. It's not about pointing a finger; it's not about laying the blame.

How can lawyers get away with this, I wondered. Hawkins had completely ignored the evidence, the discrepancies and inconsistencies of his own witnesses, presented illogical conclusions as if they were fact, and told the jury that no one had done wrong and no one should be blamed, least of all good nurses like Ruth and Anagaile.

Hawkins was upset about Frank's recommendation that the jury find Lisa's death to be a homicide.

As I prepared my remarks last night and this morning, I said right at the outset, you can rule out suicide and homicide as issues because there is no suggestion of that. That was my second remark, but based on Mr. Gomberg's submissions I do have to go further and talk about those. The Coroner will give you the definitions and explain the meaning of the words, and he will go through it, as I believe Ms. Browne will.

I would like to go briefly through it and give you my interpretation. 'Homicide' as defined is the action of killing, the action of a human being killing another, or the killing of one human being by another. By definition, homicide is an action, a positive step. It is not inaction, it is not omission, it is not failure to act. The dictionary definition is an action, somebody taking a positive step.

Whatever is stated about this case, and whatever Mr. Gomberg wants to state about this case, there is no evidence whatsoever on anything before you of a positive act taken by anybody in this case that resulted in Lisa's death. It goes far beyond any of the evidence to suggest that this in any way fits with the definition of homicide.

Trying to date it back to the act of administering morphine, in my view, far stretches and takes the definition of homicide well beyond the plain and ordinary meaning of those words, which is an act, an act causing death. And there is absolutely no suggestion, no evidence of any act. There are errors, there are errors of omission, people failing to do things. That is a far, far cry from suggesting that there is a positive act resulting in death. And that's the definition of homicide.

I think the two answers, or where the answer lies is either accidental or undetermined. And to some extent, that depends back on your determination of the how question. What is the medical cause of death, and can we conclude that there is a medical cause of death. The definition of 'accident,' again, is an occurrence or incident or event that happens without foresight or expectation.

And certainly no one has suggested anything to the contrary but that this event was unexpected and unforeseen. None of the treating professionals in any way anticipated, expected, foresaw something like this happening. Even if we accept that it's a drug reaction, we have to realize that it took the Coroner's office and the Coroner's experts some 15 or 16 months to come up with a possible explanation for a drug reaction.

And it's not surprising, and it's not difficult to see why the treating professionals did not foresee, did not expect, did not anticipate. And so on that level, if we accept drug interaction, I think the answer, and I'd agree with Ms. Posno, is accidental.

However, if we accept that the answer is undetermined on the cause of death, the answer that we may be left with, for the 'by what means' is equally undetermined. Because if we do not know the precise sequence of events, the precise medical events that lead to death, I'm not sure that we can answer the question by what means on anything other than undetermined.

And so, my view, depending on your interpretation or your decision on the cause of death, is that the answer is somewhere between accident and undetermined. Unfortunately, some of the fundamental answers to the questions are unknown, and I'm not sure that I can suggest which of the two answers it is, but it is certainly not homicide, as suggested by Mr. Gomberg.

The next morning, Margaret Browne was given the opportunity as coroner's counsel to give a final summation to the jury. Margaret had been "wearing her heart on her sleeve" during the inquest, so openly siding with us that Hawkins had complained about it to the coroner. Margaret had been mortified that he had gone over her head to her boss instead of speaking directly to her. The Hospital for Sick Children did not like Margaret Browne, and Margaret Browne did not like the Hospital for Sick Children.

We were quite surprised, then, that someone who had been so visibly angry about the hospital's actions delivered such a muted, lacklustre speech. She told the jury Lisa's death was neither a suicide nor a homicide, suggesting the jury find her death an accident. As she put it, "Nobody's perfect. There were human errors made, it was sad, and they have been faced and perhaps not to your satisfaction, but they have been faced. I wouldn't dwell on them too much. I would look at the preventative function of this inquest. Think of ways that we can avoid this. Think of ways we can not depend on things that might go wrong."

Dr. Cairns delivered his instructions to the jury, and we left the courthouse, dejected at the thought that we would find no justice for Lisa there.

31

THE MANNER OF HER DEATH

It took two weeks for the jury to finish deliberating. We knew it would come up with forceful recommendations, but what we were really waiting for was to learn how the jurors would classify Lisa's death.

Although an inquest is not allowed to assign blame, jurors can do so indirectly by their findings and recommendations, such as by ruling on the manner of death: homicide, suicide, accident, natural causes, or undetermined. The word homicide, for example, does not mean murder but does mean the killing of one person by another. If an armed suspect is about to shoot a police officer but the officer kills him first in self-defence, few would say the officer committed murder even though the death would clearly be a homicide. If this jury came back with a finding of homicide, it would be tantamount to assigning all of the blame for Lisa's death to the nurses. If the jury found her death was an accident, everyone would get on with their lives, the two nurses would return to work at the hospital and continue caring for other children, and Lisa's death would be forgotten by everyone but us.

The courthouse was mobbed. TV trucks were parked up and down the street and reporters and camera crews were waiting for us outside. As we walked in, one of the coroner's constables smiled at us and said, "It's going to be a good day today!" I thought that maybe he knew something and was trying to give us a hint, but I was afraid to dwell on it and quickly hurried inside.

Dr. Cairns began reading. "The name of the deceased: Lisa Shore. The date and time of death: October 22, 1998, between 6:20 a.m. and 7:00 a.m."

Until now, the official time of Lisa's death was 7:50 a.m., when the resuscitation efforts had been stopped and death was officially pronounced. But the jurors had put the time of death down as somewhere between 6:20 a.m. and 7:00 a.m.–after the patient care summary had printed off but before the doctors entered Lisa's room at 7:18 a.m. It looked like the jury was implying that Doerksen had read the patient care summary when it had printed off and that she had gone into Lisa's room, probably to do the 7:00 a.m. check she claimed she had forgotten. The jury was saying that Ruth Doerksen knew that Lisa was dead before the doctors ever entered her room.

I held my breath in wonder and hope, and Dr. Cairns continued. "The place of death was the Hospital for Sick Children, in Toronto. The cause of death was probable complex drug interaction leading to cardiac and respiratory arrest."

"And the manner of her death was…homicide."

I gripped Bill's hand tightly and began crying. My mother and sister were crying with me. The jury understood why Lisa had died and who was responsible for her death. They knew she should still be alive. We were consumed with grief and sadness and wildly ecstatic all at the same time.

Reporters rushed out to make phone calls and to set up their positions for the impending scrum outside the courthouse. The hospital had promised the press it would comment once the inquest was over, but now it refused to say anything except that it was holding a press conference later that afternoon. That would give it a few hours to figure out what to say yet still allow enough time for its remarks to make the evening news.

Besides figuring out how to put a positive spin on a homicide finding, the hospital had another equally difficult public relations problem which it needed to solve quickly: how to deal with the many frantic and angry parents of patients who were worried about the safety of their children.

We didn't want to be standing outdoors in February for any longer than necessary, so we had rented a room at the YMCA across the street from the coroner's courthouse in order to hold our own mini press conference. It wasn't fancy, but it worked. Frank and I sat at a table answering questions. We told everyone we felt vindicated, that the jury had confirmed what we had been saying all along, which was that the Hospital for Sick Children and two of its nurses were wholly responsible for Lisa's death. We hoped to see a criminal investigation into the actions of Nurses Doerksen and Soriano, and we felt there should be a public inquiry into the hospital's cover-up.

Some of the photographers had put their equipment down on the table in front of us. One of them was labelled with its owner's name, and I noticed it was the same surname as the jury forewoman's. On our way out, Bill and I saw the photographer and asked if he was related to her. He sheepishly admitted the forewoman was his mother. We asked him to let her know how impressed we were with her tenacity and strength, and how brilliantly she had questioned some of the witnesses. We asked him what his mother did, explaining that we guessed she was an office manager of some large company, running a very tight ship and keeping all the executives in line. "No," he laughed, "she's just a mom!" Then he added, "But that's the way she is, she'd fight like a tiger for her kids, or for anything she really believed in."

We had no idea what slant the hospital would put on all of this. We considered attending its press conference ourselves to find out, but my friend Sharon's husband volunteered to go on our behalf. Since no one knew him or his relationship to us, he walked into the hospital unchallenged, notepad in hand, and sat with the rest of the reporters. Afterwards, when one of the TV stations let us watch their tape, we were flabbergasted to see he had actively taken part and asked some very probing questions!

We thought the jury's finding would force the Hospital for Sick Children to re-evaluate itself and acknowledge responsibility for Lisa's death. We hoped it would reconsider the actions of Lisa's nurses in a new, more honest light. We prayed that notwithstanding the original cover-up and conspiracy, the hospital's board of trustees and its senior executives would finally decide to step in and do the right thing. This was the perfect time for it to rehabilitate itself in the public's eye, we thought. It could fire the nurses and show how committed it was to the safety of its patients.

It did none of these things.

A new official had taken over the role of front man from Jean Reeder. Dr. Alan Goldbloom, a hospital Vice-President and the person in charge of patient care, told the gathered press the hospital did not agree with the homicide finding. Over and over again he told everyone how it agreed with the recommendations of the Crown counsel that Lisa's death should have been considered an accident. What hypocrisy, hailing the words and recommendations of Margaret Browne, the same person it had so roundly disparaged and belittled only a few weeks earlier!

Dr. Goldbloom read a prepared speech: "While everyone here acknowledges the errors that were made and which resulted in the tragedy of Lisa's death, I don't think that there is anyone in this institution who feels that there was ever intent. Our only intent is to help children, and serve families. The finding of the jury, despite the recommendations of the Crown counsel, suggest otherwise and that I think is the shocking part for those that have committed their careers to this institution."

"Why is that shocking?" he was asked. He replied, "I think that the feeling of everybody here, as well as the Crown counsel, was that the errors that occurred were human errors, not intentional. Accidental errors. And that the cause of death which has still not been fully determined leaves us with a lot of unknowns."

The reporters didn't buy it. "It's pretty clear the jury didn't believe a word <the nurses> said. They lied. They were covering their butts. What do you say to that?" Dr. Goldbloom answered, "We believe that everybody who testified at the inquiry testified honestly."

Dr. Goldbloom extended his apologies to us, the second such dubious apology the hospital had made solely for the benefit of the assembled media. In order to show it was taking positive action in response to the homicide finding, he promised that the hospital's chief of nursing, Dr. Jean Reeder, would review all the actions and circumstances of Lisa's death. Since she was the two nurses' most ardent supporter and had been integrally involved in the hospital's strategy of denial, we knew exactly what kind of one-sided review she would perform; we wrote about this promise on our website the next day and characterized it as putting the fox in charge of the henhouse.

The rest of that day, most of that night, and the next morning were a blur of television and radio interviews. At each one I said the hospital should fire the nurses and take responsibility for Lisa's death.

As a result of the publicity, my website was now receiving close to a thousand visitors each day. I received hundreds of e-mails offering condolences, with most of them saying how appalled they were with the actions of the Hospital for Sick Children. One mother wrote that her child had frequent admissions to Ward 5A/B and had previously encountered Ruth Doerksen. The woman said that Doerksen was so careless that she had complained about her, and she would not allow Doerksen to care for her child. Many nurses—although none from Sick Kids—sent apologies and told me how upset and ashamed they were that nurses like Doerksen and Soriano belonged to their profession. Some said the detailed information I had posted allowed them to reflect on their own practices and become better nurses as a result. A master's-level nursing class in South Africa used my website as a teaching tool.

I began drafting letters of complaint to the College of Nurses of Ontario, the regulatory body whose mandate is to protect the public by enforcing nursing standards of practice. Anyone who believes that a nurse has not met those standards may file a complaint, and the College must investigate every complaint it receives except where it is found to be frivolous or vexatious. If the complaints have merit, the College is empowered to take action ranging from a letter of reprimand to outright revocation of a nurse's license.

Government regulations required that employers who fire nurses for sexual abuse of a patient, incompetence, incapacity, or professional misconduct must report those nurses to the College.[1] This regulation, designed to prevent the public from the potential danger posed by a bad nurse, had one significant flaw: it assumed that hospitals would always act in the best interest of its patients and would always fire bad nurses. Virtually all hospitals do so, but not the Hospital for Sick Children.[2] Since it had no intention of firing Doerksen and Soriano, it was under no obligation to report them to the regulatory college.

I had planned from the start to file complaints against the nurses, but Frank had advised me to wait until the inquest was over. I was in the midst of preparing them when he and I agreed to appear on a local talk show. On air, Frank mentioned the impending complaints against four nurses, surprising the interviewer who had thought there were only two nurses involved. As Frank named the four—Ruth Doerksen, Anagaile Soriano, Jean Reeder, and Mary Douglas, I thought to myself they were surely watching and I had better finish and submit my complaints immediately.

Frank summed up for the TV interviewer: "What Sharon and her husband would like is some accountability. There's no accountability. The hospital did no investigation at all. This is on their own admission. Now that we've done 22 days of evidence and the jury has reached its conclusion, the hospital has the audacity to say that they're going to kick the matter now back to the chief nurse, Dr. Jean Reeder, and Dr. Reeder is going to do an investigation. Well, there's no investigation that has to be done; what has to be done is the nurses have to be fired, and they should have been fired the instant the word 'homicide' was uttered by the Deputy Chief Coroner. Instead, they're now going to do an investigation; that's a joke."

He praised the jurors, "…these are jurors, by the way, who the hospital has maligned since the verdict. The hospital says it's shocked by the verdict; the hospital shouldn't be shocked by the verdict at all. The foreperson was very clear in the newspaper on Saturday when she was interviewed that this was a verdict of conscience;[3] this was a verdict that was reached after due deliberation on the part of the five jurors. Instead of the hospital gracefully accepting the verdict, firing the nurses, firing the cover-up artists and moving on, the hospital attacks the verdict and says it's shocked. Well, I'm shocked that the hospital is shocked."

The interviewer asked me if the nurses had expressed any remorse, regret, or contrition. I told him they hadn't, and explained about the two impersonal and insincere apologies the hospital had given us: Dr. Reeder's while testifying at the inquest, and Dr. Goldbloom's to the reporters who came to the hospital's press conference to which we had not been invited.

Hospital staff had been watching the show, all right. We were on television from 10:30-11:30 p.m., but the next morning, hours before I arrived at the College to hand in my complaints, all four nurses who had been named "self-reported" themselves. The hospital immediately issued a press release praising the nurses' actions.[4] Dr. Reeder was quoted: "My leadership and ethical conduct has been questioned publicly. As a registered nurse in a leadership role, I welcome the opportunity to be reviewed by my regulatory body and independent experts." The College of Nurses was somewhat taken aback, noting that it was not its role to conduct reviews, but to act on complaints filed by members of the public or by nursing employers.

Following several more days of publicity, I received a phone call from the hospital's head of public relations asking if Bill and I would be willing to meet privately with its president, who wished to apologize to us directly. We agreed to meet him at Frank's office.

Michael Strofolino, then CEO and president of the Hospital for Sick Children, was a commanding presence and a man accustomed to being in charge. He began with an apology that seemed sincere, and then told us that in addition to the nurses' self-reporting to the College, the hospital had also independently reported Lisa's two nurses. To demonstrate his point, he opened a binder he had brought with him. This was a clever tactic: from across the table, all we could see was a binder with some papers. He did not offer to let us read what he purported to show us, but we could tell that whatever those letters were, they were only a few lines long, much too brief to contain the details necessary for a genuine complaint. Exactly as we had surmised, the College later confirmed that both the hospital's submission letters and the nurses' self-reports had merely requested a College review and did not qualify as bona fide complaints.

I told Strofolino I was sure his apology was sincere, but it was an empty gesture unless the hospital did something to back it up. I explained to him everything the nurses had done, how they had breached the most basic standards of nursing, and how the hospital's refusal to do anything about it demonstrated it cared more about protecting its nurses than it did about protecting its patients. I told him the nurses should have been fired shortly after Lisa's death, but even if the hospital hadn't done that, at the very least it should have done so immediately after the inquest jury returned its finding of homicide. He answered that although the hospital very much regretted what had happened, the nurses were going to remain on paid leave and were not going to be fired.

We were both exceedingly polite to each other, but the meeting was a waste of time, at least for us. Not surprisingly, the hospital used it to its advantage: A relative who was asked to donate to the hospital had refused, citing her connection to us, and received a letter from the head of public relations explaining that "the Hospital has apologized to the Shore family in several venues, most recently in a private meeting between our President and CEO, Michael Strofolino, and the family".

The hospital knew that Hawkins had not done an outstanding legal job for it or for its nurses. A "friend of a friend" who worked at Hawkins' law firm reported that Strofolino's yelling could be heard through the closed doors of the boardroom. Perhaps the hospital decided it would be prudent to hire another lawyer to represent the nurses, or else some lawyers independently contacted the nurses and convinced them to assert their rights, but suddenly three of the nurses had a new lawyer.[5] The hospital still pulled all the strings, however, since it continued to pay all of the nurses' legal fees. It had filed complaints about the nurses with the College of Nurses and praised itself for doing so in a press release at the same time as it was helping the nurses defend themselves from the College's investigation and any potential findings of negligence or misconduct. It was a massive conflict of interest, not to mention a case of questionable ethics.

Elizabeth McIntyre, the new lawyer, was highly regarded by many nurses; if a nurse got in trouble she knew to call Liz. Others who had dealt with her were somewhat more sparing in their praise.

McIntyre quickly issued a press release stating that her clients had been subjected to unsubstantiated allegations of significant wrongdoing, and told a reporter that the nurses believed they had been wrongly accused and wanted an opportunity to clear their names.[6] Lisa's death was caused by a drug interaction, not a breach of nursing standards, she claimed.

After all the evidence that had come out of the coroner's inquest, this was nothing more than manipulative grandstanding. We sent out our own press release:[7]

> Nurses at the Hospital for Sick Children say they were wrongly accused at the Lisa Shore Inquest and are fighting back. The Shores wish to make clear that the inquest jury came to its finding of homicide after carefully weighing all the evidence. This evidence included the sworn testimony of all four nurses in question.
>
> The nurses say they want to 'clear their names'. The family would like to know what information the nurses will give to the College of Nurses that they did not testify to at the coroner's inquest.

PART THREE

March 2000 – May 2003

32

POLICE INVESTIGATION

After the jury found Lisa's death to be a homicide, the press demanded to know if the police would start an investigation. The police had little choice but to become involved. In theory, any unusual death going to inquest should have already been investigated by the police officers assigned to do interviews and gather information on behalf of the coroner's office. Unfortunately, Bill and I had been the only people the police had interviewed back then, because no one else had been willing to answer any questions. We half-expected the police to tell us they didn't really want to do this investigation but they had been pressured into it because of the inquest publicity.

None of us had any idea what the police would do, or what kind of criminal charges might ensue. Frank suggested we hire a criminal lawyer, someone who was well thought of by both defence lawyers and the Crown, to advocate for us and perhaps act as a liaison to the police. We weren't sure if this was a good idea, not to mention how expensive it would be, but others we spoke to all seemed to approve. Bill and I talked it over and decided that if there was any chance this could help the police take matters more seriously than they otherwise might, it would be worth the cost. Frank mulled over the names of some prominent criminal lawyers and recommended we retain Michelle Fuerst.

Michelle agreed to help us, commenting that it was a nice change to have clients she could be confident wouldn't be calling her in the middle of the night telling her they were in jail. She did some research and told us what criminal charges might be laid, and also contacted the police and the Crown attorney's office. She reported back that they seemed intent on conducting a real investigation, so we decided we no longer needed her assistance.

Detective-Sergeant Michael Davis, a highly experienced and respected homicide squad officer, was assigned to the case. He was a member of the coroner's Paediatric Death Review Committee, but had not been involved in any of its discussions about Lisa because there had been no suspicion at that time that Lisa's death might have been the result of a criminal act.

I thought it would be a good idea to provide Davis with some background information. For instance, it was important he know about the events leading up to Lisa's death, since those had not been addressed at the inquest. The fact that the nurses on Ward 5A did not like Lisa and felt her problems were all in her head was very relevant because, in my opinion, it explained *why* Ruth Doerksen and Anagaile Soriano had intentionally neglected Lisa.

Frank pointed out that our justice system operated under a policy of full disclosure. If charges were ever laid against the nurses, the police and the Crown would have to provide copies of every relevant document in their possession to the nurses and their lawyers, meaning that anything I sent to the police would end up in the nurses' hands. This full disclosure system only works in one direction: the accused gets copies of everything, but doesn't have to turn over anything to the prosecution.[1] I decided it was better the police got the information even if the nurses did too.

I guessed that Davis would start by reading the inquest transcripts. To help him make better sense of it all, I wrote up an explanation of who each witness was, what position he or she held, and in what order they had testified. I also explained the Kidcom system, the monitors, patient care plans, what constituted normal vital signs, and highlighted what I felt were the most disturbing parts of Doerksen's and Soriano's testimony.

Davis called to thank me, and after only a few minutes of discussion I could tell Michelle had been right about his intention to conduct a genuine investigation. He explained he would be able to speak with me about its progress, but only up to a point. If the case ever came to trial, I would be called as a witness, and so would he as the chief investigator. If he gave me too much information, my testimony might become "tainted". Witnesses must be able to give truthful testimony based entirely on what they saw, heard, did, or said, without anyone influencing them or interfering with their independent recollections.

Since I had been with Lisa in the hospital on the night she died, had seen all the medical records, learned the details of the coroner's investigation, and heard most of those involved testify under oath, I didn't think there was much he would find out that I didn't already know, but I understood the reasons for his concern.

This was going to be a very unique criminal investigation, with some very unusual problems. Because of the inquest, the two nurses who were the subject of the investigation had given evidence in a quasi-legal proceeding. Yet when people are charged with a criminal offence they must be presumed innocent and cannot be compelled to testify at their own trial. Most of the information surrounding Lisa's death had only come out at the inquest, so Mike had to read the transcripts including the nurses' testimony—in order to begin his investigation. But once he understood the details and the evidence, he had to disregard the testimony because none of it could be used against the nurses.

Another problem was that all the evidence introduced at the inquest, such as the medical records and the nurses' notes, had been obtained via a coroner's warrant. A coroner investigates deaths and does not have the power to convict anyone or send them to jail, and therefore has access to documents and other evidence the police cannot get without a search warrant. The police might review the inquest exhibits as part of their investigation, but if they wanted to use any of it at trial they would have to give them back to the coroner, get a search warrant, and return to the coroner's office to get them again under that warrant.

The hospital's public relations department told the media the hospital planned to cooperate fully with the police investigation, but that comment was strictly for show. Mike asked Dr. Goldbloom if the police could have access to the medical records of the other patients who were on the same ward as Lisa on the night of her death with all identifying information removed so there would be no invasion of privacy. Dr. Goldbloom refused and said the only way Mike would ever get them would be with a search warrant.

Undaunted, Mike raised the matter with the hospital's CEO, Michael Strofolino, and asked him if the hospital would at least give him the names and addresses of the patient's parents so a letter could be sent asking for permission to obtain their child's records. He refused.

Mike speculated aloud that he might have to make a public appeal to parents, and he would have to explain that this action was necessary because of the hospital's refusal to cooperate with the police.

The hospital immediately changed its mind and decided it would allow a letter to be sent to parents after all, so Mike prepared a draft. After taking several months to make some minor changes, the hospital decided Mike's letter could go out, but only as an attachment to the hospital's own covering letter. It was no shock to learn the cover letter the hospital composed was innocuous on the surface but its underlying tone was clearly meant to discourage parents from responding. Mike read me the one-page letter over the phone; it suggested in three separate places that parents were under no obligation to respond to the police request. And just in case they were considering responding, the hospital advised they first contact the hospital's Risk Manager—the same person who was one of the key behind-the-scenes players at the inquest as well as the editor of the hospital's misleading letter to the coroner.

Nine letters were sent out on July 24, 2000. Mike and I were not surprised that only one family responded—and that child had been in the Constant Care Room, nowhere near Lisa. But the hospital's attempts to obstruct the investigation would ultimately backfire: the police wanted those records, and if the hospital would not voluntarily turn them over, there were other ways to get them.

∼

With my consent, my friend Sharon had been showing Lisa's chart to various nursing colleagues, including some who worked at the Hospital for Sick Children. These nurses thought that the chart was too neat and must therefore have been falsified. That made no sense to us, since Lisa's chart showed gross incompetence. If someone was redoing or changing a chart, wouldn't she have made it look like her care was adequate?

We recalled Sharon's theory that Soriano had taken Lisa's blood pressure at 4:05 a.m. just as she had done for the boy in the next room, but did not write it down because it was better to look incompetent than negligent. However, what if she *had* written it down, and when Doerksen looked it over she had decided it would be better to redo the chart altogether, making sure the damaging information was omitted?

We didn't know if this was what had really happened, but it sounded plausible. I spoke with Mike and elaborated on the theory. He agreed it was worth investigating, and said he would contact the Centre of Forensic Sciences to arrange for the chart to be analyzed. The Centre, commonly called the CFS, is a government facility that handles all forensic testing in the province for the police, the coroner's office, and any other government departments as needed. Although its website claims it is one of the most extensive forensic science facilities in North America,[2] one of its analysts told Mike the chart could not be analyzed because the lab was not set up to handle it.

Did that mean the CFS did not have necessary state-of-the-art equipment, or had someone there decided this was not a worthwhile exercise and refused to allow the work to be done? Either way, it was time once again to do things ourselves. I called Michelle Fuerst, figuring that a criminal lawyer would know a reliable document examiner. She referred me to someone in Ottawa, who told me that based on what I told him he was sure he could perform the analysis we wanted. Since he was going to be in Toronto, he proposed to do his work at the CFS so Mike would be able to supervise it. Mike agreed.

It turned out the CFS was set up to do the analysis after all; the section head admitted afterward he felt badly about having said otherwise. Even though the work was done at the CFS, using CFS equipment, under police supervision, we still had to pay for it. The upshot of the document examination was that the expert did not believe the flowchart had been altered, although he did not have enough information to determine if that held true for the nursing notes. We still privately thought our theory was right, with one variation: the nurses had testified it was their practice to record their patients' vital signs on scrap paper and then transpose the information later onto the patient's chart. Maybe the nurses had taken Lisa's blood pressure but when preparing the chart had made a conscious decision not to include it. We could not prove anything so we dropped the issue altogether and filed the report away. We did not realize that due to Mike's involvement he would make notes about the document examination which would ultimately get disclosed to the nurses.

Mike wanted a nursing expert to review the records, but he did not know where to find one since it was apparent he could not call the Hospital for Sick Children for help. The College of Nurses told him that it too would normally have used someone from Sick Kids, so it did not have an expert either although it anticipated it would eventually get one from one of the other children's hospitals in the province. However, the College told Mike it would not share the name of its experts with the police. He was not pleased.

With Mike's okay, Frank and I tried to see if we could find a nursing expert ourselves. Frank left messages for Deans of Nursing of several American universities, but they did not return his calls. I e-mailed Dr. Berde, the Chief of Anaesthesia at Boston Children's Hospital and the head of its pain clinic. Dr. Wilder, who had been Lisa's primary doctor in Boston, had already made known his reluctance to talk to me or to become involved in any way, but his colleague Dr. Berde seemed more at ease and willing to help. He promised to talk to some senior nurses at his hospital on our behalf.

Several weeks later Dr. Berde came to Toronto to speak at a conference on RSD, and I arranged to meet him for breakfast. I discussed the progress of the police and the College's investigations and asked if he had been able to find a nursing expert. Sheepishly, he said that none of the nurses he had spoken to wished to get involved.

The jury's finding of homicide had outraged the Ontario and Canadian nursing organizations. Conveniently ignoring all the factual evidence of the nurses' negligence, these organizations had decided it was more important to stand up for its nurses than to maintain standards of professional excellence. They threw their resources into supporting Doerksen and Soriano, but did it quietly, probably suspecting the public would not be sympathetic. We could not look to any of the nursing organizations for help. Besides, many nurses in Canada with extensive paediatric experience had obtained a substantial part of that experience at Sick Kids. Even if they hadn't, anyone prominent in that community would likely be acquainted with some of the people involved in this case.

I did a search on the Internet for paediatric nursing experts, and recognized one of the names that came up as a frequent contributor to a nursing mailing list I belonged to. I had always found her comments intelligent and fair, and she lived in upstate New York, only a few hours drive from Toronto. I e-mailed her and briefly outlined the situation, and she agreed to review the file for the police. I passed on the contact information to Mike and did not speak with her again, since neither of us wanted any discussions between us which could potentially taint my testimony or hers. Mike spoke with her and told me her credentials were quite impressive, so we finally had our nursing expert!

I continued to talk to my cousin in Israel, who kept in touch with Dr. Schily. Dr. Schily agreed he would return to Toronto to testify at a disciplinary hearing if one was called. I passed that information on to the College and to Mike, assuring him that Dr. Schily would also return to testify at a criminal trial. Mike was more than a little surprised to learn about my connection to him.

Most of the preliminary police investigation consisted of reading the inquest testimony, reviewing the medical records, and interviewing Dr. Cairns and others involved in the inquest. Mike spoke with the two mothers who had been in the hospital rooms adjacent to Lisa's; one told him there had been no alarms going off that night, and the other said she had walked by Lisa's room in the night and looked in, and did not see a monitor.

Kate Hughes, McIntyre's partner, called to ask if Mike was planning to interview any of their clients; he told her he had the transcripts of their sworn testimony, so unless they had additional information to provide it wouldn't be necessary to meet with them. Hughes asked Mike for a list of the questions he would ask, prompting Mike to respond that this was a criminal investigation and he didn't give out his questions in advance. She did not call him back to arrange any interviews.

After reviewing all the evidence, Mike told me that in his opinion criminal charges were warranted. He cautioned us that the Crown attorneys would have to review the file, and they would be the ones making the final decision, not him. We were glad, however, that the police agreed with us and believed what had happened to Lisa had truly been a crime, but also very sad. Frank saw it differently, bringing us a bottle of champagne and telling us we should be celebrating. We thanked him and quietly put the bottle away as we did not feel there was anything to celebrate.

There was a long way to go and some potential obstacles to overcome before the nurses actually got charged with anything. Normally, when the police have reason to believe a crime has been committed, they arrest the suspects. In unusual or complex cases, however, the police will generally seek advice from the Crown attorney's office before proceeding. Would the Crown agree that charging the nurses was the right thing to do? It was virtually unheard of for doctors or nurses anywhere to be charged with a criminal offence. Most people felt that medical negligence belonged in the realm of civil litigation through malpractice claims and had no place in the criminal justice system.

We later heard that when Mike had gone looking for someone to take on this difficult and controversial case, all the Crown attorneys but one had closed their office doors or otherwise made sure they were unavailable. Luckily for us, the one who had the courage to agree to review the file was a senior Crown named Hank Goody, who many thought was one of the best prosecutors in the city. Mike also spoke to Paul Culver, who was Hank's boss and the head Crown attorney for the Toronto region, and elicited a promise from him that Hank would be given four uninterrupted weeks to review the files and work on the case. This was a major concession, as Crowns tend to be extraordinarily busy and may be working on many cases at any one time.

Mike was considering two possible criminal charges: Failure to provide the necessaries of life, or criminal negligence causing death. The first was usually reserved for those who didn't carry out their familial responsibilities, such as parents who neglect their children, or children who mistreat their elderly parents. Medical care is considered one of life's "necessaries", so theoretically the nurses' neglect of Lisa could fall into this category, but I had never heard of a hospital nurse being charged under this section of the Criminal Code before. The maximum penalty on conviction was two years in prison.

The second possible charge was by far the more serious, and carried a maximum sentence of life imprisonment. Criminal negligence causing death was really another way of describing manslaughter, where a person doesn't intend to murder someone but nevertheless does something that causes the death of another human being. This was one of the few crimes where you could be charged not only for committing a negligent act, but also for failing to do something you had a legal obligation to do. For example, if you were swimming in a pool and saw someone drowning and did nothing to try to save her, you would be a truly evil person but probably not legally liable because you had no special relationship or duty to rescue the drowning person. However, if you were a lifeguard at that same pool who ignored a drowning person, then you could be charged with criminal negligence causing death and also sued by the person's family, because you had a legal responsibility towards her.[3]

Criminal negligence causing death is the type of charge commonly laid against people who kill somebody while driving dangerously or while drunk (although the Criminal Code has now broken out those actions into distinct offences). To be criminally negligent, your actions have to be "wanton or reckless". Skidding on ice during a snowstorm and smashing into a car is likely not wanton or reckless, but smashing into a car because you were driving at 180 kilometres per hour and lost control is. Accidentally running over a child who darts out from between parked cars may not be wanton or reckless, but racing past a school bus with its red lights flashing and killing a child who is crossing in front of the bus is. What differentiated the reckless and wanton act from the merely irresponsible or stupid? The test is whether the person knew—or more importantly, should have known—that what he did could cause harm or death to someone. The speeding, tailgating driver might never have consciously thought what he was doing was going to cause an accident and kill someone, but any normal, reasonable person would have.

Ruth Doerksen and Anagaile Soriano ought to have known that taking charge of a patient who had come up from Emergency without checking the doctors' orders could result in harm to that patient. Any reasonable, competent nurse would have known, and that was the standard they would be held to. What medications had been ordered for the patient? What kind of monitoring was required? A nurse needed to have doctors' orders to follow when caring for a patient on a ward. If the orders were there to be read and she didn't read them, then she was putting her patient's life in danger. If she had a hospital manual with written protocols that she was very familiar with but did not follow, then her actions—coupled with the failure to check the doctor's orders—were reckless and wanton. What about responding to Lisa's failing vital signs? A reasonable nurse would have known Lisa was dying, even based on the incomplete vital signs that were recorded. And if Mike believed me, as well as the inquest jury and the two mothers in the adjoining rooms, that there had been no monitor in Lisa's room, then he also believed the nurses were lying. If they were lying there could be no argument that they hadn't known exactly what they were doing.

Soriano's and Doerksen's actions and omissions were definitely wanton and reckless, and if the Crown could prove they had led to Lisa's death, then there was a real possibility of a successful conviction. There was no doubt in my mind that criminal negligence causing death was the appropriate criminal charge.

33

NURSING INVESTIGATION

We ordered inquest transcripts from the court reporter, and sent them to the College of Nurses along with a copy of the same detailed information I had already given to Mike. The investigator was very appreciative and said that my complaints were the most thorough the College had ever received.

She explained what happened when the College received a complaint from a member of the public. An investigator would speak with the various people involved, such as the complainant, nurses, doctors, administrators and other hospital staff, family members, and other witnesses. She warned me, however, that in this case she would not be able to interview Doerksen or Soriano since McIntyre never allowed the College to interview any of her clients. The investigator would then compile these interviews into one detailed report, which would be sent to a Complaints Committee along with the medical records and other relevant documents. The report was carefully written to be as neutral as possible to allow the Committee to draw its own conclusions based strictly on the evidence before it.

The Complaints Committee dismisses about half of the complaints it reviews without taking any action.[1] Some complaints are found to be groundless, while others cannot proceed due to insufficient evidence. If a complaint is found to have merit and there is supporting evidence, the nurse might receive a Letter of Caution–what I would call a letter of reprimand–or be asked to enter into a participatory program where the parties jointly work out an acceptable solution. For the most serious offences, such as theft, fraud, or assault against patients, nurses can be charged with professional misconduct and ordered to appear before a disciplinary hearing.

A disciplinary hearing is conducted much like a criminal trial, with several key differences: the nurse is compelled to testify, whereas in a criminal trial the accused does not have to take the stand. Instead of a judge, the tribunal is presided over by a panel of nurses and laypersons, although the panel has its own lawyer to provide it with guidance on legal issues as they arise. If the College finds someone guilty of professional misconduct, it cannot send that person to jail but it can mete out punishment by temporarily or permanently revoking the nurse's right to practice.

Lawyers for both the nurse and the College will meet frequently before the hearing starts to see if they can agree on some of the facts and issues, which simplifies matters for all parties. It is not uncommon for both sides to agree on what happened and work out a "sentence" that is acceptable to everyone, exactly like a pre-arranged plea bargain in criminal court.

The College had to establish which of the complaints it had received in this matter were valid, before it could begin its investigation. There were the ones I had filed against Doerksen, Soriano, Reeder, and Douglas alleging multiple acts of professional misconduct;[2] the hospital had filed complaints against Doerksen and Soriano asking the College to investigate their actions but making no allegations against them; and Reeder, Doerksen, Soriano, and Douglas had all proudly "self-reported" themselves, making sure they received ample media coverage in the process. The College knew that none of the complaints except mine had any substance and planned to completely disregard the nurses' self-reporting. It told the hospital that unless it was prepared to file valid complaints, its "non-complaining" complaints would also be dismissed.

If the hospital's complaints were dropped, it would no longer be a party to the matter and it would lose its right to obtain information about the College's investigation. It solved its problem in an act of utmost irony: the Hospital for Sick Children added its name to my complaints so it could piggy-back on them and be entitled to copies of all correspondence between the College and me, at the same time that it was publicly defending the nurses who were the subjects of those complaints.

At the inquest, we had argued against having one lawyer representing the hospital and all the nurses, but did not pursue it because we hadn't wanted to hold things up while lawyers fought it out. We had hoped that this time, nurses who had to answer to the College of Nurses would feel more pressure to be truthful knowing their licenses to practice were on the line. But with McIntyre representing Doerksen, Soriano, and Douglas, they would work as a united group with one unalterable version of events, no matter how illogical and improbable those events seemed.

What was readily apparent to everyone except McIntyre's clients was that notwithstanding her official status as their lawyer, she was really only working for Ruth Doerksen, arguably the most culpable individual of all. A lawyer looking out for Soriano's best interests would see that Soriano had some real bargaining power: she was an inexperienced new nurse, had not been Lisa's primary nurse, and had only been relieving Doerksen. In exchange for Soriano telling the truth and implicating Doerksen, the College might agree not to lay any charges against her, giving her a chance to walk away with her nursing career intact. We would have been willing to accept that as the price of learning the truth and obtaining justice. Even Mary Douglas, who was absurdly loyal to Doerksen, could be made to understand by a good lawyer that her best chance of putting all of this behind her was to come forward with the truth. Three good lawyers, representing three separate clients, might jump at the chance to be the first to get some kind of deal in exchange for the truth. As Frank always said, this kind of thing was usually a one-time offer; the first to come forward was the only one who got it.

But McIntyre could not allow Soriano or Douglas to make a deal like that, because if either of them told the truth then Doerksen, McIntyre's primary client, would inevitably be found guilty of misconduct and likely permanently barred from nursing. McIntyre did not want that to happen, so Soriano and Douglas would not learn about the one real chance they had to walk away from all of this virtually unscathed. The only defence McIntyre would provide to her clients was the "all-for-one-and-one-for-all" strategy required to protect Doerksen.

And if McIntyre's conflict of interest wasn't problematic enough, there was still the problem of the Hospital for Sick Children working both sides of the street by having signed on to my complaint and also continuing to pay all of McIntyre's fees. If Soriano or Douglas became whistleblowers, the ensuing publicity would destroy what little would be left of the hospital's reputation. Ruth Doerksen's interests and the hospital's interests coincided: it would be bad for both of them to have the truth revealed. The hospital did not want Soriano or Douglas to know that confessing was one of their options any more than McIntyre did.

The College agreed that McIntyre had a major conflict of interest but felt there wasn't anything it could do about it. We were getting tired of hearing those words, because they usually signified the organization in question did not want to do something rather than it couldn't, which in turn made us all the more determined to get it done. We asked the foremost lawyer in the province in the area of legal ethics and conflicts of interest for his professional opinion. If Gavin MacKenzie decided the Hospital for Sick Children and Elizabeth McIntyre were in a conflict of interest, nobody would dispute it.

As we had expected, Gavin agreed there was a conflict between Doerksen and the other nurses, and between the nurses and the hospital.[3] We gave his letter to the College of Nurses, who sent it to its outside counsel and to McIntyre. The College's lawyer advised us it would not do anything about the problem unless and until the nurses were sent to a disciplinary hearing, even though Gavin believed the conflict arose as soon as negotiations between the parties began.

The College's lawyer suggested we file a complaint against McIntyre with the Law Society, the lawyers' professional body. But all we really wanted was for the nurses to have separate lawyers who would look after the interests of only their own client and nobody else, and making a complaint would do nothing to accomplish this. As much as we disliked McIntyre's operating style, we had seen too much bad behaviour already on the part of the hospital, its employees and its lawyers. We chose not to file a complaint against McIntyre, and hoped instead the College would eventually use Gavin's opinion letter to force her to represent only one nurse.

Before the College could commence its investigation, it had yet another important issue to deal with: a significant portion of my complaints centred on the nurses' inquest testimony. Just as the police could not legally use a person's testimony against her in criminal proceedings, the College felt it could not use it either. Gavin was bothered by this decision, saying that if a lawyer testified falsely at a coroner's inquest he would immediately be brought before the Law Society on professional misconduct charges. His instinct told him that professionals must still be accountable to their regulatory bodies even if their testimony was not admissible civilly or criminally. But the College disagreed and told me to resubmit my complaints without reference to inquest testimony.

This wasn't too hard to do for Doerksen and Soriano, because the medical records supported my allegations of professional misconduct. However, a large part of my complaint against Douglas related to her outlandish testimony where she tried to convince the jury that Lisa got acceptable nursing care and that Lisa's deteriorating vital signs did not give any cause for concern. It had been my submission to the College that someone who held such distorted views of what was acceptable nursing practice had no business being a nurse, let alone a nurse-educator.

If I couldn't use Douglas's inquest testimony, my grounds for complaint were no longer as strong as they had been. I resubmitted a revised complaint, concentrating instead on her actions at the hospital on the morning of Lisa's death, and how she had coached Doerksen while sitting as a spectator in the courtroom–actions which had nothing at all to do with her sworn testimony.

34

PROFESSIONAL SOLIDARITY

Chief of Nursing Dr. Jean Reeder continued making her taped messages of support for her nurses, but they were growing increasingly frantic and disjointed. She acknowledged she had received criticism about her leadership from some nurses at the hospital and complained it would be more helpful to receive feedback directly rather than through anonymous messages.

Reeder also referred to my website and warned listeners that not everything on it was factual.[1] She said she wasn't calling me a liar, although in reality that was exactly what she was doing. That amused me, since I had taken great care to ensure the website was as accurate as possible and any opinions and perceptions were clearly labelled as such. I posted every newspaper article about the case whether I liked it or not, in order to be totally fair. The website infuriated the hospital, yet it could do nothing about it; if it tried to shut me down it would only look like a bully, not to mention giving me a lot of publicity. I was still receiving large volumes of supportive e-mail, including some from parents with children in that hospital.

Several days later, Reeder recorded a new message telling her nurses she had decided to visit her family in Arizona. Three weeks later, the hospital announced she would be voluntarily leaving her position as Chief of Nursing, even though her five year contract didn't expire for another six months. The head of public relations told the media her departure was "absolutely not" connected with the inquest in any way.

The Hospital for Sick Children had been handed yet another opportunity to correct its previous errors in judgment: with Reeder out of the way, it could repudiate the two nurses, accept responsibility for Lisa's death, and be regarded as having made the best of a bad situation.

In retrospect, it was more likely the hospital was simply looking for a scapegoat to blame the inquest fiasco on, and Jean Reeder was it. When we had met privately with Michael Strofolino shortly after the inquest so he could extend his apologies to us, he had made a cryptic comment about the problem with Reeder being resolved shortly. It hadn't made sense at the time, but now we understood what it had meant: Strofolino knew Jean Reeder was going to be leaving the hospital "voluntarily" before Jean Reeder knew it herself.

We doubted, however, that the hospital would seize this opportunity. We wondered if there was an internal campaign to disseminate misinformation so that staff really believed the newspapers were reporting untruths, the coroner's jury was misguided, and my website was full of inaccuracies, or whether there was an atmosphere of fear and intimidation in which people were afraid that if they spoke up they might lose their jobs.

~

There were two large nursing organizations in the province, the Ontario Nursing Association, or ONA, and the Registered Nurses Association of Ontario, or RNAO. Although both had elected not to make any public statements about the case, the RNAO wanted to show that its membership stood behind Doerksen and Soriano. A former RNAO president gave a presentation at one of the large local hospitals entitled "When Bad Things Happen to Good Nurses",[2] and spoke at length about two such good nurses, namely Doerksen and Soriano. The presenter taught at one of the local nursing schools, and had also attended the coroner's inquest on the day Jean Reeder was slated to testify, in a show of support for Reeder.

My friend Sharon worked at that hospital, and guessed what was in store as soon as she saw the notice about the upcoming presentation. She attended with a tape recorder in plain view, planning to merely sit and listen. Sharon, however, was not one who could easily keep silent when she felt a wrong was being committed, and was so outraged by what she heard that she felt compelled to speak up.

When the presenter talked about orders that were written for Lisa in the Emergency Department that "for some reason" did not get electronically sent to the ward and "for some reason" did not get checked, Sharon leapt to her feet and told her the orders did make it electronically to the ward and the only reason they weren't checked was because the nurses didn't bother to do so.

The lecturer told her audience that the nurses monitored Lisa throughout the night, and mentioned the many important issues that had come up during the inquest such as the coroner's late arrival on scene, the unreliability of the hospital's apnea monitors, and nurse-patient ratios and understaffing. Not only was she factually wrong about these having been important issues at the inquest, it was notable that nothing on her list had anything to do with the actual nursing care Lisa received. Sharon spoke up again in protest, "The nurses were incompetent. The vital signs that were taken indicated that Lisa had respiratory depression, and they never responded to that. I have been intimately involved in the case, and it was very clear that the nurses did not respond properly and Lisa should not have died."

Unable to argue with someone who knew the facts, and unwilling to admit the nurses had done anything wrong, the presenter defended herself by invoking moral superiority. In spite of her previous willingness to comment on the inquest and the nursing care without knowing any of the facts or the evidence, she piously chirped, "We weren't there on the shift so we can't say what happened. I don't feel comfortable judging the practice of another nurse unless I have seen all of the evidence."

I was quite upset when I heard Sharon's tape. I immediately wrote a letter to the RNAO's Executive Director telling her that her organization had every right to present its opinions but it also had a moral and ethical obligation to ensure its facts were correct.[3] I noted that the mere act of marking down data without taking necessary corrective action did not constitute monitoring by any standard of acceptable nursing practice, and the repeated failure of nurses to take the blood pressure of a patient who was in obvious respiratory and cardiac distress was an act of gross negligence. I sent her Lisa's medical records, and suggested some reflection on the RNAO's mission statement "to promote excellence in nursing practice" would be in order.

The RNAO, evidently hoping that platitudes would satisfy me, responded with a patronizing letter that did not bother to address a single one of my concerns.[4] I wrote back again and bluntly asked whether it was going to stop giving out incorrect and misleading information when discussing the case, and said, "The RNAO needs to decide whether its mandate is to protect all nurses no matter how negligent their actions or whether it truly wants to use its influence to strive for excellence in nursing practice. It cannot do both".[5]

This time, the director wrote back that the RNAO would no longer discuss the subject.[6] The real question was why this battle had to be fought in the first place. The RNAO was always lobbying, advocating, holding press conferences, and issuing press releases promoting its unceasing efforts to ensure high quality nursing and to safeguard the public's health. A member of the public would think that such an organization, on learning a coroner's inquest jury had concluded that grossly negligent nursing care was responsible for a child's death, would be appalled and ashamed; conceivably, an organization with principles and standards might choose to distance itself from two such dangerous health care practitioners in its midst rather than rushing to embrace them. At a minimum, a group with such noble motives would want to get its facts straight before resorting to proselytizing, and if it didn't have the courage or integrity to denounce bad nursing practice it would at least want to keep quiet and make no comment at all.[7]

∼

Several months later, the Complaints Committee at the College of Nurses concluded that Doerksen and Soriano should face a disciplinary hearing. We had been hoping for this, but were always mindful that things did not always turn out as expected. This decision meant I was no longer a party to the proceedings; the College of Nurses now "owned" the complaint and had levelled its own charges of professional misconduct against the nurses. I asked the investigator if the nurses had stuck to the story they had given at the inquest, and she answered that they had. I asked if they had accepted any responsibility for Lisa's death; they had not.

The Complaints Committee issued Jean Reeder a Letter of Caution[8] and also ordered her to appear before it to receive an Oral Caution, which I understood to be the equivalent of a stern lecture. I was disappointed she was not going to face a disciplinary hearing, because I felt her efforts to excuse and cover-up gross nursing negligence were a violation of the most fundamental ethical principles of the profession, all the more so given her leadership position both at the hospital and in the nursing community at large. Doerksen and Soriano were responsible for Lisa's death, but Reeder was in large part responsible for the moral bankruptcy that followed. On the other hand, Frank congratulated me and said it was unheard of for a Chief of Nursing of a major hospital to be censured by her governing body, and I should be proud of what I had accomplished.

Mary Douglas also got a Letter of Caution.[9] That disappointed me too, because even though my complaint was weaker without her inquest testimony, I had hoped it was strong enough for the committee to recommend professional misconduct charges.

When I read the Complaints Committee's decisions, it was apparent to me it had looked at matters piecemeal and failed to consider the complete picture. The nurses' answers may have been satisfactory in response to each separate allegation, but didn't the Committee notice that some of the individual responses directly contradicted one another?

For example, where I had said that Reeder had failed to investigate Lisa's death and allowed potentially unsafe nurses to continue caring for other patients, she responded that Doerksen and Soriano had told her they recognized they had made errors in judgment and provided substandard care.[10] In other documents Reeder sent to the College she said just the opposite: she hadn't been able to obtain any details of what had happened because Doerksen and Soriano were advised by the hospital's lawyer not to speak about this case with anybody including her.[11]

The College of Nurses advised me, Reeder, and Douglas that if we felt the Complaints Committee's decision had been wrong we could file appeals with the Health Professions Appeal and Review Board (HPARB), the government regulatory tribunal empowered to review the decisions of Complaints Committees of twenty four different health professions, including doctors and nurses. I thought the Committee's findings were too lenient and the nurses' lawyers felt there should have been no penalties at all, so each of us—Reeder, Douglas, and me—appealed and cross-appealed.

HPARB sends copies of every document pertaining to an appeal to all parties as part of the process of full disclosure. I received many I had not seen before, including the College's interviews with Michael Strofolino, Jean Reeder, and Alan Goldbloom, who had recently been promoted to the position of chief operating officer of the hospital.[12]

Strofolino had expressed some concern about nurses Doerksen and Soriano and acknowledged the possibility Lisa's death might have been preventable. Not so with Dr. Goldbloom, who rationalized, excused, and justified everything that had occurred. Nurses who did not check doctors' orders or follow hospital protocols were not of any concern to him because "even without looking at the admitting orders, Ms. Doerksen already knew what nursing measures were required because she knew the protocols well". When Doerksen and Soriano had testified, they had implied Lisa was a different kind of patient than they usually saw so they were justified in treating her differently. This had outraged the jury, but Dr. Goldbloom had no qualms about making essentially the same comment. He said that "Lisa was a different kind of admission from the type of patients usually seen on the unit. She was experiencing a lot of pain, and was on a number of other medications already. Her diagnosis of RSD was somewhat uncommon… Patients with this diagnosis have pain that is very difficult to treat."

Any competent physician would tell you that a patient with unusual symptoms who was taking unfamiliar drugs required a much higher level of monitoring than other patients precisely because she might be at greater risk of potentially dangerous drug side effects or medical complications. If nurses didn't have much information about a patient, they would need to watch her more carefully rather than less carefully, just to be safe. That a paediatrician of many, many years experience like Dr. Goldbloom could imply that Lisa's differences justified a lower standard of care, rather than a higher one, was abhorrent. The things that made Lisa different from the other patients could in no way explain or justify the poor nursing care Lisa received. She had been asleep and not in pain the entire time she was under Doerksen's and Soriano's care, and her deteriorating vital signs were indicative of impending medical disaster by every reasonable standard of care, regardless of any underlying illness or any medications she was taking.

In addition to Dr. Goldbloom's insupportable opinions, his interview with the College contained some inconsistencies. For instance, he said that the hospital did not do an investigation into Lisa's death because the coroner had taken the original records and the hospital thought it did not have a copy, while explaining in another paragraph how the Anaesthesia department discovered that there were no doctor's orders while it was reviewing Lisa's records.

When conducting an interview, a College investigator makes detailed notes of everything the interviewee says, then prepares a draft for the interviewee to review. As shocked as I was to see what a senior hospital executive was prepared to commit to writing to justify his nurses' negligence, I later learned that after Dr. Goldbloom saw the investigator's draft and realized how bad his original remarks sounded, he had heavily edited and sanitized them; I had been reading the milder, toned-down final version.

35

NOT WANTED AT THE INQUEST

In September 2000, seven months after Lisa's inquest ended, a 17 year-old girl named Sanchia Bulgin died unexpectedly at the Hospital for Sick Children on Ward 5A/B, the same ward as Lisa. Sanchia had sickle cell disease and had been admitted in the morning for what was supposed to be routine gall bladder surgery. After the surgery, she suffered internal bleeding and shock, and like Lisa, her deteriorating vital signs were charted and ignored for hours until she finally died early that evening. The coroner, whose office had evidently learned nothing from Lisa's death, waited until the next day to go to the hospital to investigate.

Two months later, a Toronto Star reporter learned of the girl's death and thought it warranted a news story given its apparent similarities to Lisa's and its occurrence so soon after the inquest. In order to be thorough and fair, the reporter contacted the hospital to obtain its comments. As soon as the hospital learned the story was going to appear the next day, it immediately issued a press release acknowledging the girl's death and taking full responsibility for it.[1] The press release became the lead story in the evening news, effectively preempting the reporter's scoop. It was a masterful public relations coup: the hospital's apparent *mea culpa* drew almost universal accolades for its humility, conscience, and social responsibility.

Yes, the new ethical paradigm was to own up to one's mistakes, but there was a moral imperative which was supposed to accompany it that the hospital sorely lacked: one must make the confession as soon as one finds out about the problem, not two months after the patient has died and hours before imminent public exposure by the news media.

Dr. Cairns was assigned to the investigation, and this time he knew exactly what questions to ask and what to look for. An inquest was called, and Chief Coroner Dr. James Young was quoted in the press that the decision was at least in part due to the apparent similarities between Sanchia's death and Lisa's.[2]

I spoke at length with Sanchia's mother, who had retained Frank as her lawyer. After much thought and discussion, I decided to ask for standing at the upcoming inquest. With standing I would have the right to question witnesses, address the jury, and propose recommendations. It was important to find out whether the hospital had implemented the recommendations from our inquest, and whether any that hadn't been implemented had affected the care Sanchia received. Sanchia's family was there to find out what happened to Sanchia, but I needed to learn what was going on at the hospital generally, not only for Lisa but for other children who would come to the hospital in the future.

Would I be brave enough to stand up in court and ask tough questions of witnesses who would be supported by experienced lawyers? Would I even be able to think of any questions to ask? Could I make an effective closing address to the jury? I knew I would be terrified, but I had to try.

Dr. Young was going to preside over this inquest, which was no surprise since the last inquest involving the Hospital for Sick Children—ours—had been very controversial and generated much adverse publicity. It would be far easier to ensure that nothing like that happened this time around if he maintained control over the proceedings himself.

Dr. Young didn't like me very much, nor I him, but I hoped that would not interfere with my request for standing. One must have an "interest" to get standing at a coroner's inquest, but it is up to the coroner to decide what constitutes that interest. The family of the deceased always has an interest, as does anyone whose testimony might subject him or her to any express or implied criticism. The engineering expert who testifies about an accident reconstruction is likely not going to be criticized for his testimony and is therefore not entitled to have standing, although he may be allowed to have his own lawyer there for the duration of his testimony. However, the driver involved in a car accident that caused someone's death may indeed be the subject of criticism and would therefore be entitled to have a lawyer present throughout the entire proceedings to protect his interest. At Lisa's inquest, standing had been given to us, the hospital and its employees, doctors, and the manufacturer of the Corometric monitor.

I drafted a letter to Dr. Young with five reasons why I believed I qualified as having an interest: The circumstances of Sanchia's death had many similarities to Lisa's; some of the jury recommendations from Lisa's inquest may have had a bearing on the circumstances and issues surrounding Sanchia's death; suggestions made at Lisa's inquest were rejected by the hospital and might need to be revisited; because the hospital had been so adversarial at Lisa's inquest, we had been able to contribute to the investigative process and help uncover information the hospital did not voluntarily disclose; and Lisa's death should not be in vain.[3]

A pre-inquest meeting was held at coroner's court for everyone who had standing or was applying for it, to go over the timing of the inquest and other administrative matters. The hospital's lawyer was someone from Patrick Hawkins' firm, but not him. This time the hospital had prudently decided to retain a separate lawyer, Elizabeth McIntyre, for its nurses; she was the one representing Doerksen and Soriano before the College. Since McIntyre and I would be seeing each other often during the upcoming disciplinary hearings, I thought it would be a nice gesture to introduce myself to her. After all, if Dr. Goldbloom and I could nod cordially to each other, McIntyre and I could do the same. When I offered her my hand, she shook it and blurted out how nice it was to meet me. She would go to great lengths in the future to be rude and discourteous to me, so I can only assume in hindsight that I startled her and she had responded automatically without having had time to think about it.

Dr. Young advised everybody there would be another meeting specifically to cover issues of standing, and added that any related written materials had better be sent to him in advance. Some of the lawyers appeared to misinterpret his comments to mean that submission of written materials was mandatory, so law firm faxes were constantly in use over the next few days as copies of documents were sent to each of the lawyers.

I had already distributed copies of the letter I had sent to Dr. Young requesting standing to every lawyer who attended the pre-inquest meeting. Although it was Dr. Young who would make the ultimate decision, every party who already had standing—the hospital, the doctors, the nurses, and the family—was entitled to either support or oppose any other party's request for standing.

The Hospital for Sick Children and Elizabeth McIntyre did not support me. At 4:15 on Friday afternoon, two working days prior to the standing meeting, the lawyer for the hospital faxed over sixteen pages explaining why my request should be denied.[4] Shortly afterwards, at 5:30 p.m. that same afternoon, McIntyre faxed me ten pages opposing my standing request.[5]

The hospital had prepared an affidavit—a sworn statement—by Dr. Goldbloom that said if I was given standing, my "ongoing campaign" and the "aggressive position I had taken against the hospital" would place an unwarranted burden on hospital staff and increase their anxiety. The only evidence he offered to demonstrate this aggressive position was the first sentence on my website: "In memory of Lisa Celine Shore, who died senselessly and tragically because of two negligent nurses at the Hospital for Sick Children in Toronto, Canada. The hospital continues to employ the two nurses".

McIntyre's opposition had been expected, but its viciousness stunned me. Her submission was much more detailed than the hospital's and undoubtedly had kept several law students busy researching old inquests and court cases. She really should thank me, I thought with tongue-in-cheek, because her efforts to fight me were generating a lot of extra revenue for her firm.

Her letter referred to my "ongoing hostile attitude" toward the nursing staff on the unit, my "spurious allegations" against those involved in the prior inquest, claimed I was on a "crusade" against the nurses and continued to engage in an unprecedented and unfair attack on them, and the accusation I found the most offensive, that "it would be dangerous to grant my application for standing".

This kind of legal machination was beyond anything I had ever dealt with. I had no legal expertise, and decided that I needed a lawyer of my own to argue my right to obtain standing. It would cost several thousand dollars, but it would at least give me a fighting chance of getting to the inquest in the first place.

Frank couldn't act for me because he was already representing Sanchia's family, but he recommended somebody else. My new lawyer decided I should submit my own affidavit explaining why I wanted standing.[6] My statement was simple: it denied I was on any campaign or "witch hunt" against the hospital or its nursing staff, and explained that my opinions were consistent with the evidence presented at the inquest. The affidavit described some of the hospital's poor behaviour at our inquest, and noted that its current assurances that nothing like that would happen again were somewhat self-serving.

The standing hearing was a travesty. McIntyre and her colleague Kate Hughes, both of whom did not acknowledge my presence, appeared on behalf of Doerksen and Soriano to protest not only my request for standing but my affidavit as well. It was apparently all right for them to claim I was a danger, but unacceptable for me to defend myself against their accusation. They argued that my words were prejudicial to their clients and requested my affidavit not be allowed to be filed. Their efforts to plead their case were almost comical, because they didn't want to quote from my affidavit and thereby allow its contents to become known, all the while exclaiming how terrible it was.

What were those terrible, prejudicial statements I allegedly made about nurses Doerksen and Soriano? Only one paragraph even mentioned them, and not by name:

> I have at all times held the view and publicly expressed the view that there are many fine doctors and nurses at the Hospital for Sick Children and that it is an important institution that provided a great benefit to our community. It has, instead, been my position throughout that two nurses in particular were negligent and that their negligence led directly to the death of my daughter and I have publicly pressed for their dismissal. I have also publicly taken the position that the hospital was not forthcoming with information concerning the facts surrounding the death of my daughter Lisa and that there is every reason to believe that even as of this date the Hospital for Sick Children is lacking in any real insight into the fundamental problems of nursing education, training and diligence that led to the death of my daughter. These views, all of which I have publicly espoused, are certainly reasonable and entirely borne out by the evidence at the inquest and the position the hospital has taken before, during and after the inquest.

Dr. Young agreed with McIntyre and Hughes and decided to "seal" my affidavit, thereby forbidding anyone to read or discuss it.[7] Although there was nothing defamatory or prejudicial in it, Dr. Young was in charge and did not have to justify his decision. With the affidavit sealed, McIntyre's and Hughes' concern for their clients' reputations was satisfied for the moment.

Dr. Goldbloom then took the stand. He had conceded in his affidavit that the care provided to Lisa had fallen below the appropriate standard, and my lawyer attempted to question him on it. "And I suggest to you, sir, that in the case of Lisa Shore, the major way in which the care fell below the appropriate standards was in the area of the monitoring in response to information raised from the vital signs while she was on Ward 5A/B. Do you agree?"

Before Dr. Goldbloom could answer, an apoplectic Kate Hughes stood up to object to the reference to her clients, who weren't there to defend themselves. Dr. Young agreed, and told my lawyer to try to keep specific people and conclusions out of it.

My lawyer continued this futile exercise. He tried to get Dr. Goldbloom to clarify what falling below the standard of care really meant, but Dr. Goldbloom had been well-prepared for this line of questioning. It could mean something trivial, he answered, or that something wasn't done on time, or an accidental error, and none of those would imply any negligence.

"Well, sir, falling below the level of the professional standard of care is what negligence is all about. You know that, don't you?"

Dr. Goldbloom disagreed. "Again, I would go back to what I said before, that I didn't talk about individuals. I said that her care fell below the standard, the standard that we would expect."

My lawyer was getting exasperated by Dr. Goldbloom's doublespeak. "I'm sure this care wasn't provided by the paint or the brooms or the janitor, was it? It was provided by the nurses, right?"

Up popped McIntyre to object to "the inappropriate line of questioning".

My lawyer told Dr. Young, "Well, sir, the doctor says she's aggressive, and the proof of her aggression is, he says, her words on the Internet—two nurses were negligent in the death of <her> daughter. I am surely, with respect, entitled to cross-examine…<to show that>

no weight should be given to that because a) it's true, and b) it's a perfectly reasonable position that a lot of people might take."

Dr. Young said my lawyer had made his point and he would consider it in his submission, and suggested he move along. My lawyer moved along, and I grew angrier and angrier at the mockery unfolding before me. Dr. Goldbloom had also stated in his affidavit that the nurses were fearful of being questioned by me, so my lawyer asked him, "And what do you think Mrs. Shore is going to do with these witnesses? Do you think she's going to get up and beat them with a rubber hose?"

Dr. Goldbloom answered, "…it is their perception, regardless of Mrs. Shore's intent…that they are under attack."

At that, McIntyre and Hughes vigorously bobbed their heads up and down several times in agreement, with the pronounced exaggeration of bobble-head dolls. What unprofessional behaviour, I thought to myself.

The discussion about nurses currently on staff at the hospital gave Dr. Goldbloom the opening he had been waiting for. He tried to bring up some nursing statistics, except that my lawyer wasn't interested and he needed his own lawyer's help to get the information out. The hospital lawyer began his well-scripted and well-rehearsed questions, enabling Dr. Goldbloom to tell Dr. Young how nursing turnover on Ward 5A/B had been so abnormally high since October 1998 that elective surgery had to be reduced by 25%. "Of the normal staff complement of 60 nurses for 5A and 5B, they've had, since October '98, they've had 34 nurses leave."

In case anyone missed it the first time, the lawyer repeated the really important part. "Since October of 1998?"

Goldbloom answered, "Since October of 1998."

I persisted in believing that the hospital and its administration would eventually get tired of acting deviously, but it never seemed to run out of underhanded ideas. The plan had evidently been to use the nurses' fear of being questioned by me to bring up the high nursing turnover and the elective surgery delays, and then to make sure everyone associated the problem's origin with October 1998, when Lisa died. The inference the hospital wanted everyone to draw was obvious: my "campaign" and aggressive stance against the nurses since

Lisa's death had led to them being fearful, which led to their quitting, which forced the hospital to cancel surgery. Dr. Goldbloom and his lawyer wanted Dr. Young and everyone else to draw the misleading conclusion that this was all the fault of Sharon Shore.

The truth behind the hospital's nursing problems was a little more complex. Jean Reeder, who was interviewed by the College of Nurses of Ontario in response to my complaint against her, told its investigator the hospital began suffering a shortage of nurses in 1997.[8] Since the hospital did not suffer any adverse publicity until the inquest began at the end of 1999, and Doerksen and Soriano continued caring for children on Ward 5A/B until then, it was ludicrous to associate any abnormal nursing turnover with Lisa's death one year earlier.

Dr. Goldbloom also did not allow for the possibility that some nurses had left not because of my so-called crusade, but because they were upset by the actions of the Hospital for Sick Children.[9] Many of the outlying suburban hospitals had been greatly expanding their paediatric departments and there were many more job opportunities for experienced paediatric nurses than there had been in a long time.

It was evident Dr. Young was not happy about what was going on—not because I was being railroaded, but because my mere presence was causing so much controversy that he was unable to conduct the quiet, uneventful inquest he had planned. Frank stood up and said a few words in my support, but that carried no weight with Dr. Young. The lawyers who were representing the other doctors and nurses all stood up to say I should not get standing, but not one of them had the decency to provide any reasons.

The final submission was made by the assistant Crown attorney, to whom I referred as Dr. Young's lawyer. He worked full-time for the coroner's office, and primarily for Dr. Young. He was supposed to represent the public interest—that is, the people of Ontario—but the only interest he really represented was that of his boss, Dr. Young. As soon as he began speaking, I knew right away that my chances of getting standing had gone from 10% at most right down to zero. Rather than presenting arguments carefully weighing all the considerations both for and against granting me standing as I had expected, the assistant Crown attorney argued that my request for standing should be denied. Why would Dr. Young not listen to his own counsel's advice to deny me standing, particularly when Dr. Young himself had consistently muzzled my lawyer and prevented him from effectively arguing my position? At that point, only the most naïve could possibly believe that Dr. Young's decision was not already a foregone conclusion, not to mention one that had already been made long before I entered the courtroom.

Luckily for me, the press was there. A Toronto Star columnist wrote a page 2 story entitled, "Hospital battles to rebuff Lisa's mother".[10] She ended her column with "How lucky for them, and Sick Kids, that they have a whole bunch of high-powered lawyers to defend their interests, without concern for cost. Unlike the mother of a dead child".

As expected, Dr. Young issued his ruling soon afterwards explaining why I would not be getting standing.[11] He accepted Dr. Goldbloom's argument that my presence might disrupt the nursing care provided to children on Ward 5A/B given the ward's nursing shortage. He agreed with McIntyre and Hughes that my participation might potentially reopen the earlier inquest with other parties–their clients–not present or protected. He felt that the coroner's counsel was there to protect the public interest, and that my interest was only personal. As for as the similarities between Sanchia's and Lisa's deaths, arguably one of the main reasons for calling the inquest, there would be expert witnesses whom the various lawyers could cross-examine. That was almost funny: most of the lawyers there had a vested interest in not addressing the similarities between the two deaths, and Dr. Young had already said on the record that he did not want to reopen the earlier inquest.

The real loser was the public. If no one looked deeply into the root causes of the deaths of two young girls on the same ward of a hospital, then no one would solve the underlying problems and it would only be a matter of time until another tragedy occurred.

The inquest into Sanchia Bulgin's death began. I attended almost every day, listening in amazement as incident after incident of unbelievably poor care was recounted. The surgeon did not inform the clinic that handled Sanchia's ongoing treatment for sickle cell disease that she was coming in for surgery, so the clinic did not order the blood transfusion that was essential for her to have. When the anaesthetist expressed concern that the patient had not had a transfusion and there were no recent blood tests,[12] the surgeon allayed her concerns and told her everything was all right; she deferred to him and did not investigate further. The nurses who were supposed to go through a pre-operative checklist did not notice there was no blood work.

After surgery when Sanchia was due to be transferred from the recovery room to the ward, she had to wait an additional forty-five minutes until ward nurses were ready to receive her. None of the recovery room nurses checked on her during those forty-five minutes, and by the time she arrived on Ward 5A/B her vital signs already showed she was in shock,[13] a life-threatening condition in which the heart cannot circulate enough blood to the body. Just like in Lisa's case, Sanchia's nurse took her blood pressure when she first came to the floor but never again. The vital signs that were charted nonetheless showed her rapid deterioration, but although four different nurses added information to the flowsheet not one of them noticed or took any action. Ironically, Sanchia was on a vital signs monitor, but when the monitor's alarm went off the nurses thought the monitor was malfunctioning.

When the surgeon came by on rounds a few hours later, he only stood at the doorway of Sanchia's room. He claimed he saw her from the door and she didn't look pale—an indicator for shock—although he couldn't satisfactorily explain how paleness could be determined from a distance in a child with black skin who was covered with a blanket and wearing an oxygen mask. He didn't bother to look at her chart or discuss her condition with any of the nurses, so he, too, never noticed his patient was near death.

Sanchia's mother had told the nurses that her daughter's hands and feet were cold. This is one of the known signs of shock, when the patient's hands and legs become cold as blood is diverted to the internal organs to try to keep them going. What had the nurses done about Sanchia's cold feet? They brought her blankets and warmers to warm her hands and feet up, which reduced her body's ability to protect its vital organs and possibly even hastened her death.

Although conducted in the same courtroom, this inquest was very different from Lisa's. Lawyers from the hospital, the coroner's office, the doctors, nurses, and even Sanchia's family (who had released Frank and retained a different lawyer) all worked together like a mutual admiration society. Everyone was cooperative and collegial, except for one lawyer who represented the Sickle Cell Association of Ontario. But every time she tried to explore a meaningful issue or make a valid point, one of the lawyers representing the hospital, the doctors, or the nurses would object. Every single time a lawyer objected, Dr. Young agreed with the objection and made her stop her line of questioning. There was to be no controversy at this inquest. The poor lawyer was utterly marginalized and there was nothing she could do about it. It didn't seem very fair or just.

Why were the lawyers being so nice to each other? Perhaps the lawyers representing the hospital and its doctors and nurses figured that solidarity was the best tactic. So many people had made so many mistakes that what would hurt one would hurt them all. Even the family's lawyer did not delve into the underlying causes of Sanchia's poor care in the manner I would have expected. Maybe Sanchia's mother, a deeply religious woman, had instructed her lawyer to avoid conflict. Another possibility was that the hospital had offered a much higher than usual financial settlement to Sanchia's family to enable it to pay the inquest legal fees. Our civil suit with the hospital had taken place before the inquest had started, and Frank had requested the hospital help us defray his inquest fees, but the hospital had refused. The amount usually paid to a parent for the wrongful death of a child was too low to cover the legal fees for the two months that Sanchia's inquest took, so paying those fees would eliminate the adversarial relationship between the family and the hospital and reduce the likelihood of adverse publicity.

Whatever lay behind the strategy of cooperation, it worked. The recommendations from the Shore inquest were barely referred to. Because everyone readily accepted that mistakes had been made, few expert witnesses testified; who needed anyone to confirm what all the parties had already agreed on? The similarities to Lisa's death were never explored, which may have benefited the hospital but did not allow the jury to understand the full picture when trying to formulate effective recommendations. The mantra was that everybody made mistakes, no one person was at fault, it was a bad, bad thing to blame anybody, ad nauseum. In spite of the fact that anyone who had taken an elementary first aid course could have given Sanchia better nursing care than her primary nurses did, the hospital did not plan to take any action against them other than giving them a bit more training.[14]

I was quite certain, however, that none of the hospital's senior administrators, physicians, or lawyers would knowingly let those particular nurses anywhere near *their* children.

Attending the inquest did teach me more about McIntyre, who worked very hard at pretending I didn't exist. Day after day we walked by each other and day after day she looked right past me. Even when we stood two feet apart in the very small ladies washroom, she acted as if I were invisible. I initially thought she was nearsighted, but after a while it became obvious she was doing this intentionally. It was surprising to see a grown woman behave that way, but the College of Nurses investigator said I shouldn't feel I was special; McIntyre treated the investigators the same way.

Sanchia's inquest jury concluded that her death was accidental, a decision even I agreed with. The errors that in combination caused her death were mainly due to arrogance (the surgeon's) and incompetence (the nurses), but there was no intentional flouting of procedures and protocols and none of the overt lies permeating the testimony of hospital employees as had been the case with Lisa. At our inquest, everybody including the hospital administration denied they had done anything the least bit wrong, a position they continued to maintain in spite of all the evidence to the contrary. At this inquest, while no nurse or doctor individually took any responsibility, senior staffers and department heads acknowledged errors which in combination had led to Sanchia's death. It was easier for the hospital to accept responsibility when it could attribute it to multiple causes, but much harder when, as in Lisa's case, there were only two nurses involved and their actions only made sense in the context of gross negligence.

When the inquest concluded, the Toronto Star asked me to write an opinion piece on what I thought of the jury's recommendations. In it, I pointed out that a number of the inquest recommendations were almost identical to the recommendations made at Lisa's inquest. I asked why the recommendations necessitated that the hospital teach its nurses to be nurses, when command of the basic skills of a profession should be a given. I wrote that a wholly blame-free philosophy was nothing more than a "get-out-of-jail-free"' card if the system included unsafe practitioners who weren't capable of doing their jobs.[15]

36

PASSING MUSTER

It took over a year after Lisa's inquest ended for the Crown to decide whether or not to lay criminal charges. First, Mike Davis had needed about six months to complete his investigation. He had recommended charging the nurses and passed on all his materials to Hank Goody. Hank was busy with a number of other cases and it was several months until he had the time to review the information. Once he began, it took another six weeks for him to go through everything.

Hank explained that he was appalled by what he was reading but cautioned that this did not necessarily translate into criminal charges. He was quite impressed with both Frank and the monitor manufacturer's lawyer. He said they had been very restrained at the inquest, much more so than he would have been, and just reading the testimony made him want to yell out. He told me if charges were laid I would become an important witness, so he would not be able to speak with me too often to ensure my testimony could not be inadvertently influenced.

Several weeks later, Mike called to tell me that he and Hank had met to discuss the case, along with Hank's boss Paul Culver. Culver wanted to meet with us, and if everything went well after our meeting they would consider charging the nurses.

"Charge them with what?" I asked, expecting to hear it would be the less serious charge of "failure to provide the necessaries of life". When he answered, "Criminal negligence causing death," I considered for the first time opening up the celebratory bottle of champagne Frank had bought us months earlier.

The second question I asked was why we had to meet with Crown attorneys before charges could be laid. Did things depend on whether or not they liked us? I thought charges were laid whenever the police had reasonable and probable grounds to believe a crime had been committed, so why did we need to be interviewed first?

Mike explained that Culver wanted to find out what we expected from all of this. There had been an inquest, a lawsuit against the hospital, and the nurses were being prosecuted at a disciplinary hearing by their regulatory body, so Culver wanted to see why it was we felt criminal charges were also necessary. I instinctively understood that everyone knew this was going to be a very difficult and high-profile case, and the Crown was not prepared to take it on unless they could be sure we would be cooperative. Hank and Culver wanted to meet me to determine how good a witness I would make.

The meeting took place on March 2, 2001, at the Crown attorney's office in the city's main courthouse. Bill and I were nervous and worried about saying something that might make them change their decision. We were also upset: we were the victims, so why did we have to prove ourselves worthy before the police would lay charges?

Mike met us at the courthouse and escorted us to a boardroom where Hank and Culver sat waiting, along with Culver's boss, John McMahon. The Crown attorney's office was paying attention to this case at the highest levels.

There was no doubt we were under intense scrutiny. It seemed as if they were actively trying to discourage us. McMahon did most of the talking, telling us how hard it was in general to get convictions against health care professionals like doctors and nurses and that their office had a very poor success rate in such cases. Although he mentioned no names, I knew he was referring to a recent high-profile case where a newborn baby had starved to death and the mother and the social worker had been charged with criminal negligence causing death.[1] There had been a lot of publicity, and the judge had thrown the case out at the preliminary hearing stating in essence that it was society's fault the baby had starved and not the accused's. Many people had not liked that decision, including the Crown attorney's office, and it was afraid of another such fiasco.

Hank was confident about the prospect of obtaining a conviction, and said there was a great deal more evidence in this case than in the other one. He spoke with great enthusiasm, and we knew charges would be laid tomorrow if it were entirely up to him.

McMahon asked Bill and me how we would feel if the nurses were acquitted. I said I realized the hospital would consider it a public relations bonanza, but asked how the Crown felt when people who they knew were guilty were acquitted. Bill added we would never know whether or not that would happen unless charges were first laid.

"They'll never go to jail, even if there is a conviction," they told us. They were nurses, first time offenders, solid citizens who were no threat to the community. We said it didn't matter whether they went to jail or not; we wanted justice, not punishment, and justice would be served by a conviction.

They reminded us of Susan Nelles, a nurse who had been wrongly charged over twenty years earlier with murdering young babies on the cardiac ward of the Hospital for Sick Children. The police and the Crown had been heavily criticized for their actions, and the public had never forgotten it. If the nurses were charged, nurses everywhere would claim this was another Nelles case and that the nurses were being unfairly persecuted. I didn't care. "That will change once everyone sees the evidence," I insisted.

They were also concerned about the website and all the information I had made available on it. They worried the defence might argue it wouldn't be able to find an impartial jury and get a fair trial, since many potential jurors would have seen and been influenced by the site. I told them I would take the site down the moment charges were laid, to alleviate that concern. They seemed sceptical that I would do it, and repeated several times how important it was I obey their request. They didn't realize that when I say I will do something, I do it.

They discussed amongst themselves which lawyers, or rather, which "high priced teams of lawyers" would represent the nurses, aware that the defence teams would be backed by the powerful resources of the Hospital for Sick Children.

We were told the trial would take about three months, and the preliminary hearing about half that long. The two nurses would have separate lawyers but would be tried together, to avoid the potential miscarriage of justice that could arise if one accused was found guilty by one court and the other acquitted by a different court.

This meeting had evolved from probing questions to talking as if the laying of charges was a fait accompli. We had passed the test.

I spoke with Mike a few days later. Everything was in process and charges would definitely be laid—eventually. First the police needed to prepare some search warrants, one of which would be for Lisa's original medical records which were in the possession of the coroner's office. A second search warrant would be served on the Hospital for Sick Children to obtain the nursing records for the other patients on the ward on the night Lisa died—the same records the hospital had previously refused to give to the police and had discouraged parents from providing.

Mike predicted it would take him a month or two to prepare the warrants. He told me that the usual practice when executing a search warrant on a hospital was to drop off the warrant and come back later to pick up the information, but not in this case. An officer would serve the warrant and stand there waiting while the hospital got the documents. And, he added, the warrant would be served before charges were laid. If the nurses or the hospital discovered charges were coming, the records the police wanted might mysteriously disappear.

The police didn't trust the Hospital for Sick Children any more than we did.

Mike's prediction turned out to be a little off, and his month or two of preparation lasted seven months. The Crown expected the warrant against the hospital would be challenged by defence lawyers because it concerned patient records and privacy issues, and wanted to make it as "bullet-proof" as possible. Accordingly, Mike's draft had to be reviewed by an expert before it could be finalized. There could no longer be any doubt the Crown was taking matters very seriously and committing as many resources to this case as necessary. The only problem with doing such a good job was the length of time it took and the resultant delay in laying charges. I felt sorry for Mike, though: the government lawyers kept making changes to the warrants, and each time he had to redo them—again and again and again.

37

APPEALS

The Health Professions Appeal and Review Board had scheduled Jean Reeder's and Mary Douglas's appeals for July 2001.

The investigator from the College of Nurses could not attend but she gave me some advice. I had been thinking of retaining Frank to speak for me, but she felt the Board looked more favourably on people who represented themselves. I worried I would be out-matched by the lawyers, but she said not to worry, the panel members would handle that if it occurred. They get frustrated with people who go on and on, she said, as some lawyers tend to do. I would be given one chance to present my position, another to rebut my opponent's arguments, and I might be asked questions by the panel at any time.

I had previously submitted my written reasons for appealing the College's decisions to HPARB, and was surprised to learn I would have to stand before the panel and make oral arguments. Couldn't they just read the materials and base their decision on that? I had no idea what I could say that I hadn't already written about. I was also nervous about the rebuttal, especially when I learned the panel expected a response as soon as the other party finished speaking. Lawyers are good at things like that, I thought, not me. I was committed to seeing this appeal through, however, so I began working on my presentation. I didn't want to re-read aloud what I had already submitted in writing, so I tried to summarize and re-emphasize my most important points.[1]

Reeder arrived with Patrick Hawkins. We had expected McIntyre to represent Douglas, but her colleague Kate Hughes showed up instead. Hawkins and I politely acknowledged each other, as did Reeder, but Hughes had evidently taken the same course on social graces as McIntyre and refused to make eye contact with me.

The HPARB panel consisted of three men, all lawyers. We began with Douglas's appeal. As the complainant, I spoke first, and asked the panel if I could show them a picture of Lisa to give them an idea of what this case was really about. They admitted it was unusual but said it would be all right. Bill was watching Hughes, who made a grimace of disgust as I walked up to the panel with the picture.

Douglas's Letter of Caution had censured her for coaching a witness during the inquest, but she had been absolved of any other misconduct. I explained to the panel how the reprimand was insufficient, because the only way a witness could be coached by a member of the audience was if the two parties coordinated it in advance. Douglas's actions were a pre-meditated attempt to deceive the court and in my view should have been considered a disgrace to the nursing profession sufficient to warrant a disciplinary hearing. I also tried to show why my other allegations of misconduct, which the College had dismissed, had merit and should be re-considered. I spoke for perhaps ten minutes, and then Hughes began her arguments.

She started talking, and she kept on talking. She talked so much that Bill muttered, "Is she getting paid by the word?" She expounded at length on Mary Douglas's sterling career history. She described Lisa's care in painstaking detail, and after every statement she said "…and Mary had no involvement with that". She seemed ready to go through each of the inquest recommendations too, except that one of the panel members finally told her, "We get your point, please move on."

I was frantically scribbling notes as she talked, preparing my rebuttal. Stick to the big things, I told myself, there isn't time to get creative. It was not as bad as I feared it would be; once I began speaking I was too busy to be nervous, and after all, I knew my subject better than anyone else.

The panel was not happy with Douglas. Its members felt Hughes was picking and choosing her arguments: in one breath she emphasized how Douglas was not involved with Lisa's case in any way, but in the next explained how Douglas had unselfishly decided to help Doerksen by going into Lisa's room to check the monitor settings. Was she involved or wasn't she?

They took issue with Douglas's assertion that since she had reported her concerns to the ward manager, any duty she had to report nursing concerns to anyone else was discharged. Since the manager was not a nurse, he was not accountable to a health profession regulatory body and may not have understood the implications of what Douglas was telling him.

The panel members most definitely did not like the fact Douglas had coached a witness at the inquest. Hughes, speaking for Douglas, emphatically denied her client had done any such thing. But as part of the College's investigation into my complaint, it had interviewed the jury forewoman, who had reported that it was the jury members who first noticed what was happening and brought it to the coroner's attention. Hughes told the panel the forewoman's interview should be disregarded because she was biased. The panellists were incredulous. "Can you think of anyone more likely to be objective than the forewoman of the jury?" they asked. Hughes, undaunted, answered, "They had a certain point of view."

Hughes went on and on until even the panel members were visibly squirming. They asked how much longer she planned to be—which anyone with any sense would have known was an invitation to cut things short—and she told them she still had quite a few more things to cover. I probably spoke for no more than twenty minutes in all, but the hearing lasted well over three hours because of her nattering. This was problematic because Reeder's appeal was scheduled to follow and it looked like it might have to be postponed—a hardship to Reeder who had come from the west coast specifically for it.

Finally and to everyone's great relief, Hughes finished. Her performance had not helped her client any, but it had been an epiphany for me. I had always been in awe of lawyers, believing them to be much smarter than I. But observing Hughes had made me realize lawyers were not necessarily as smart as I had thought. I had just represented myself at an official hearing, and believed I had done it reasonably well. For the first time, I began to seriously consider becoming a lawyer myself.

We all agreed to stay late to finish Reeder's appeal. Her Letter of Caution had cited her for failing to conduct an investigation as soon as she became aware there were nursing issues involved in Lisa's death. The College felt this could have endangered other patients and given the appearance she was putting the interests of nursing colleagues ahead of those of patients.

I again went first, discussing the general lack of an investigation and then Reeder's own failure to do one. One of the hospital's rationales for not investigating Lisa's death had been that everyone there initially believed it had been due to a morphine overdose. To that I said, "So how about doing an investigation to try to figure out how such a thing could have happened? How about the need to take steps to ensure that such a thing didn't happen to anyone else? Why *wouldn't* anyone do an investigation?"

One of Reeder's arguments for not personally investigating Lisa's death, according to the disclosure materials I received, was that nurses Doerksen and Soriano refused to give her any information based on advice they received from their lawyer, and that this refusal had effectively limited the scope of her investigation. Emulating Frank's cross-examination technique which he had used so effectively at the inquest, I asked rhetorically, "Remember, the nurses are not talking to an outside party here. They're not talking to the coroner, to the police, or to a lawyer representing the family. They're talking to the Chief of Nursing at the hospital. Why didn't Reeder call up Hawkins— who was acting for the nurses and also for the hospital—and say, Mr. Hawkins, this is ridiculous, tell your nurses to talk to me!" The panel liked that question and put it to Reeder, who explained she felt it would have been inappropriate because it would be coercive.

By the time the hearing was over, I think the panel members understood quite well what had gone on at the hospital following Lisa's death. They had asked probing questions, noted that many of the answers they received were inconsistent or implausible, and honed in on the key issues. I was impressed with them, but also realistic enough to predict the panel would likely take the middle road and neither rescind the Letters of Caution as the nurses wanted nor send the nurses to a disciplinary hearing as we wanted. It took the panel members six months to render their decision. I was right: the Letters of Caution stayed.

When we stood up to leave the hearing, Reeder came over to me and said, "Mrs. Shore, I want you to know that I think about what happened every single day of my life." I wanted to ask her, "What exactly do you think about—my daughter who should still be alive and isn't, or your lost career?" But I said nothing.

I could understand why Reeder thought about what happened every day. Her life had profoundly changed. In a relatively short period of time, she had gone from being the Chief of Nursing at a large, well-known hospital, with a cross-appointment to the Faculty of Nursing at the University of Toronto, to unemployment. She had been highly respected in the nursing field, and had served on a number of boards and committees. The hospital had ended her contract early because it didn't like the way she had handled the Shore inquest, even if it refused to publicly admit it. The adverse publicity from the extensive media coverage and the jury's finding of homicide likely affected its fund-raising, frightened the parents of its patients, and harmed its reputation, and the hospital needed a scapegoat. However I felt personally about Jean Reeder, there was no doubt she had been fiercely loyal to her nurses and to the hospital, and she could only have seen her dismissal as a betrayal.

I don't know if she chose not to seek other employment, or if she could not find anything suitable because gossip and rumours about what had happened in Toronto followed her. Whether or not by desire, she began to do consulting, speaking regularly at nursing and medical conferences all over North America. Ironically, her subject of choice was patient safety. It was difficult to understand how someone who was cited by her profession's governing body for not conducting an investigation into nursing issues surrounding a patient's mysterious death, and who emphatically defended negligent nursing care, could present herself as an expert on the subject. I wondered how often she faced questions from her audience about what had happened at Sick Kids.

Ten months after the hearing, Jean Reeder committed suicide. I suspected but would never know for sure if Lisa's death and its aftermath had anything to do with her decision to end her life.

38

ONLY ONE RECOMMENDATION NECESSARY

Inquest recommendations are just that: recommendations. No laws compel anyone to implement them. If an organization promises to implement a recommendation there is nothing in place to verify whether or not the organization keeps its promise. If recommendations are implemented, there is no monitoring mechanism to ensure the organization maintains what it has implemented. Some organizations eagerly embrace inquest recommendations, while others choose which they wish to adopt. Without any ongoing system of evaluation, reporting or audit, and feedback, inquest juries are doomed to keep addressing the same issues again and again.[1]

Approximately one year after an inquest concludes, the coroner's office issues a report on the status of the jury's recommendations, thus ending the responsibility of all parties involved in the inquest. Since most of the recommendations from Lisa's inquest were addressed directly to the Hospital for Sick Children, the hospital prepared a progress review for the coroner in July 2001.[2]

The report discussed each of the 29 recommendations aimed at the hospital, but in a vague sort of way that left a reader unable to determine whether or not the recommendation had been implemented. I did an analysis and posted it on my website, classifying each recommendation as Implemented, Not Implemented, or Unable to Determine.[3] Only 10 of the recommendations had been implemented exactly as proposed.

Twelve recommendations had not been implemented, including those we believed to be the most important, the ones that attempted to ensure the rules and protocols which were not followed for Lisa, were followed in the future. Recommendation 2 suggested the hospital implement an automated warning system if there were orders in the system that had not been checked after a period of time following a patient's admission from Emergency. The hospital replied that the need for an automated warning was eliminated because suspended orders automatically printed off at the nursing station. It had already told that to the inquest jury and the jury had made the recommendation anyway, aware that a nurse who did not bother to check the computer for orders could not be relied upon to check the printer for them. The purpose of an automated warning system was not to remind a nurse to do what every competent nurse already knew to do, but to warn others it had not been done. The hospital had no intention of following this recommendation because none of its nurses ever forgot to check orders—except for Ruth Doerksen when she looked after Lisa Shore.

The inquest jurors had heard that Doerksen had entered basic information on Lisa into the computer system while sitting in the Constant Care Room, even though she had not bothered to read the doctors' orders that were on the same system. The jury felt a good way to ensure orders always got checked was to prevent someone from doing what Doerksen had been able to do: the recommendation was to prohibit staff from updating the patient's records where there were orders in the system that remained unread. The purpose was not to forbid access to the system but to accomplish exactly the opposite—by not allowing updates, anyone who tried would instantly be aware there was a serious problem and would have to take remedial measures. In Lisa's case, for example, had Doerksen been unable to update the system unless she first read the orders, she would have been forced to look at them. The hospital subverted the recommendation's intent by stating that blocking access to the chart would compromise patient safety, even though there had never been any suggestion that access should be denied. It congratulated itself on meeting the intent of the recommendation by having suspended orders automatically print off at the nursing station, the same thing it had offered as an ineffective solution to recommendation 2, and a solution that the jury had already rejected.

Recommendation 9 was that monitoring orders for patients on PCA pumps be improved and clarified. The hospital did clarify some ambiguity in the orders, but it looked as if it had concurrently introduced a change that could only be described as detrimental to patient safety. Lisa's blood pressure had been checked only once in violation of the then-existing monitoring protocols which required it be taken every 4 hours. The hospital had apparently decided the best solution to nurses not taking a patient's blood pressure when they were supposed to was to change the rules so that blood pressures no longer needed to be taken at all. I categorized the hospital's action in this case as "Action Worsened the Problem".

Another recommendation proposed that doctors ask nurses for all vital signs during any telephone consultations, and the hospital said this had been implemented in March of 2000. Yet Sanchia Bulgin died in September 2000, and according to testimony at her inquest, her nurses had had several telephone consultations with doctors. Had any of the doctors asked for Sanchia's vital signs—or had any of the nurses offered them—the doctors would have known immediately she was close to death. We categorized this one as "Implemented but not Followed".

The Hospital for Sick Children had cherry-picked the recommendations it wanted to implement. That was within its rights, of course, although there was only one logical conclusion to be drawn about the ones it had chosen to implement and those it had decided to ignore: the hospital knew what Doerksen and Soriano had done was so out of the ordinary that it was a one-time occurrence, and therefore it did not need to expend time and resources on recommendations aimed at preventing recurrences.

Had the hospital truly wanted to make itself safer for its patients, it only needed to implement the one recommendation I had been proposing since we had first learned about the nurses' negligence two years earlier: fire the two nurses!

39

NURSING PROPAGANDA

The search warrants finally met with everyone's approval. On Monday morning, October 22, 2001, three years to the day of Lisa's death, the police served a warrant on the coroner's office to take possession of Lisa's original medical records and other inquest documents. It caused quite a commotion, but that was nothing compared to what went on at the Hospital for Sick Children when a warrant was served on it the next day. It wasn't the warrant that was the problem, it was what it meant: nurses Doerksen and Soriano were about to be charged with criminal offences.

Due to the high profile of the case and the low risk to public safety, Mike called McIntyre to give her advance notice. He knew the press would find out soon enough, so he allowed the nurses to surrender themselves quietly without the public embarrassment of a formal arrest. The lawyers made arrangements to go down to the police station with their clients on Thursday morning. I knew about it but had agreed not to say anything.

Wednesday morning, the day before the nurses were to be formally charged, my phone began to ring at 6:00 a.m. One of the newspapers had broken the story of the impending criminal charges on its front page,[1] and a radio station was calling for confirmation. I was worried the police would mistakenly think I had been the source of the leak, but the article contained details even I hadn't known.

I had told the Crown that once the nurses were charged my website would be taken down, and I kept my promise. I also agreed to refrain from making any public comments, because as an important witness it would be inappropriate. Frank and I figured, however, that a few innocuous comments from him would give the press the quotes they wanted without jeopardizing my promise to be silent.

Frank fielded call after call from the media, politely telling everyone he couldn't say anything about the criminal charges until he received official confirmation. McIntyre must have been equally beleaguered, and ultimately provided confirmation. Reporters and camera crews crowded into Frank's office for an impromptu press conference.

McIntyre denounced the criminal charges as outrageous and said the case did not belong in the criminal courts, which made Frank so angry he threw away his prepared comments and told everyone she was misguided and it was not her place to say whether or not criminal charges were appropriate. Always quick with an analogy, he remarked that if he were to walk into a liquor store with a gun and rob it, he would be in trouble with the Law Society but that wouldn't excuse him from facing criminal charges.

The police were upset with McIntyre's comments, because calling the criminal charges inappropriate and outrageous was essentially saying the police and the Crown were incompetent and didn't know what they were doing. Mike told me, "The police and the Crown can't say anything; Frank's our voice. Tell him to keep up the good work."

The nurses did turn themselves in the next morning, but to a different police station than originally planned. Somebody inside the station must have alerted the press anyway, because the nurses were surrounded by waiting media by the time they left.

Two lawyers attended with the nurses: Elizabeth McIntyre, now representing only Soriano, and Marlys Edwardh, representing Doerksen. Edwardh was a highly regarded criminal lawyer, reputed to be among the best in the country. The Crown had correctly guessed she would be the one the hospital hired to defend its nurses.

Why was McIntyre, who was a labour lawyer and not a criminal lawyer, representing Soriano in the criminal courts? From the little I knew about law, it seemed akin to hiring a dermatologist to perform a heart transplant. I told Mike about the ongoing conflict of interest with McIntyre representing Soriano for the criminal case and both nurses before the College of Nurses. Because the College case had been ongoing for some time, McIntyre had obtained privileged information from Doerksen that as Soriano's lawyer she would not otherwise have been entitled to. In turn, she could potentially use this knowledge to help her client, Soriano, at Doerksen's expense. Mike discussed it with Hank, but I got the impression the Crown was happy with the status quo and preferred to deal with one good criminal defence lawyer instead of two.

McIntyre continued to publicly complain about how outrageous the criminal charges were. Edwardh, the experienced criminal lawyer, knew it was better to maintain a good working relationship with the Crown prosecutors that McIntyre was so vociferously disparaging, and wisely said nothing other than she would vigorously defend her client.

A friend of a nurse at Sick Kids reported to us that its nurses were telling everyone that Doerksen and Soriano had nothing whatever to do with Lisa's death and that I had caused my own daughter's death. These comments, if true, were sad and appalling: these nurses' extraordinary efforts to remain wilfully blind were exceeded only by their eagerness to believe the unbelievable. Didn't any of them have the capacity for independent, critical thinking? Had anybody read the many newspaper accounts of the inquest or looked at Lisa's chart which was posted on my website for almost two years–a website they were encouraged to disregard but which many surreptitiously visited late at night?[2] Did they really think the Deputy Chief Coroner for Ontario, the physicians on the Paediatric Death Review Committee, the five laypeople who made up the inquest jury, the College of Nurses of Ontario, the Toronto police homicide squad, and the Crown attorney's office had all been duped?

Michelle Fuerst, the criminal lawyer we had retained for advice after the inquest, called to say that Edwardh had asked if she wanted to work with her on the case. She had declined because of the obvious conflict of interest. Edwardh had asked for specifics,[3] which Michelle would not provide other than to confirm that we had retained her.[4] We assumed that would be the last of the matter.

The day before the nurses' first scheduled court appearance, Edwardh sent Frank a letter saying the comments he had made to the media after the charges had been laid were inappropriate and risked undermining the nurses' right to a fair trial.[5] We knew the timing was no coincidence; she just wanted to put Frank on notice that he had better not say anything on a day when the nurses would again be in the news. Frank wrote back disagreeing with her characterization of his comments and said they were made only in response to McIntyre's remarks; had she stayed quiet, he would have too.[6]

The nurses made their court appearance surrounded by their supporters: Doris Grinspun, the RNAO's executive director, Dr. Janet Rush, the hospital's new Chief of Nursing, and a gaggle of nursing colleagues. Dr. Rush talked to the press about system problems and human error and how nurses everywhere had been affected by these criminal charges.

Edwardh complained to the press that she wasn't able to decide whether the nurses would elect trial by judge or jury because the Crown hadn't given her full disclosure. When I asked Mike what information she hadn't received, he laughed and said she was missing four pages of inquest transcripts of the pharmacologist's testimony. They were missing from the police copy too, he told me. I laughed, telling him that McIntyre had ordered all the inquest transcripts and therefore the Defence had its own originals of those missing pages. "Those are the kind of games they play," he told me.

The public was in favour of a criminal prosecution,[7] but not the nursing organizations. The Ontario Nurses' Association issued a press release echoing McIntyre, saying that Ontario's demoralized nurses were angered at criminal charges filed against their Sick Kids' colleagues, and the appropriate place to deal with matters like this was at the College of Nurses.[8] The RNAO, having seen Lisa's medical chart in the course of my previous correspondence with it, took a more subdued approach and issued a less strident release, merely terming the charges against the nurses as "sad".[9]

Not content with issuing press releases, the nursing organizations began the propaganda war in earnest. The RNAO published a lengthy article by its Executive Director[10] in its member's magazine, emphasizing its unwavering commitment to safe and high-quality care and its long-standing tradition of supporting nursing colleagues in times of crisis. The writer explained how the nurses were sending Anagaile and Ruth cards of support, and gave the e-mail address for readers to send their own cards and letters. And just as Hank and John McMahon had predicted, she revived the ghost of the Susan Nelles case, encouraging readers to draw their own comparisons between a nurse wrongly accused of murder more than twenty years earlier and the two nurses charged in the present-day.

Nursing leaders adopted two themes to spread its message: the mantra that nurses should never be the subject of criminal charges, and the Sick Kids inspirational homily that Doerksen and Soriano were just in the wrong place at the wrong time and what happened to them could have happened to any other nurse.

Canadian Nurse magazine talked about strained working conditions and how anyone could be held liable for negligence despite having little or no control over her working environment.[11] Frank wrote back to say that Lisa's death was the direct result of nurses ignoring systems that were in place, and it was a people problem, not a systems problem. To suggest otherwise was to miss the point, he explained, one that was manifestly clear to the five member coroner's jury. It was the mandate of the police and the Crown to decide when criminal charges were appropriate, not the mandate of the College of Nurses, Canadian Nurse magazine or Elizabeth McIntyre.[12]

Janet Rush wrote an article for an issue of the RNAO magazine explaining the many things Sick Kids was doing to support its two nurses.[13] My friend Sharon, herself a member of the RNAO, was so upset at how Doerksen and Soriano were constantly being portrayed as innocent victims that she sent a letter to the editor and demanded it be printed in the next issue:

> The thrust of Dr. Rush's article is that these charges caused shock, disbelief, fear and concern among nurses across Ontario and the entire country, that it was outrageous that such a thing could have happened, and how important it was for the nursing community to support these two nurses in every way possible.
>
> Dr. Rush has neglected to mention that the College of Nurses of Ontario is vigorously prosecuting these two nurses on multiple charges of professional misconduct relating to the care they provided to the child. I wonder whether Dr. Rush has familiarized herself with the nursing details of this case, or if her comments are simply a knee-jerk response to having two of her hospital's nurses charged with a serious criminal offence. It is undisputed fact that these two nurses admitted the child to their ward from the Emergency Department on a very quiet night, yet never once checked the doctor's orders nor followed the applicable Hospital for Sick Children written protocols.

Dr. Rush writes that the prevailing sentiment among Sick Kids' nurses is, 'This could happen to any of us'. If Sick Kids' nurses truly believe that they could easily have provided the same level of nursing care to their own patients, then those patients would be far safer if they stayed away from the hospital. The nurses that I know are proud of their nursing skills, their dedication to their profession and their patients, and they would never find this type of nursing acceptable.

When this case comes to trial, nurses will have to make a choice: quality nursing or solidarity at any cost. It appears that Dr. Rush has already made her choice.[14]

The RNAO confirmed to Sharon that it would print her entire letter, but reneged on its promise and published an edited version which deleted the important sentence pointing out that the nurses had neglected to read the doctors orders or follow the hospital's protocols.[15] Without including the underlying facts on which Sharon's opinions were based, her words sounded vindictive and mean-spirited and her criticisms without foundation.

The RNAO claimed to represent registered nurses in the province, but it seemed to want to represent only those who believed that nurses should never be subject to criticism no matter how egregious their deeds.

It was remarkable how the less people knew about the facts the more they felt qualified to give their opinions. The nurses were one thing, but it was another when the remarks were made by lawyers under the guise of legal analysis and comment. The Medico-Legal Society of Toronto is an interest group consisting primarily of doctors and lawyers which publishes a semi-annual newsletter with articles of interest to its members. Its Fall 2001 issue included a submission from an articling law student entitled "A Nurses' Dilemma: Criminal Sanctions in the Hospital Setting"[16] in which she parroted the nurses' catchphrases. Frank wrote back to the Medico-Legal Society saying the student was not aware of the facts when she expressed her opinion that criminal charges were unfair. Where the student had written that the legal outcome of this "unfortunate incident" would clarify how legal liability would be apportioned between the individual and the system, Frank said the only thing the criminal case would clarify was whether the nurses were merely negligent or whether they were criminally negligent; either way the verdict would not be a reflection on the province's health care system.[17]

Frank requested the Society print his response in its next newsletter, and sent a copy of it to the articling student as a courtesy. The student worked at a law firm that frequently defended doctors who had been sued for malpractice, and his letter prompted a hasty phone call from the firm's senior partner trying to convince him to withdraw his submission. I told Frank that no articling student would submit an article to a journal under her firm's name without it having first been read and approved by senior staff. The partner did not apologize for the article or say it was inappropriate and should not have been submitted, she just did not want her firm to look foolish.

Frank's rebuttal ran in the newsletter's next issue.

40

DEEP POCKETS

The College of Nurses had scheduled the disciplinary hearing for Doerksen and Soriano for December 2001, but McIntyre requested it be postponed until after the trial. Some people suggested the College hearings were no longer necessary because the matter would be now be dealt with by the criminal justice system, but the College believed that nursing practice issues needed to be addressed regardless of the trial's outcome.

A hearing was convened so an adjournment could be formally requested. The two nurses did not attend, but McIntyre submitted affidavits on their behalf. She told the panel her clients were most anxious to testify before the College, but they had a right not to have their testimony used against them. In the interim, while her clients did not accept the charges laid by the College or criminally, the nurses were not at present involved in patient care activities and there were no patient safety issues.

The adjournment was duly granted, and I went over to the hearing's coordinator to request copies of the nurses' affidavits. The tribunal is a public hearing and as a member of the public I am entitled to see the evidence. McIntyre, who had taken great pains not to look in my direction or acknowledge my presence, abruptly marched over to the prosecutor who was sitting nearby. She angled herself so that her back was to me and demanded to know what was happening. When the prosecutor explained I wanted copies of the affidavits, she sniffed, "I don't think that's appropriate." Told there were guidelines to follow, McIntyre said disapprovingly, "Well, okay then!" and walked out.

The College's rules stated that anyone wanting copies of exhibits must put their request in writing. I submitted my request the next day with a promise to keep any material strictly confidential, and sent copies of my letter to all the involved parties including McIntyre.[1] I didn't think there could be anything of great importance in affidavits that merely requested a postponement, and doubted that even she would want to waste her time fighting such a trivial matter.

I was wrong; McIntyre was very much opposed. But her opposition had an ulterior motive: she told the College prosecutors she would drop her objection to my seeing the nurses' affidavits if I would turn over copies of Lisa's Boston records to her. McIntyre and Edwardh were evidently fishing around hoping to dig up something useful, because I knew they had already tried unsuccessfully to get those records from the coroner's office. Because the Boston visits had nothing to do with Lisa's death, neither the coroner's office nor the police had felt it necessary to review them.

The College pointed out to McIntyre that objecting to my getting copies on one hand and being willing to withdraw her objection on the other hand was inconsistent, to say the least. I was surprised she didn't already have the Boston records, since Patrick Hawkins had copies as part of our civil proceedings against the hospital and I assumed he had given his case file to her when she took over as the nurses' lawyer. I told the College that if she didn't already have them, I was not going to let her extort them from me.

McIntyre prepared a response opposing my motion.[2] She sent copies to the Discipline Committee, to the hearings administrator, and to the College's prosecutors–but not to me. Lawyers always send copies of their materials to every party in a case, and for McIntyre to deliberately not send them to me was not only discourteous but also a violation of the legal profession's standards of practice. The College and the prosecutors did not think too highly of her actions and immediately sent me a copy of McIntyre's response.

Her submission was strikingly similar to what she had said when she opposed my request for standing at the Sanchia Bulgin inquest, except this time she had combined her arguments and the hospital's into one vitriolic document. She reiterated the assertions Dr. Goldbloom had made about my aggressive and immoderate position and how fearful the nurses were because of me, and added some brand new accusations: I consistently used the media as part of a well-publicized campaign against the hospital's nursing staff, I used all documents that came to my attention to discredit and defame Doerksen and Soriano, and I would likely misuse any records and transcripts the College would give me in a way that would bring disrepute to the Committee's processes.

To substantiate her claims, she included Dr. Goldbloom's affidavit from the Sanchia Bulgin standing hearing,[3] my letter to the coroner requesting standing at that inquest, and numerous pages printed off from my website–a website that had been taken down several months earlier when criminal charges had been laid–that related the story of what had happened to Lisa and why I believed Doerksen and Soriano were responsible. I was flabbergasted that McIntyre would voluntarily provide such detailed information, told from my point of view, to the disciplinary panel.

According to the rules, I was entitled to file a response to her response. I rebutted her accusations,[4] regretfully excluding any mention of McIntyre's "offer" to withdraw her objection in exchange for the Boston information, which I had been told by the College was made strictly off-the-record. The College prosecutors submitted their own response to McIntyre supporting my motion and my right to get copies of the evidence.[5]

The Disciplinary Committee considered the various arguments and agreed I was entitled to obtain copies of the nurses' affidavits, although it warned me to keep them confidential. The prosecutors were somewhat displeased with that cautionary note because they felt exhibits should be publicly available unless there was good reason otherwise, but it didn't matter to me.

Doerksen's and Soriano's affidavits stated that compelling them to testify at a disciplinary hearing in advance of the criminal trial would interfere with their constitutional right and ability to have the fullest possible defence. There was no rational explanation for McIntyre's opposition to my seeing them.

The legal profession uses the term "deep pockets" to refer to clients who are willing to pay for the best legal services regardless of cost, but even the wealthiest of clients usually demands value for his or her money. The deep pockets of the Hospital for Sick Children were paying for frivolous and wasteful legal services and no one seemed to mind. Unfortunately, the Hospital for Sick Children was ultimately funded by the taxpayers, who might have minded–had they only known about it.

41

PREPARING FOR TRIAL – THE CROWN

The law is designed to protect the rights of the accused in every way possible, although in reality it is only the wealthy, the well-connected, and those backed by powerful organizations like the Hospital for Sick Children who can retain the best lawyers and who have the resources and knowledge to effectively use those protections. In order to be acquitted at trial, the accused does not have to prove he or she is innocent, only that there is a chance he or she might be; the Crown has to prove the guilt of the accused beyond a reasonable doubt. Hank would have to convince a judge and jury that his version of events was 99% likely to be true, whereas all the defence had to do was raise the possibility that it wasn't.

Even a small mistake on the Crown's part, or on the part of the police, can give rise to the possibility of doubt, and result in the accused going free. Many cases are thrown out on technicalities, but no one should be fooled into thinking that necessarily means the accused was not guilty of the crime with which he or she was charged. Most people are pleased if a police officer mistakenly transposes one letter or number on a parking or speeding ticket because they know it means the ticket will get thrown out and they will not have to pay the fine or incur demerit points, but how many people realize the same principles could potentially apply, say, to a charge of murder?[1]

The best outcome the Defence could achieve for their clients, even better than an acquittal, would be to have the charges dismissed without having to go through a trial. The Hospital for Sick Children would save hundreds of thousands of dollars in legal fees, avoid the embarrassing publicity a trial would bring, and enable the nurses to criticize the Crown by claiming the dismissal was proof they were innocent and charges should never have been laid in the first place.

No one knew precisely how the Defence would go about trying to get the charges dismissed, but much could be intuited by the questions they were asking potential witnesses, the documents and materials they sought, the unique circumstances of this case, and the Crown's past experience with criminal defence lawyers.

We were sure one tactic would be an attempt to get the charges thrown out as having been an "abuse of process". This catch-all phrase includes, among other things, errors in procedure, and is an accusation commonly made by an accused against Crown attorneys and the police when alleging they acted improperly or maliciously.

We believed the Defence would argue that the entire inquest had been nothing but a sham, an excuse to gather information and force witnesses to testify, a fishing expedition by the police and the Crown to see if there were sufficient grounds to lay charges. They had already alleged that the police had done no independent investigation and the criminal charges had been laid solely because I had pressured them into it. Hank would have to spend so much time trying to disprove such allegations that he would be hard-pressed to find sufficient time to prepare and present the case itself.

At one point, the Defence unsuccessfully tried to compel Hank to testify about his involvement in the case. Had they succeeded, Hank would have been forced to step down because he could not simultaneously be both witness and prosecutor. Since none of the other Crowns had wanted to take on this case before, it was questionable whether any of them would be willing to do so now. Even if someone had agreed to take it on, his or her arrival so late in the case would mean that he or she would never have been able to attain Hank's level of knowledge. A new Crown would be at a great disadvantage when matched against the Defence, which we guessed was the point of the whole exercise.

I still kept in touch with my cousin in Israel, who periodically spoke with Dr. Schily. He had originally promised to come to Canada to testify at the trial, but began to vacillate as time went on. In one conversation he would say he was coming because he wanted to do the right thing, in the next he had changed his mind and wasn't coming, and in the next he would be reconsidering. Dr. Schily eventually confessed to my cousin that a senior Sick Kids physician had once intimated to him he had better toe the line if he ever wanted to work in Canada. Now we understood: Dr. Schily was afraid to testify.

Mike told me the Defence were going to allege Dr. Schily had altered his Emergency Department note after Lisa died. I wasn't sure exactly what they would claim had been changed, but guessed it had to be that the instruction to "see Kidcom orders" had been written post mortem. That would be yet another ludicrous accusation. Ward nurses were automatically and without exception supposed to check for doctors' orders every time a patient was admitted from Emergency; there should not be any need to be told. Defence lawyers often used tactics like this to make Crown witnesses look bad: inventing spurious allegations could make even a saint look like a liar.

If Dr. Schily didn't testify, it would be difficult for Hank to prove accusations such as these false, and the Defence might succeed in their efforts to raise reasonable doubt. I asked my cousin to tell Dr. Schily if he wanted to protect his career and his reputation, he needed to testify and face his accusers rather than hide from them. When Dr. Schily's lawyer officially informed the Crown her client would not return voluntarily to Canada to testify, the Crown considered his testimony far too important to abandon. Many countries in the world have Mutual Legal Assistance Treaties, whereby they agree to assist each other in criminal investigations by conducting searches, gathering evidence, or getting people to testify. Canada and Israel signed such a bilateral agreement in October 1999.[2] However, seeking another country's assistance is not a simple matter: the federal government must apply to the government of the foreign country and hope the foreign government agrees there are sufficient grounds to compel its citizen's testimony. This case had received attention at the highest levels of the Crown attorney's office in Ontario, but now it was being elevated further, all the way to Ottawa.

The American nursing expert retained by the Crown had reviewed the medical records and prepared a forty page report strongly condemning Doerksen and Soriano.[3] While defence lawyers can look for expert after expert and use only the ones whose opinions they like, the Crown has to disclose all expert reports to the Defence regardless of how favourable or unfavourable they are. Mike would not tell me the report's contents because it was evidence and I was to be a witness, but I got the sense he and Hank were pleased with it. He did say the expert had called Doerksen's and Soriano's care "grossly negligent" and had verbally told him that "those nurses ought to be hanged".

Hank had the one nursing expert, but he worried the Defence might claim nursing standards were different in the US than in Canada and thereby attack the expert's credibility and qualifications. The accusation might have had merit had the standards in question related to highly sophisticated or controversial medical treatments, but the basic standards of nursing practice in Rochester, New York, where the expert lived, were no different from those in Toronto, a three hour drive away. Health professionals would know that, but a shrewd defence lawyer might be able to convince a judge otherwise.

The Crown needed a Canadian nursing expert with unassailable credentials. As we had already discovered in our various skirmishes with Canadian nursing organizations, they wholeheartedly supported Doerksen and Soriano. Anyone willing to testify for the Crown would need extraordinary fortitude and strength of character because she was likely to be ostracized by her peers, and potentially the entire Canadian nursing community. My friend Sharon volunteered, but Hank turned her down, explaining that she lacked the required paediatric background and that her long and excellent nursing career would be overshadowed by the Defence claiming her relationship with me made her biased.

I knew Hank was getting worried about not having a Canadian expert. Since he did not have the means to find one on his own, I decided to see if I could help. I contacted a highly respected professor at the University of Manitoba with whom I had exchanged e-mails in the past. He knew of a nurse with the perfect credentials: she taught at the university's Faculty of Nursing and had a background in paediatrics, and the professor described her as articulate, with great integrity, and someone who was not easily intimidated. He contacted her and she agreed to help.

It took a long time for the Canadian nurse to produce her report. She was initially hesitant about putting her opinion in writing, worrying the nurses might go to jail, asking if the nurses' behaviour had been condoned by the hospital, questioning if the nurses had been tired and whether there had been system problems. Ultimately, however, she agreed that the nursing care provided by Doerksen and Soriano to Lisa Shore had been negligent and there was no justification for what they had done.[4]

Hank began the long process of interviewing all the potential witnesses, including those who worked at the Hospital for Sick Children. The hospital tried to make things as difficult as possible, causing Hank to describe its actions as outrageous. One management-level nurse told the Crown that the hospital's PCA protocols were only "optional guidelines". If what she said had really been true, it would have meant that the Hospital for Sick Children had no rules, no procedures and no protocols, only optional guidelines which nurses were free to follow or not at their whim. It is up to judges to weigh the testimony of those who appear in court before them and determine the witness's credibility, but even the most experienced judge might be fooled into believing a high-ranking Hospital for Sick Children nurse no matter that what she said was nonsense.

One staff doctor called the CMPA, the legal group that acts for physicians, for advice before agreeing to be interviewed by the Crown. The CMPA told her she did not need a lawyer and she could speak freely, but when the hospital found out it refused to allow her to speak unless its own lawyer was present. Since the hospital controlled her work environment, it was impossible for her to refuse its demand.

Many hospital employees were openly hostile to the Crown and to the police. Some refused to speak to them at all, claiming the hospital's lawyer had been present at every discussion where Lisa was mentioned so all those conversations were therefore privileged and confidential. This was untrue, as the rules of privilege between a lawyer and his or her client apply only when the lawyer is giving legal advice and not simply because there is a lawyer in the room. The tobacco companies claimed attorney-client privilege for many years in their attempts to cover up the dangers of tobacco products until the courts forced them to disclose their secrets,[5] and it seemed ironic but fitting that hospital employees were trying a similar ruse to cover up the truth about Lisa's death.

The only positive interview was Dr. Catre's, who told the Crown that when he touched Lisa she was very cold and he thought she had been dead for at least an hour, thus proving that the vital signs that Ruth Doerksen had charted at 6:00 a.m. were false.

Both the Crown and the Defence wanted one of the Boston doctors who had treated Lisa to testify. Hank wanted someone who could describe to a court the disease Lisa had suffered from, how it was treated, and the medications she was prescribed. The Defence likely wanted the doctors' testimony in the hope it could somehow be used to discredit Lisa or me. Since the doctors were resident in another country, they could not be compelled by subpoena to testify, and would have to come voluntarily unless the Mutual Legal Assistance Treaty with the US was invoked. Hank was not prepared to go that route, but Mike told me the Defence was; he called it a sign of their desperation.

When the Crown had contacted Dr. Wilder, Lisa's main Boston physician, he had categorically refused to have anything to do with the case. I was not surprised, since he had agreed to review Lisa's chart shortly after she died and had then refused to speak with me once he saw it. Dr. Berde, the head of the pain clinic, had initially been willing to testify but had changed his mind on advice from his counsel. The explanation given for this was that the Boston hospital's lawyers felt that laying criminal charges against nurses was extreme and they did not want Dr. Berde to have anything to do with it.

Mike asked me to speak to Dr. Wilder and Dr. Berde to see if I could convince them to change their minds. Dr. Wilder was a lost cause as far as I was concerned, but I thought Dr. Berde might be approachable. I wrote him a letter explaining that the criminal charges were laid after a lengthy police investigation and prosecutorial review, both of which had concluded that based on the evidence a criminal act had likely been committed. I said it was difficult to understand how lawyers who knew few of the facts felt qualified to act as both judge and jury by deciding the criminal charges were unwarranted. My letter ended with a final entreaty for him to come testify: "Your life has been based on treating children's pain. It takes compassion and brilliance to have achieved what you have. But it takes courage and integrity to do the right thing, even when it isn't always the easiest thing to do".[6]

Dr. Berde never responded.

42

PREPARING FOR TRIAL – THE DEFENCE

I did not attend any of the nurses' numerous court appearances, believing it would be emotionally difficult and only serve to antagonize them and their supporters. After one such appearance, McIntyre and Edwardh cornered a Toronto Star reporter who had been following the case, and Edwardh grilled him about whether I had been putting pressure on him to write his stories. The reporter told her that many people put pressure on him, but it was laughable to suggest I was one of them. He was upset at the accusation, and told me he felt that Edwardh's tone was vicious and offensive.

It didn't surprise me, although I had hoped that Edwardh would not attack me the way McIntyre had. It was true that reading the various newspaper articles left one with a negative impression of the nurses, but that was because what they had done was quite appalling. It was only the nursing magazines that portrayed them as saintly by omitting material facts, attacking the police and the Crown, and sugar-coating the truth.

I expected the Defence would go to great lengths to try to discredit me. In keeping with the hospital's and McIntyre's accusations against me thus far, it was a safe guess they intended to claim I was so determined to obtain revenge that I would do or say anything and therefore my testimony should not be believed. Although I was nervous at being cross-examined by Edwardh at the trial, I was confident that everything I had written or said after Lisa's death had been carefully thought out and was not, as the Defence would surely allege, obsessive and irrational.

McIntyre and Edwardh were working together, but Edwardh was undeniably the one in charge. She began peppering the Crown with demands for me to turn over various documents. Every time I got a phone call from Mike or Hank, I would ask myself, "What does she want this time?"

Her first letter demanded the legal opinion Gavin MacKenzie had given us regarding McIntyre's conflict of interest, the transcript of a television talk show I had appeared on, the Boston records, and my personal notes.

The College of Nurses had previously given Gavin's letter to McIntyre, and the transcript of the television show had been posted on the Internet where the Defence must have seen it or they wouldn't have known to ask for it. Why did they want things they already had? Edwardh was too smart for that, so there had to be an ulterior motive. It wasn't too hard to figure out: if I refused to turn documents over, no matter how irrelevant they were to the case or even if they already had copies, Edwardh would attack me in court and argue I had withheld evidence and prevented her clients from being able to properly defend themselves.

I told Mike he could have the opinion letter and the transcript if the Defence really wanted them, and I sent him the Boston records. My notes, which were not much more than a log of which doctor had seen Lisa, when, and what he or she had said, were personal. I explained there was nothing in them that was different or inconsistent with anything I had said, but they had been written in the expectation of privacy and I did not intend to turn them over.

The Defence wanted it badly enough to fight for it. I was only a witness in these proceedings, and generally a third party's private information is considered confidential. For example, if a passer-by witnesses an assault, defence counsel could not subpoena that person's employment records or medical records to fish for information which could be used to discredit him or her. Edwardh would have to make a special application before a judge and convince her or him that her need to have my diary to better defend her client outweighed my right to privacy. I reread the diary and decided that a judge might indeed find it relevant. It would be foolish and a waste of time to fight a battle I had a reasonable prospect of losing, so I sent the diary to Hank voluntarily. He told me he found it quite helpful because it clearly laid out the chronology of events.

Edwardh wrote a letter to Hank demanding all of Lisa's medical records back to early childhood, saying that "...based on a review of the records, the Defence will explore the role of the Shore family in the treatment of and its ultimate impact on Lisa".[1] We didn't know what she meant by this until it was reported to us that some Sick Kids' nurses were telling people that I suffered from Munchausen's Syndrome by Proxy, or MSBP.

MSBP is a rare but deadly mental illness whereby a parent, usually the mother, surreptitiously injures her child in order to induce serious illness and then basks in the attention she receives as her sick child's loving and devoted caregiver. Invariably, these mothers start abusing their children when they are babies, and the children often die before their sixth birthday. Edwardh likely wanted to see Lisa's old records to see if she could find a history of illness which she could use as the basis for alleging MSBP. I authorized release of those records, knowing they dashed the Defence theory because they showed that Lisa was an unusually healthy child with few visits to the doctor other than for routine checkups.

The next letter to arrive in Hank's office from Edwardh was more than a little peculiar. She had apparently come across an Internet site that contained information about Lisa's death,[2] and accused me of being behind it. She wrote that its content "...of course draws any reader to a conclusion of negligence. This could not be further from the truth..." As Hank read the letter to me he muttered that it was exactly the truth. He was much angrier and more offended by the letter's tone than I was; I was so used to being the subject of McIntyre's attacks that to me it was just more of the same.

The Internet site had nothing to do with me, as anybody who took even a few minutes to explore it would quickly realize. It was run by a grandmother who gathered news stories from around the world concerning the wrongful deaths of children, and one of the thousands of stories posted was Lisa's. The site was filled with angels and Christian imagery, and our family is Jewish–as Edwardh and McIntyre well knew. Hank wrote Edwardh back eloquently telling her I had no involvement with the website: "This is manifestly a Christian-oriented site. Wherever the Shores believe Lisa is now, I can assure you that it is *not* in Jesus' arms".

Hank warned me he believed Edwardh planned to accuse me of deliberately overmedicating Lisa. He expected her to allege I had taken Lisa to multiple doctors to obtain additional medication, and that I had asked Dr. Laxer to increase Lisa's Gabapentin dosage at my own whim in order to obtain more drugs for her. Hank also felt that Edwardh would claim that when I brought Lisa to Boston a few weeks before her death, the doctors had told me there was nothing wrong with her and discontinued all medications but that I had nevertheless continued to supply Lisa with drugs.

Most of the Defence's tactics and ideas to date had been so absurd they barely merited serious consideration; Mike had been right when he called them acts of desperation. But if the Defence really planned to allege I was deliberately poisoning my own daughter, there was clearly no limit to how low they would go to get their clients acquitted. To forestall their allegations, I prepared a spreadsheet showing every one of Lisa's prescriptions, when they were filled, who had prescribed them, and the quantity and dosage. The schedule included Carbamazepine, the new drug Dr. Wilder had prescribed for Lisa on our last trip to Boston, thus proving he had not discontinued her medications. As far as the claim that I had asked Dr. Laxer to increase Lisa's medication on my own, my phone bills confirmed I had called Dr. Wilder in Boston just a few days before seeing Dr. Laxer, which was when he had suggested increasing her dosage.

This was not the end of the absurdity. Hank told me that since the monitor found in Lisa's room was not on, I should also expect to be accused of being the one who turned it off. I now understood exactly what the phrase "blaming the victim" meant.

The Defence next complained that the Boston records I had sent in were incomplete. Lisa had seen Dr. Wilder in the summer of 1998 when she had been feeling quite well, but there was no note about that visit in the file. Furthermore, there were scant records in the file relating to the September 1998 visit made only a few weeks before Lisa died: no admission records, no nursing notes, no write-up by Dr. Wilder, and no consult note from Behavioral Sciences although there was a doctor's note recommending they see her.

I wrote to the Boston hospital for a copy of Dr. Wilder's missing reports, but nobody in the medical records department could find anything. Dr. Wilder appeared to have made no notes in the file about Lisa's June visit, nor had he written anything up about the September visit even though he had seen Lisa extensively. There were no admission or nursing records for that period because Lisa had been seen as an outpatient. There were no Behavioral Science consult notes because according to my recollection our visit there had been brief and unofficial. We had asked for a referral to a Toronto biofeedback clinic, one not affiliated with Sick Kids, and Dr. Wilder had sent us to a psychologist who he thought was more likely to know the right people and would be able to recommend someone to us.

The emphasis on the Boston records, however, did remind me of a painful moment I had long buried and forgotten: the neurologist's note I had torn up in grief and anger a few weeks after Lisa died. The doctor had written that Lisa was suffering from conversion disorder, meaning he believed that her problems existed only in her mind. The neurologist had made a psychiatric diagnosis that he was unqualified to make, and one that was terribly wrong.

I knew that nothing in the neurologist's note mattered to the case. Lisa was sleeping—or rather, dying—the entire time Doerksen and Soriano had been responsible for her. Whether Lisa was black or white, polka-dotted or striped, happy or depressed, well-rounded or mentally unstable, she was a child who deserved competent nursing care.

I had convinced myself that the note was unimportant and irrelevant.

The worst mistake of my life was bringing Lisa to the Hospital for Sick Children on October 21, 1998. Not saying anything about the neurologist's note was second.

43

LEGAL MANOEUVRING

Criminal trials are held in either the provincial courts or the superior courts.[1] In most cases, where the crime's maximum penalty is less than five years, the trial is held in Provincial Court in front of a judge and without a jury. For more serious charges, the accused can choose a trial in Provincial Court with a judge alone, or a trial in Superior Court either with a judge and jury or with a judge alone. Criminal negligence causing death had a maximum penalty of life imprisonment, so Doerksen and Soriano could choose any of these three options.[2]

Defence lawyers consider a number of factors when deciding whether or not to choose a trial by jury, and one of the most important is an assessment of how a jury is likely to feel about their client. If the accused is, say, a sole support single mother living in abject poverty who was terribly abused by her former spouse, chances are excellent her lawyer will opt for a jury trial. Where the accused has a deviant lifestyle or stands accused of a heinous crime that jurors might find morally repugnant, then a trial by judge alone is often the preferred choice.

Doerksen and Soriano belonged to a profession customarily held in high regard by the community, and neither had prior criminal records. Normally a good defence lawyer would be able to play on that to make the nurses seem like the finest and most upstanding of citizens, but there was one major problem: these nurses had already appeared before a jury at the coroner's inquest, and one had only to read the inquest transcripts to see how much the inquest jury had disliked them. Given the impression the nurses had made on the first jury, it would be risky to put them in front of a second.

Another potential problem with a jury trial was that the Crown's most important witness was the mother of a dead child, and the jury would feel sympathy for me and not for the accused. Any attempt by the Defence to attack me—which seemed to be its main strategy—would make a jury, many of whom would probably be parents themselves, very angry.

The Defence asked Hank how he would feel about a judge-alone trial.

Since a trial without a jury could take place in either Provincial or Superior Court, the Defence still had to decide which court they wanted. The accused has the right not only to make the choice, but also the right to make it at any time until almost the very last minute.

If there is to be a criminal trial in Superior Court, it must be preceded by a preliminary hearing, often referred to as the "prelim".[3] The prelim is held in Provincial Court before a judge who hears the Crown's case and decides if there has been enough evidence presented for a jury to possibly find the accused guilty. The evidence doesn't have to be so strong that a guilty verdict is probable, just enough so that it is at least a theoretical possibility. The bar is quite low, and provided there are no surprises, preliminary hearings almost invariably result in the accused being committed for trial.

There is no inherent equality between the Crown and the accused at a preliminary hearing. The Crown must present its entire case, but the Defence doesn't have to present anything. The Defence can and usually does cross-examine all of the Crown's witnesses at the preliminary hearing, and does it again at the trial with all the advantages a second chance brings. Defence lawyers use the preliminary hearing to assess and attack the credibility of the Crown's witnesses, try out different strategies and tactics to evaluate their effectiveness, and look for weaknesses in the Crown's case.

Another important factor that defence lawyers had to consider when deciding between a Superior Court trial or one in Provincial Court was who the presiding judge would be.

Judges are appointed for life. They judge others, but they themselves are not judged except in the breach when there have been allegations of serious misconduct. There are no performance appraisals, reviews, or ratings, or at least none that are public. People often have a misperception that a judge is a judge is a judge, but the truth is they are no different from any other group of people: some are brilliant and some are of distinctly lesser ability, some are tough "law and order" types while there is at least one who is known to be extraordinarily lenient and quick to attribute the accused's crimes to his environment and upbringing rather than to any individual blameworthiness. Everyone in the system knows who is who, and criminal defence lawyers routinely engage in behind-the-scenes judge-shopping to try to avoid the hardliner judges. Technically nobody can pre-select a judge, but in practice there is much finagling and manoeuvring which frequently accomplishes the same objective.

McIntyre and Edwardh very much wanted the judge who was famous for her leniency to hear the case. She worked at Provincial Court, and if they could get her, the Provincial Court proceeding would be a trial; if not, the lower court proceeding would be a preliminary hearing followed by a Superior Court trial.

They were unsuccessful; Provincial Court Justice Ramez Khawly was selected to preside over the preliminary hearing or trial. I heard Justice Khawly described as unpredictable, a judge whose rulings might provide multiple grounds for appeal by both the Crown and the Defence.

The Crown had rethought its position vis-à-vis McIntyre representing Soriano. Although it believed that facing a lawyer with little or no criminal court experience would give it an advantage, McIntyre nonetheless posed a potential problem because the conflict of interest Gavin MacKenzie had warned us about still existed. McIntyre was representing Soriano criminally, but was defending Soriano and her co-defendant, Doerksen, before the College of Nurses. If the nurses were convicted, the Crown did not want to give them a reason to appeal the verdict by claiming their lawyers had provided ineffective representation.

Hank brought a motion before the court asking that McIntyre be removed as Soriano's counsel. Khawly heard the motion, giving ample opportunity for the Crown and Defence to see him in action. Doerksen and Soriano both took the stand and testified they knew, understood, and agreed that McIntyre and Edwardh were conducting a joint defence, and swore that neither of them would ever incriminate the other. Now that it was on record, this potential ground for appeal had been eliminated.

Although judge-shopping was not officially allowed, it seemed that judge-bargaining, at least for Superior Court judges, was sometimes tolerated. Since both the Crown and the Defence wanted someone other than Khawly to preside over the trial, they were willing to negotiate. The Defence claimed they wanted someone with a medical background and proposed to send the Crown a list of those whom they found acceptable, but Hank was not prepared to risk appearing before an unknown judge whose knowledge of civil law might have exceeded his or her knowledge of criminal law. He counter-proposed Mr. Justice David Watt.

Justice Watt was highly respected by both the Crown and the defence bar, and he had indicated his willingness to hear the case. The Defence was amenable, but there was one problem: Watt was married to Michelle Fuerst, the criminal lawyer we had retained following the inquest.

Watt told the Crown he and his wife had not discussed the matter and he could hear the case without conflict. Nevertheless, this offered Edwardh an opportunity she was quick to seize: she sent Hank another letter, this time telling him it was "essential to have a detailed description and the nature of the legal advice" Michelle had provided to me.

Edwardh had succeeded in obtaining my diary, but I refused to waive privilege and provide this information to her. Michelle had been retained long after Lisa died, had represented us for a short period of time, and had given us a brief legal opinion which we had not relied on. The only reason Edwardh wanted to know all the details was because she was trying to accumulate information she hoped could be used to discredit me.

Hank desperately wanted to have a Superior Court trial with Watt presiding, and he pressed me to turn over the correspondence between Michelle and me. I compromised and wrote a letter confirming that all Michelle had done was provide a legal opinion which had not been relied on,[4] but Hank said that wasn't enough to satisfy Edwardh. I told him she was bluffing: she knew Watt was as good a choice as any for trial judge, he had not discussed the case with his wife, and a legal opinion which had not been used for any purpose was irrelevant to the nurses' defence.

Hank was afraid to call her bluff. If I continued to refuse to waive privilege, Edwardh would only be able to get the information if she could convince a judge her need for it outweighed my right to communicate confidentially with my lawyer. I doubted she would be successful, but I also knew that if I didn't give her what she wanted she would continue dragging things out. Hank really wanted to settle the matter about what kind of trial he faced, in which court, and before which judge. I felt indebted to him for taking on this case and persevering in spite of how difficult the Defence was making it for him, and decided that helping him was paramount no matter how much Edwardh's demand offended me.

Criminal lawyers hold that privilege between them and their clients is sacred, but it seemed they didn't much care about principles if it weren't *their* client's privilege at stake. I wrote a letter describing in very great detail the opinion Michelle had provided.[5]

Everyone agreed there would be a preliminary hearing in front of Justice Khawly, followed by a Superior Court trial presided over by Justice Watt.

44

A MOTHER'S MISTAKE

About one week before the preliminary hearing was scheduled to begin, another letter arrived from Edwardh. The Defence wanted to interview Dr. Desparmet, the Pain Service physician who had treated Lisa at Sick Kids, but Desparmet's lawyer would not allow her to speak to them without my permission.

If I refused to allow it, the Defence would claim I was concealing something. If I gave Desparmet permission to speak freely, the Crown would want to interview her too. I doubted Hank would appreciate having to go to Montreal, in the midst of his trial preparation, to interview Dr. Desparmet. I didn't know exactly what she would say, but the relationship between us had been cool at best and I figured the Defence would somehow try to manipulate that to their advantage. Dr. Desparmet had treated Lisa when she was alive but had not had anything to do with her care when she died. Nothing she had said or done had anything to do with Doerksen and Soriano and the charges against them. I was going to be viciously attacked by the Defence no matter what I did, so why should I help them if I had any choice in the matter? I refused to give permission for Edwardh to speak to Dr. Desparmet.

The preliminary hearing began on Monday, April 15, 2003, with Bill as the first witness. I could not attend because I would be testifying later and my testimony had to be completely untainted by anyone else's evidence. For the same reason, Bill and I could not discuss any part of his testimony. This would not be easy for a long-married couple used to talking everything over, but we knew Edwardh would test me on it.

I had started law school that year and was in the middle of intense studying for upcoming exams. Because studying consumed so much of my time, I was too busy to have any long discussions with Bill. In spite of that, there were still many awkward conversations, prolonged silences, and sentences hastily cut off in mid-word.

According to what Bill related to me afterwards, the proceedings opened with administrative minutiae. Khawly told the nurses they did not have to sit on the hard uncomfortable benches where the accused usually sat, and invited them to come sit with their lawyers where they could be more comfortable.

The judge was quite displeased to learn that the hearing might not be finished by the end of June when he had scheduled his vacation. He mercilessly berated Hank, even though the main reason for the preliminary hearing's extended running time was the Defence's lengthy proposed cross-examinations. Khawly told everyone to cancel their vacations and make sure they were available every day so the hearing could be finished on schedule.

His zeal for working hard lasted only until 3:45 p.m. that afternoon when Edwardh took a minute to check her notes and then told Khawly she was just about finished cross-examining Bill. Khawly responded, "That's music to my ears!" and suggested everyone call it a day.

Because Khawly had decided to adjourn the hearing so early, Bill had to return the next day and testify for no more than forty-five minutes, a third of which was spent answering variations of the same questions Edwardh had asked the previous day.

At one point in his testimony Bill asked Edwardh to clarify a question, but instead of doing so she launched into a tirade about me. Bill said that had he been a bystander who didn't know me, he would have thought I was a crazy person both from what she said and the tone in which she said it. My mother, who had attended the proceedings to lend emotional support to Bill, had not been aware that demonizing me was one of the main defence themes, and was stunned and horrified at what she heard.

Bill could see that some of Edwardh's questions were merely laying the groundwork for her planned attack on me. She asked him about the lisashore.com website, but quickly moved on once she learned he had no direct involvement with it. She wanted to know when he and I had first talked about criminal charges, when we had met with the

Crown attorneys, and what we had talked about at the meeting—most likely as a prelude to alleging that the criminal charges were laid because I had somehow pressured the Crown into it.

Edwardh asked Bill if any of the doctors in Boston had told us that Lisa had conversion disorder. Bill asked her what conversion disorder was, which took her aback. She did not answer his question, and Bill told her he didn't remember anyone saying that. Had she asked me, I could have told her with certainty that no one had ever discussed with us conversion disorder, or anything else that hinted of a mental illness; my internal warning system was fine-tuned to these kinds of inferences ever since our dealings with the orthopaedic surgeons at the Hospital for Sick Children.

Edwardh asked whether we had brought the Boston records to Sick Kids with us when we took Lisa to the Emergency Department. Bill replied that we did not see those records until after Lisa's death. That wasn't her point: just as Hank had told us, she wanted to make the allegation that we had been told by the Boston doctors that nothing was wrong with Lisa, and that we had gone to Sick Kids and deliberately withheld this knowledge from the hospital's doctors and nurses.

This was just as ludicrous as their other allegations, but that didn't seem to matter. If the doctors in Boston had no longer wanted to treat Lisa, Dr. Wilder would not have started her on a new pain medication. We had no interest in Lisa's medical records, and never asked for them until after she died. If we hadn't tried to obtain the records from Sick Kids, where Lisa received abysmal care, why would we have wanted the records from Boston, where we believed Lisa received excellent care? Most important of all, what possible difference would this have made to anything? Lisa was given a lot of morphine at the Hospital for Sick Children, and Ruth Doerksen and Anagaile Soriano had an obligation to properly care for her, an obligation which they did not fulfil and which resulted in her death. Did the Defence think it was acceptable for their clients to neglect Lisa because she didn't "deserve" to get any morphine?

The Defence came up with yet another devious ploy. We knew that Edwardh and McIntyre were aware of the forensic document examination of Lisa's flowchart that we had previously commissioned, since they had received full disclosure from the Crown over a year earlier.

The disclosure materials contained reference to the report's existence, but no copy of the report; had it contained anything of relevance the Defence would have been provided with a copy. While Edwardh had spent much of the past year demanding all kinds of information from me on anything even remotely related to the case, she had deliberately not asked for this–until Bill began testifying. He had no idea where the report was, so he was given special permission to discuss this part of his testimony with me.

I immediately recognized this as the sleazy stunt it was. Every other avenue Edwardh had pursued to try to destroy my credibility had gone nowhere, so she was going to accuse Bill and me of deliberately withholding important evidence, even though the document forming the basis of her allegation was neither important nor evidence.

I dug the report out of a box and gave it to Bill to bring to court the next morning.

Because my law school studies consumed virtually all my time and energy, I was too busy to think about my upcoming testimony. I must have been the only student around who did not celebrate the completion of her exams. Once I finished them and began to think about what awaited me, I began to get frightened. I could see from the stressful effect that Edwardh's cross-examination had on Bill that she was very skilled at it; a lawyer I knew had told me she could even make Mother Theresa look bad. I had also just experienced her willingness to engage in tactics which many might term under-handed, and knew she would subject me to a vicious and ugly cross-examination.

Everything I had ever said about the night Lisa died was true. Doerksen had not looked at me or talked to me when we arrived and Soriano had said very little. Lisa had not been put on any monitors, and because there were no monitors there were no alarms, false or otherwise. The monitor found in the room in the morning did not alarm when Lisa's heart stopped because it was never turned on. One or both of the nurses had brought that monitor into the room in the early hours of the morning and attached it to her, but the only logical explanation for going to all that trouble and then not turning it on was because Lisa was already dead. Doerksen lied in the nursing notes she wrote up after Lisa's death when she said Lisa had been on a monitor all night, and she and Soriano had lied throughout their inquest testimony. Neither of them ever bothered to even look for doctors' orders, neither followed the hospital's protocols, and neither took action when they saw Lisa's abnormal vital signs. The inquest jurors had been so right: Doerksen and Soriano were responsible for Lisa's death.

But for all the security and confidence brought by knowing I was telling the truth and the nurses were liars, I still had one secret gnawing away at me: I had never disclosed the neurologist's note. I had told myself—over and over and over again—that the note made no difference to anybody or anything except Lisa's memory. I had convinced myself that no one would ever ask me about it, but I began to think about how intent Edwardh was on dissecting everything I had ever said or done and realized this was no longer a safe assumption. It was probable that Edwardh would thoroughly grill me about Boston. I knew I would answer all her questions truthfully when I testified no matter how painful they were, because lying under oath was unthinkable to me.

Once I faced up to reality, I knew I had to tell Hank about the note right away, before I testified. I began to have nightmares and trouble sleeping, afraid of the consequences of what I had done as a grieving mother to protect my child in life and in death.

I went down to the courthouse to confess. As soon as Hank realized I was there for more than polite conversation, he asked a policewoman who had been assisting him to take my statement. Through my tears, I told the story of how I had read the neurologist's report while enveloped in grief, and what I had done with it to protect my daughter from being wrongly labelled as mentally ill.

I ordered the Boston records again. When they arrived, I re-read the neurologist's report for the first time in four and one half years. I decided I had been an idiot and a fool, so intent on preserving Lisa's memory that I had lost sight of the fact that whatever was or was not wrong with her had nothing to do with how Ruth Doerksen and Anagaile Soriano had caused her death in the early morning hours of October 22, 1998.

But I knew Marlys Edwardh would argue otherwise.

45

DEATH BY A THOUSAND CUTS

The preliminary hearing continued, but no one called me and I did not know what was going on. I did hear that Dr. Schily had come in from Israel and the nurse who had seen Lisa in the Emergency Department had come in from England, but knew nothing more than that.

After the preliminary hearing had been going on for a month, but before I was due to testify, Mike called me to say Hank wanted to meet with Bill and me the next day at the Crown attorney's office. My heart began pounding and I immediately asked him if Hank was planning to drop the charges. He said he would let Hank explain, and I knew I had to be right.

Bill and I went to the meeting and brought Frank with us, more as our friend than as our lawyer. We returned to the same boardroom we had been in two years earlier when the Crown told us it was planning to lay criminal charges. Now we were here to learn why it was dropping them.

Even the same people were present: Mike Davis and another detective, and the three Crown attorneys: Hank Goody, Paul Culver, and John McMahon. Hank and McMahon did all of the talking.

I was right; they were dropping the charges. Hank called it "death by a thousand cuts", explaining that Bill's testimony had been the high point of the preliminary hearing and it had gone downhill from there.

The Canadian nursing expert–the Crown's main expert witness–had backed out in the middle of the preliminary hearing and refused to testify.

Dr. Catre refused to repeat under oath what he had told the Crown in his previous interview. Where before he was sure that Lisa was so cold when he found her that she had been dead for over an hour, in the witness box he could no longer remember whether she had been warm or cold. He had also told the Crown that the monitor was not on when he entered Lisa's room, but in his courtroom testimony he decided he could not say whether it had been off or on.

Dr. Schily's testimony was different from what it had been at the coroner's inquest. Before he had blamed the nurse who spoke with him for giving him incomplete or inaccurate information and had defended his actions, but now he accepted partial responsibility and said he should have asked the nurse for more information. He also said he was up on the ward in the morning but did not look at Lisa's chart because he knew doing so would be wrong, but the ward manager and one of the nurses had told the Crown in their interviews that he had asked for the chart and had even been provided with a room in which to sit and review it.

The Boston neurologist's diagnosis of conversion disorder had assumed great importance, just as I had feared. Dr. Schily told the court that had he known Lisa had conversion disorder he would not have given her morphine. Bill's assumption about what the Defence would allege was correct: According to them I had been told in Boston that Lisa's problems were all in her head and had intentionally withheld this information from Sick Kids. Had I told Sick Kids the truth, Lisa would have been sent home from the Emergency Department without treatment.

I sat very still, knowing that if I tried to say anything I would start crying uncontrollably. "If only they had sent Lisa home," I thought. "If only they had not believed she was in pain. If only they had not given her morphine. Oh, God, if only!" I could not believe what I had just heard. That Dr. Schily and the Defence had said it, yes; that the Crown was talking as if it made a difference, no. Do nurses treat a lung cancer patient who was formerly a heavy smoker differently than the lung cancer patient who never smoked? Whatever the reason why Lisa had been given morphine, she needed to be cared for by her nurses just like any other patient on morphine.

There was more, Hank explained. Somewhere between the inquest and the preliminary hearing the Hospital for Sick Children had unearthed a policy no one had known about before. The policy showed that Dr. Schily's orders were invalid because they had not been countersigned by someone in Orthopaedics. The flawed logic was that because the orders were invalid, therefore there were no orders, therefore the nurses hadn't done anything wrong by not following them.

"This is pathetic!" I thought silently. "How could the Crown have bought into this? The nurses didn't look at the orders in the first place, so it didn't matter if they were in hieroglyphics! Had anyone known about such a policy—and they hadn't, that was certain, or it would have been brought up at the inquest—it would have made no difference. Any competent nurse who didn't have orders, or who had invalid ones, would be after the doctors to give them orders they could use."

The Crown seemed to have forgotten another relevant fact: there were other suspended orders in the system besides Dr. Schily's.[1] The orthopaedic resident in the Emergency Department had also entered orders for Lisa even though he had not seen her, but no one had deemed them important because they covered minor matters such as which IV solution to use. Even under the hospital's newly discovered and patently absurd policy, the nurses had not read or followed the "valid" orders which did not require countersigning, and had not administered the correct IV solution.

And what about the written protocols the nurses didn't follow? Or did the hospital decide after all that its rules were only optional guidelines which didn't have to be followed?

Hank and McMahon continued explaining how their case had fallen apart. Dr. Roy had looked at Lisa's nursing flowsheet and said he didn't see any cause for concern. I recalled the inquest where Mary Douglas had tried the same thing, but in that case the jury had not been fooled. Were Dr. Roy to repeat this comment in front of his colleagues—a most unlikely scenario—those colleagues would react in shocked disbelief. Hank told me that my previous remarks to him about Dr. Roy had been right, but it was small consolation to learn the Crown thought as little of him as we did.

Another Sick Kids physician, one who had worked on Lisa during the resuscitation attempt, said essentially the same thing as Dr. Roy and Mary Douglas: yes, Lisa's earlier respirations were concerning but they had levelled off and looked all right. What about the heart rate, she was asked. Well, yes, Lisa was tachycardic, anything over

100 was tachycardic, but she would have just assumed it was because Lisa was in pain.

The Defence had found a new expert witness on biomedical engineering to revive the theory the hospital had advanced and then abruptly discarded at the inquest after the coroner's office said the theory was ludicrous: that Lisa's heart could have given off electrical rhythms after she was dead which fooled the monitor into thinking there was a heart beat and therefore accounted for the machine not alarming. That theory would have had no chance of success if Dr. Catre had been willing to tell the truth about Lisa's body being very cold when he found her, but truth seemed to be a scarce commodity when Hospital for Sick Children doctors and nurses were testifying.

They saved the most painful for last—me. By withholding the neurologist's note, the Crown believed my credibility had been irreparably damaged. They were unwilling to let me testify, expecting that Edwardh would be able to destroy me in the process.

McMahon's tone of voice was neutral, but it was also very cold. He had lost all respect for me. I, who had tried so hard to be honest and decent when it seemed like everyone around me had been dishonest and immoral, had been relegated to a lower category of human being.

Edwardh, the nurses, the doctors, and the Hospital for Sick Children had outwitted the Crown. The nurses had caused the death of my little girl and succeeded in getting away with it. The hospital and its staff had acted unscrupulously and unethically in order to protect them, evade responsibility, and cover up the truth—and they got away with it too.

46

JUSTICE PREVAILS?

Mike Davis called me afterwards to tell me how sorry he was. I knew he believed, as we did, that the nurses had been criminally responsible for Lisa's death. He had recommended to Hank that in spite of the potentially damaging effect my recent revelation about the Boston records might have had on my credibility, he should put me on the stand and let me take my chances with Edwardh. Hank hadn't wanted to; I guess he had been too discouraged to continue.

The last thing Mike told me was that if all parents took care of their children the way Bill and I had taken care of Lisa, the world would be a better place.

It took me a long time to stop crying.

Hank stood up in court on Friday, May 17, 2003 and told Khawly that the Crown no longer believed it had a reasonable prospect of conviction and it was not going to present any further evidence. Khawly adjourned the proceedings for thirty minutes, an unnecessary break since his written judgment had been prepared in advance; he returned with it already typed up and with multiple photocopies ready for distribution.

Khawly's judgment was so riddled with trite phrases and clichés that a casual reader would be hard-pressed to figure out what he was saying.[1] He implied that the Crown's case was all about revenge, "the determination to affix accountability for perceived wrongdoings" and "the rage and demand for criminal responsibility for a life cut so short". Not content to stop there, he added that "...part of the resulting cacophony included accusations of documents being withheld and tampered with". Since it seemed that I was the main person being accused of withholding documents, and I had not testified, Khawly had never had the chance to assess my credibility. The accusations he was referring to had no evidentiary basis, and most judges would not have included unproven defence allegations in their judgment.

Outside the courthouse, McIntyre and Edwardh distributed a previously-prepared press release to the gathered media entitled "Justice Prevails", in which they repeated what they had been saying since criminal charges were first laid: the police had not done an independent investigation, the Crown should never have laid charges, and the nurses were innocent.[2]

We knew they would say that and had tried to prepare ourselves as best we could. We weren't surprised when one of the nursing organizations hastily issued its own press release parroting McIntyre and Edwardh.[3] Sick Kids issued a press release too, saying that justice had been done—and with unbelievable audacity, claimed that "the hospital cooperated fully with the police investigation and Crown counsel".[4]

If we told people how we really felt and what a miscarriage of justice had occurred, we would sound bitter and angry and possibly even irrational. We were bitter and angry, but we had always attempted to act with dignity and decided to keep our feelings of loss and devastation to ourselves. Instead, we sent out our own press release expressing our sadness and reminding people that the nurses still faced a disciplinary hearing at the College of Nurses.[5]

Toronto has four large circulation newspapers, and each reported the story differently. One devoted a full page to it and interviewed the nurses and me in depth,[6] and another buried it in its back pages,[7] but both attempted to present a balanced point of view. The third newspaper was somewhat sympathetic to me and included a quote from the woman who had been jury forewoman at the coroner's inquest: "Lisa's death was not a mistake…If these people <*the nurses*> have souls—if they have souls—and are ever alone with their souls, I hope they cringe".[8]

The fourth newspaper article[9] was so unconscionable that I seriously considered suing. The Globe & Mail made no attempt to comply with fundamental standards of journalistic integrity but simply gave McIntyre and Edwardh a soapbox from which to rant. The reporter wrote that a document examiner's expert report had been suppressed, the nurses' not reading the doctors' orders had been an innocent act, and the Boston records had been relevant to the case. Where Khawly had mentioned accusations of documents withheld and tampered with, this reporter repeated the phrase but omitted the words "accusations of". He went on to personally attack me by repeating one of McIntyre's and Edwardh's offensive canards, but he cowardly attributed it to the proverbial anonymous sources <italics mine>: "*Several of those caught up in the case* cited Lisa's mother–Sharon Shore–and her lawyer as a major force behind the criminal charges." The article's headline was "Charges against two nurses collapse", but rather than printing a picture of the nurses, the paper ran a large, three-year-old, highly unflattering picture of me.

Our press release had included a telephone number where I could be reached. Every newspaper and major television station in the city but the Globe & Mail had called, come to interview me, or used information from the press release.

I left a phone message for the newspaper's editor-in-chief, but he did not return my call. Frank wrote a letter to the editor pointing out that even in the free marketplace of ideas there were boundaries of accuracy which needed to be adhered to;[10] his letter was not acknowledged.

Frank and I appeared briefly on a morning news show, following which he received a letter from Edwardh stating that our comments had been libellous and we had better cease talking about Soriano and Doerksen.[11] Frank wrote her back respectfully disagreeing with her characterization of our remarks, and added, "I congratulate you on the success you achieved for your clients. Your clients are lucky to have both of you. Had they performed as well as the two of you did, they would never have needed you."[12]

47

NO MORAL CONSCIENCE

This has been the story of Lisa Shore, the little girl—my little girl—who deserved to live, and play, and laugh, and love, and grow up.

The "what-ifs" will haunt me forever: What if I had not brought her to the Hospital for Sick Children that night? What if she had not been given morphine? What if she had been assigned to even marginally competent nurses? What if I had stayed awake all night? What if Dr. Schily had asked what Lisa's vital signs were when the nurse paged him at 4:00 a.m.?

Those are the questions I will ask myself for the rest of my life, as I mourn my beloved child. But there are other questions that also need to be asked.

Some have no answers, or at least none we will ever learn. Why didn't Ruth Doerksen and Anagaile Soriano read the doctor's orders, follow the hospital protocols, or take action when they saw Lisa's vital signs deteriorating? Did they act out of malice, or was there some other unknown motivation? I believe—I have to believe—that they only intended to neglect Lisa and never realized that their neglect would have such deadly consequences, for to think otherwise is to call Lisa's death a murder.

Although there cannot be any justification or rationalization for their actions according to any objective standard—no matter how loudly their supporters argue otherwise—one can make reasonable guesses about why they decided to lie afterwards: Sheer panic, for one thing. Fear they would lose their jobs, for another. That they were willing to go to such extremes to cover up their roles in a child's death is testament to their own flawed characters. That all of the people surrounding them—colleagues, superiors, doctors, managers, administrators, and lawyers—chose to help them conceal the truth, chose to collectively deny any responsibility, and chose to demonize the mother of the child whose death they caused is nothing less than an abomination.

The Hospital for Sick Children's problems are manifold: it puts its own reputation before the welfare of its employees, which it, in turn, puts before the health and safety of the community it serves; it condones health-care negligence; and it willingly engages in deceitful practices to conceal information from parents, police, and others. The hospital does provide top quality medical care to many children, but it will go to almost any length to make sure no one finds out about the mistakes it makes and the problems that arise along the way.

Sick Kids basks in its stature as a world-class paediatric hospital. It commands respect from the public, the government, and the health care community. Corporations, community groups, the rich and famous, and the man on the street all donate generously. It attracts brilliant researchers and pioneers groundbreaking medical treatments. The hospital believes these are the things that matter, and they are right. But there is one more quality that must be present to earn the word "world-class", and the Hospital for Sick Children does not have it: a moral conscience.

Increased patient safety is a laudable goal. Systems can always be improved upon, and those improvements will reduce errors and save lives. But no one should confuse the current buzzwords of "patient safety", "medical error", and "systemic problems" with what happened to Lisa. No one mistakenly inserted a decimal place in the wrong position leading to a medication overdose, or accidentally nicked an artery during surgery, or misread an X-ray. All the systems were in place when Lisa came to the hospital: doctors were to enter orders and nurses were to read and implement those orders. If there were problems with the orders the doctor needed to be contacted and hospital protocols followed in the interim.

Lisa's death was not about patient safety and medical error, it was about gross negligence: the intentional disregard of rules and procedures, and the violation of universal and fundamental standards of nursing practice. Just as no one of sound mind would blame the road traffic system when a driver deliberately runs a red light, responsibility for the actions of Ruth Doerksen and Anagaile Soriano lies foremost with themselves. Doctors and nurses and hospital administrators and lawyers who cannot or will not distinguish between accidental error and outright negligence do not deserve our respect, and should not be entrusted with our lives or the lives of our children.

Why did no one have the courage to speak up for Lisa? Why did none of the hospital's decision-makers, its board of trustees, or its senior staff publicly voice their opposition to the dishonourable actions of the institution they worked for or with? Why did so many doctors and nurses and administrators and lawyers act unethically to protect two bad nurses, and why did everyone else stay silent?

The names of corporations like Enron and Worldcom are etched upon the public consciousness. People were shocked to learn how shareholders and employees alike were cheated out of their livelihoods and their life savings by greedy and unethical executives. Scandals erupted, criminal prosecutions ensued, and governments brought in legislation to ensure such things could not happen again. Today, auditors worriedly scrutinize every business transaction fearing for their own reputations, executives are forced to take personal responsibility for the veracity of their books and records, and the catchword of the day is "corporate governance".

Where is the equivalent for the health-care profession and for health-care corporations? Where powerful executives play with money, doctors and nurses play with patients' lives. There are no legislated disclosure requirements, no Securities Commissions, and no media scrutiny to ensure public accountability.

The regulatory colleges are largely ineffective. They are quick to prosecute sexual misconduct, billing improprieties, assaults and thefts, but rarely do anything beyond the proverbial "slap on the wrist" when it comes to practice issues. How can they, when those whom they are supposed to regulate cannot be trusted to regulate themselves, and others who have not committed misdeeds themselves become complicit in covering them up?

The Hospital for Sick Children, its lawyers, and the nurses of Ontario all believe that different standards of justice apply to health care professionals than to the rest of the world. They believe that no matter what they do, provided it occurred while they were engaged in practice, they should never under any circumstances be held criminally accountable and responsible.

The Crown laid criminal charges because it believed Lisa's death was the result of a criminal act. It did not anticipate that nurses across the country would be unwilling or afraid to testify. It did not expect health care professionals would refuse to speak to them, be willing to dramatically shade the truth, or develop selective amnesia. It did not foresee the Hospital for Sick Children would care more about protecting its reputation than it would about the wrongful death of a ten-year-old child.

The Hospital for Sick Children and its lawyers succeeded in their mission. Thanks to the hospital's willingness to spend well over a million dollars of taxpayers' money[1] to protect two negligent nurses, the Crown was so badly battered that no Crown attorney anywhere in the country will ever again be willing to prosecute a doctor or nurse who harms a patient, no matter how criminal the deed. There are now two standards of justice in this country: one for the health care professions and one for everybody else.

EPILOGUE

As of September 3, 2004, more than four years after my complaints against Ruth Doerksen and Anagaile Soriano were submitted to the College of Nurses of Ontario, no starting date has been scheduled for their still-pending disciplinary hearing on charges of professional misconduct.

Any updates to this information will be posted on www.lisashore.com.

The Ontario Health Insurance Plan, which had deferred its decision about paying our claim for reimbursement of Lisa's Boston medical expenses until the inquest's conclusion, eventually decided to reimburse us. Its decision had nothing to do with the merits of our case and everything to do with the inquest's homicide finding, public sympathy and support for us, the relatively low dollar value of our claim, and the sure knowledge that the circumstances of this case were so unusual that no precedent would be established by paying us. We used the money to set up an endowment fund at a local high school; the annual interest provides scholarships each year in Lisa's memory to two of the school's graduating students, for excellence in art.

NOTES

[All referenced documents may be found online
at www.lisashore.com]

CHAPTER ONE
[1] Hospital for Sick Children Annual Reports 2001-2002 and 2002-2003, Internet: <www.sickkids.ca/annualreport2001_2002; www.sickkids.ca/annualreport2002_2003>.
[2] Alan J. Gayer, CEO and President of the Hospital for Sick Children, as quoted in the Toronto Star, May 29, 2003, page G4, "Sick Kids is one of the three or four best children's hospitals in the world. Over the next five years we plan to make it the best in the world."
[3] Isabella J. Mori, Pain medication used by persons suffering from Reflex Sympathetic Dystrophy, Literature review and pilot study of 45 RSD sufferers, April 5, 1998; Hooshang Hooshmand and Masood Hashmi, Complex Regional Pain Syndrome (Reflex Sympathetic Dystrophy Syndrome): Diagnosis and Therapy-A Review of 824 Patients, Pain Digest, 1999.
[4] Quote by Dr. S. Weir Mitchell, Internet: <history.nih.gov/exhibits/pain/docs/page_09.html>.
[5] Lisa Shore's Hospital for Sick Childen medical records <*Lisa's HSC records*>, radiology report by Dr. J. Ash (Feb. 26, 1998) <**Ref#1-5**>.
[6] Robert T. Wilder, Charles B. Berde et al: "Reflex Sympathetic Dystrophy in Children, Clinical Characteristics and Follow-up of Seventy Patients", Journal of Bone and Joint Surgery, July 1992 at 917

> "...Although bone-scanning has been reported to be helpful in the diagnosis of reflex sympathetic dystrophy in adults, studies have shown that the findings can vary in children who have reflex sympathetic dystrophy. We suggest that the role of plain radiography and bone-scanning in the work-up of a child who apparently has reflex sympathetic dystrophy is not to make the diagnosis but rather to rule out other conditions..."

Article's availability in HSC library was confirmed by a resident.
[7] A fellow is a physician who has completed his or her residency and is doing post-graduate training in his or her chosen field.
[8] *Lisa's HSC records*, nursing progress note, J. Savoie (Feb. 25, 1998): "On many occasions during shift, writer looked in patient's window and patient appeared to be playing with no distress, eating with no distress. As soon as patient noticed writer,

expression of pain appears and when writer opens door, patient moans" <**Ref#1-8**>.
[9] *Lisa's HSC records,* nursing progress note, D. Clark (March 2, 1998) <**Ref#1-9**>: "...Patient told distraction techniques for pain management, then mother interrupted with following statement; "Oh that's what they tell pregnant women, but it doesn't work". Explained to mother her statement was not helpful... Assessment: Unrelieved pain from fracture of tibia. Great anxiety in mother with respect to daughter's pain; hospitalization. Plan: Continue to monitor pain level and tolerance. Suggest conference and strategy including family so consistent info and approach is maintained between doctors, nursing, other medical personal <sic> and family..."
[10] *Ibid,* nursing progress note by student nurse, signature unclear (Feb. 27, 1998) <**Ref#1-10**>.
[11] Information about pain clinics generally and at Hospital for Sick Children specifically was provided by Dr. Robert Wilder, Children's Hospital, Boston, Dr. Joelle Desparmet, HSC, and by the author's observations and questioning of various physicians and nurses.
[12] Naproxen, an over-the-counter pain reliever also known as Anaprox, and Lorazepam, a prescription anti-anxiety drug also known as Ativan.
[13] *Lisa's HSC records,* Pain Service note by Dr. D. Szpisjak (March 2, 1998) <**Ref#1-13**>.
[14] *Lisa's HSC records,* resident's neurology note on behalf of Dr. MacGregor (Mar. 6, 1998) <**Ref#1-14**>.
[15] *Lisa's HSC records,* psychiatry note, Dr. M. Jeavons (March 6, 1998) <**Ref#1-15**>. Medications proposed were Carbamazepine and Gabapentin.

CHAPTER TWO
[1] *Lisa's HSC records,* psychiatry progress note, Dr. N. Westreich (March 17, 1998) <**Ref#2-1**>.
[2] *Lisa's HSC records,* psychiatry note, Dr. N. Westreich (not dated, but note is headed "Date Seen: March 17, 1998") <**Ref#2-2**>.
[3] Per manufacturer's (Pfizer) monograph: "Acute oral overdoses of Neurontin up to 49 grams have been reported. In these cases, double vision, slurred speech, drowsiness, lethargy and diarrhea were observed. All patients recovered with supportive care." 49 grams equals 49,000 milligrams, approximately 80 times Lisa's prescribed dosage of 600 milligrams, Internet: <www.pfizer.com/download/uspi_neurontin.pdf>.
[4] Per conversation with the author's sister, Dr. Cindy Grief.
[5] *Lisa's HSC records,* discharge orders (March 25, 1998) <**Ref#2-5**>.

CHAPTER THREE
[1] Letter from Sharon Shore to Dr. Joelle Desparmet (April 12, 1998) <**Ref#3-1**>.
[2] Letter from Dr. Mailis to Dr. Lee Ann Gallant (dated March 30, 1998 but received by mail at end of April) <**Ref#3-2**>.
[3] *Time* magazine, Fall 1997 Special Issue.
[4] *Health Insurance Act,* R.R.O. 1990, Reg. 552 Amended to O. Reg. 422/01, s. 28.4(2).
[5] Letter from Dr. Lee Ann Gallant to OHIP (May 5, 1998) <**Ref#3-5**>.
[6] Letter from Sharon Shore to Dr. Angela Mailis (April 28, 1998) <**Ref#3-6**>.

ENDNOTES

CHAPTER FOUR
[1] Children's Hospital Boston, Office of Public Affairs: Press Room, Internet: <www.childrenshospital.org/cfapps/CHdeptPagePressDisplay.cfm?Dept=Press%20Room&PageNbr=96&ParentPage=1>.
[2] *Ibid*, Pain Treatment Services, Internet: <www.childrenshospital.org/cfapps/CHprogDisplay.cfm>.
[3] Lisa's Boston records, Pain Management Clinic note by Dr. R. Wilder (May 18, 1998) <**Ref#4-3**>.
[4] Letter from Ontario Health Insurance Plan to Dr. Lee Ann Gallant (May 12, 1998) <**Ref#4-4**>.
[5] Treatment Summary letter from Dr. Frederick Rocco (June 10, 1998) <**Ref#4-5**>.

CHAPTER FIVE
[1] Letter from Dr. Ron Laxer (June 17, 1998) <**Ref#5-1**>.
[2] Parano E, Pavone V et al, Reflex sympathetic dystrophy associated with deep peroneal nerve entrapment, Brain & Development 20 (1998) 80-82, Elsevier Science B.V.
[3] The Terry Fox Foundation, Internet: <www.terryfoxrun.org>.

CHAPTER EIGHT
[1] Letter from Frank Gomberg to Dr. William Lucas (Nov. 11, 1998) <**Ref#8-1**>.
[2] Letter from Dr. William Lucas to Frank Gomberg (Nov. 17, 1998) <**Ref#8-2**>.

CHAPTER NINE
[1] Conversion disorder — Information from the Diagnostic and Statistical Manual of Mental Disorders, Fourth Edition (DSM-IV)

    300.11 Conversion Disorder: Diagnostic criteria
- A. One or more symptoms or deficits affecting voluntary motor or sensory function that suggest a neurological or other general medical condition.
- B. Psychological factors are judged to be associated with the symptom or deficit because the initiation or exacerbation of the symptom or deficit is preceded by conflicts or other stressors.
- C. The symptom or deficit is not intentionally produced or feigned (as in Factitious Disorder or Malingering)
- D. The symptom or deficit cannot, after appropriate investigation, be fully explained by a general medical condition, or by the direct effects of a substance, or as a culturally sanctioned behavior or experience.
- E. The symptom or deficit causes clinically significant distress or impairment in social, occupational, or other important areas of functioning or warrants medical evaluation.
- F. The symptom or deficit is not limited to pain or sexual dysfunction, does not occur exclusively during the course of Somatization Disorder, and is not better accounted for by another mental disorder.

    300.11 Conversion Disorder: Diagnostic Features

…Conversion symptoms are related to voluntary motor or sensory functioning and are thus referred to as "pseudoneurological." Motor symptoms or deficits include impaired coordination or balance, paralysis or localized weakness, aphonia, difficulty swallowing or a sensation of a lump in the throat, and urinary retention. Sensory symptoms or deficits include loss of touch or pain sensation, double vision, blindness, deafness, and hallucinations. Symptoms may also include seizures or convulsions. The more medically naïve the person, the more implausible are the presenting symptoms. More sophisticated persons tend to have more subtle symptoms and deficits that may closely simulate neurological or other general medical conditions.

A diagnosis of Conversion Disorder should be made only after a thorough medical investigation has been performed to rule out an etiological neurological or general medical condition. Because a general medical etiology for many cases of apparent Conversion Disorder can take years to become evident, the diagnosis should be viewed as tentative and provisional...

300.11 Conversion Disorder: Specific Culture, Age, and Gender Features
Conversion Disorder has been reported to be more common in rural populations, individuals of lower socioeconomic status, and individuals less knowledgeable about medical and psychological concepts. Higher rates of conversion symptoms are reported in developing regions, with the incidence generally declining with increasing development...

[2] Lisa's Boston medical records, Neurology consult note by Dr. C. Menache on behalf of Dr. R. Rust (Oct. 4, 1998) <Ref#9-2>.
[3] *Lisa's HSC records*, nursing flowsheet for Oct.22, 1998 <Ref#9-3>.
[4] According to the inside back cover of Whaley & Wong's Nursing Care of Infants and Children, by Wong, Hockenberry et al, 6th ed., 1999, Mosby Inc., normal heart rate for a resting or sleeping child of Lisa's age is 50-90 beats per minute.
[5] *Ibid*. Normal respiratory rate for a child of Lisa's age is 19 breaths per minute.
[6] *Lisa's HSC records*, Ruth Doerksen's nursing progress note (Oct. 22, 1998, 01:50 hours) <Ref#9-6>.
[7] *Ibid*. Ruth Doerksen's added nursing note (Oct. 22, 1998, 0900 hours) <Ref#9-7>.
[8] *Ibid*. Death Summary by Dr. James Wright (Nov. 6, 1998) <Ref#9-8>.
[9] Letter from Frank Gomberg to Dr. William Lucas (Dec. 11, 1998) <Ref#9-9>.

CHAPTER TEN
[1] Letter from Sharon Shore to the Solicitor-General of Ontario et al (March 11, 1999) <Ref#10-1>.

CHAPTER ELEVEN
[1] Letter from Hospital for Sick Children, no author identified, to Dr. M. Reingold, Office of the Chief Coroner (March 3, 1999) <Ref#11-1>.
[2] Covering letter from Marion Stevens to Dr. M. Reingold (March 3, 1999) <Ref#11-2>.
[3] HSC Department of Nursing Education, Dec. 1991, revised 05/92, 05/94, 03/95 & 07/98 <Ref#11-3>.
[4] Letter from Sharon Shore to Dr. James Young (March 17, 1999) <Ref#11-4>.
[5] Tracey Tyler and Harold Levy, *The Toronto Star*, <Ref#11-5>.

CHAPTER TWELVE
[1] *Lisa's HSC records*, doctor's orders, Dr. Markus Schily and Dr. Joel Lobo (Oct. 21, 1998) <Ref#12-1>.
[2] HSC note to Dr. William Lucas re Lisa Shore file (Jan. 28, 1999) <Ref#12-2>.

CHAPTER THIRTEEN
1. Per on-line search of Quicklaw Ontario Reports (search terms: inquest, testimony, perjury), June 1, 2003.

CHAPTER FOURTEEN
1. *To v. Toronto Board of Education*, [2001] O.J. No. 3490, (2001) 55 O.R. (3d) 641 <QL>.
2. *Athey v. Leonati*, [1996] S.C.J. No. 102, [1996] 3 S.C.R. 458 <QL>.
3. The mandatory mediation process began in Toronto and Ottawa in 1999, and has since been expanded to Windsor. Our mediation was voluntary and occurred without Frank having sued the hospital. Had the mediation been unsuccessful, he would have issued a statement of claim and formally launched a lawsuit.
4. Doctors are considered self-employed, independent practitioners.
5. Letter from Dr. Jean Reeder to Investigator at the College of Nurses in response to complaint by Sharon Shore (Oct. 27, 2000) <Ref#14-5>.
6. *Ibid* at 8 <See ref#14-5>.

CHAPTER FIFTEEN
1. Divisional Court is part of the Superior Court of Justice. It hears appeals and reviews of decisions by government agencies, tribunals and boards, including the coroner's office. Internet: <www.attorneygeneral.jus.gov.on.ca/English/about/pubs/courts_annual_03/ch2.pdf>.

CHAPTER EIGHTEEN
1. Falconer, Julian and Macklin, Richard, "Current Issues on Standing" at B16 in *Inside Inquests* (Law Society of Upper Canada Department of Continuing Education program of Oct.12, 1993).
2. Dick Chapman, *Toronto Sun* (Nov. 10, 1999) <Ref#18-2>.
3. Natalie Southworth, *The Globe and Mail* (Nov. 10, 1999) <Ref#18-3>.

CHAPTER TWENTY
1. Mary Douglas, 5A Incident, Nov. 12, 1998, Lisa Shore inquest exhibit #21 <Ref#20-1>.
2. Office of the Chief Coroner, Paediatric Death Review Committee, Final Report on Lisa Shore, appendices 1 and 2, Jan. 2000, Lisa shore inquest exhibit #22 <Ref#20-2A, 20-2B>.

CHAPTER TWENTY-ONE
1. Hospital for Sick Children, Admissions from Emerg–Kidcom Orders, Aug. 1994, Lisa Shore inquest exhibit #25A <Ref#21-1>.
2. HSC, Admissions from Emergency–Kidcom Orders, January 2000, Lisa Shore inquest exhibit #25B <Ref#21-2>

CHAPTER TWENTY-THREE
1. Typed transcriptions of Ruth Doerksen's notes of Oct. 23, 1998, and Anagaile Soriano's notes of Oct. 25, 1998, Lisa Shore inquest exhibits #38B and 44B <Ref#23-1A, 23-1B>.

² Interview by College of Nurses of Ontario with the inquest jury forewoman (Oct. 30, 2000) <Ref#23-2>.

CHAPTER TWENTY-FIVE
¹ Kerry Gillespie, *The Toronto Star* (Nov. 9, 1999) <Ref#25-1>.
² Natalie Southworth, *The Globe and Mail* (Jan.18, 2000) <Ref#25-2>.
³ Rick Vanderlinde, *The Liberal*, Thornhill edition (Jan.18, 2000) <Ref#25-3>.
⁴ Harold Levy, *The Toronto Star* (Jan. 20, 2000) <Ref#25-4>.
⁵ Harold Levy, *The Toronto Star* (Jan. 28, 2000) <Ref#25-5>.

CHAPTER TWENTY-SIX
¹ Death Summary dictated by Dr. Joel Lobo for Dr. James Wright on Oct. 29, 1998, inquest exhibit #56 <Ref#26-1>.

CHAPTER TWENTY-SEVEN
¹ Harold Levy, *The Toronto Star* (Feb. 4, 2000) <Ref#27-1>.

CHAPTER TWENTY-NINE
¹ Dick Chapman, *The Toronto Sun* (Feb. 2, 2000) <Ref#29-1>.
² Tracy Huffman, *The Toronto Star* (Feb. 5, 2000) <Ref#29-2>.
³ Harold Levy, *The Toronto Star* (Feb. 9, 2000) <Ref#29-3>.

CHAPTER THIRTY-ONE
¹ *Regulated Health Professions Act*, 1991, S.O. 1991, c. 18, Schedule 2, section 85.5.
² The majority of nurses reported to the College of Nurses of Ontario on bona fide grounds have been dismissed by their employers.
³ Harold Levy, "Juror supports probe", *The Toronto Star* (Feb. 27, 2000) <Ref#31-3>.
⁴ Hospital for Sick Children, Canada Newswire press release, "Sick Kids and nurses report to College of Nurses of Ontario" (March 6, 2000) <Ref#31-4>.
⁵ Dr. Jean Reeder continued to be represented by Patrick Hawkins; the new lawyer represented the other nurses.
⁶ Elizabeth McIntyre, Cavalluzzo Hayes Shilton McIntyre & Cornish press release (March 6, 2000) <Ref#31-6>.
⁷ Shore family, Canada Newswire press release (March 7, 2000) <Ref#31-7>.

CHAPTER THIRTY-TWO
¹ This rule holds true at all times except where the defence is in possession of incriminating physical evidence, i.e. "the smoking gun", in which case it must be disclosed to the Crown. This is best illustrated by the saga of the infamous Bernardo videotapes, where Bernardo's lawyer did not disclose their existence to the Crown and was later charged with (but subsequently acquitted of) obstruction of justice.
² Internet: <www.mpss.jus.gov.on.ca/english/pub_safety/centre_forensic/about/intro.html>.
³ The two are not mutually exclusive: If you are successfully sued because of your negligence you will have to pay damages to the victim or his family; if you are convicted on criminal charges you could go to jail. Think of OJ Simpson, who was acquitted in criminal court of the murder of his wife Nicole Brown Simpson and her

friend Ron Goldman, yet was successfully sued by the victims' families for wrongful death and ordered to pay them millions of dollars in damages.

CHAPTER THIRTY-THREE
[1] The College of Nurses of Ontario's 2002 annual report itemizes the Complaints Committee Dispositions as 7% being referred to discipline, 42% as having no action taken, 9% complaints withdrawn, and 7% dismissed as frivolous and vexatious. The remaining 35% enter into participatory resolution, are referred to Quality Assurance, or receive a reminder, advice, or letter of caution.
[2] Aug. 10, 2000, re Ruth Doerksen <**Ref#33-2A**>, Anagaile Soriano <**Ref#33-2B**>, Mary Douglas <**Ref#33-2C**>, and Jean Reeder <**Ref#33-2D**>. Note: Complaints of professional misconduct were initially filed on March 3, 2000 against these four nurses and against two additional nurses, but the College decided that inquest testimony could not be used to form the basis for a complaint. The latter two complaints were then dropped and the four main ones revised.
[3] Letter from Gavin MacKenzie to Sharon Shore (June 2, 2000) <**Ref#33-3**>.

CHAPTER THIRTY-FOUR
[1] The complete transcription of what we heard of Dr. Jean Reeder's recorded messages is included with the complaint to the College of Nurses, ref#33-2D. The specific reference to the website not being factual is found on the transcription dated March 6, 2000.
[2] Presentation by Sue Williams at Sunnybrook and Women's College Hospital, Sept. 26, 2000.
[3] Letter from Sharon Shore to Doris Grinspun (Sept. 27, 2000) <**Ref#34-3**>.
[4] Letter from Doris Grinspun to Sharon Shore (Oct. 5, 2000) <**Ref#34-4**>.
[5] Letter from Sharon Shore to Doris Grinspun (Oct. 11, 2000) <**Ref#34-5**>.
[6] Letter from Doris Grinspun to Sharon Shore (Nov. 1, 2000) <**Ref#34-6**>.
[7] Sad to say, the RNAO's response was in many ways quite typical of the manner in which organizations "close ranks" to protect themselves from outsiders.
[8] Letter of Caution from College of Nurses to Dr. Jean Reeder (Feb. 6, 2001) <**Ref#34-8**>.
[9] Letter of Caution from College of Nurses to Mary Douglas (Feb. 6, 2001) <**Ref#34-9**>.
[10] See Ref#14-5 at page 6.
[11] College of Nurses interview with Dr. Reeder (Oct. 11, 2000), page 3 <**Ref#34-11**>.
[12] College of Nurses interviews with Michael Strofolino (Sept. 6, 2000) <**Ref#34-12A**>, Alan Goldbloom (Sept.6, 2000) <**Ref#34-12B**>, and Jean Reeder <**see Ref#34-11**>.

CHAPTER THIRTY-FIVE
[1] Hospital for Sick Children, Nov. 9, 2000, Internet: <www.sickkids.on.ca/releases/release00/unexpected.asp>.
[2] Sonia Verma and Harold Levy, "Something wrong in death of Sanchia", *The Toronto Star* (May 22, 2001) <**Ref#35-2**>.
[3] Letter from Sharon Shore to Dr. James Young (Jan. 19, 2001) <**Ref#35-3**>.
[4] Affidavit of Dr. Alan Goldbloom (April 20, 2001) <**Ref#35-4**>.

[5] Letter from Elizabeth McIntyre to Dr. James Young et al (April 20, 2001) <Ref#35-5>.
[6] Affidavit of Sharon Shore (April 30, 2001) <Ref#35-6>.
[7] Although the Chief Coroner ordered the document sealed, the restriction no longer applies once the inquest proceedings have concluded.
[8] College of Nurses of Ontario interview with Jean Reeder (October 11, 2000) on page 2 <see Ref#34-11>: "In 1996, the hospital experienced a drop in its census, and as a result, the experienced casual nurses were not getting enough work. Then in late 1997, the census went back up, and the hospital was caught with a shortage of nurses, especially in the critical care areas."
[9] I was given the name of one nurse who left the Hospital for Sick Children for a position at a suburban hospital expressly because she was disgusted with its conduct.
[10] Rosie DiManno, *The Toronto Star* (May 3, 2001) <Ref#35-10>.
[11] Dr. J. Young, Inquest into the death of Sanchia Bulgin standing application ruling (May 4, 2001) <Ref#35-11>.
[12] Because Sanchia had no pre-surgical blood work, there were no recent hemoglobin levels nor any blood typing and cross matching done.
[13] 17-year-old Sanchia's vital signs as charted on admission to Ward 5A/B: temperature 35.2, pulse 120, respiratory rate 44, and blood pressure 80/40. Over the next few hours, Sanchia's pulse and respiratory rates increased to >160 and >60 respectively; no further blood pressures or temperatures were taken.
[14] In Oct. 2003, the College of Nurses held a disciplinary hearing and imposed 30-day suspensions on Sanchia's two primary nurses. The College may have been acting on a complaint received from a family member, or it may have initiated its own investigation as a result of media reports.
[15] Sharon Shore, "Focus on personnel, not system", *The Toronto Star* (July 20, 2001) <Ref#35-15>.

CHAPTER THIRTY-SIX
[1] *R. v. Heikamp*, [1999] O.J. No. 5382.

CHAPTER THIRTY-SEVEN
[1] Presentation by Sharon Shore to HPARB panel re Mary Douglas (July 16, 2001) <Ref#37-1A>; re Jean Reeder (July 16, 2001) <Ref#37-1B>.

CHAPTER THIRTY-EIGHT
[1] The inquests of Lisa Shore and Sanchia Bulgin are but two examples. Others are the inquests into the deaths of Arlene May in 1998 and Gillian Hadley in 2001, murdered respectively by a former boyfriend and the husband from whom she was separated. Still other examples: the 1994 inquest into the death of Lester Donaldson and the 1999 inquest into the death of Edmond Yu; both men belonged to visible minorities, were mentally ill, and were shot to death by police during confrontations.
[2] Review of Progress on the Recommendations of the Coroner's Jury which Investigated the Death of Lisa Shore, The Hospital for Sick Children, April 25, 2001 <Ref#38-2>.
[3] Analysis of the hospital's status report on the inquest recommendations, posted on www.lisashore.com from July to October 2001 <Ref#38-3>.

CHAPTER THIRTY-NINE

1. Christie Blatchford, "Two nurses to face criminal charges", *National Post* (Oct.24, 2001) <**Ref#39-1**>.
2. According to my lisashore.com website statistics, the most frequent organizational visitor to the site was Sick Kids. Over 125 unique computers from the hospital accessed the site, with a significant portion of these visits coming between midnight and 6:00 a.m.
3. Letter from Marlys Edwardh to Michelle Fuerst (Oct. 29, 2001) <**Ref#39-3**>.
4. Letter from Michelle Fuerst to Marlys Edwardh (Oct. 30, 2001) <**Ref#39-4**>.
5. Letter from Marlys Edwardh to Frank Gomberg (Nov. 21, 2001) <**Ref#39-5**>.
6. Letter from Frank Gomberg to Marlys Edwardh (Nov. 22, 2001) <**Ref#39-6**>.
7. Radio station CFRB ran a phone-in poll, and 77% of callers were in favour of the charges.
8. Ontario Nurses Association, Canada Newswire press release (Oct. 25, 2001) <**Ref#39-8**>.
9. Registered Nurses Association of Ontario *(RNAO)*, Canada Newswire press release (Oct. 25, 2001) <**Ref#39-9**>.
10. Doris Grinspun, "RNAO: With you every step of the Way!" *Registered Nurse Journal* (Nov./Dec. 2001) <**Ref#39-10**>.
11. "Criminal charges laid three years after girl's hospital death" *Canadian Nurse* (Jan. 2002), Vol. 98, No. 1 <**Ref#39-11**>.
12. Letter from Frank Gomberg to Canadian Nurse (Feb. 22, 2002) <**Ref#39-12**>.
13. Janet Rush, "Criminal charges rattle RNs" *Registered Nurse Journal* (March/April 2002) <**Ref#39-13**>.
14. Letter from Sharon Deutsh to the Managing Editor, RNAO Journal (May 19, 2002) <**Ref#39-14**>.
15. RNAO Journal Mail Bag (May/June 2002) <**Ref#39-15**>.
16. Theodora Theodonis, Tremayne-Lloyd Partners, *Medico-Legal Society of Toronto, On Examination* (Fall 2001) <*On Exam*> <**Ref#39-16**>.
17. Frank Gomberg, letter to the editor, *On Exam* <Spring 2002> <**Ref#39-17**>.

CHAPTER FORTY

1. Letters from Sharon Shore to College of Nurses of Ontario (Dec. 5, 2001 and Jan. 28, 2002) <**Ref#40-1A, 40-1B**>.
2. Elizabeth McIntyre, Response to the Motion for Access to Exhibits (March 8, 2002) <**Ref#40-2**>.
3. Dr. Goldbloom's affidavit contained an assertion that it was prepared for the standing hearing and for no other purpose, therefore its use in McIntyre's submission to the College was technically improper.
4. Sharon Shore, Response to Materials Submitted by Elizabeth McIntyre Opposing Motion for Access to Exhibits (March 21, 2002) <**Ref#40-4**>. Note that copies were sent to all parties including McIntyre.
5. Linda Rothstein, Paliare Roland Rosenberg Rothstein, Reply Submissions of the College of Nurses of Ontario re: Shore Motion to Access Exhibits (March 28, 2002) (factum only) <**Ref#40-5**>.

CHAPTER FORTY-ONE

[1] This over-simplistic analogy is used to illustrate the point. While it is generally true, in reality, the more serious the crime the more serious the mistake has to be for the court to throw the case out.

[2] *Canadian Jewish News*, Nov. 4, 1999, Internet: <www.cjnews.com/pastissues/99/nov4-99/front1.htm>.

[3] Expert report prepared by Louise Cardillo, RN, Dec. 16, 2002 (obtained by author after the criminal proceedings had concluded) <**Ref#41-4**>:

Conclusions:

Based upon my review of the medical records of Lisa Shore, the medical records of patients on Ward 5A, the testimony of Dr. Schily at the inquest it is my opinion that the care received by Lisa Shore at <the> Hospital for Sick Children in Toronto, Ontario led to her death.

The lack of care provided to Lisa based upon her medical history, the medications she had administered prior to her admission at home and in the emergency room has a direct causal relationship to her death.

If in the event that Lisa Shore had received closer monitoring via vital signs, oximetry, apnea monitor, her condition would have been noted in a timely fashion. Based upon the autopsy findings the treatment of Narcan, supportive care, oxygen and monitoring would have saved her life. Thus, if not for failures to act, omissions and commissions of Ms. A. Soriano and Ms. R. Doerksen, Lisa Shore would be alive and here today.

[4] Expert report prepared by Carla Shapiro RN, MN, Dec. 10, 2002, obtained by author after the criminal proceedings had concluded <**Ref#41-5**>.

Conclusion:

...While clinical judgement applies to every aspect of patient care, there is an expectation that nurses will follow protocols and guidelines that are in place to ensure the safety of their patients Based upon a review of the materials provided to me, it is my opinion that the nursing care provided to Lisa Shore at the Hospital for Sick Children in Toronto fell below the standard of care expected from reasonable and prudent Registered Nurses.

...Had the nurses or nurses who had a duty of care to Lisa Shore carried out interventions according to appropriate policies and procedure (thus meeting the expected standard of care), I believe that the tragic outcome to this child and her family could have been avoided.

[5] See e.g. Geoffrey C. Hazard, *"Tobacco Lawyers Shame the Entire Profession,"* The National Law Journal, 5/18/98, A.22.

[6] Letter from Sharon Shore to Dr. Charles Berde (July 5, 2002) <**Ref#41-6**>.

CHAPTER FORTY-TWO

[1] Copy of letter is not available; Hank Goody read it over the phone.

[2] The website is www.littlestangels.net/Stories475.html.

CHAPTER FORTY-THREE

[1] In Ontario, the provincial courts are called the Ontario Courts of Justice, and the higher courts are the Superior Courts of Justice. The highest Ontario court is the Ontario Court of Appeal.

[2] Murder charges must be heard in Superior Court before a judge and jury, but those accused of other serious crimes may choose judge alone or judge and jury.
[3] The Crown can bypass this requirement by "preferring a direct indictment" with the approval of the Attorney General for Ontario, but it is rarely done.
[4] Letter from Sharon Shore to Detective-Sergeant Michael Davis (Jan. 20, 2003) <Ref#43-4>.
[5] Letter from Sharon Shore to Detective-Sergeant Michael Davis, (Jan. 23, 2003) <Ref#43-5>.

CHAPTER FORTY-FIVE

[1] See Ref#12-1, *Lisa's HSC records*, suspended orders of Dr. Joel Lobo (October 21, 1998) <Ref#45-1>.

CHAPTER FORTY-SIX

[1] Judgment of the Honourable Mr. Justice R. Khawly, Ont. Court of Justice (May 16, 2003) <Ref#46-1>.

...Such forces are synonymous with two powerful locomotives converging on the same track. One carries within it the rage and demand for criminal responsibility for a life cut so short. The other, in its mighty boilers, carries one of the lynch pins of our democracy namely, the requirement of "proof beyond a reasonable doubt" of criminal wrong doing.

When these two leviathans finally collided some eighteen months later in this forum, part of the resulting cacophony included accusations of documents being withheld and tampered with.

I must conclude that it is partly as a result of sifting through this wreckage that the Crown is now asking the Court to terminate the proceedings.

[2] Marlys Edwardh and Elizabeth McIntyre, press release, May 16, 2003 <Ref#46-2>.
[3] Ontario Nursing Association, Canada Newswire press release (May 16, 2003) <Ref#46-3>.
[4] Hospital for Sick Children, press release, May 16, 2003 <Ref#46-4>.
[5] Shore family, Canada Newswire press release (May 16, 2003) <Ref#46-5>. As of Sept. 1, 2004, the College of Nurses has not yet proceeded with the disciplinary hearing.
[6] Michelle Shepard and Harold Levy, "Negligence charges against nurses dropped" *The Toronto Star* (May 17, 2003) <Ref#46-6A>; Harold Levy, "Sharon Shore changes focus" *The Toronto Star* (May 17, 2003) <Ref#46-6B>.
[7] Jonathon Kingstone, "Sick Kids case over" *The Toronto Sun* (May 17, 2003) <Ref#46-7>.
[8] Christie Blatchford, "Mother's mistake ends case" *National Post* (May 17, 2003) <Ref#46-8>.
[9] Kirk Makin, "Charges against two nurses collapse" *Globe and Mail* (May 17, 2003) <Ref#46-9>.
[10] Letter from Frank Gomberg to *The Globe and Mail* (May 18, 2003) <Ref#46-10>.
[11] Letter from Marlys Edwardh and Elizabeth McIntyre to Frank Gomberg (May 21, 2003) <Ref#46-11>.
[12] Letter from Frank Gomberg to Marlys Edwardh and Elizabeth McIntyre (May 22, 2003) <Ref#46-12>.

CHAPTER FORTY-SEVEN

[1] This is a highly conservative estimate, considering the hourly billing rates of Patrick Hawkins, Marlys Edwardh, and Elizabeth McIntyre (all partners in their respective firms), the number of other lawyers, students and clerks who could reasonably be expected to have worked on the case with them, the estimated time preparing for and appearing at the coroner's inquest, the Sanchia Bulgin standing hearing, the College of Nurses of Ontario proceedings, the Health Professions Appeal and Review Board hearings, and the criminal case which included about one month of court time for the preliminary hearing alone. Significant additional expenses include payroll costs for Ruth Doerksen's and Anagaile Soriano's wages, who were placed on paid leave from the hospital in November 1999, the salaries of the many nurses who attended the inquest and the cost of hiring replacements for them, and the compensation the hospital had to have paid Jean Reeder for terminating her contract six months early.

At the time this was written, the Hospital for Sick Children continues to incur legal expenses on behalf of the two nurses as their lawyers prepare for the still pending College of Nurses disciplinary hearing.

ISBN 1-41204346-8